BROKE

BROKE

How Debt Bankrupts the Middle Class

Edited by Katherine Porter

STANFORD UNIVERSITY PRESS
STANFORD, CALIFORNIA

Stanford University Press
Stanford, California

Printed in the United States of America on acid-free,
archival-quality paper

Library of Congress Cataloging-in-Publication Data

Broke : how debt bankrupts the middle class / edited by
Katherine Porter.
     pages cm
  Includes bibliographical references and index.
  ISBN 978-0-8047-7700-1 (cloth : alk. paper) —
ISBN 978-0-8047-7701-8 (pbk. : alk. paper)
  1. Bankruptcy—United States. 2. Debt—United States.
3. Consumer credit—United States. 4. Middle class—
United States. 5. Finance, Personal—United States.
I. Porter, Katherine (Katherine M.), editor of compilation.
  HG3766.B76 2012
  332.70973—dc22
                                     2011015040

Typeset by Bruce Lundquist in 10/13 Sabon

This book is dedicated to Teresa Sullivan,
Elizabeth Warren, and Jay Westbrook,
who taught us about studying families in bankruptcy.

CONTENTS

PART III   Hurting at Home

CHAPTER SEVEN

CHAPTER EIGHT

PART IV   The Hard Road Out

CHAPTER NINE

CHAPTER TEN

PART V   The Once and Future American Dream

CHAPTER ELEVEN

CHAPTER TWELVE

APPENDIX

BROKE

CHAPTER ONE

Driven by Debt

Bankruptcy and Financial Failure in American Families

Katherine Porter

The waiting room is ordinary enough—lined with rows of simple metal chairs and barren of decoration other than a government poster of rules and regulations. The people in the room are ordinary too. They wear jeans and work boots, simple sun dresses and sandals, khaki pants and button-down shirts, or uniforms from retail stores. A few navigate into the room with a walker, and others try to find a space to accommodate a baby stroller. The room could be a local Social Security office or a parking permit bureau, just another pedestrian pause in daily life, but its atmosphere is the giveaway. Rather than the heavy stickiness of boredom, the room is filled with quiet anxiety. Conversations are hushed and brief. Many people twist their hands or study their shoes. The scene is like the waiting area in an emergency room, and for good reason.

This is the room where people wait to be diagnosed with a financial emergency—bankruptcy. The bankruptcy trustee calls people inside a small examination room and quickly reviews their debts, assets, income, and expenses. The trustee asks few questions; it's an easy diagnosis of flat broke in most cases. The need for these families to have legal help with their debts is obvious from their bankruptcy court records. Credit card debts, medical debts, and other unsecured debts typically total more than an entire year of the family's current income, and more than half of them are behind on their mortgage or car payments, facing foreclosure or repossession. Satisfied in most instances that the family qualifies for bankruptcy relief, the bankruptcy trustee sends husbands and wives, mothers and fathers, widows and young singles back to work or home.

As they leave the trustee's office, most people ask their attorney, "What's next?" They have typically struggled seriously with their debts for the previous one to two years. In fact, many households spent months simply scraping together the money and paperwork needed to file a bankruptcy petition. Most are skeptical that their problems just ended. What comes next in bankruptcy varies with people's circumstances. Some will receive a discharge of their debts in a few weeks, while others will struggle to repay creditors for years. Some will save their houses and see bankruptcy as a miraculous cure. Others will suffer continued hardships, skid farther down the economic ladder, and view bankruptcy as a plea for help that went unanswered.

Nearly all of these families will remember their few minutes with the bankruptcy trustee as one of the most painful moments of their lives. Bankruptcy is a head-on encounter with promises to pay that cannot be honored and privations suffered trying fruitlessly to make ends meet. These families' aspirations of middle-class security evaporated under pressure from debt collectors. At least for now, their version of the American Dream has been replaced by a desperate hope that things do not get even worse. Driven by debt, these families are at rock bottom.

• • •

Anthropologist Katherine Newman asserts that there are no ceremonies to mark downward mobility.[1] This is a stark contrast to the graduation ceremonies and housewarming parties that mark upward mobility. But meeting the bankruptcy trustee is exactly such a ceremony. It is a visible group experience characterized by a routine series of events that tangibly marks a decline in class status. Bankruptcy is a public declaration that a family has "fallen from grace," to borrow Newman's characterization of Americans who skid down the economic spectrum.

In the waiting rooms of bankruptcy trustees across the United States, in 2010 approximately 1.5 million families endured the bankruptcy ritual.[2] Their experiences are evidence that some people lose the borrowing game that has become the American economy. Increased consumption was largely financed by debt, rather than by increases in wages or appreciation of assets. The consumer spending that drove the economy at the end of the twentieth century was not costless. It was bought and paid for with interest charges, late fees, increased stress about making ends meet, and sometimes, the humiliation of bankruptcy.

The debt loads that are commonplace among today's families would have been unthinkable a mere generation ago. The Great Recession that began in mid-2007 has widened the scope of the financial pain caused by overindebtedness, but the problem predated the large-scale economic meltdown that captured headlines. And all indicators are that consumer debt will be a defining feature of middle-class families in years to come. The "deleveraging" process of paying down debt and increasing savings has just begun. Along the way, more families will lose their homes or cars, trade off family time for second jobs, endure dunning from debt collectors, and slip farther down the economic ladder.

This book exposes the underbelly of consumer debt. It tells the stories of families who filed for bankruptcy in early 2007. Even at that time when the economy was still strong, some households could not make ends meet. The plight of the bankrupt families in this book illustrates the financial pain that the Great Recession inflicted on tens of millions of middle-class families as the economy crashed in late 2007.[3] A survey by RAND researchers found that between November 2008 and April 2010, 39 percent of families had experienced one or more indicators of financial distress: being unemployed, having negative equity in their homes, or being two months behind on their mortgage or in foreclosure.[4] This "new normal"—a world of layoffs and job losses, cuts in social programs, and continued housing depreciation—only means that more people will find themselves collapsing under the weight of debts incurred in brighter economic times.[5]

Bankruptcy is a public window into how consumer debt has reshaped the middle class and its economic and social life. The staples of middle-class life—going to college, buying a house, starting a small business—carry with them more financial risk than ever before because they require more borrowing and new, riskier forms of borrowing. This book is about the endgame for those who borrowed in the hope of prosperity but could not sustain the heavy debt burdens of middle-class life. In telling these stories, we use empirical data. The figures and tables in this book reveal who suffers serious financial distress, how they get to that point, the hardships they face as they deal with overwhelming debt, and the difficulty they have righting their financial lives. Real people stand behind these statistics. This book tells the stories of their financial failures, exposing a part of middle-class life that is often lost in the success stories that dominate the American economic narrative.

DEBT: THE NEW MIDDLE-CLASS STATUS SYMBOL

The middle class is a powerful concept. Historically, the size and prosperity of the American middle class has been heralded as a great social and economic achievement. Membership in the middle class is associated with homeownership, educational opportunity, comfortable retirement, access to health care, and last but certainly not least, an appetite for consumer goods.[6] The middle class also has political appeal, as demonstrated by President Barack Obama's decision during his very first week in office to establish a Middle Class Task Force.[7] As chair of the task force, Vice President Joe Biden explained that middle-class life is the "old-fashioned notion of the American Dream" and that he and the president had "long believed that you can't have a strong America without a growing middle class. It's that simple. It's that basic."[8] The task force has focused its energy on job creation, retirement security, work-family issues, and higher education.[9]

But the task force has ignored entirely a revolutionary change in the lives of middle-class Americans: the increase in household debt. In the mid-1980s, the ratio of debt to personal disposable income for American households was 65 percent. During the next two decades, U.S. household leverage more than doubled, reaching an all-time high of 133 percent in 2007.[10] Measured in the aggregate, the ratio of household debt to gross national product reached its highest level since the onset of the Great Depression.[11] This record debt burden, which crested just as the financial crisis began, set up families to suffer deeply as foreclosures, unemployment, and wage stagnation set in for the years to follow.

The consumer debt overhang, however, began long before the financial crisis and recession. Exhortations about subprime mortgages reflect only a relatively minor piece of a much broader recalibration in the balance sheets of middle-class families. Debt began to climb steeply beginning in about 1985, with its growth accelerating in nearly every subsequent year. The run-up in consumer debt coincided with a period of deregulation of financial institutions and the preemption of state usury laws that capped interest rates. Unfortunately for American families, the debt binge was not accompanied by meaningful increases in disposable income. While income crept up, debt shot up, as Figure 1.1 illustrates. As debt grows relative to income, fami-

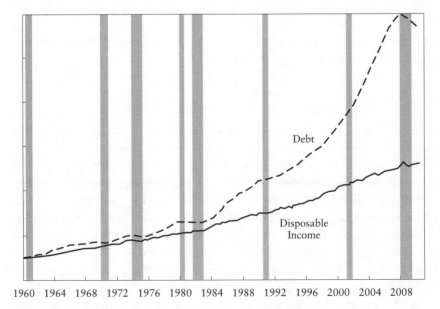

Figure 1.1   Real household debt and income, 1960–2010

SOURCE: Glick and Lansing, "U.S. Household Deleveraging"; updated data through Q1:2010 courtesy of Federal Reserve of San Francisco.

NOTE: All series normalized to 1960:Q1. Recession periods are shown in gray.

lies must stretch their dollars farther to pay for current consumption, while keeping up with debt payments. At some point, income simply becomes insufficient, and families must either curtail spending or default on debt.

The growth in debt outstripped the appreciation of assets during this same period. In other words, increases in liabilities—mortgage debt, home equity lines of credit, student loans, and credit cards—collectively grew faster than increases in assets—houses, cars, stocks, or cash savings. Edward Wolff of the Levy Economics Institute has calculated that as far back as 1995, the amount of mortgage debt began to increase faster than house values.[12] The result of the increased borrowing was to constrain or retard growth in household wealth. Indeed, between 2001 and 2004, the typical (median) American household's wealth actually declined.[13] This was an unprecedented event because the wealth decline occurred during a period of economic expansion. Household debt outstripped household asset accumulation for the middle class. For households with wealth between the 20th and 80th percentiles of the entire distribution, the debt-to-equity ratio climbed from 37.4 in 1983 to 51.3 in 1998, and then topped off at 61 percent in 2004 and 2007.[14] Whether assessed against income or assets, debt grew in proportion to other changes in families' balance sheets.

The boom in borrowing spans social classes, racial and ethnic groups, sexes, and generations. Every age group, except those seventy-five years or older, had increased leverage ratios between 1998 and 2007.[15] Similarly, African Americans, Hispanics, and non-Hispanic whites all saw their leverage ratios grow from 2001 to 2007.[16] This is not to suggest that the debt explosion was equally distributed. For example, between 2004 and 2007, typical people who lacked a high school diploma and typical households headed by a person between ages sixty-five and seventy-four experienced particularly sharp increases in their debt burdens.[17] In particular periods, some groups saw modest declines in consumer debt, but the overwhelming trend was increased amounts of debt among nearly every type of family. By 2007, when debt burdens peaked, 77 percent of American households had some type of outstanding debt.[18] Consumer debt has become one of the most common shared qualities of middle-class Americans, usurping the fraction of the population that owns a home, is married, has graduated from college, or attends church regularly.[19]

TOO BIG TO FAIL AND TOO SMALL TO SAVE:
MIDDLE-CLASS FAMILIES IN CRISIS

As debt increases, so too does the risk of financial failure. This is as true for American families as it is for large corporations, where the catchy phrase "highly leveraged" captures a profound tilt into the red on a company balance sheet. Over the long haul, increases in consumer debt seem to explain a significant portion of the increased numbers of consumer bankruptcies.[20]

The escalation in debt has turned the smart financial decisions of the prior generation, such as purchasing a home or taking on student loans, into high-stakes economic gambles for middle-class families. Today, millions of Americans are losing those bets, struggling to avoid financial collapse. This statement was as true before the Great Recession as it is today. As President Obama explained in January 2010, "Too many Americans have known their own painful recessions long before any economist declared a recession."[21] The per capita bankruptcy rate, shown in Figure 1.2, provides one example of this phenomenon. Bankruptcy has become more frequent in the American population over the past three decades, although the filing trend of the past few years reflects the major reform of the bankruptcy laws in 2005.

Other markers of debt problems have also increased in recent years. The percentage of consumers who experienced a third-party debt collection activity has grown steadily in the past decade, doubling from 7 percent in 2000 to 14 percent in 2010.[22] Foreclosure filings, for example, climbed in the 1980s and 1990s.[23] The crisis in the mortgage markets sharply escalated the foreclosure rate; in 2009, one in forty-five homeowners received a foreclosure notice.[24] Debt collection was the leading complaint to the Federal Trade Commission in each of the past several years.[25] Credit card charge-offs, while highly sensitive to economic conditions, have generally crept higher (see Figure 1.3). The volatility of debt default has also increased. The Great Recession is causing a spike in credit card charge-offs that is much larger than other recent recessions.

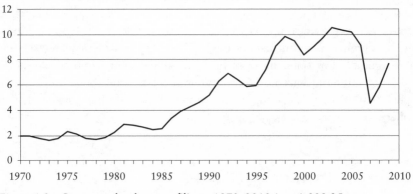

Figure 1.2   Consumer bankruptcy filings, 1970–2010 (per 1,000 25- to 64-year-olds)

   SOURCE: Calculations by Robert Lawless and Katherine Porter from U.S. Census Population Estimates and Administrative Office of U.S. Courts data.

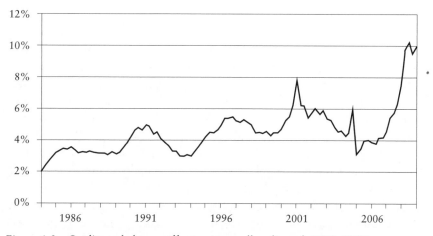

Figure 1.3   Credit card charge-off rate, seasonally adjusted, 1985–2009
SOURCE: Federal Reserve Bank Statistical Release.

Subjective measures of prosperity tell a story similar to the hard data: Americans' insecurity about their financial lives is on the rise. A New York Times/CBS poll found that in 1995, about one in six people did not think they would reach the "American Dream," as they defined it, within their lifetime. In 2005, more than 25 percent of people said the American Dream would remain out of their reach.[26] In 2008, the Pew Research Center reported data from surveys asking whether people were better off, the same, or worse than they were five years before, noting that the responses reflected "the most downbeat short-term assessment of personal progress in nearly half a century of polling."[27]

Despite the ubiquity of debt problems, most people in financial distress suffer silently.[28] The Great Recession may have shifted this cultural norm somewhat, particularly in locations where job loss or foreclosure is relatively common. But it is hard to dispute the fact that the media, Congress, and pundits have spent more time on the financial collapse of big banks than of everyday families.[29] At a conference I attended, someone quipped that while banks were "too big to fail," families were "too small to save." In part, this comment reflects the powerful importance of the risk frame in public policy: small incidences of harm rarely receive the attention of large ones, even if the accumulation of small harms dwarfs the single large harm. This preference to prioritize single large events over multiple smaller ones shortchanges middle-class families. The U.S. Treasury's bold intervention in the capital markets is a stark contrast to its anemic response to foreclosures at the family level: the Home Affordable Modification Program (HAMP), which has been criticized as inadequate.[30]

The inattention to the financial well-being of American families existed long before the collapse of Bear Stearns or Lehman Brothers demanded the attention of policymakers. Alan Greenspan's surprise at the number of sub-prime mortgages that originated during his tenure as chairman of the Federal Reserve is an example of the failure of government to monitor consumer finance at the household level.[31] When consumer credit did come to the fore, concerns about the dangers of borrowing were met with dogged claims that credit regulation would only lead to less availability of credit and no appreciable benefits to consumers.[32] In retrospect, retrenchment in borrowing seems like a good idea. The blind eye that policymakers turned to the risks of consumer borrowing has cost the world economy dearly.

Although the Great Recession had many causes, recent research demonstrates a link between household balance sheets and the economic downturn. Using cross-sectional, county-level data, finance professors Atif Mian and Amir Sufi conclude that their analysis supports "the hypothesis that the initial economic slowdown was a result of a highly-leveraged household sector unable to keep pace with its debt obligations."[33] The borrowing binge has certainly slowed; household debt contracted for the first time in the fourth quarter of 2008.[34] Since 2009, middle-class families have made efforts to pay down debt and to save,[35] although this progress remains small given the lopsided nature of families' balance sheets. This reduced debt may improve the stability of the overall U.S. economy in the long term, but the inability of families to keep borrowing to make ends meet will plunge some into hardship. A 2011 study found that if faced with a financial emergency, half of families could not come up with $2,000 from savings, family or friends, or borrowing. This evidence of widespread financial fragility illustrates the risks facing middle-class families during the recovery from the recession.[36] Decreased debt also will mean decreased consumer spending. Yet, middle-class consumption is the major driver of growth in the postindustrial economy. Families' efforts to pare down their debts by substituting repayment for spending, or their decision to forego repayment entirely by walking away from their mortgages or filing for bankruptcy, are likely to be drags on any economic recovery in the foreseeable future.[37]

Ultimately, we may recognize that in the U.S. economy, the middle class is too big to fail. This emerging insight will challenge the idea that consumer debt is too small of a subject to study deeply and with rigor. In exploring the plight of families whose debt problems drove them to bankruptcy, this book suggests the kinds of policies that might prevent or remediate unmanageable consumer debt.

THE 2007 CONSUMER BANKRUPTCY PROJECT

While bankruptcy is only one measure of serious financial distress, it is the most visible sign of financial catastrophe. It is a public place for seeing financial pain that is largely endured in private, behind closed doors. And because it represents a particularly extreme form of financial distress, it is a useful barometer of the financial suffering of American families. This book uses bankruptcy data to examine how growth in consumer debt undermines financial security and prosperity.

Researchers have studied families in bankruptcy for at least forty years.[38] Much of that work documented the financial profiles of people in bankruptcy, their demographic characteristics, and people's self-reported causes of their financial problems. This book updates and extends that literature. The dataset used in this book is the most recent iteration of the Consumer Bankruptcy Project (CBP), which was conducted in 2007. The CBP did its first study in 1981 and conducted expanded versions of similar studies in 1991 and 2001 (see the appendix for more details).

The 2007 CBP collected data on bankruptcy cases filed in the first few months of 2007. A random sample of about five thousand households was drawn from all Chapter 7 or Chapter 13 consumer bankruptcies, and these households were mailed a four-page written survey that asked for demographic information and reasons for bankruptcy.[39] On this survey, debtors were asked whether they would be willing to complete a telephone interview about their bankruptcies. More than twenty-four hundred households returned completed surveys, for a response rate of approximately 50 percent. The CBP researchers then completed telephone interviews lasting sixty to ninety minutes with 1,032 of these households about six to twelve months after they had filed for bankruptcy. Information on financial characteristics from these debtors' bankruptcy court records also was coded. Collectively, the three instruments (written surveys, bankruptcy court files, and telephone interviews) gathered thousands of pieces of data. The 2007 CBP is both the largest and the most comprehensive study ever conducted of families in bankruptcy.

The 2007 CBP coprincipal investigators came from several disciplines and had a wide array of research questions (see the appendix). Reflecting this diversity, the data are expansive in their scope. The CBP collected data on demographics, such as age, education, race, and marital status; financial characteristics at the time of bankruptcy, such as current income, current expenses, debts owed and names of creditors, and assets and their values; causes of bankruptcy, assessed both by self-reporting and by specific inquiries about certain bankruptcy triggers, such as a pending foreclosure; and experiences in financial distress and bankruptcy, such as effects on children and marriages, emotional reactions to debt, and assessments of the bankruptcy process. This book provides comprehensive coverage of these areas; several other published works also use the 2007 CBP data.[40]

The appendix provides a more detailed methodology of the 2007 CBP. It describes the data collection process, calculations of response rates, and tests for response bias. The addendum to this introduction is a primer on consumer bankruptcy and will be particularly useful for those without legal training or who are not familiar with the prior literature on consumer bankruptcy. It describes the bankruptcy filing process, differences between the Chapter 7 (liquidation) and Chapter 13 (repayment plan) types of bankruptcy, and outcomes from bankruptcy.

FAILURE STORIES

Bankruptcy is contested terrain. One measure of this fact is that Congress spent ten years debating reforms to the consumer bankruptcy system before they ultimately became law in 2005. Some see bankruptcy as the refuge of the profligate, impulsive, or greedy—a symbol of consumption excesses and weakening moral fiber. Others see bankruptcy as the locus of the fallout from decades of structural changes in the allocation of financial risk among families, businesses, and the government—a symbol of a weakened social safety net and shifts in wealth away from the middle class.

This book's purpose is to counter the rhetoric about bankruptcy by providing data on the real families who file for bankruptcy. In analyzing their financial situations, we identify gaps and inconsistencies in the law, policy, and economics of consumer credit. Each chapter examines a different slice of the bankruptcy system, but the chapters together give a useful overview of the severe financial distress that plagues many American families struggling with their debts.

Part I. The Debtor Next Door

The book opens with an inquiry into who files for bankruptcy. In Chapter 2 Elizabeth Warren and Deborah Thorne describe the "bankrupt tribe,"[41] the families who live and work among us and whose financial problems remain largely invisible. They examine the socioeconomic status of families and show that measured by enduring socioeconomic characteristics such as education, occupation, and homeownership, more than 90 percent of bankrupt people are members of the middle class. Because their incomes at the time of bankruptcy hover between poverty and working class, these families are experiencing dramatic reversals of fortune when they collapse into bankruptcy. Their stories are a rare opportunity to observe downward mobility, a phenomenon that is widespread in modern America but is much less studied than upward mobility.

Because the families in bankruptcy look so much like the rest of us, their problems—job instability, illness and injury, and family breakup—serve as a case study of the economic vulnerabilities of America's middle class. The bankruptcy data suggest that the old strategies for wealth building—home-ownership, a well-regarded job, and college attendance—are increasingly correlated with <u>financial insecurity</u>. The demographics of bankruptcy in 2007 reflect the economic insecurity that plagues middle-class Americans, even during the best of times for the overall economy. The data also suggest that the path to middle-class prosperity may be perilous as traditional strategies for economic security do not offer insulation from financial distress.

The bankrupt are only one category of those with financial problems; millions of other households are financially vulnerable but not bankrupt. Brian Bucks in Chapter 3 compares bankrupt households with households in the general population using data from the CBP and the Federal Reserve's Survey of Consumer Finances. As alternatives to bankruptcy in understanding the breadth of household economic insecurity in the United States, he develops four <u>measures of financial distress</u>: households with very low financial assets, households with high debt payments relative to their incomes, households that were turned down for credit, and households that were delinquent on debt payments. The relatively small overlap between these groups and bankrupt households highlights the challenges for designing policies that take aim at reducing the overall level of financial vulnerability among Americans.

Part II. Starting Right, Ending Wrong

The causes of bankruptcy are complex. For most families, a confluence of factors rather than a single decision or event explains their overwhelming debts. The groundbreaking research of Teresa Sullivan, Elizabeth Warren, and Jay Westbrook pointed to <u>three</u> major <u>life events</u> that families frequently experience before bankruptcy: job problems, such as unemployment or a reduction in hours; illness or injury; and a major change in family structure, such as divorce or the death of a spouse.[42] This book explores three other life decisions that have a powerful influence on a family's risk of bankruptcy: owning a home, attending college, and <u>starting a small business</u>. Although these are typically viewed as "smart" financial decisions, they bring with them serious consequences for one's financial situation, largely because homeownership, college, and business startups today are financed with large amounts of debt. The data on the bankruptcies of these households are reminders that pursuing opportunity for upward mobility can itself lead to <u>downward mobility</u>.

L♂

In the years after the housing bubble burse in 2007, it is painfully easy to observe the risks of homeownership. The American economic landscape is littered with families who bought too much house with too little income and too little understanding of their mortgage obligations. Foreclosures remain at or near their highest levels in fifty years.[43] Underwriting criteria have constricted, closing off or at least significantly delaying homeownership for young families or those with limited savings;[44] and governments continue to reduce services to neighborhoods in the wake of declines in tax revenues and strain on social programs.[45] The fallout from the mortgage excesses of the 2000s has created a dire need for research that helps to identify the appropriate level of financial risk for homeowners.

In Chapter 4 Jerry Anthony explores the housing cost burdens of families in bankruptcy, including how those burdens vary by demographic factors. Among other findings, he identifies the higher likelihood of widowed or divorced people having high housing cost ratios and significant differences in ratios by age, a finding that has implications for financial planning over the lifecycle. He also analyzes whether housing cost ratios are associated with how households and lenders react to loan default. The findings have implications for designing policy responses to foreclosure.

Chapter 5 examines the intersection of education and bankruptcy risk. For the past several decades, policymakers have embraced the mantra that "college pays."[46] I test this idea against the educational experiences of bankrupt people and do not find the expected linear relationship between more education and less bankruptcy. In fact, the people who attended college but did not graduate with a four-year degree are overrepresented in bankruptcy. While this outcome does not seem to be driven by student loan debt, it nonetheless suggests the existence of long-term financial consequences of attending college without earning a bachelor's degree. Advocates of more vocational or community college attendance may want to reevaluate policies to expand college attendance if further research bears out a relationship between some college attendance and financial insecurity and bankruptcy. This chapter's analysis does not purport to be causal, but it challenges conventional ideas about the traditional paths to middle-class prosperity.

Robert Lawless, in Chapter 6, tackles another example of how assumptions about the path to achieving the American Dream may mask the hard realities of financial risk taking. His analysis finds that self-employed people are overrepresented in the bankrupt population. Furthermore, when these people collapse into the bankruptcy system, they do so with very large debts, even compared with other bankrupt families. His data are a powerful reminder that starting a business may pay big dividends, but like all things with the potential for higher-than-average financial returns, it carries a higher-than-average level of risk. He juxtaposes the failures of the self-employed whom he observes in bankruptcy against the dominant narrative of successful entrepreneurship.

Part III. Hurting at Home

Bankruptcy is a profound financial event that has the potential to rewrite a family's balance sheet, eliminating some debts and forcing the surrender of some assets. These financial changes should not undercut the ways in which bankruptcy is also a social and emotional phenomenon. In this part of the book, Marianne Culhane and Deborah Thorne describe the personal, not merely the financial, consequences of financial distress.

Between 2007 and early 2010, 6.6 million families had foreclosures initiated on their homes.[47] This number is only a rough estimate and may miss families who surrendered or sold their houses because of financial pressures. In Chapter 7 Marianne Culhane uses the bankruptcy data to reveal what happens to families who lose their homes. She shows that many of them return to renting or live with family or friends for a significant period—if not for the rest of their lives. Using debtors' own words, she documents the reasons that families desperately wanted to hang on to their homes. For Americans, their own home is an anchor in the social landscape. Without this mooring, many families are fearful about their futures and experience a loss of place that leaves them disoriented in their social worlds.

Marriage is to be "for better or for worse"; for many couples, bankruptcy and the financial distress that precedes it is a time of "for worse." Sociologist Deborah Thorne in Chapter 8 connects the emotional experiences of men and women in bankruptcy to the literature on gendered patterns of work. Women in financially distressed families overwhelmingly bear both the responsibility for paying bills and the emotional fallout of trying (but failing) to make ends meet in the years before the family files for bankruptcy. Thorne exposes how gender-neutral legal systems, such as bankruptcy, rarely operate in ways that affect men and women equally. Financial distress seems to hurt nearly everyone who falls into that condition, but these two chapters suggest that homeowners and women experience particularly acute emotional pain.

Part IV. The Hard Road Out

Bankruptcy is not itself supposed to be a problem. By design, it is meant to be a solution to the problem of financial distress. But like most policies, it is far from a perfect solution. Those who look to bankruptcy for easy relief are surely disappointed. The data show that the bankruptcy system is expensive, complicated, and sometimes unjust in its operation. The financial crisis may provoke a renewed interest in designing a better safety valve for families with overwhelming debts. Chapter 9 by Angela Littwin on the importance of attorney representation in bankruptcy, and Chapter 10 by Dov Cohen and Robert Lawless on racial disparities in the bankruptcy system, point to two important considerations in any redesign of the bankruptcy system.

Although one would expect consumer law to be accessible to consumers, bankruptcy may be the poster child for the failure of the law to achieve that criterion. Bankruptcy law is, in fact, quite complex, at least in part because it is designed around a one-size-fits-all system that accommodates the insolvency of both multimillion-dollar corporations and the family next door. Littwin's analysis shows that unrepresented debtors, those who file pro se without lawyers, fare significantly worse in bankruptcy than their counterparts who have lawyers. She documents who foregoes a lawyer and shows a surprising effect: it is not the poorest or least sophisticated debtors who attempt bankruptcy on their own, but rather those who seem to believe that the high cost of a lawyer is an expense they can forego. The data show the folly of that hope. Even in the simpler form of bankruptcy, Chapter 7, the lack of an attorney increases by ten times the likelihood that a debtor will fail to receive a discharge of debt. In Chapter 13 bankruptcy, the outcome of doing it oneself is near certain dismissal of the case without substantial debt relief. The stakes are high in bankruptcy, and families who take the bankruptcy gamble by themselves are certain to suffer.

On its face, bankruptcy law is race blind; it has no equivalent to financial affirmative action or discrimination imbedded in it.[48] The system's operation may not be neutral as to race, however—a possibility that has particular cultural resonance in the United States where African Americans have long suffered financial disadvantages. Cultural psychologist Dov Cohen and law professor Robert Lawless find that African American households file Chapter 13 bankruptcy at more than double the rate of debtors of other races. Because Chapter 13 debtors, as compared with Chapter 7 debtors, are less likely to receive a discharge of their debts, more likely to pay higher attorneys' fees, must stay in the bankruptcy system longer, and typically must repay some of their debts, the differential in chapter choice translates to differential debt relief among racial groups. Cohen and Lawless link their findings to a long literature on "local legal culture" in bankruptcy and suggest that racial bias may be a hitherto unforeseen aspect of legal decisions.

Part V. The Once and Future American Dream

The last two chapters of the book put financial distress from unmanageable debt in a larger perspective. In Chapter 11 Kevin Leicht provides historical and social context for the remarkable growth in household borrowing. The expansion in debt coincided with two other powerful economic phenomena:

a stagnation in wages and a sharpening of inequality between the richest households and middle-class households. His statistical simulation shows how the debt burdens of today's families would have been unthinkable in the prior generation. Leicht describes how debt is used as a tool to simulate social class. He conceptualizes debt as a buoy to keep middle-class lifestyles afloat in the face of trends such as stagnant wage growth that would otherwise undermine middle-class consumption desires. In this way, the book reconnects firmly to its opening focus on the way in which debt is ubiquitous in the middle class.

Chapter 12 locates bankruptcy risk in the context of an overall decline in economic security for American families. Political scientist Jacob Hacker describes the need for a twenty-first-century social contract that protects families against the most severe risks they face, including problems such as job dislocation, medical bills, family care-giving obligations, and retirement insecurity, which can push families into overwhelming debt and even bankruptcy. He argues that economic security is a necessary component of economic opportunity and that an improved social safety net requires a redistribution of economic risks among families, private industry, and government.

PROTECTING MIDDLE-CLASS PROSPERITY

America's relationship with borrowing is at a turning point. Lenders have tightened underwriting standards, and households are reducing their spending and saving more of their incomes. Even the federal government has taken decisive action with the creation of a new regulator, the Consumer Financial Protection Bureau, which is specifically charged with monitoring the functioning of the consumer credit markets.[49] The open question is whether this retrenchment will endure or accelerate. In the early twenty-first century, debt is still near record levels, relative to income, and twice as high per family as in the 1980s.[50] Will the United States reverse more than two decades of reliance on consumer borrowing and gradually work its way back to debt burdens of the post–World War II period of prosperity? Or will the borrowing habit return in a few years as the Great Recession recedes, with another boom in borrowing replacing the past few years of bust? The choice between these paths has profound consequences for the economic security of America's middle class.

The bankruptcy data illustrate the deep economic pain experienced by millions of middle-class families. Consumer debt is not the only reason for the increasing financial vulnerability of Americans; stagnant wages, increased volatility in the labor market, health-care and college costs that outpace inflation, and longer lifespans that strain retirement savings all play a role. Consumer debt is particularly useful as a lens for middle-class prosperity, however, because in the past two decades debt was the crutch of families wounded by other economic harms. Debt smoothes consumption over time; for example, it can ease the uneven income that characterizes the rising cadre of temporary and contract workers in the country. Debt substitutes for cost controls in markets gone astray; for example, people increasingly must finance medical bills because they overwhelm their monthly budgets. Debt fills gaps in people making ends meet when social programs erode; for example, people may borrow from a payday lender to cover utility bills as local governments eliminate energy subsidy programs.

These functions for debt are not inherently bad. To the contrary, debt has long been a lynchpin of opportunity in our society. But there is concern that too many Americans have borrowed too much and that they have often taken on debts that will worsen, rather than improve, their financial situations. This book exposes the harms of consumer debt because those harms are one piece of information needed to regulate consumer credit markets. The cost of debt is not just the annual percentage rate charged to a family; it is also the social costs of some borrowers becoming hopelessly mired in debt and the macroeconomic effect of overleveraged households. Those costs are being paid by today's middle-class families during the Great Recession and will likely continue to be paid in the upcoming decade. Economic models of the amount that families would need to save to push the debt-to-income ratio down to 100 percent over the next ten years show that such dramatic changes in household behavior would subtract about three-fourths of a percentage point from annual consumption growth each year in the next decade, relative to the savings rate remaining at its 2008 level of 4 percent.[51] The cumulative result of households' addressing their unstable and risky debt burdens will be to drag down economic growth for the entire nation.

Going forward, we cannot afford to adopt a blind belief that more debt equals more prosperity. We cannot sustain national economic prosperity while unmanageable borrowing undermines the prosperity of American families. But neither can we afford to limit opportunity and shunt upward mobility for the middle class by buying into fear that all borrowing is bad. The challenge is to figure out how to calibrate consumer credit markets to balance the harms described in this book against the benefits of borrowing.

ADDENDUM: A PRIMER ON BANKRUPTCY

Bankruptcy is one of the most common legal processes in the United States. In 2010, about one consumer bankruptcy case was filed for every 76 households in the country. Put differently, if you were to drive past one thousand houses in a subdivision that was representative of the U.S. population, you would pass thirteen households that had just filed for bankruptcy. But despite its widespread use by everyday people, bankruptcy is a complicated process. The public understanding of bankruptcy is mired in myths and misunderstandings, often by those who see its relief as a panacea for all financial ills. While many of the authors of the chapters in this book are legal experts on bankruptcy, others write as outsiders to the system. This book is designed to be accessible to anyone who wants a better understanding of the problems of consumer debt in American families and who has some familiarity with social science statistics. Particularly for people interested in legal policy or methodology, however, a basic knowledge of bankruptcy may be useful. Here I outline the broad contours of the consumer bankruptcy system, describing the relevant law on the books and the empirical data about how that law operates in reality.

Nearly all consumer bankruptcies in the United States are voluntary. The process usually begins with people contacting a bankruptcy attorney, or less commonly, making the decision to file without an attorney representation. The bankruptcy attorney will typically gather information about the family's financial characteristics, such as assets, debts, and income. The family will often describe the particular problems that triggered their decision to seek bankruptcy relief. The most common pressures are repeated contact with debt collectors or concern about losing a home to foreclosure.[52]

Attorneys will counsel debtors on which type, or chapter, of bankruptcy to file.[53] About two-thirds of consumer bankruptcy cases are filed under Chapter 7, with the remaining one-third being Chapter 13 cases.[54] Chapter 7 differs greatly from Chapter 13; the choice of which chapter to file influences everything from the cost of legal fees and the length of the bankruptcy to the substantive type of debt relief available. Table 1.1 shows the main differences between Chapter 7 and Chapter 13.

Chapter 7 is the more familiar "liquidation" bankruptcy. The trustee reviews the debtor's assets and determines what, if any, property the law permits to be sold to satisfy debts. The makeup of this "exempt property" varies depending on the debtor's state of residence but often includes things thought to be necessary for basic existence, such as clothing, modest household furnishings, or a single household vehicle. The two most important exemptions are probably the amount, if any, of protection for a family home ("homestead exemption") and for cash (often a pending tax refund) because these are often the most important property of debtors. If debtors want to avoid the sale of property that is not exempt, they may choose to file Chapter 13 instead.

In the vast majority of Chapter 7 cases, there are no nonexempt assets for the trustee to liquidate.[55] In other words, the debtor does not have any

TABLE 1.1

Major differences between Chapter 7 and Chapter 13 bankruptcy

	Chapter 7	Chapter 13
Type of procedure	Liquidation ("sell off")	Reorganization ("pay out")
Exempt property	Nonexempt property sold and proceeds distributed to creditors	Retain all property regardless of exemptions
Treatment of collateral	Must be current on payments or creditor usually will be permitted to foreclose/repossess	Can be retained even if behind on payments; can catch up on missed payments over repayment plan
Payments to creditors	No payments required to unsecured creditors; debtor retains all future income	Payments made to unsecured creditors out of future income; payment amounts vary
Court involvement	Minimal; often only if debtor reaffirms a dischargeable debt or a creditor contests discharge	Moderate to heavy; court must approve repayment plan; debtor's plan is administered by trustee
Discharge	About four months after filing	After plan completion (three to five years)
Attorneys' fees	Usually $1,000–$1,500	Usually $2,000–$4,000

property that can be sold to repay unsecured creditors. The trustee examines the debtor at the meeting described in the opening of this chapter and files a report that there are no assets, and the debtor's unsecured creditors receive no repayment from the bankruptcy. If there are nonexempt assets to sell, the trustee will sell them and distribute the sale proceeds pro rata to the debtors' creditors. This means that each unsecured creditor receives a share of the proceeds that is in proportion to how much it is owed as a share of the total unsecured debt.

Secured creditors, such as mortgage companies or car lenders, have taken collateral to secure repayment of the debt, so they are treated differently in bankruptcy. They have more rights, including most fundamentally the right to repossess the property if the debt remains unpaid during the bankruptcy proceedings. In Chapter 7, debtors are often current on their mortgage or car payments and simply continue making the payments. Alternatively, debtors will be required to reaffirm the debt in order to keep the property. A reaffirmation is a legally binding promise to repay the debt. These agreements must be filed with the bankruptcy court. Sometimes debtors cannot afford to keep the collateral. They may have been behind on payments when they filed for bankruptcy or not be able to keep up with payments during or after the bankruptcy. In these situations, the secured creditor will repossess the collateral (or foreclose on the home). The creditor gets the property or its value upon sale. A bankruptcy discharge, however, means that the debtor will not owe the creditor the deficiency amount; this is any amount that remains due to the creditor after the collateral is sold.

Chapter 7 bankruptcies usually last only four months. The debtor files the required paperwork, the trustee reviews the case, and the debtor receives a discharge from the bankruptcy court. The discharge is an injunction that forbids the debtor's creditors from attempting to collect the discharged debts. The discharge is powerful relief, letting the debtor off the hook for many common debts, including credit card bills, hospital and medical bills, and deficiency obligations. A bankruptcy discharge is not complete relief, however, from all financial problems. Student loans, certain tax debts, and some obligations incurred shortly before bankruptcy usually are not discharged. Just as importantly, debtors emerge from Chapter 7 back into their regular lives, having to make ends meet on whatever income they earn. Many debtors continue to struggle financially, largely because the majority of bankrupt people have low incomes.[56]

Chapter 13 bankruptcy operates on a different premise from Chapter 7. Debtors can retain all of their property, regardless of whether the law exempts it, but they in turn must commit to using all of the disposable income they have during the next three to five years to repaying their creditors. Some debtors cannot file Chapter 13 because they do not have any income at all, or more commonly, they do not have enough income to confirm a repayment plan. The operative issue in Chapter 13 is usually whether the debtors' proposed treatments of their secured creditors are in accord with the requirements of bankruptcy law. Debtors must have enough income to keep up with payments on any property they want to keep, such as their house or car, and also to catch up on any missed past payments. While the law has some flexibility to adjust the terms of these debts, it is fairly limited, especially for mortgage debts. Successful Chapter 13 debtors need to have enough money to keep up with their regular, ongoing secured debt payments; find additional money in their budgets to make up missed payments; and keep their households supplied with food, clothing, gas, and other necessities. Perhaps because of these challenges, some Chapter 13 debtors do not confirm a repayment plan, either dropping out of bankruptcy entirely or converting their cases to Chapter 7.[57] Many Chapter 13 debtors do confirm a plan but then stumble as they try to make the required payments for the three- to five-year plan period. In Chapter 13, the discharge of unsecured debts does not occur until the end of the repayment plan. Only one in three Chapter 13 filings gets to this point.[58] The norm in Chapter 13 is not discharge (the standard outcome in Chapter 7) but instead continued liability for unsecured debts, along with temporary relief during the attempted repayment plan.

Chapter 13 cases require more intensive court and trustee involvement. The court must approve the Chapter 13 repayment plan, finding that it is feasible and that it provides the required treatment to secured and unsecured creditors. If in the trustee's judgment the debtor's budget does not look reasonable or does not propose to pay all disposable income to unsecured creditors, the trustee may object to the plan being confirmed. Courts are also often asked to rule on whether a secured creditor can repossess collateral or a case should be dismissed. The trustee collects the debtor's payments in the repayment process, distributing them as appropriate to secured creditors, unsecured creditors, and the debtor's attorney. The trustee will move to dismiss the case if the debtor misses payments.

In both kinds of bankruptcy, debtors file extensive paperwork—typically about fifty pages.[59] This paperwork is complicated and often completed with the help of an attorney. It includes a petition with basic information about the debtor, with the debtor's signature indicating under penalty of perjury that the paperwork filed in the case is correct. The debtor also files various schedules, which are essentially lists of the debtors' assets, debts, income, expenses, and significant past financial events. These court records are public, but the court system requires a nominal fee and password for someone to access them electronically or a trip to the courthouse for someone to see them for free in person. Bankruptcy is reported to credit-reporting agencies and can stay on a debtor's records for up to ten years.[60]

The complex legal choices and paperwork requirements of the consumer bankruptcy system mean that legal fees are fairly expensive. In 2007, the median Chapter 7 debtor paid $1,000; the median Chapter 13 debtor paid $2,500.[61] On top of these charges, debtors must pay about $300 in filing fees to the bankruptcy court. In Chapter 7, the attorneys' fees are paid up front, usually requiring debtors to save them up over several months or to delay filing until they have some extra income, such as a tax refund. In Chapter 13, debtors usually pay only a small fraction (often $200) of the total attorneys' fees at the time of filing. The attorney collects the rest in the form of disbursements from the trustee during the debtor's repayment plan.

Nearly everything just discussed is subject to dozens of exceptions, some resulting from legal loopholes, but primarily because bankruptcy practice varies tremendously across the country. On paper, bankruptcy is federal law, codified in Title 11 of the U.S. Code. Indeed, even back in 1787, the people who drew up the U.S. Constitution recognized that interstate commerce would necessitate "uniform laws on the subject of bankruptcies throughout the United States."[62] In reality, however, the practices of judges, trustees, attorneys, and even debtors themselves vary.[63] For example, Chapters 9 and 10 in this book describe variation in the proportion of pro se (no attorney) cases and in the fraction of cases that are Chapter 13s. The number of people who have previously filed for bankruptcy also varies by location, but an estimate for the national rate of repeat filings is 8 percent.[64]

Some readers will notice that the centerpiece of the 2005 amendments to the bankruptcy laws, the so-called means test, has not been mentioned in the discussion thus far. This omission is intentional and reflects the fact that the largest discernable effect of the means test seems to have been to dramatically increase attorneys' fees, rather than to force large numbers of debtors to repay their debts. The basic thrust of the means test is to apply standardized criteria to determine whether debtors have sufficient income to repay their debts and therefore should be forced to file Chapter 13 or abstain from bankruptcy relief altogether. The financial profiles of bankruptcy debtors did not change dramatically because of the means test.[65] Most debtors have incomes that are low enough to allow them to remain eligible for Chapter 7 bankruptcy, and most of the remaining group has expenses that the law permits them to deduct to avoid being screened into Chapter 13. Of course, we do not know how many families may be deterred from bankruptcy because of the means test. We see only those who do file. This is another reminder that people who file for bankruptcy represent only one segment of people in financial distress; for every family who files for bankruptcy, more families narrowly scrape by without bankruptcy or hover only one financial event from collapse into bankruptcy.

ADDITIONAL RESOURCES FOR THIS BOOK

This book has a website, *www.sup.org/broke*. It contains additional tables and data for some chapters. The book is designed to be useful as a reader for a course in law or social stratification. The website contains two sample syllabi that may be reproduced in their entirety or may serve as models for instructors wishing to design their own courses around the book. One syllabus is for an upper-class seminar in a law school; it contains descriptions of writing assignments and in-class exercises as well as a complete reading list for the semester. The other syllabus is appropriate for a graduate course in public policy, sociology, or similiar disciplines. Assigning one chapter for each of the twelve weeks of the course provides students with continunity of material and exposure to different disciplines that study consumer debt issues.

PART I

THE DEBTOR NEXT DOOR

CHAPTER TWO

A Vulnerable Middle Class

Bankruptcy and Class Status

Elizabeth Warren and Deborah Thorne

Bankruptcy has become a defining event for millions of families, taking a place alongside college graduation and divorce as a turning point in modern American life. Each month, more than one hundred thousand middle-class families—people who went to college, got respectable jobs, and bought homes—file for bankruptcy. They publicly declare themselves flat broke, losers in the great economic game of life. By the time they file for bankruptcy, unemployment has often decimated their incomes, and their debts are inflated beyond all hope of repayment. But their educations, jobs, and home addresses give some clues about the lives they once lived and the dreams they pursued.

Studies conducted by the Consumer Bankruptcy Project (CBP) in 1991, 2001, and 2007 consistently demonstrate that bankruptcy is a largely middle-class phenomenon.[1] Educational levels, occupational status, and rates of homeownership make it clear that most bankruptcy debtors are squarely in the middle class. These enduring measures of class status indicate that it is ordinary Americans, rather than the marginalized underclass or high-stakes gamblers, who are most apt to experience financial failure.

The only measure that initially seems inconsistent with middle-class status is the income of bankrupt families. Their incomes at the time of filing for bankruptcy situate substantial numbers of them well below the national average for the middle class. But the data also show that shortly before filing, many people lost their jobs or saw their work hours reduced, two economic blows that often are central to part of the crisis that pushes households into bankruptcy. As such, we contend that because income levels often reflect recent declines, income is an unreliable indicator of class status for those in bankruptcy.

Because the families in bankruptcy look so much like the rest of us, their troubles and struggles—job instability, illness and injury, and divorce—can serve as a case study of the economic vulnerabilities of much of middle-class America. The data presented here update studies of bankrupt households from 1991 and 2001. The basic finding remains constant: when measured by enduring criteria, most of the families in bankruptcy are legitimate members of the middle class, even if their incomes are relatively quite low. But the data also reveal two important differences: compared with those earlier bankruptcy filers, debtors since 2001 are more likely to have gone to college and more likely to have bought a home. This suggests that these two traditional strategies for building wealth—college attendance and home-ownership—are increasingly divorced from financial security. In the past, we have assumed that these markers of the middle class strongly protected Americans from the economic instability that often leads to bankruptcy. It appears, however, that the financial tables have turned. Benefits enjoyed by those Americans with some college education or by those who have bought homes have been undermined, so that neither college attendance nor home-ownership seems to correlate with reduced rates of bankruptcy.

It appears that the debts taken on by students and homeowners may turn an otherwise prudent economic move into a high-risk gamble that, for a growing number of people, does not pay off. Now that these time-honored wealth-building strategies fail to provide substantial economic protection, the middle class may face even greater economic instability in coming years. These data suggest that in the modern economy, the path to prosperity may be far more perilous than anyone previously imagined.

THE MIDDLE CLASS DEFINED

Who holds a place in the middle class? Income has long been a leading measure for identifying middle-class status.[2] Scholars frequently define the middle class as those whose household earnings fall in the three middle quintiles, between the bottom 20 percent and the top 20 percent. This approach is easy to calculate and aligns closely with our collective perception that the American middle class is a large group. Although some researchers amend the cutoff points—for example, expanding the criteria to include the middle 80 percent or 90 percent of the distribution—the dominant metric remains squarely focused on income as a proxy for class status.[3]

Our inquiry into who goes bankrupt indicates that the families who filed for bankruptcy in 2007 had a median gross household income of $32,988.[4] In contrast, the median gross household income for all families in the United States that same year was $50,233.[5] This suggests that in 2007 many of the bankrupt households were trying to make ends meet on considerably less income than the average American household.[6]

Dividing these populations into quintiles highlights the sharp disparity in incomes between bankrupt households and the general U.S. population.

At every quintile in the income distribution, the breakpoints for the U.S. population were higher than for the families in bankruptcy. As Figure 2.1 illustrates, U.S. households and bankrupt households in the bottom quintile had similarly low incomes—$20,300 and $18,240, respectively. However, the gap between those in bankruptcy and those in the general population increased considerably up the income scale. At the top quintiles, the incomes of those in bankruptcy were only about 60 percent that of the population generally. Indeed, the benchmark for the top 20 percent of bankrupt households ($57,228) was not that much greater than the 50 percent benchmark for the U.S. population, with its median income of $50,233.

These data make it clear that, compared with the incomes of all American households, the incomes of those in bankruptcy are visibly concentrated in the lower quartiles. This should come as no surprise. After all, bankruptcy is designed to help those in financial trouble. Lost income is deeply disruptive to a household's economic security, leaving the family more vulnerable to financial failure.

Although income is a readily available metric for determining class status, it has serious limitations. For example, careers that most Americans would classify as middle or even upper-middle class can have relatively low salaries. For instance, in 2007, mental health counselors, who are required to have either a master's or doctoral degree, earned average pretax incomes of a mod-

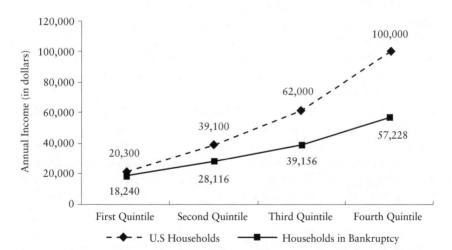

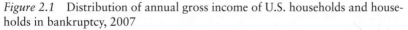

Figure 2.1   Distribution of annual gross income of U.S. households and households in bankruptcy, 2007

SOURCE: U.S. Census Bureau, Current Population Survey, Table HINC-05; Consumer Bankruptcy Project 2007.

NOTE: Income figures are at the upper cut-points for 20th, 40th, 60th, and 80th percentiles (to correspond to each quintile). For calculation of gross income of households in bankruptcy, payroll deductions were added to net income ("combined monthly total income" on Schedule I of bankruptcy court records).

est $39,450, or approximately $19.70 an hour.[7] In contrast, some jobs that do not necessarily carry middle-class status and prestige pay relatively high incomes. For example, in 2009, the median annual income for a United Parcel Service tractor-trailer truck driver was $70,550.[8]

Another problem with using income as a sole measure of social class is that over relatively short periods of time, income can fluctuate greatly. For example, a high school math teacher who quits teaching to enroll in a graduate program will immediately experience an income decline that will likely leave her hovering near the poverty level, but her class status will improve as her education increases. Furthermore, income as a measure of social class is uniquely problematic among bankrupt households, as incomes tend to be highly variable shortly before filing. Two-thirds (65 percent) of the households in bankruptcy reported job problems during the two years before they filed for bankruptcy.[9]

The income difficulties faced by families who filed for bankruptcy in 2007 are not the exclusive product of the recession. When our data were collected in the first quarter of 2007, the national unemployment rate was 4.5 percent.[10] Although that rate more than doubled in the following two years, the families filing for bankruptcy in 2007 reported the same concentration of job problems that plagued families who filed for bankruptcy in previous years. In the 1981, 1991, and 2001 CBP studies, bankrupt debtors also reported that their household incomes fluctuated sharply before they filed. When given the chance to explain the reasons behind their bankruptcy filings, a large proportion of bankrupt families in those years also identified job losses and cutbacks in the number of work hours.[11]

As the examples above illustrate, a meaningful definition of class requires more than income measures. Consequently, social scientists combine other criteria, such as education and occupational prestige, to provide a more accurate indication of social class status, particularly when studying people who experience sharp income fluctuations. Using these well-established variables, Martin Marger concludes that there are three levels of middle class—upper-middle, lower-middle, and working class—and when all three are combined, 68 to 80 percent of Americans are situated, broadly speaking, in the middle class.[12] By merging these criteria, the size of the middle class remains about the same as the rough income comparisons, but the composition shifts somewhat (see Table 2.1 in the note).[13] Sociologists Melvin Oliver and Thomas Shapiro expanded the calculus used to determine social class by adding homeownership—a common proxy for wealth, economic security, and social status.[14]

The critical point for our purposes is that for families in bankruptcy, income is often sharply disrupted near the time of filing, and it is out of synch with other indicia of class status. Because of the problems associated with using income as an indicator of class status for bankrupt households, we believe that the alternate criteria of social class—educational achievement, job status, and homeownership—are more valid measures of middle-class membership. For the remainder of this chapter, we use each criterion to compare the people who file for bankruptcy with the U.S. population. In addition, because we collected similar data from earlier years, we are also able to compare the status of bankrupt debtors today with their counterparts from 1991 and 2001. The data point toward a solidly and consistently middle-class group of households that file for bankruptcy.

EDUCATION MATTERS

The link between education and social class is long established in the social sciences.[15] As Marger notes: "The relationship is quite simple: The higher the number of years of education, the greater the probability of upward mobility."[16] Generally speaking, people with advanced degrees (professional degrees and graduate degrees) enjoy not only higher earnings, but also greater life chances, especially compared with those without a high school diploma.[17] In a nutshell, as a person's level of education increases, so too does his or her social class.

People who file for bankruptcy today are considerably more educated than they were just fifteen years ago. Figure 2.2 illustrates this clear trend. For example, compared with their 1991 counterparts, those filing for bankruptcy in 2007 were half as likely to have dropped out of high school and were much more likely to have attended some college. Overall, in 1991, the proportion of bankrupt people who had some college coursework, a college diploma, or an advanced degree comprised 46.5 percent of all of those in bankruptcy. By 2007, that proportion increased to 58.9 percent.

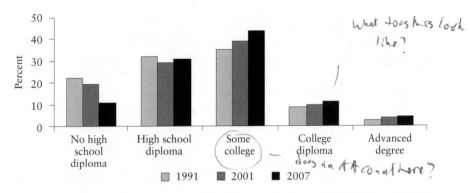

Figure 2.2   Educational attainment of people in bankruptcy, 1991, 2001, and 2007
SOURCE: Consumer Bankruptcy Projects, 1991, 2001, and 2007.

Not only are people who filed for bankruptcy in 2007 better educated than those who went bankrupt nearly two decades ago, they continue to be better educated than the general population. For example, between 1991 and 2007, the percentage of the U.S. adult population who had attended college increased from 39.2 percent in 1991 to 53.4 percent in 2007 (see Table 2.2 in the note).[18] And although this reflects a positive trend, the total remains notably smaller than the 58.9 percent of bankrupt debtors who had attended college in 2007 (Figure 2.3).

People who file for bankruptcy are also less likely to be represented at either end of the educational spectrum than the U.S. population. As Figure 2.3 illustrates, people in bankruptcy were less likely to drop out of high school, but they were also less likely to have earned advanced degrees from universities. Instead, people in bankruptcy were far more likely to be bunched in the middle—having attended college, but not having graduated.

The spike in "some college" shown in Figure 2.3 reflects a persistent trend among bankrupt debtors: compared with the general population, they were more likely to have attended college, but less likely to have completed their college degrees. People in bankruptcy were 60 percent more likely than Americans generally to have attended college but to have left without a diploma. When a person attends college but fails to graduate, the benefits that typically accompany the credential are less forthcoming. As Katherine Porter reports in Chapter 5, it is not mere college enrollment but a bachelor's degree that dramatically increases income.

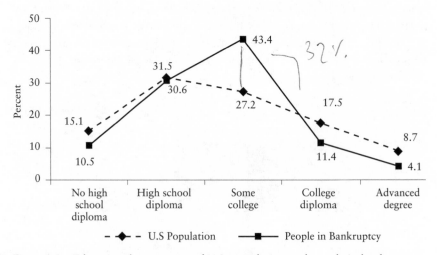

Figure 2.3   Educational attainment of U.S. population and people in bankruptcy, 2007

SOURCES: U.S. Census Bureau, Current Population Survey, Educational Attainment: 2007, Table 1; Consumer Bankruptcy Project 2007.

Nonetheless, for the purposes of determining class status, college attendance remains a significant event; it signals both aspirations and experiences that are distinctly middle class. When college attendance is used as a measure of social standing, nearly six of ten 2007 bankrupt debtors are in the middle class. As a group, people in bankruptcy appear to have the same or higher educational attainment than the general population, reinforcing the appropriateness of categorizing bankrupt debtors as a middle-class demographic.

THE ALL-IMPORTANT JOB

People often define themselves, and others, by their jobs. Our work shapes our minds, our bodies, and the rhythm of our daily lives. And equally importantly, our work also shapes the prestige others accord to us and our own sense of social standing.[19]

Occupational prestige is a matter of such importance that social science surveys have been used for decades to calibrate, and recalibrate, the status affiliated with virtually every job in the United States. On the basis of results from these surveys, jobs are assigned occupational prestige scores, which range from 0 to 100. For example, the occupation of custodian has been assigned a prestige score of 16; hair stylist, a score of 33; registered nurse, a score of 62; and physician, a score of 84. Not surprisingly, income and educational level are highly correlated with occupational prestige.[20] But there are important exceptions. For example, the occupation of professor is assigned a higher prestige score than a plumber, even though plumbers often earn considerably more money than professors. Because of such divergences, occupational prestige is an important alternative to income for measuring middle-class status.

In 1991, 2001, and 2007, the CBP asked debtors to describe their work and then assigned the corresponding occupational prestige score.[21] The median occupational prestige scores held constant at approximately 36, which is associated with jobs such as clerks, nurses' aides, office administrators, and brick masons. The most prestigious occupations of those in bankruptcy, which included social workers, guidance counselors, and computer programmers, had a score of 51 and were also constant across all three time periods. Most people in bankruptcy had jobs associated with the middle class, which often require some advanced training or specialized job skills beyond a high school diploma.

As Figure 2.4 illustrates, in 2007, all workers in the United States and workers who filed for bankruptcy shared a similar occupational prestige score distribution. The figure plots the break points for occupational prestige scores for each decile of the two populations and shows how the bankruptcy scores trail the U.S. population by only a few points at each interval.

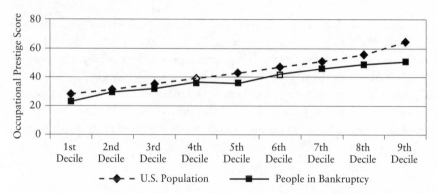

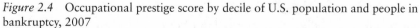

Figure 2.4 Occupational prestige score by decile of U.S. population and people in bankruptcy, 2007

SOURCES: National Opinion Research Center, General Social Surveys, 1972–2006; Consumer Bankruptcy Project 2007.

Bankrupt debtors are moderately concentrated in lower prestige jobs and are underrepresented at the upper end of the distribution in the higher prestige occupations, such as doctors, lawyers, and engineers. As a group, the individuals in bankruptcy in 2007 had somewhat less prestigious jobs than their counterparts in the population generally, but the magnitude of the difference was modest at most. People who file for bankruptcy are typically working right alongside other Americans.

The pattern of occupational prestige scores for people who filed for bankruptcy in 2007 is virtually identical to those patterns in the 1991 and 2001 CBP studies. Data from 1991 and 2001 also reveal similar patterns of occupational prestige scores between bankrupt individuals and the U.S. population: there is generally a proportional representation among the middle class, a small overrepresentation among the lowest class, and a more noticeable underrepresentation among the highest class (see Table 2.3 in the note).[22]

As our data illustrate, the occupational status of households that file for bankruptcy has remained relatively constant. Likewise, the distribution of occupational prestige scores for all Americans changed very modestly between 1991 and 2007. Nationally, median occupational prestige scores rose only slightly from 1991 to 2001 and then flattened out from 2001 to 2007. The similarity of the patterns reinforces an important and enduring trend: bankrupt Americans tend to have jobs similar to their nonbankrupt counterparts in the general population.

If occupational prestige scores are a marker of class status, then it is possible to demarcate points on the scale that reflect membership in the middle class. For purposes of locating the bankrupt debtors within the larger population, we suggest that the upper 80 percent of 2007 occupational prestige scores nationwide represent people who made it to the middle class. This criterion translates into an occupational score of 32 or higher. By this definition, people with occupational scores of 31 or lower (people working in retail or as delivery drivers, factory and assembly line workers, cooks and waiters, and landscapers) are excluded from the middle class. Because of the concentration of bankrupt debtors near the middle of the national occupational prestige scores, 77 percent of people in bankruptcy exceeded this threshold with an occupational score greater than 31 and therefore have a claim to middle-class status.[23]

For those who might draw the boundaries of middle-class membership more generously, including assembly line workers and others with scores of 30 or 31, for example, then the proportion of bankrupt debtors with middle-class occupations rises to 80.2 percent. For those who might draw a boundary at the other end of the spectrum, declaring those with occupational prestige scores in the top decile (occupational scores of 51 or higher) to be upper class rather than middle class, then the proportion of debtors with middle-class jobs shrinks by 5.4 percentage points. In the latter case, however, it is noticeable that much of the discussion of consumer bankruptcy centers around the issue of whether the people filing have achieved middle-class status—not whether they have exceeded it.

OWNING A HOME

During the housing boom that peaked in 2007, the government-sponsored mortgage agency Fannie Mae ran a series of advertisements depicting itself as being in the "American Dream business." That campaign tapped into the long-held belief that people who could purchase a home, who could put down roots and secure their financial futures, surely had accomplished the American Dream—even if they had borrowed every dollar needed to get there. While real estate agents and mortgage brokers were eager to point out the financial benefits of homeownership, sociologists Oliver and Shapiro stressed that owning a home has traditionally been an enduring, as well as a highly visible, symbol of middle-class achievement.[24]

For whatever combination of economic and social motives, families across the country have acquired homes in ever-growing numbers. From 1991 to 2007, homeownership in the United States expanded from 64.1 percent to 68.4 percent (Figure 2.5). For families in bankruptcy, the rise in homeownership was far more remarkable. The proportion of bankrupt families who were, or had recently been, homeowners jumped from 43.9 percent in 1991, to 50 percent in 2001, to 66.3 percent in 2007.[25] These data suggest that the housing bubble that began to inflate in the early 2000s included a

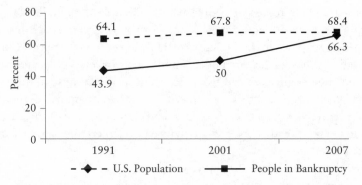

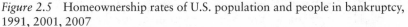

Figure 2.5   Homeownership rates of U.S. population and people in bankruptcy, 1991, 2001, 2007

S O U R C E S : U.S. Census Bureau, Housing Vacancies; Consumer Bankruptcy Projects 1991, 2001, and 2007.

growing number of homeowners who found themselves in bankruptcy even before the housing bubble burst.

Unlike the education and occupation statistics, the housing numbers are not directly comparable between all Americans and the bankrupt population. For the U.S. population generally, the proportion of homeowners is a measurement taken at a cross section in time, for example, during the month of March in 2007. But families in bankruptcy are in economic turmoil, and part of that turmoil may include losing a home through foreclosure, short sale, or surrender to a lender. A measure of homeownership that extends over a period of time is more likely to accurately capture a household's enduring living situation and class status. For this reason, families in bankruptcy were asked whether they owned a home at the time of filing for bankruptcy *or* had owned a home, but had lost it for financial reasons, in the five years before bankruptcy.

Figure 2.6 shows the 2007 homeownership rates of the U.S. population and people in bankruptcy. Slightly more than half (51.2 percent) of the families owned their homes at the time of bankruptcy, while a sizeable fraction, another 15.1 percent, had lost their homes for financial reasons within the five years preceding their bankruptcy filings. There is no comparable number for how many families in the general population lost their homes during the five years before 2007. The foreclosure rates in those years remained less than 1 percent, suggesting a small effect, but there is no accurate measure of the number of short sales or other arrangements that occurred outside the formal legal system to end homeownership. As a result, direct comparability about past homeownership is not possible.

If we limit our comparison strictly to current homeownership at a single point in time, the bankrupt population is substantially behind their counterparts in the general population. Homeownership rates among those in bankruptcy were about 25 percent lower than in the population generally. Even so, the fact that 66.3 percent of the households in bankruptcy either were current homeowners or had been homeowners in the past five years suggests middle-class aspirations and accomplishments—much like those who went to college but did not graduate. The tangible accomplishment of buying a home suggests middle-class status, even for those who were unable to hang on to their houses.

We pause to consider the relationship between our findings and the mortgage boom and bust of the late 2000s. The bankrupt sample was drawn in the first quarter of 2007, just before housing values crashed and home mortgage foreclosures skyrocketed. In the first quarter of 2007, at about the time our data were collected, the number of foreclosures was estimated at 437,000, considerably fewer than the 799,064 posted in the fourth quarter of 2010.[26] Consequently, our data were drawn at the tail end of the housing bubble, when the maximum number of families had been offered easy credit to buy homes, but before they began to lose those houses in large numbers. This means that the "lost home" category, which had already hit 15.1 percent in early 2007 for families in bankruptcy, is likely to have grown substantially during the subsequent years, as the housing market plummeted and mortgage credit evaporated. Put another way, the number of "lost homes" among families in bankruptcy in 2007 is likely an underestimate of the effect of dangerous mortgage practices because these homes were lost well before the housing market crashed.

Before the housing bubble of the 2000s, it would have been plausible to use homeownership as an indicator of families' economic security. Back in the 1970s and 1980s—when average first-time buyers put up 18 percent of a home's purchase price to get a mortgage,[27] and when applications for

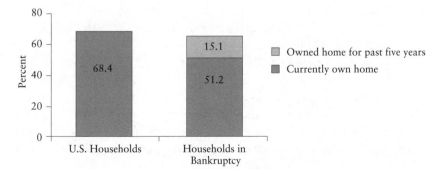

Figure 2.6 Homeownership rates of U.S. households and households in bankruptcy, 2007

SOURCES: U.S. Census Bureau, Housing Vacancies; Consumer Bankruptcy Project 2007.

home mortgages required detailed inquiries about income, length of employment, and credit history—homeownership signaled that people had passed
considerable economic scrutiny.[28] By 2005, however, with the median down
payment at zero and rampant use of so-called liar's loans (loans in which
there was no verification of borrower's income, often leading to inflated
income and higher loan amounts), teaser rate mortgages, and other exotic
devices, buying a home might have actually become an unreliable indicator
of the buyer's financial stability.

In his acceptance speech to the Republican National Convention in
2004, George W. Bush announced: "Another priority for a new term is to
build an ownership society, because ownership brings security and dignity
and independence. Thanks to our policies, home ownership in America is at
an all-time high. Tonight we set a new goal: seven million more affordable
homes in the next ten years, so more American families will be able to open
the door and say, 'Welcome to my home.'"[29] The data make it clear that
families in bankruptcy, much like most American families, embraced the
dream of homeownership. By 2007, two-thirds of all those filing for bankruptcy had punched their admission ticket for the middle class by buying a
home. Unfortunately, some people's homeownership dream proved fleeting
and elusive; the bankruptcy data show that financial problems led to many
families losing their homes even before the housing bubble burst.

ADDING THE WAYS TO THE MIDDLE CLASS

There are multiple paths to the middle class. Income is a frequent proxy for
class status, but it fails to capture the complexities of the class status of people
in financial trouble, particularly of those whose income has recently dropped.
Enduring criteria of class—education, occupation, and homeownership—
offer a clearer sense of the lives that bankrupt debtors once lived and the lives
to which they will again aspire. We use these enduring criteria to determine
what proportion of the *households* in bankruptcy might reasonably claim
membership in the middle class.

Couples who file joint bankruptcies present a particular statistical challenge when the number of middle-class bankruptcies is being calculated.
Couples living together share a home; thus they share class status based
on homeownership. But education and occupation are individual accomplishments. To describe accurately the class status of households in bankruptcy—and to avoid overcounting results from married couples—we rely
on household, rather than individual, data. We follow the convention that
the highest status associated with either spouse of a married couple living
together applies to the household.[30] This means, for example, that if a mar-

ried couple files for bankruptcy and one spouse is a college graduate and the other has earned high school diploma, the household is assigned the higher status of the college graduate. Similarly, if one spouse is a corporate manager and the other is a substitute teacher, the household is assigned the higher occupational prestige score of the manager. Because of this, *households* had somewhat higher occupational prestige scores and higher proportions in which someone had gone to college than the proportion of *individuals* evidencing those same criteria.

With the household as the unit of analysis, homeownership and education each qualify about two-thirds of the households in bankruptcy as middle class (Figure 2.7). Occupational prestige sweeps in a larger group, with 82.9 percent of bankrupt households composed of at least one family member whose occupation is among the top 80 percent of occupational scores in the United States.

With these criteria, more than nineteen of twenty households in bankruptcy could be classified as middle class: 95 percent reported at least one measure of middle-class status. This is an increase from 2001, when similar calculations revealed that 91.8 percent showed at least one indication of middle-class status. The data suggest that families in bankruptcy have been drawn largely from the middle at least since 1991, and the proportion with middle-class credentials continues to rise.

The strength of the claim these families might make on middle-class status can be further tested. Of the households that had at least one indicator of middle-class status, 38.7 percent met two of the criteria and 41 percent met all three criteria.

These three indicia of middle-class status are highly correlated, with no single criterion dominating. Homeownership and occupational status combined would classify 90.6 percent of all the filers as middle class. Homeownership and some college would identify 87.2 percent as middle class.

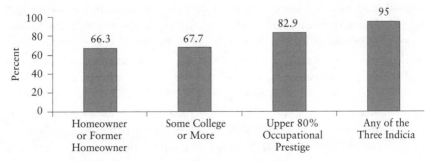

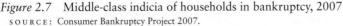

Figure 2.7   Middle-class indicia of households in bankruptcy, 2007
SOURCE: Consumer Bankruptcy Project 2007.

Some college and occupational status would peg 88.4 percent as middle class. These recombinations demonstrate the tight correlation among the variables. Of course, the correlations are expected because these class identifiers tend to reinforce each other, as people with better educations often end up in better jobs, and those with better jobs are more likely to buy houses.

There are no data that combine the indicia of middle-class status for the general U.S. population, making it impossible to carry out a direct, cumulative comparison between the bankruptcy population and the general population. Despite this limitation, the bankruptcy numbers are useful in themselves. They reveal that people who file for bankruptcy graduated from high school and went on to college. They got good jobs. They bought homes. They may trail other Americans at the margins, with fewer bachelor's and graduate degrees and fewer very-high-status occupations, but collectively they have enduring indicia of middle-class achievement. People in bankruptcy accomplished a great deal before their financial collapse, and they reflect a class status that is much like their counterparts around the country.

IMPLICATIONS OF THE DATA

The headline finding is unmistakable: bankruptcy is used primarily by middle-class families in financial distress. With more than nine in ten of all households in bankruptcy achieving middle-class status by virtue of education, occupational status, or homeownership, bankruptcy cannot be dismissed as one more tragedy in lives beset by chronic poverty and limited choices. Bankruptcy has become a clear marker of how far middle-class people are falling from a once-solid economic rung on the American class ladder.[31]

The most disturbing finding in these data may be the trend lines. To the extent that a trend is discernible from the three studies in 1991, 2001, and 2007, the data suggest that the proportion of middle-class families turning to bankruptcy is increasing. The most notable increases were in two areas: the proportion of respondents with "some college," and the proportion who were, or had recently been, homeowners. Compared with the number of bankruptcy filers in 1991, by 2007 the number of filers who owned homes had increased 20 percentage points, and the number who had "some college" had increased 10 percentage points.

The irony is inescapable. To an earlier generation, more education and homeownership spelled economic security. But these traditional paths have become far more treacherous. With more students than ever before taking out student loans, the stretch for an advanced education is considerably riskier. For those who are unsuccessful in their efforts to earn a bachelor's degree, the lack of a credential combined with higher student loan debt and years of deferred earnings from delayed job market entry may spell financial disaster later in life. Furthermore, the financial risks of higher education may be exacerbated by the increased presence of private student loan lenders—who charge higher interest rates and fees than federally backed loans—and by the increasing need for students to rely on credit cards to cover college expenses.

The data also suggest that the economic implications of homeownership are changing. The homeownership rates of bankrupt households showed a marked increase, approaching that of the general population. The housing bubble was inflated by easy money, which meant that down payments vanished; loans became highly leveraged; and borrowers absorbed even more risk by taking on mortgages with adjustable rates, interest-only payments, and teaser rates that reset in two or three years. At the same time, the country saw an expansion of unscrupulous lending practices, with many homeowners deceived about the costs and risks associated with buying a home. The bankruptcy data offer a crucial warning that, absent proper regulation of the mortgage industry, homeownership may actually undermine a family's social class rather than elevate it.

Most Americans will never seek protection from their creditors through bankruptcy.[32] For example, in 2007, the year of this study, there were 112 million households in the United States.[33] That same year, 827,000 bankruptcies were filed—most by households rather than by large corporations. Translated, this means that only seven-tenths of 1 percent (which is less than one in one hundred) of the households in the United States filed for bankruptcy in 2007.[34] Because the percentage numbers are small in any given year, we might expect a sharp deviance from the general population. However, the fact that these data show a strong similarity between bankrupt debtors and the middle class reveals important aspects of the economic and social health of American families. Bankruptcy data are a barometer of financial failure. Knowing that middle-class America is at risk suggests problems that run to the very heart of the American economy.

The findings in this chapter warn of a United States in which "middle class" is no longer synonymous with "financial security," a discontinuity that Jacob Hacker explores in Chapter 12. Instead, the bankruptcy data reveal an increasingly vulnerable middle class that plays by all the rules—going to college, finding decent jobs, buying homes—and whose members still find themselves in economic collapse.

CHAPTER THREE

Out of Balance?

Financial Distress in U.S. Households

Brian K. Bucks

Data on bankruptcy filers provide a natural basis for studying families facing financial difficulties. Nonetheless, looking only at those who have filed for bankruptcy may provide an incomplete perspective on financial distress. Because bankruptcy is fairly rare—generally less than 1 percent of adults file for bankruptcy in a given year—data on filers may shed light on only the most extreme forms of financial distress.[1] Families may also be financially constrained or distressed in ways that do not necessarily lead to or that are not remedied by filing for bankruptcy. Indeed, many individuals default on debt without filing for bankruptcy, and debtors who default on debt but do not file for bankruptcy appear to differ from bankruptcy filers.[2]

To examine the relationship between bankruptcy and other dimensions of household financial distress, this chapter draws on data from the Consumer Bankruptcy Project (CBP) of 2007 and the 2007 Survey of Consumer Finances (SCF). It contrasts the balance sheets of bankruptcy filers in the CBP with those of households in the SCF that might be considered financially vulnerable by other, nonbankruptcy measures, namely, families who (1) have been turned down for credit, (2) have high debt payments relative to income, (3) have fallen behind on debt payments, or (4) have limited assets to draw on when faced with an adverse financial event.

This comparison reveals that bankruptcy filers' finances generally differ from those of households that meet other criteria for financial distress. As might be expected, for instance, bankruptcy filers tend to have greater debt and, in particular, greater unsecured debt than the typical U.S. household. But bankruptcy filers also typically have more debt and unsecured debt than other types of financially distressed households in the SCF.

The financial characteristics of nonbankrupt, financially distressed families also vary across the SCF subgroups, a finding that suggests the potential benefit of using multiple measures for identifying households in financial distress. To the extent that the four subgroups of SCF families are distinct, this chapter also highlights the potential difficulty of formulating policies to reduce financial vulnerability.

In Chapter 2, Elizabeth Warren and Deborah Thorne conclude that, by multiple measures of socioeconomic status, most bankruptcy filers are middle class. In contrast, this chapter finds that bankruptcy filers' finances differ sharply from those of other families, including the finances of families who might be considered financially distressed. Consequently, an exclusive focus on bankruptcy filers likely captures only a particular and possibly unrepresentative segment of vulnerable households, and filing rates may undercount the number of households facing financial difficulties.

In considering the potential implications of the results, the chapter notes the difficulty of drawing strong conclusions based on the CBP and SCF data alone. In light of these limitations, the chapter closes with a discussion of how comprehensive data on the finances, experiences, and decisions of families could yield a fuller understanding of the variety of forms that financial distress might take and of the factors that may affect a decision to file for bankruptcy.

FINDING FINANCIAL DISTRESS: DATA AND DEFINITIONS

Consumer Bankruptcy Project

For data on bankruptcy filers, this chapter draws on data from bankruptcy court records in the 2007 CBP. The sample consists of roughly twenty-four hundred consumer filings under either Chapter 7 or Chapter 13 of the U.S. Bankruptcy Code. The CBP extracted detailed data from each respondent's bankruptcy court records on assets, liabilities, income, and expenses. With few exceptions, the data reflect the financial position of the filer at the time of the bankruptcy filing. To provide estimates that are representative of cases filed during the sample period in early 2007, the analysis in this chapter utilizes weights for the CBP sample that were constructed to ensure that the distribution of cases across the eight categories defined by bankruptcy chapter (Chapter 7 or Chapter 13) and Census region (Northeast, Midwest, South, and West) matches the distribution estimated from administrative data.[3]

Survey of Consumer Finances

For data on U.S. families as a whole and on financially vulnerable, nonbankrupt families, this chapter uses the 2007 SCF, the most comprehensive and highest quality data on U.S. household wealth. The survey collects detailed household-level microdata on assets and liabilities in addition to data on income, demographics, credit market experiences, expectations and attitudes, and employment. The Federal Reserve Board conducts the SCF every three years, and the data are reported as of the time of the interview, except the data on income, which refer to the prior calendar year. The most recent SCF cross section, conducted in 2007, included 4,422 households.

The SCF sample comprises a standard, geographically based random sample and a list sample.[4] The list sample, which oversamples households likely to be relatively wealthy, makes up about a third of households in the final sample. The full SCF data include sample weights, which are used for all estimates in this chapter, to provide estimates representative of all U.S. households.[5]

The analysis includes families in the SCF who had previously filed for bankruptcy. Since the 1998 survey, the SCF has asked whether the household head or that person's spouse or partner had ever filed for bankruptcy and, if so, the date of the most recent filing.[6] In the 2007 SCF, roughly 12 percent of families had previously filed for bankruptcy. These households are included in the analysis (although I refer to families in the SCF as "non-bankrupt" families) because for many of them the filing was several years earlier. Of families who reported having previously filed for bankruptcy, about 13 percent had filed fewer than three years earlier, and nearly half had filed ten or more years earlier.[7] In addition, bankruptcy may not fully eliminate financial pressures, so even families who include a recent bankruptcy filer may be financially vulnerable.[8] Indeed, as shown below, families who reported a prior bankruptcy filing are more likely to be classified as financially vulnerable by the criteria detailed below.

Beyond Bankruptcy:
Defining Financial Vulnerability of Families in the SCF

A family's financial security may depend on several factors, including the degree of economic risk its members face (such as the probability of a job loss or of a sizable unanticipated expense), the family's outstanding debt, and the resources available to it when faced with a financial shock. For example, a family confronting an unexpected expense might draw on savings, borrow, or spend more of its current income. A household with low savings, limited ability to borrow, or large debt repayment obligations relative to its income may have difficulty overcoming an adverse economic shock and, as a result, may default on debt or forgo potentially essential purchases. This concept of financial security guides this chapter's definition of four subgroups of families who might be considered financially vulnerable.

The first subgroup is families who may have limited access to credit. More specifically, it comprises families who reported they had, at some time in the past five years, either (1) applied for credit but were turned down or received less credit than they sought, or (2) considered applying for a loan but chose not to because they thought they would be turned down.[9] Earlier studies have found that these SCF questions about credit application decisions and outcomes provide an indicator that a household is potentially credit constrained.[10] About 21 percent of households in the 2007 SCF are classified as *credit constrained* on the basis of these criteria.[11] These families most frequently cited financial or credit characteristics, such as a poor credit rating, lack of credit history, or inability to repay, as the primary reason they were turned down or anticipated that they would be turned down for a loan.[12]

The second subgroup of families is those who recently may have faced difficulty in meeting debt payments. This group is defined as families with outstanding debt who reported having fallen behind on any loan payment by two months or more in the previous year. More than 5 percent of all households—about 7 percent of households with debt—fall into this *late payments* group.

The third subgroup is families who may be facing difficulty in servicing debt obligations because they have high debt payments relative to income.[13] In identifying this group, I exclude payments on mortgage debt (loans secured by either the primary residence or other real estate) because households with mortgage debt payments that are a large fraction of income differ notably from the other groups that I consider.[14] Families with a non-mortgage debt payment-to-income ratio (PIR) greater than 25 percent are classified as "high nonmortgage PIR," or simply *high PIR* households.[15] This group comprises less than 6 percent of SCF households.

The final subgroup of financially vulnerable families is defined by comparing a family's assets with the savings that the family considers sufficient to cover unanticipated expenses. Differences in responses to this question appear to reflect, in part, differences in risk preferences, access to credit, and the degree of economic risk that families face.[16] Gauging the adequacy of households' savings requires defining the set of resources that a family could draw on when faced with an adverse economic shock, and there are several measures that could be used. One common choice is financial assets, but, as Arthur Kennickell and Annamaria Lusardi note, this measure may be too narrow.[17] Families might be able to draw on some nonfinancial assets by, for instance, taking out a home equity line of credit. Families might also be unwilling or unable to liquidate all financial assets, such as balances in individual retirement accounts (IRAs) or defined-contribution pension plans. In light of these considerations, and similar to Kennickell and Lusardi, the measure of available assets used is in this chapter includes (1) all liquid financial assets that are not held in retirement plans, (2) a third of equity in primary residences and other real estate, and (3) a third of the value of certificates of deposit, IRAs, and defined-contribution or similar retirement accounts.[18] By this measure of the adequacy of households' assets, 19 percent of U.S. families have *low savings*.[19]

Looking across all four proposed criteria that define families who might be considered financially vulnerable—those who are credit constrained and those with late payments, high PIR, or low savings—36 percent of households meet at least one of the definitions of financial distress (Figure 3.1). Although these measures overlap, they appear to capture somewhat different dimensions of household financial vulnerability. As shown by the shaded portions of the bars in Figure 3.1, about 12 percent of all families—or a third of families classified as economically vulnerable by at least one measure—meet more than one criterion. Only 1 percent of households that meet at least one criterion meet all four. The same pattern generally holds when looking at each criterion separately. Roughly half of families who are credit constrained or have low savings are not financially distressed by any other measure, for example. An exception is families who had late debt payments, three-quarters of whom meet at least one other criterion.

As noted earlier, the analysis of SCF families includes those who reported

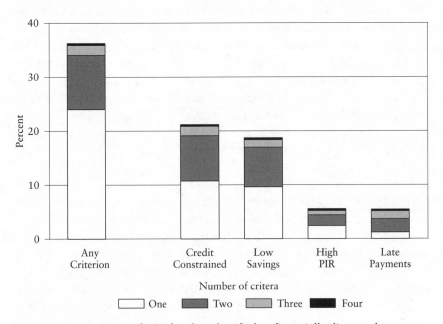

Figure 3.1   Percentage of SCF families classified as financially distressed

SOURCE: 2007 Survey of Consumer Finances.

NOTE: Height of each bar indicates total share of families classified as distressed on the basis of each criterion. For each criterion, the shaded portions indicate the fraction classified as financially distressed by multiple criteria.

that the household head or that person's spouse or partner had previously filed for bankruptcy, and these families are disproportionately represented among financially vulnerable households as defined here. A third of families in which neither the head nor the spouse/partner had previously filed for bankruptcy meet at least one measure, but nearly 58 percent of families in which the head or spouse/partner had ever filed and two out of three households that had filed in the previous ten years are classified as financially vulnerable by one or more of the criteria.[20]

Table 3.1 shows the distribution of household income by the financial distress criteria and indicates that financial distress as defined by these criteria is not synonymous with low income. Families in the credit-constrained or late-payments groups disproportionately fall into the second and third income quintiles (between the 20th and 60th percentiles), whereas families with high debt payments relative to income and those with low savings are overrepresented in the first and second income quintiles. Nonetheless, more than a quarter of the families in these latter two groups might be considered middle- to upper-income given that their income falls in the third or fourth income quintiles.

Bankruptcy filers in the 2007 CBP typically have lower income than U.S. families as a whole, a finding that is consistent with the results of Warren and Thorne in Chapter 2 as well as those of Teresa Sullivan, Elizabeth Warren, and Jay Westbrook for earlier waves of the CBP.[21] The distribution of income for bankruptcy filers is broadly similar to the income distributions for families who are credit constrained or who have missed debt payments, but bankruptcy filers tend to have higher incomes than families with low savings or high PIRs.

TABLE 3.1

Distribution of household income by financial distress criterion

Percentile of income for all U.S. families	SCF				CBP
	Credit constrained	Late payments	High PIR	Low savings	Bankruptcy filers
Less than 20	20.4	21.4	35.9	35.8	19.7
20–39.9	30.7	32.8	29.9	33.3	32.9
40–59.9	25.9	26.1	21.4	19.8	28.0
60–79.9	16.8	15.8	10.3	8.1	16.3
80–100	6.3	4.0	2.6	3.1	3.1

SOURCES: 2007 Survey of Consumer Finances (SCF) and Consumer Bankruptcy Project (CBP) 2007.

NOTE: Income quintiles are calculated over all U.S. households based on the 2007 SCF. Income excludes Social Security payments. PIR indicates payment-to-income ratio.

Challenges in Aligning and Comparing Data Sources

The CBP and the SCF provide comparatively high-quality data on household balance sheets. The accuracy of the CBP financial data should be high because the data are drawn from bankruptcy court records, for which misreporting could lead to severe legal penalties. The SCF takes several steps to maximize the quality of the survey data, including careful sequencing and framing of questions, training of interviewers, review of the data by Federal Reserve staff, reassuring respondents of the confidentiality of their data, and giving respondents the option to provide ranges if they are unable or unwilling to report exact dollar amounts.

Nevertheless, comparison of data from different sources is generally difficult. Divergent values of seemingly similar variables in any two datasets may stem, for instance, from differences in the conceptual framework and implementation of the surveys or in the postcollection processing and editing procedures.[22] Definitions used in administrative data (the source of financial data in the CBP) can differ from respondents' understanding in a survey such as the SCF. Moreover, comparison of financial data may be especially difficult because classification and valuation of assets and liabilities can be complex. These concerns along with the issues described below suggest a cautious interpretation of differences in the estimates of the balance sheets of bankruptcy filers in the CBP and nonbankrupt households in the SCF.

The CBP and SCF differ in their design and execution. One critical difference is the unit of observation, namely, a bankruptcy case in the CBP and a household in the SCF. About a third of married individuals in the CBP file a single petition. In such instances, which represent about 14 percent of all bankruptcy filings in the CBP, the bankruptcy filing collects information on some assets and debts that are likely held only by the filing spouse, such as credit card debt or retirement account balances. An exception is the measure of income in the CBP that is used in this chapter, which generally includes income earned by a nonfiling spouse.

By contrast, the SCF captures all assets and debts of both members in a couple (whether married or unmarried), and, with few exceptions, it is not possible to determine the value of the share owned by each spouse or partner. To address this discrepancy between the CBP and SCF, one might consider adjusting the CBP, for example, by assuming an equal division of assets and debts or by allocating wealth in proportion to the earnings of each member of the couple. However, both of these assumptions would be ad hoc, and neither would take into account either any allocation of assets and debt to maximize the economic value of filing for bankruptcy or gender differences in holdings of assets and debts.

The two data sources also differ in their treatment of missing data. Missing values in the SCF are imputed five times, yielding five complete datasets. The uncertainty in predicting missing values in the SCF can be readily estimated and incorporated into calculations of statistical significance.[23] Missing values are not imputed in the CBP and are excluded from the CBP analysis in this chapter. This approach is valid only under the strong assumption that the probability of nonresponse in the CBP does not depend on the characteristics of the bankruptcy filer or case.[24]

Differences in definitions of financial variables may likewise complicate this chapter's comparisons. I seek to align the definitions of each variable as closely as possible, and the conclusions appear to be robust to alternative definitions. The construction of each of the balance sheet measures is detailed elsewhere, but the definitions of income, credit card debt, and medical debt are particularly worth noting.[25]

Bankruptcy court records include information on income from several time periods, including for the six months before the bankruptcy filing and for the previous calendar year. Although the prior-year income amount in the CBP matches the timeframe covered by the SCF income measure, I use the annualized six-month value because it is available for a greater share of filers and it generally includes spousal income, which is not reported in the calendar-year income for married petitioners.[26] This six-month income measure excludes Social Security payments, as required by bankruptcy law, so I subtract an estimate of Social Security income for SCF households when comparing incomes in the SCF and CBP.

Annualized income for the six-month period preceding the bankruptcy filing may be lower than income in the prior calendar year if the decision to file was precipitated by a drop in income or if bankruptcy filers intentionally reduced earnings in anticipation of filing to reduce legal challenges to the bankruptcy case based on ability to pay creditors or to satisfy the means test.[27] A comparison of both income amounts, though, suggests that there is likely little systematic difference. For filings that included income for both time periods, annualized median income for the prior six months is roughly $31,800, and median income for the prior calendar year is $30,400. Similarly, the median ratio of income in the prior calendar year to annualized income based on the six-month measure is essentially 1.[28]

Bankruptcy filers must list all unsecured debts in the filing, but credit card obligations are not clearly distinguished from other unsecured claims. The CBP provides two measures that probably serve as lower and upper bounds for credit card debt. The first amount, "definite credit card debt," comprises the total debt specifically reported as, for example, "credit card," "charge account," or "revolving credit." The second amount, "probable credit card debt," includes a broader set of debts such as amounts owed to one of the largest card issuers.[29]

Neither the SCF survey nor the bankruptcy court records specifically measure medical debt. Households' medical debt in the SCF is estimated as the total of reported debts for which either (1) the loan purpose is coded as "medical/dental/veterinary expenses; attorney's fees" and the lender was not a lawyer, or (2) the debt is owed to a "doctor or hospital; dentist; veterinarian." Under this definition, medical debt in the SCF may appear as an equity extraction on a first mortgage, a second mortgage, a home equity loan, a line of credit, or an "other loan." Other loans in the SCF include nonmortgage installment loans taken out for a purpose other than educational expenses or vehicle purchase, including outstanding bills that are more than thirty days past due. This approach to identifying medical-related debt is similar to that used to code medical debt from the bankruptcy petitions in the CBP.

This measure of medical debt may understate the actual fraction of household debt attributable to medical expenses for at least three reasons. First, although SCF respondents are generally reminded to include medical bills and similar debts that are more than thirty days past due when asked about "other loans," some respondents may not consider outstanding bills to service providers as loans and therefore may not report them.[30] Second, as in the CBP, it is not possible to identify the types of expenses financed on credit cards, so any such outstanding medical debt is instead classified as undifferentiated credit card debt.[31] Third, debt is fungible: when faced with a medical expense, families may choose to forgo paying on, say, a car loan to pay a medical bill, or vice versa.

DIFFERING SHADES OF RED? THE FINANCES OF BANKRUPTCY FILERS AND OTHER FINANCIALLY VULNERABLE FAMILIES

This chapter's comparison of bankruptcy filers with nonbankrupt families focuses on balance sheet components, including income, net worth, and specific types of assets and debts. The comparison uses three statistics to characterize the financial position of an individual or family: the ownership rate, the conditional median, and the "equivalent quantile." The *ownership rate* is the fraction of families with a given asset or debt.[32] The *conditional median* is the median value for those families with a given asset or debt. The conditional median of mortgage debt, for instance, is the median amount of mortgage debt for families with a mortgage. Estimates of the median are often statistically less sensitive than estimates of the mean for variables whose distribution is skewed (with a small proportion of very large values), as is the case for many assets or debts. The median may also be a more intuitively appealing measure of a "typical" value within a skewed distribution. Unlike means, however, medians are not additive: median net worth, for instance, is not the difference between median assets and median debt. Differences in conditional medians across groups can also be difficult to interpret when ownership patterns differ. If ownership rates differ sharply between two groups, then the conditional median values correspond to individuals in different parts of the overall, unconditional distributions.[33]

The *equivalent quantile* offers an alternative basis of comparison that is useful when ownership rates differ sharply. In particular, whereas conditional medians allow comparison of filers and families who are at the same position in their respective *conditional* distributions (namely, the 50th percentile), the equivalent quantile allows comparison of filers and families at the same position in their respective *unconditional* distributions. To determine the value of the equivalent quantile for a given asset or debt, I first calculate the unconditional quantile in the CBP corresponding to the conditional median in the CBP. The equivalent quantile is then defined by determining the value for the given asset or debt at the same unconditional quantile of the distribution for a given SCF comparison group.

To take an example, as shown in Table 3.2, the conditional median amount of debt for bankruptcy filers is $89,100 dollars. By comparison, the conditional median among all SCF households is nearly $22,000 lower, at $67,300. The difference in typical debt levels is larger, however, if one adjusts for differences in the shares of bankruptcy filers in the CBP and families in the SCF that have any debt by comparing the conditional median in the CBP with the equivalent quantile in the SCF. Because nearly all bankruptcy filers have debt, the conditional median amount of debt is nearly identical to the unconditional median.[34] Correspondingly, the equivalent quantile in the SCF is roughly the median of the unconditional SCF debt distribution. In contrast to the near-universal debt ownership among bankruptcy filers, only 77 percent of SCF families have debt, so the equivalent quantile is much lower—$27,900—because this unconditional distribution includes the 23 percent of SCF families with no debt. Thus, the difference in the equivalent quantiles between the CBP and the SCF is $61,200, or nearly three times the difference in the conditional medians.

The Bottom Lines

The median bankruptcy filer, perhaps not surprisingly, has negative net worth, with debt that exceeds assets by $24,400 (see Table 3.2). In contrast, median net worth for each of the financially distressed SCF subgroups is greater than zero and ranges from $2,200 for households with low savings

TABLE 3.2

*Conditional medians, ownership rates, and equivalent quantiles
of net worth, assets, debts, income, and selected ratios:
CBP filers, all SCF families, and SCF subgroups*

		Net worth	Assets	Debt	Leverage ratio (%)	2006 income[a]	Debt/2006 income[a] (%)
CBP							
Bankruptcy filers	Cond. median	−24.4	57.7	89.1	155.9	31.6	309.5
	Percent with	100.0	99.7	99.9	100.0	100.0	100.0
SCF							
All families	Cond. median	120.6**	221.5**	67.3**	20.4**	44.0**	68.8**
	Percent with	100.0	97.7**	77.0**	100.0	100.0	100.0
	Equiv. quantile	120.6**	214.7**	27.9**	20.4**	44.0**	68.8**
Credit constrained	Cond. median	11.9**	45.1*	30.6**	49.3**	32.4	58.8**
	Percent with	100.0	95.9**	83.0**	100.0	100.0	100.0
	Equiv. quantile	11.9**	37.7**	17.5**	49.3**	32.4	58.8**
Late payments	Cond. median	9.6**	54.2	28.0**	69.5**	31.9	124.4**
	Percent with	100.0	96.8**	100.0	100.0	100.0	100.0
	Equiv. quantile	9.6**	47.8	28.0**	69.5**	31.9	124.4**
Non-mortgage PIR >0.25	Cond. median	33.7**	128.4**	50.1**	65.2**	23.7**	267.1
	Percent with	100.0	98.7	100.0	100.0	100.0	100.0
	Equiv. quantile	33.7**	128.4**	50.1**	65.2**	23.7**	267.1
Low savings	Cond. median	2.2**	9.2**	11.1**	34.4**	21.5**	12.8**
	Percent with	100.0	88.8**	65.4**	100.0	100.0	100.0
	Equiv. quantile	2.2**	7.3**	2.5**	34.4**	21.5**	12.8**

SOURCES: 2007 Survey of Consumer Finances (SCF) and Consumer Bankruptcy Project (CBP) 2007.

NOTE: Figures are thousands of 2007 dollars except where noted. "Cond. median" is the conditional median, i.e., the median value for those with a given asset or debt; "Percent with" is the share of filers or households with nonzero holdings; "Equiv. quantile" is the equivalent quantile, i.e., the SCF quantile that corresponds to the unconditional percentile of the CBP conditional median. PIR indicates payment-to-income ratio. Leverage ratio is the ratio of debts to assets.

[a]Income excludes Social Security payments, but Social Security payments are included in the calculation of nonmortgage PIR.

*$p < 0.05$, **$p < 0.01$. Asterisks indicate significance of differences for each SCF group relative to bankruptcy filers. Standard errors are bootstrapped with 999 replicates. SCF replicates are drawn in accordance with the sample design, and the standard errors are adjusted for imputation uncertainty.

to $33,700 for those with a high PIR. These median values are well below the $120,600 median net worth of all U.S. households in 2007.

Nearly 80 percent of bankruptcy filers have negative net worth (not shown), a fraction that is more than twice the corresponding share for each of the SCF subgroups and ten times the share of households with negative net worth in the population overall. Although families with low savings and families with a high PIR have the lowest and highest median net worth, respectively, among the SCF subgroups, the shares with negative net worth are identical for the two groups (24 percent). Together, these estimates point to differences in the distribution of net worth for these two groups. More specifically, the dissimilar medians and identical shares with negative net worth can be reconciled by noting that a relatively large share of families with limited savings have low, but positive, net worth.

Bankruptcy filers' lower median net worth is primarily due to their greater debt as reflected by both a large fraction with debt and higher typical amounts of debt. As might be expected, nearly all bankruptcy filers have debt. In this respect, bankruptcy filers are comparable to families in the late-payments and high-PIR groups, whose debt ownership is 100 percent by construction. By comparison, the debt ownership rates for credit-constrained families and for those with low savings are significantly lower.

The differences in the typical level of debt are arguably more striking. As detailed above, the conditional median for bankruptcy filers is $89,100, about $22,000 more than the median for all U.S. households that have debt, and the difference is almost three times greater if the median debtor in the CBP is compared with the household at the equivalent quantile of the SCF debt distribution. The conditional median in the CBP is also substantially higher than that for debtors in each of the subgroups of financially vulnerable households and is, for instance, about 75 percent greater than the median for high-PIR families—the SCF subgroup with the highest conditional median amount of debt.

Relative to these stark differences in the levels of indebtedness, bankruptcy filers' asset ownership and asset holdings are somewhat more similar to those of financially distressed SCF households. A large majority of households in each group have assets, but bankruptcy filers are in fact more likely to have assets than both U.S. families overall and financially distressed families in each of the SCF subgroups (although the difference in ownership rates is not statistically significant relative to high-PIR families). The conditional median of assets in the CBP of $57,700 is roughly comparable to the conditional median for the late-payments group, a bit higher than that for credit-constrained families, and substantially greater than the $9,200 conditional median for families classified as having limited savings. In contrast, the conditional median for bankruptcy filers is about a fourth of that for families overall and less than half of the conditional median among families with high debt payments relative to income.

The greater prominence of debt on bankruptcy filers' balance sheets is more pronounced when debt is measured as a share of assets or income. The median leverage ratio (the ratio of debts to assets) among bankruptcy filers, 156 percent, is significantly greater than the corresponding median leverage ratios for households overall and for each of the subgroups of SCF families. In fact, it is more than twice the median leverage ratio for families with late debt payments, whose median leverage ratio of 69.5 percent is the highest of the SCF subgroups. Similarly, the median bankruptcy filer has debt that totals slightly more than three times annual income, whereas the median debt-to-income ratios are significantly lower—less than 125 percent—for all groups of SCF households (including all families), with the exception of the high-PIR group.

The conclusion that bankruptcy filers hold substantially more debt than other households is not specific to the comparison of conditional medians. Instead, filers typically have comparatively large amounts of debt relative

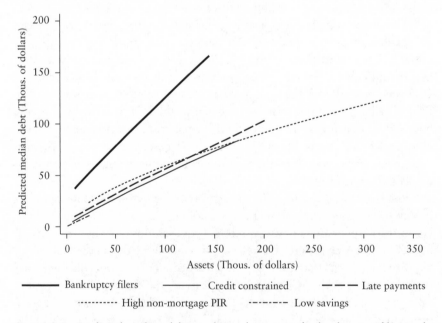

Figure 3.2   Predicted median debt conditional on assets for bankruptcy filers and financially vulnerable households

SOURCES: 2007 Survey of Consumer Finances; Consumer Bankruptcy Project 2007.

NOTE: Predicted values are plotted between the 25th and 75th percentiles of the respective asset distributions for bankruptcy filers and for households in each SCF group.

to assets across a range of asset values. To illustrate this, Figure 3.2 plots the relationship between assets and debts for bankruptcy filers and the four groups of financially vulnerable families.[35] The predicted median values of total debt are plotted for asset values between the 25th and 75th percentiles of the unconditional assets distribution for each of the subgroups. Bankruptcy filers have higher predicted debt than families with comparable asset holdings in each of the SCF subgroups. A bankruptcy filer with $50,000 in assets, for example, is estimated to have total debt of $77,000, about twice the predicted debt of a high-PIR household with the same value of assets. Comparison of the 25th and 75th percentiles of assets—the endpoints of each line—reinforces the conclusion from the conditional medians and ownership rates discussed above that families with low savings, perhaps not surprisingly, tend to have markedly lower asset holdings. In addition, it suggests that bankruptcy filers, by and large, are slightly more concentrated at lower asset levels than households in the other three groups of financially distressed families.

Unsecured, but Not Unburdened

The comparatively high debt of bankruptcy filers as a proportion of assets reflects a further distinguishing feature of their balance sheets, namely, substantially greater unsecured debt. The median leverage ratio among filers, for example, indicates that total debt exceeds total assets by about 56 percent for the median bankrupt debtor. Since the value of assets available as collateral limits the amount of secured debt an individual or family may have, this high debt-to-asset ratio suggests that a large proportion of filers' debt is likely unsecured.

Indeed, nearly all those who file for bankruptcy have unsecured debt, and the conditional median in the CBP is $32,500 (Table 3.3). By comparison, 87 percent of high-PIR families—the group with the most similar holdings of unsecured debt—have unsecured debt, and the conditional median in this group, $15,000, is less than half that of bankrupt debtors. The largest differences between the CBP and SCF comparison groups are for families with low savings; nearly half of these families have no unsecured debt, and the median amount owed by those who do have unsecured debt is $4,800.

Measured at the median, unsecured debt represents 47 percent of all outstanding debt for bankruptcy filers, a fraction that is about ten times the ratio for all U.S. families and more than twice the median shares of unsecured debt for families in the credit-constrained, late-payments, and high-PIR groups. The median share for families with low savings is similar to that for bankruptcy filers, but the equivalent quantile is significantly lower (2 percent of total debt), largely because of the fact that roughly a third of families with low savings have no debt.

TABLE 3.3

Conditional medians, ownership rates, and equivalent quantiles of unsecured debt and unsecured debt as a share of total debt: CBP filers, all SCF families, and SCF subgroups

		Unsecured debt	Definite credit card debt[a]	Probable credit card debt[a]	Education debt	Medical debt	Unsecured debt/total debt[b] (%)
CBP							
Bankruptcy filers	Cond. median	32.5	14.2	16.3	9.2	1.5	46.8
	Percent with	98.6	78.8	87.8	17.1	50.8	99.9
SCF							
All families	Cond. median	5.7**	3.0**	3.0**	12.0*	1.8	4.8**
	Percent with	55.9**	46.1**	46.1**	15.2*	3.7**	77.0**
	Equiv. quantile	0.5**	0.4**	0.1**	10.0	0.0**	1.0**
Credit constrained	Cond. median	6.4**	2.0**	2.0**	10.0	1.9	16.3**
	Percent with	67.6**	48.8**	48.8**	26.6**	7.7**	83.0**
	Equiv. quantile	1.8**	0.5**	0.3**	20.0**	0.0**	6.6**
Late payments	Cond. median	8.3**	2.8**	2.8**	9.0	3.8	16.7**
	Percent with	79.8**	45.7**	45.7**	33.1**	19.4**	100.0
	Equiv. quantile	5.6**	0.3**	0.1**	14.6	0.0**	16.7**
Non-mortgage PIR >0.25	Cond. median	15.0**	10.2**	10.2**	10.3	4.8	21.7**
	Percent with	86.6**	69.6**	69.6**	26.3**	8.9**	100.0
	Equiv. quantile	11.0**	8.0**	6.0**	24.0	0.0**	21.7**
Low savings	Cond. median	4.8**	1.6**	1.6**	9.5	3.4	50.2
	Percent with	52.2**	34.5**	34.5**	17.4	6.3**	65.4**
	Equiv. quantile	0.3**	0.0**	0.0**	9.5	0.0**	1.9**

SOURCES: 2007 Survey of Consumer Finances (SCF) and Consumer Bankruptcy Project (CBP) 2007.

NOTE: Figures are thousands of 2007 dollars except where noted. "Cond. median" is the conditional median, i.e., the median value for those with a given asset or debt; "Percent with" is the share of filers or households with nonzero holdings; "Equiv. quantile" is the equivalent quantile, i.e., the SCF quantile that corresponds to the unconditional percentile of the CBP conditional median. PIR indicates payment-to-income ratio.

[a]"Definite credit card debt" includes debt reported in the bankruptcy filing that was thought with high confidence to be owed on a credit card; "probable credit card debt" additionally includes a broader set of debts that were identified as likely to be credit card debt.

[b]Ratio of unsecured debt to total debt is calculated for CBP filers and SCF families with any debt.

*$p < 0.05$, **$p < 0.01$. Asterisks indicate significance of differences for each SCF group relative to CBP bankruptcy filers. Standard errors are bootstrapped with 999 replicates. SCF replicates are drawn in accordance with the sample design, and the standard errors are adjusted for imputation uncertainty.

The differences in holdings of unsecured debt between filers and financially distressed households vary, however, by the specific type of debt. Relative to families in each of the SCF groups, a greater fraction of bankruptcy filers have credit card debt, and filers' conditional median balances of roughly $14,000 to $16,000 are significantly higher than the conditional medians for each SCF group. This pattern does not hold, however, for education or medical debt. Bankruptcy filers are less likely to have education debt than each of the groups of financially distressed families except those with low savings, who are about as likely to have education debt.

Conversely, filers are much more likely than families in each of the SCF groups to have medical debt; half of them have such debt, compared with 19 percent of families with late payments and less than 10 percent of families in each of the other three SCF subgroups. Because few SCF families have any medical debt, the equivalent quantile is zero for each of these groups. Conditional on having student loan or medical debt, however, the median amounts in the CBP are generally comparable to those for nonbankrupt households.

To further examine the concentration of unsecured debt on bankruptcy filers' balance sheets, Figure 3.3 plots the predicted median value of unsecured

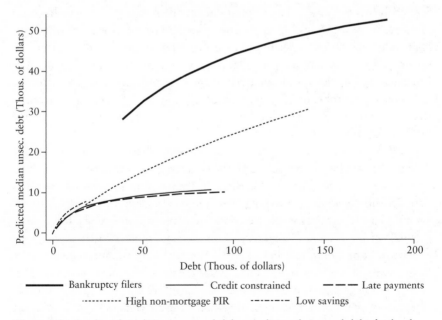

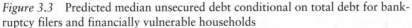

Figure 3.3   Predicted median unsecured debt conditional on total debt for bankruptcy filers and financially vulnerable households

SOURCES: 2007 Survey of Consumer Finances; Consumer Bankruptcy Project 2007.

NOTE: Predicted values are plotted between the 25th and 75th percentiles of the respective debt distributions for bankruptcy filers and for households in each SCF group.

debt as a function of total debt using the same methodology as Figure 3.2. The figure highlights that, throughout the range of total debt levels shown, bankruptcy filers have higher predicted median amounts of unsecured debt when compared with financially vulnerable households in the SCF that have similar total debt. Furthermore, the figure illustrates bankruptcy filers' greater debt, as the middle 50 percent of the debt distribution for filers is clearly greater than the corresponding ranges for each of the SCF subgroups.

There's No Asset Like Home

Housing plays an important role in many families' finances, as the home is often the household's largest asset and mortgage debt the largest liability. Indeed, housing accounts for more than half of total assets for homeowners in every group in Table 3.2, with the fraction ranging from 63 percent for all U.S. homeowners to 86 percent in the CBP.

A comparison of bankruptcy filers' home equity relative to the home equity of nonbankrupt families may be of particular interest for at least two reasons (Table 3.4). First, homestead exemptions are generally larger than personal property exemptions, which may provide an incentive for people contemplating bankruptcy to shift assets into housing and home equity.[36] Second, borrowers who have defaulted on their mortgages may have an incentive to file for bankruptcy to stop collection or foreclosure efforts or to gain additional funds by discharging unsecured debt. Furthermore, although mortgage loans on debtors' principal residences cannot be modified, debtors can catch up on missed mortgage payments over time and avoid foreclosure in Chapter 13 bankruptcy. As a result of these considerations, a substantial share of homeowners who file for bankruptcy might be expected to have little or negative home equity.[37]

Just over half of bankruptcy petitioners own their home, a rate similar to that for families who had late debt payments or who have a high PIR, and greater than the shares of credit-constrained and low-savings families that are homeowners. However, the homeownership rate among bank-ruptcy filers is significantly lower than the overall homeownership rate in the SCF of 69 percent.[38] Bankrupt homeowners tend to own slightly less expensive homes than families in any of the SCF groups, and they typically have slightly higher mortgage debt. Most of the differences in the median values of homes and mortgage debt across the CBP and SCF groups are not statistically significant, but there are significant differences in median home equity. Bankrupt homeowners' median home equity is $7,100, whereas the median values of home equity for homeowners who have a high PIR, are credit constrained, or had late debt payments range between $40,000 and

TABLE 3.4

Conditional medians, ownership rates, and equivalent quantiles of home equity, house values, mortgage debt, and home value as a share of total assets for homeowners: CBP filers, all SCF families, and SCF subgroups

		Home equity	Home	Mortgage debt	Home/assets if own home (%)
CBP					
Bankruptcy filers	Cond. median	7.1	113.0	110.4	86.4
	Percent with	52.0	52.0	49.1	52.0
SCF					
All families	Cond. median	105.0**	200.0**	107.0	63.1**
	Percent with	68.6**	68.6**	48.7	68.6**
	Equiv. quantile	150.0**	250.0**	106.0	72.4**
Credit constrained	Cond. median	40.0**	125.0	100.0	79.2**
	Percent with	45.1**	45.1**	36.0**	45.1**
	Equiv. quantile	27.0**	105.0	65.0**	72.7**
Late payments	Cond. median	45.9**	125.0	81.0*	80.5
	Percent with	49.6	49.6	42.3*	49.6
	Equiv. quantile	40.0**	120.0	67.0**	79.0
Non-mortgage PIR >0.25	Cond. median	60.0**	154.5**	94.0	67.9**
	Percent with	56.8	56.8	44.8	56.8
	Equiv. quantile	73.0**	175.0**	89.0*	70.9**
Low savings	Cond. median	14.0	136.0	106.0	79.6**
	Percent with	16.7**	16.7**	14.0**	16.7**
	Equiv. quantile	0.0**	0.0**	0.0**	0.0**

SOURCES: 2007 Survey of Consumer Finances (SCF) and Consumer Bankruptcy Project (CBP) 2007.

NOTE: Figures are thousands of 2007 dollars except where noted. "Cond. median" is the conditional median, i.e., the median value for those with a given asset or debt; "Percent with" is the share of filers or households with nonzero holdings; "Equiv. quantile" is the equivalent quantile, i.e., the SCF quantile that corresponds to the unconditional percentile of the CBP conditional median. PIR indicates payment-to-income ratio.

$*p < 0.05$, $**p < 0.01$. Asterisks indicate significance of differences for each SCF group relative to CBP bankruptcy filers. Standard errors are bootstrapped with 999 replicates. SCF replicates are drawn in accordance with the sample design, and the standard errors are adjusted for imputation uncertainty.

$60,000; only homeowners with low savings have median home equity that is comparable (in the sense that the difference is not statistically significant).

These estimates offer some suggestive evidence consistent with the view that the incentives noted above potentially affect the decision to file for bankruptcy.[39] The favorable treatment of home equity in bankruptcy in most states may help to explain the finding that homes account for a comparatively large fraction of total assets for homeowners in bankruptcy. At the same time, however, bankruptcy filers who own a home tend to have lower priced homes and to have relatively little home equity, at least at the median, which suggests that the effect of the incentives on these dimensions may be limited. Consistent with the argument that homeowners facing foreclosure or default may file to gain time or financial flexibility to catch up on past-due amounts, 29 percent of bankrupt homeowners have negative equity, a proportion that is considerably higher than the fraction of families with negative home equity in each of the SCF groups (not shown).[40]

DISCUSSION AND IMPLICATIONS

This chapter's comparison of the financial profiles of bankruptcy filers in the CBP with financially vulnerable families in the SCF suggests that the finances of bankruptcy filers are not representative of the broader set of financially distressed households, at least as defined by the criteria used in the chapter. Those in bankruptcy tend to have lower net worth and greater debt compared not only with U.S. families overall, but also with nonbankrupt, financially vulnerable families. The greater debt of bankruptcy filers is even more pronounced when debt is measured against assets, when debt payments are measured against income, or when focusing more narrowly on unsecured debt. This conclusion that bankruptcy filers and nonbankrupt financially distressed households differ with respect to many financial characteristics complements the finding of earlier studies that debtors who enter "informal bankruptcy" (that is, who default on debt without filing for bankruptcy) differ from debtors who seek legal relief from the bankruptcy system.[41]

As argued above, these differences should be interpreted with caution because of the difficulty of comparing estimates across surveys and the specific differences between the SCF and CBP. Nonetheless, the differences in net worth and debt between bankruptcy filers and households as a whole are not surprising. It is perhaps less clear whether one would expect these differences in balance sheet components to persist, as this chapter shows is the case, when filers are instead compared with families who meet the financial distress criteria examined in this chapter. Regardless of one's expectation, however, the chapter offers one of the first comprehensive attempts to estimate these differences.

The analysis of SCF families' balance sheets also indicates that the criteria used to classify SCF households as financially vulnerable capture different dimensions of distress. Only a third of families in the SCF who are classified as financially distressed meet more than one of the four financial-distress criteria. Furthermore, which of the SCF subgroups is most vulnerable depends on the measure of financial well-being. Families with limited savings have the lowest median net worth and the highest fraction of debt that is unsecured, for instance, but high-PIR households have the highest median debt, and families with late payments have the highest leverage ratio. The values for credit-constrained families tend to fall within the range of estimates for the other subgroups.

The differences in financial characteristics across the four subgroups of financially vulnerable SCF families suggest that it may be difficult to craft policies that could reduce vulnerability on each of these dimensions. Effective policymaking would likely require weighing the relative merits of the different measures of financial vulnerability and focusing on a narrower set of households, since the four distress measures together capture more than a third of all households. One might, for example, focus on households that meet more than one of this chapter's criteria. A more appealing approach, however, would be to weigh the criteria based on, for example, their correlation with continued deterioration in households' financial situation. This latter approach would likely require longitudinal data, a point I return to below.

DEEPENING OUR UNDERSTANDING OF FINANCIAL SECURITY

Many prior studies of household bankruptcy have focused, broadly speaking, on two classes of explanations for people's decisions to file for bankruptcy. The first view is that bankruptcy is a strategic and potentially anticipated choice that borrowers make after weighing the costs and benefits of filing. The second is that borrowers file for bankruptcy after suffering an unforeseen, financially devastating shock. These views are of course not mutually exclusive, but discerning their relative importance from cross-sectional data is likely quite difficult.[42]

Several of the differences noted in this chapter could be seen as offering support for a strategic view of bankruptcy. For example, bankrupt households are relatively more likely to have credit card debt and generally owe greater amounts on credit cards. The median amount of mortgage debt owed by bankruptcy filers, in contrast, is more similar to the amounts owed by financially vulnerable families in the SCF. This pattern could be partly due to the fact that most types of unsecured debt may be discharged during bankruptcy, whereas home mortgage debt usually may not be discharged. Similarly, bankruptcy filers are less likely than families in most of the SCF subgroups to have education debt, which is generally not discharged in bankruptcy.

Nonetheless, one cannot rule out either perspective on the bankruptcy-filing decision on the basis of these findings alone. These data are consistent with the possibility that at least some people shift the composition of their balance sheets to hold more unsecured debt in anticipation of bankruptcy. But these same patterns of debt could also reflect the fact that bankruptcy is not equally beneficial to all households and that those who would gain the greatest benefit from the legal relief provided by bankruptcy may be the most likely to take advantage of it. Even if its current situation were not the result of strategic decisions, a household with high amounts of mortgage debt may not benefit much from filing for bankruptcy and might not file, whereas a household with an equal amount of credit card obligations would do so.

This chapter's findings on medical debt further illustrate this point. Bankrupt households are much more likely to have medical debt than any of the other groups of financially vulnerable households. On the one hand, this could be seen as evidence that people file for bankruptcy in the aftermath of a severe medical problem. On the other hand, the higher prevalence of medical debt among bankrupt households could be seen as evidence that, in preparation for filing for bankruptcy, some people shift the composition of their balance sheets by, say, stopping payment on routine medical bills in anticipation of being able to discharge unsecured debt in bankruptcy. Of course, the relative importance of each of these factors may well differ across borrowers.

Recognizing the challenge in distinguishing between these hypotheses suggests the kind of data that would be necessary to do so. First, because any comparison across datasets is complicated, the ideal data source would include identical survey and data collection procedures for nonbankrupt households. This approach would likely have to be combined with the collection of detailed retrospective data, since it is hard to predict who will file for bankruptcy. Indeed, the CBP followed this strategy in collecting retrospective survey and interview data about prebankruptcy decisions and life events. However, retrospective data can be less reliable, and more difficult and expensive to obtain, than information on current circumstances.

In addition, discerning the extent to which households are "pushed" into bankruptcy by adverse shocks and the degree to which families structure their balance sheets to maximize the returns of a bankruptcy filing would likely require panel data at a relatively, and potentially infeasibly, high frequency. Such a dataset would quantify the frequency and magnitude of various economic shocks and capture information on households' decisions regarding payments on various types of debt and expenses.

Moreover, panel data could support analysis based on a variety of approaches to defining financial vulnerability. The measures of financial distress examined in this chapter are intended to gauge families' ability to weather adverse economic shocks, but as noted, it is unclear from these cross-sectional data alone how strong an indicator of financial distress each criterion is. Comprehensive data on family finances collected at regular intervals could be used to examine the dynamics of distress and, for example, to estimate the likelihood that a family with late debt payments is able to recover or, instead, that their financial position deteriorates further.

Survey data are unlikely to be able to provide this detailed information for a broad range of types of families. One possibility for gathering this type of information, at least in theory, may be administrative data. Combining, for example, Social Security earnings records and credit bureau data could provide historical information on income, debt, and debt payments, and it would likely offer much larger samples than would be obtained through surveys. Access to and combination of administrative data sources are often restricted. If such an approach proved feasible, however, these types of administrative data could provide a basis for substantially broadening our understanding of families' financial security and of the factors that may lead to bankruptcy as well as to other forms of financial vulnerability.

PART II

STARTING RIGHT, ENDING WRONG

CHAPTER FOUR

Home Burdens
The High Costs of Homeownership

Jerry Anthony

Homeownership is heralded for its financial benefits, and indeed, homes are the largest asset of most Americans. But homeownership also comes with burdens. For almost a century, government and private entities have measured the burden of homeownership by relying on ratios of households' housing costs to their incomes. Government entities have used housing cost ratios for many purposes, including most recently as guideposts for loan modifications aimed at preventing foreclosure. Private sector institutions, including the mortgage industry, have used such ratios to determine whether households are qualified for home mortgage loans and to determine loan amounts.

Housing cost burdens are crucial measures of the financial well-being of Americans. For most families, the cost of housing is their single largest expenditure.[1] If households spend a disproportionate share of their incomes on housing, then they may not have enough money for other expenses, such as health care, child care, or transportation, that are essential for a decent standard of living. Homeowners who spend a high fraction of their incomes on mortgage payments and related housing costs also are at a higher risk for default and foreclosure. Because housing consumes a disproportionate share of their incomes, these families have limited budget flexibility to respond to increases in expenses and may be at heightened risk of financial distress.

The U.S. housing market meltdown of the late 2000s—driven quite significantly by mortgage defaults of households with unaffordable loans—sparked much debate about mortgage underwriting standards and the risks of homeownership. One of the legacies of the foreclosure crisis is likely to be years of upcoming debate about homeownership policy. Housing cost burdens can usefully inform policymakers how to regulate homeownership markets to ensure that homeownership enhances, rather than jeopardizes, the economic security of American families. Already, the Dodd-Frank Wall Street Reform and Consumer Protection Act requires mortgage lenders to consider a borrower's ability to repay mortgage loans as a condition of under-writing. Data on the housing cost ratios of families who faced foreclosure and sought relief in bankruptcy can inform the development of an ability-to-repay standard.

This chapter uses data from bankruptcy cases filed by homeowners in 2007 to assess the housing cost burdens of families trying to save their houses from foreclosure. Just less than half (45 percent) of homeowners in bankruptcy had unaffordable housing costs. The existence of a high housing cost ratio at the time of bankruptcy may help predict whether a family can complete a bankruptcy repayment plan or save their house from foreclosure. The prevalence of high housing cost ratios varied among bankrupt homeowners with different demographic factors and loan characteristics. These are the first findings on the intersection of housing cost burdens and demographics such as age, income, race, and marital status. The analysis in this chapter may help inform policy discussions about the "acceptable" or "optimal" housing cost burden for mortgage loans as policymakers also consider America's commitment to make homeownership accessible to as many families as possible. Using interviews with homeowners in bankruptcy, I examine whether housing cost ratios explain how households and lenders react to loan defaults. Surprisingly, given that high housing cost ratios are thought to reduce the sustainability of homeownership, there was no measurable relationship between default-mitigation strategies and homeownership costs. These findings add to concerns that loss mitigation and foreclosure prevention programs are not being applied in consistent and sensible ways.

MEASURING THE COSTS OF HOMEOWNERSHIP

Researchers and policymakers have diligently grappled with how to measure the costs of homeownership since the 1930s. Much of the existing literature on housing affordability examines housing price trends, but changes in housing prices are not an accurate measure of changes in housing affordability. If incomes rise in proportion to housing price increases, housing affordability will remain unchanged. A better measure of housing affordability is the ratio of a household's housing cost divided by its income. Housing costs include rent or mortgage payments (principal, interest, property tax, and insurance) and utility payments (electricity, water, sewage, storm water, and gas), and income is measured as gross (before-tax) income from all sources. The resulting ratio of these numbers reflects the degree of burden that homeownership imposes on a household's income.

The calculation of housing cost ratios is relatively straightforward, but defining the benchmark for an "affordable" ratio is subject to considerable judgment. In the 1950s and early 1960s, an expenditure of up to 20 percent of income on housing was deemed affordable. This ratio fluctuated significantly during the 1970s and early 1980s.[2] From the late 1980s onward it has remained at 30 percent, with households that spend more than 30 percent of their income on housing costs considered to be housing-cost-burdened. All federal housing programs use this standard to determine affordability. For example, rents for public housing units and tenant contributions to housing choice vouchers are set at 30 percent of household income. Most state and local housing programs do likewise. More recently, the federal government's loan modification programs (such as the Home Affordable Modification Program, or HAMP) aimed to reduce housing cost ratios to 31 percent of household income as a way to prevent foreclosures. Although some studies acknowledge the need to parse out households with higher housing burdens in more detail—for example, by dividing people into groups with housing cost ratios at 30 percent or less, 31 to 40 percent, and more than 40 percent—the most widely used benchmark for home affordability based on income is binary: whether the housing costs are 30 percent or less or more than 30 percent.

People in bankruptcy are required to disclose extraordinary details about their financial lives, including all information needed for calculating housing cost burden ratios. The 2007 Consumer Bankruptcy Project (CBP) coded financial data from bankrupt households' court records and supplemented that information with extensive telephone interviews with bankruptcy debtors (see the appendix for details). Among the 1,032 telephone respondents, 911 households reported rent or mortgage expenses. Of these, 511 were homeowners when they filed for bankruptcy, and the remaining 400 were renters or lived with family or friends. I exclude these nonhomeowner debtors from my analysis and use data from the 511 bankrupt homeowners to document the housing cost burdens of families in bankruptcy, to explore factors that correlate with housing cost burdens of bankrupt families, and to assess whether housing cost burdens explain how homeowners and lenders react to mortgage loan delinquency.

WHO PAYS TOO MUCH FOR HOMEOWNERSHIP?
DEMOGRAPHIC VARIATION IN HOUSING COST RATIOS

A family's financial burdens are shaped by the needs, desires, and opportunities of its members—and the extent to which their earnings can support their expenses. Demographic factors such as income, race, age, marital status, wealth, and education may affect housing cost ratios. Families with some characteristics may be more likely to arrive in bankruptcy struggling with very high housing costs relative to their incomes. This section describes the prior research on variation in housing cost burdens and presents data on whether these variations are replicated among bankrupt homeowners. Because bankruptcy is a common refuge for homeowners facing foreclosure, these families are a useful subpopulation of homeowners for research on housing cost burdens.

Income

Past research shows that lower income households are more likely to have high housing costs than higher income households. Using data from the 1990 Census, Michael Stone provides compelling evidence about the disproportionate burden that housing imposes on poor people.[3] More recent evidence is presented in the 2009 report *State of the Nation's Housing*, which finds that about 16 percent of households that earn less than $20,000 per year in wage income spend more than half of that income on housing costs.[4] But only 4 percent of households with incomes higher than $50,000 spend half their incomes on housing. While there are many reasons for this disparity, the most important one is that higher income households have the financial capacity to bid on a larger number of homes with fewer location constraints than lower income households.[5] This forces lower income households to pay a higher proportion of their incomes to compete for relatively scarce housing. Do households in bankruptcy, which generally have very low incomes at the time of filing compared with the general population (see Chapter 2), reflect this pattern?

Net Wealth

Homeownership is presumed to increase household wealth. This is because housing equity, a long-term consequence of homeownership (notwithstanding the equity losses since 2007 caused by falling housing prices) is the single largest source of wealth for U.S. households. Indeed, homes are often the only asset for low-income households.[6] Housing equity is much more evenly distributed across the income distribution of all households than other forms of wealth, making widespread homeownership particularly important in addressing social inequalities. In 2007, 43 percent of households in the lowest income quartile had equity in their homes, while only 17 percent of the poorest households held stocks. In the top income quartile, 85 percent of the households had home equity, and 90 percent held stocks.[7] In 2007, the median value of home equity for homeowners was more than ten times the median value of stock wealth among stockholders. But what is the precise nature of the relationship between household wealth and homeownership? Specifically, are homeowners able to increase household wealth through purchasing a home even if they have high housing costs? If cost-burdened households can build the same amount of wealth as households with lower housing costs, then perhaps some of the increase in default risk associated with unaffordable homeownership costs would be mitigated. If households are allocating a high amount of their incomes toward housing costs to facilitate wealth accumulation, the effect may be largely a change from liquid to nonliquid financial assets (cash to home equity) and may be a positive transformation of income to wealth.

Race

Considerable evidence documents a racial gap in home buying and lending, mortgage refinancing, and homeownership rates. In all instances, the data consistently point to hardships for nonwhite households. Nonwhites are rejected at higher rates than whites for home mortgages, and when approved for loans, they pay higher interest rates and are required to make larger down payments.[8] This racial disparity in lending terms is reflected in homeownership rates. In 2009, when the national homeownership rate was 67.4 percent, the rate for whites was 71 percent, and the rates for blacks and Hispanics remained at less than 50 percent (46 percent and 48 percent, respectively).[9] Some of the homeownership gap is due to lower incomes and wealth of nonwhite households, but the effect of racial biases in determining the racial gaps cannot be discounted.[10] For example, William Apgar and Allegra Calder report that in 2001 prime loans accounted for only 70.8 percent of home refinancing for high-income African American households, and they accounted for as much as 83.1 percent of home refinances by low-income white homeowners.[11] That is, relatively wealthy African Americans were more likely to receive a subprime loan than relatively poor whites. Raphael Bostic and Brian Surette contend that for homeownership, "the racial disparity remains even after controlling for family demographic and financial characteristics."[12] The research supports an inference that at least a significant part of the gap can be attributed to discrimination and predatory lending. Race-based lending practices could increase housing cost burdens because nonwhite households could be steered into higher-cost loans compared with white households with the same incomes. The result would be inflated housing ratios for nonwhite families, increasing what they pay for homeownership and heightening their risk of default on their mortgages. But thus far no study has examined variations in housing cost burdens by race. The CBP data on bankrupt households offers an unusual combination of detailed demographic and financial information, permitting me to offer data on demographic variations in housing cost burdens.

Age

Older homeowners should have lower housing cost ratios than younger homeowners. Owning a home tends to reduce housing cost burdens over time because payments for mortgage loans (that are amortized over thirty years) remain unchanged even as incomes generally increase. On the other hand, increases in rent outpace income growth, which leads to renters' housing cost burdens increasing over time. Consequently, as homeowners age their housing cost ratios could be expected to steadily decline. If they purchased homes at a relatively young age with traditional mortgage loans, their housing cost ratios should have declined as their incomes increased when they reached peak earning potential. This expectation is consistent with the lifecycle model of consumption and borrowing articulated in the seminal works of economists Franco Modigliani and Milton Freidman.[13] Here, I explore the hypothesis that older homeowners in bankruptcy should have lower housing cost burdens than younger homeowners. One reason to question this hypothesis is that many bankrupt families have experienced dramatic shocks in income caused by job loss or adverse health in the year or two before filing for bankruptcy.[14] These income losses could increase housing cost burdens and unwind the anticipated effect of age. In these situations, the benefits of fixing homeownership costs over time with a mortgage loan are undercut by income problems that occur in midlife or later.

Family Structure

Although it is difficult to clearly establish the effect of family structure on housing cost burdens, many scholars associate household dissolution with financial stress. For example, Teresa Sullivan, Elizabeth Warren, and Jay Westbrook cite change in family structure such as divorce, death of a family member, or birth of a child as a leading cause of bankruptcy.[15] Households with married adults also can be expected to have more financial resources (wealth to make a down payment at purchase) and more stable income (with perhaps two wage earners) than households headed by a single adult who has never been married or is divorced, separated, or widowed. Bostic and Surette report that in the highest two income quintiles, 88.7 percent and 79.1 percent of the households are married couples.[16] The effects of lost income from changes in family structure and of lower incomes for one-adult households may be to produce lower housing cost burdens for married households. Empirical evidence examining marital status and housing costs is virtually nonexistent; the bankruptcy data again offer a new opportunity for understanding demographic variation in housing cost burdens.

Education

Higher education is supposed to enhance financial prosperity, but as Katherine Porter explores in Chapter 5, more education does not necessarily ensure greater economic security. In the context of housing burdens, education might insulate a person from underestimating the complete costs of homeownership and may provide some protection from impulses to borrow heavily in order to own a home. For example, educated households might keep housing cost burdens at the lowest level possible to maximize flexibility regarding nonhousing expenses and to permit them to diversify their wealth accumulation by investing in other financial assets such as stocks or retirement programs. Borrowing can be a wise financial strategy, but taking on very high housing debt as a means of building household wealth is a high-stakes game that could result in a loss of shelter from foreclosure. Households with more education may recognize this risk and have lower housing costs relative to their incomes than households with less education. On the other hand, scholars have noted that debt, and perhaps most ubiquitously mortgage debt, has become an acceptable and necessary part of American culture,[17] and the American cultural pressure to become a homeowner to achieve middle-class status may most strongly influence college-educated individuals.

The Analysis

To begin analysis of the way in which demographic variation may occur in housing cost burdens, I divided the bankrupt sample of homeowners into two groups: those with homeownership cost ratios equal to or less than 30 percent of their incomes, and those with homeownership cost ratios that exceed 30 percent of their incomes. Table 4.1 presents descriptive data on the CBP sample of homeowners in the bankrupt population in these two groups. Households that exceed the traditional 30 percent benchmark for housing affordability differ significantly on several demographic characteristics, including standardized income, median years of college education, marital status, and mean standardized net wealth. Low-housing-cost and high-housing-cost families in bankruptcy do not seem to differ on the basis of race and age.

The differences are particularly notable for the two demographic characteristics that measure financial well-being. The median standardized income of households in the sample is 56.7 percent of area median income. Clearly, these are families with severe income shortages who are filing for bankruptcy to cope with debts that overwhelm their low incomes. Indeed, households at the income level of the typical bankrupt family are income-qualified for most federal rental housing programs. Standardized income is sharply higher for

TABLE 4.1
Characteristics of bankrupt homeowners

		Housing cost burden ≤30%[a]	Housing cost burden >30%[b]
Demographic factors			
Income	Standardized annual household income from all sources	60.5% of area median income	52.7% of area median income
Net wealth[c]	Median	−89.45%	−86.5%
	Mean	−108.26%	−150.69%
Race	Nonwhite (either spouse or single person)	23%	27%
Age (years)[d]	Median	48	49
	Mean	49.7	50.0
Marital status	Percent married	44	34
Education[e]	Median	4	5
	Mean	4.75	5.48
Home loan characteristics			
Loan-to-value ratio[f]	Median	105.12%	97.35%
	Mean	145.03%	99.12%
Has adjustable-rate mortgage	Yes	19.26%	23.24%
Had second mortgage at home purchase	Yes	16.67%	10.79%
Has home equity loan	Yes	32.22%	30.71%
Owns mobile/ manufactured	Yes	24.44%	22.82%

SOURCE: Consumer Bankruptcy Project 2007.

NOTE: N=511 households.

[a]A total of 270 households had cost burdens less than or equal to 30 percent of income, with a median cost burden of 21.45 percent (mean = 20.303, standard deviation = 6.232, lowest value = 0.41).

[b]A total of 241 households had cost burdens greater than 30 percent of income, with a median cost burden of 40.08 percent (mean = 48.69, standard deviation = 41.83, highest value = 526.23 [which means that the housing cost was more than five times income]).

[c]Difference between all assets and all debts was considered "wealth"; this amount was standardized using household income to account for the difference in true value of the same dollar amount of net wealth for households of different financial status (i.e., $10,000 in net wealth is more valuable for a household with a total income of $40,000 than for a household with a total income of $140,000).

[d]Oldest nondependent adult in household.

[e]Number of years of college-level education of all adults in the household.

[f]Ratio of all home loans of a household at the time the bankruptcy was filed to the household's home value at that time.

those with affordable (30 percent or less) ratios of housing cost to income. Although household wealth is often measured as the difference between assets and debts of households, a more accurate measure in comparative research is standardized household wealth, computed by dividing the difference between assets and debts by the household's annual income. The typical (median) bankrupt household that owns a home has a net standardized wealth of about –87 percent; that is, its debts exceed its assets by 87 percent of its annual income. This finding reflects the degree to which households that file for bankruptcy are deep in debt, owing amounts approximately equivalent to a year's income. One would expect bankrupt households to have large debt burdens, but Robert Lawless et al. find that median net worth of households in the 2007 CBP sample is substantially negative (at –$24,000).[18] The lack of wealth of these bankrupt homeowners is a reminder that purchasing a home may not necessarily lead to wealth accumulation, an achievement that requires sustaining homeownership for many years.

The descriptive findings above may reflect correlations between variables; for example, the finding on marital status may simply reflect the fact that married couples are also more likely to earn higher standardized incomes. To examine the data in a more robust way, I used a multiple logistic regression model with a yes/no binary dummy for housing cost burden ("yes" if higher than 30 percent and "no" otherwise). The other variables were demographic factors in categories. For this analysis, I also introduced a variety of loan characteristics as explanatory variables.

Table 4.2 shows the results of the logistic regression analysis. Several of the demographic factors were statistically significant. Household income was, as expected, statistically significant. If a household's income was less than half the median for the area of the household's residence, that household was more than two-and-a-half times as likely as a household with income above the area median to have high housing costs relative to its income. However, there was no statistically significant difference in the probability of a household with an income between 50 percent and 100 percent of the area median being housing-cost-burdened.

The analysis provides a crude quantification of when lower income begins to affect housing cost burdens and reinforces past findings. While low- and moderate-income households (between 50 percent and 100 percent of area median) do not seem particularly apt to suffer high housing cost ratios, the very poorest families are particularly likely to be paying too much of their incomes for homeownership. Given the low amount of income of these families in absolute dollars, the situation of these households may be quite grim. With housing costs eating up more than roughly a third of their incomes, these families may not have enough residual income after paying housing costs to avoid a poverty-level standard of living. The

TABLE 4.2
Logistic regression of demographic and loan characteristics associated with high housing cost burdens among bankrupt homeowners

		Odds ratio	Standard error
Demographic characteristics			
Income	<50% Area median income	2.650*	0.027
	50–100% Area median income	1.362	0.451
	>100% Area median income	Reference	
Net wealth[a]	Net negative wealth >100% of income	1.334	0.418
	Net negative wealth 0–100% of income	1.692	0.143
	Net positive wealth	Reference	
Race	Both spouses race unknown	0.974	0.970
	Both spouses white	0.851	0.635
	One or both spouses nonwhite	Reference	
Age (years)[b]	<40	0.481*	0.025
	40–65	0.589	0.074
	>65	Reference	
Marital status	Never married	1.566	0.250
	Widow(er)	2.137**	0.008
	Divorced/separated	2.625**	0.007
	Married	Reference	
	No	Reference	
Education[c]	<Associate level	0.316**	0.000
	College level	0.809	0.524
	Highly educated	Reference	
Loan characteristics			
Loan-to-value ratio[d]	Unknown	1.317	0.463
	<100%	4.254**	0.001
	100–120%	3.981**	0.002
	>120%	Reference	
Has adjustable-rate loan	Yes	1.409	0.211
	No	Reference	
Had second mortgage at home purchase	Yes	0.594	0.121
	No	Reference	
Has home equity loan	Yes	0.924	0.749
	No	Reference	
Owns mobile/ manufactured home	Yes	0.672	0.141

SOURCE: Consumer Bankruptcy Project 2007.

NOTE: N = 511 households. $*p < 0.05$, $**p < 0.01$.

[a]Difference between all assets and all debts was considered "wealth"; this amount was standardized using household income to account for the difference in true value of the same dollar amount of net wealth for households of different financial status (i.e., $10,000 in net wealth is more valuable for a household with a total income of $40,000 than for household with a total income of $140,000).

[b]Oldest member of the household.

[c]Number of years of college-level education of all adults in the household. If this total was less than two, then the household's level of educational attainment was classified as "<Associate level"; if equal to four or five, then as "College level; and if six or more, then as "Highly educated."

[d]Ratio of all home loans at bankruptcy filing to home value at that time.

finding on income underlines the dire need for reasonably priced homes for low-income homebuyers.

In the logistic regression model, net wealth did not emerge as a strong predictor of unaffordable homeownership. This may be an artifact of the sample. Households in bankruptcy may have drawn down on any available assets during their financial struggles before filing for bankruptcy. Alternatively, the lack of a detectable relationship between net wealth and housing cost ratio may reflect broader trends in declining wealth and increasing consumer debt among U.S. households.[19]

Age did not strongly affect the probability of a family having an unaffordable housing cost ratio. There was no statistically significant difference in the housing cost burdens of people older than sixty-five years and those forty to sixty-five years old. Households whose oldest adult was younger than forty were significantly less likely to be housing-cost-burdened compared with households whose oldest adult was older than sixty-five. These findings contradict the assumption that housing costs as a percentage of income decrease over time as people age. Barry Bosworth and colleagues and Karen Dynan and colleagues posit that the traditional model of lesser debt as a person ages needs to be revised because middle-aged and older households have shown a greater propensity to be in debt and a lesser propensity to save in the past three decades.[20] The finding here illustrates their concern about the economic security of older Americans.

Marital status had a statistically significant relationship to housing cost burden, with homeownership seeming to be particularly expensive for people who are not married. Households headed by a widow or widower were twice as likely as married households to be housing-cost-burdened. Similarly, households headed by a divorced or separated adult were more than 2.5 times as likely to be housing-cost-burdened as married households. Although these findings are not unexpected, the magnitude of the effect of not being married, even after one controls for household income, net wealth, and other factors, is striking. Several possible hypotheses might explain the hardships of unmarried homeowners. Perhaps married couples make more informed or wiser choices about the homes they can afford on their incomes; two decision makers may be better than one in resisting urges to choose housing beyond what a household's income can support. Alternatively, married couples may have more choices regarding the size and location of their homes compared with other types of households that may be smaller or may have some location-based constraints that drive up housing expenditures. The idealized American homeowner as a married couple with 2.2 children and a family dog may drive home builders and communities toward offering a larger supply of housing suitable for that ideal. A more likely explanation may relate to the effects of family dissolution. Couples may buy homes when they are married, but then after divorce or separation, one person may hold on to the family home. Such reluctance to surrender a family home may reflect concerns about dislocating children or a desire to retain the home in which family memories were made (see Chapter 7), but the outcome may be to burden divorced or separated adults with unaffordable housing costs. The likelihood of this situation may result from income declining after divorce or separation, as one earner needs some of his or her income to support a separate household. The bankruptcy data cannot resolve these questions about the high housing cost ratios of homeowners who are not married, but they do highlight the need for further research for a better understanding of economic risks related to family structure.

Education is a statistically significant factor in predicting unaffordable homeownership costs, but the direction of the effect was counter to expectation. More education usually has been associated with improved financial outcomes for households, but in this analysis, households with less education (fewer than two years of college total for all adults in the household) were half as likely as households with four or more years of college-level education to have housing costs that exceed 30 percent of their incomes. More educated households may be more likely to be aware that debts secured by their homes have lower costs than other types of debts, such as credit cards, a difference reflecting both lower interest rates for secured loans and the ability to deduct mortgage interest on tax returns. Households with more educated adults might be more sensitive to these cost differentials and therefore have consolidated nonmortgage debts into a home loan, lowering payments on other debt obligations but raising their mortgage payments, and by extension, their housing cost ratios.

It is noteworthy that while researchers have found that race has a significant effect on homeownership rates and access to credit, it does not have an effect on housing cost burdens in this sample of bankrupt households. Because racial disparities have been documented in many other aspects of homeownership, the lack of a measurable effect on home cost burdens is notable. Future research should replicate this demographic analysis on a sample from the general (nonbankrupt) population.

In summary, lower income households are more burdened by unaffordable housing costs than moderate income and higher income households; younger households are more burdened than older households; and households that are headed by single people who are divorced or separated or widowed are more likely to be stressed by housing expenses than households headed by married couples. The bankruptcy data suggest that demographic characteristics may predict higher housing costs.

THE BURDENS OF BORROWING:
LOAN CHARACTERISTICS AND HOUSING COSTS

A family's financial well-being is directly affected by the costs and terms of their debts. Loan characteristics shape how much is owed, how rapidly the debts must be repaid, and the extent to which a borrower has equity in the collateral securing the debt. In the late 1990s and first half of the 2000s, the traditional thirty-year fixed-rate mortgage, obtained after a home buyer paid 20 percent of the house's value as a down payment, gave way to a proliferation of alternative arrangements. Mortgage loans with some characteristics may be more likely to be associated with unaffordable housing costs. This section presents the findings of the logistic regression analysis to examine the ways in which variations in mortgage borrowing may shape housing cost burdens. Because home mortgage loans normally cannot be modified in bankruptcy,[21] the extent to which loan characteristics lead to high housing cost burdens may be an important explanatory factor in understanding why many homeowners who file for bankruptcy do not save their homes (see Chapter 7 for an estimate of home loss during the first year after bankruptcy filing).

The mortgage industry makes widespread use of loan-to-value ratios to assess the risk of borrowers defaulting and to price mortgage products accordingly. Conventional underwriting criteria that were widely used before the early years of the 2000s held that the higher the loan-to-value ratio, the higher the default risk and therefore the higher an interest rate should be charged on a mortgage. The traditional model for a prime loan required a homeowner to put down 20 percent of a house's value, producing a loan-to-value ratio of 80 percent at loan origination. The subprime lending boom pushed standards lower, albeit with private mortgage insurance, resulting in a significant number of loan originations or refinancings during the housing bubble in which homeowners borrowed more than 100 percent of a home's value. However, lower requirements for down payments should merely convert the wealth constraint for homeownership to an income constraint for homeownership because lower down payments increase the amount of the mortgage loan, and a larger loan makes a correspondingly bigger demand on income. No research has examined the relationship of loan-to-value ratios to housing cost ratios, even though both calculations are measures of default risk and are interrelated (a higher loan-to-value ratio should result in a higher housing cost ratio). Because the CBP data were collected during the first few months of 2007, before housing prices began to plummet, the dataset is ideal for exploring whether and how the two ratios are related in a "normal" economy with rising or stable housing costs. These findings may help inform whether future regulations should focus on down payment requirements or housing cost ratios to reduce default risks.

The proportion of adjustable-rate mortgages in all segments of the mortgage industry—prime, Alt-A, and subprime—grew significantly in the early 2000s. While interest rates were fairly stable during that period, the adjustable-rate mortgages in the years of the housing bubble were notable for offering introductory "teaser" interest rates that were much lower than the fully indexed rate that kicked in two or three years after loan origination. These rate resets often increased housing payments to unaffordable levels and have been blamed for contributing to the spike in foreclosures in the subprime and prime segments that began in 2007. Because adjustable-rate mortgages have been associated with unsustainable home loans, there may be a relationship between adjustable-rate loans and high housing costs.

As recently as the late 1980s, home equity loans were regarded as loans of last resort for consumers because a failure to repay them could result in foreclosure. In the late 1990s, many lenders began to encourage Americans to use financial products such as home equity loans because banks' returns on home equity loans are much higher than on signature consumer loans. Many banks rolled out slick, well-funded advertising campaigns promoting home equity loans (for example, Citibank's $1 billion "Live Richly" campaign and Banco Popular's "Make Dreams Happen" campaign with the tagline "Need Cash? Use Your Home").[22] These campaigns were clearly successful in enticing American families to take out home equity loans. The 1986 Tax Reform Act also added incentives for tapping home equity. The law included the gradual elimination of the tax deduction for interest paid on nonmortgage debt, while allowing the deduction of interest paid on home equity loans. This change gave consumers an incentive to switch from other forms of consumer debt to home equity debt.[23] Outstanding home equity loan amounts increased from about $1 billion in 1982 to $188 billion in 1988 and approximately $1 trillion in 2007. As a percentage of homeowners' disposable income, equity extraction from homes increased more than threefold, from about 3 percent of disposable income in 1991 to 11 percent of disposable income in 2005.[24] The effect of such increases in home lending was to ratchet up the amount of mortgage debt, thus pushing up the demands on consumers' incomes to pay mortgage loans.

The 1990s also saw the rise of second mortgages on homes at the time of purchase. These so-called piggyback loans were issued in conjunction with a conforming (80 percent loan-to-value) mortgage that was saleable to government-sponsored enterprises (such as Fannie Mae). This double-loan structure reduced the loan-to-value ratios on the large loan to a level that avoided the need for primary mortgage insurance. The average size of mortgage packages that featured piggyback loans in the 1990s and early

2000s was about 40 percent higher than those with single loans.[25] The use of piggyback loans enabled households without sufficient assets (to own a home with size and amenities they desired) to buy a home by essentially substituting their asset shortage for an increased burden on future income. While piggyback loans are a lower cost alternative than mortgage insurance, they are more likely to lead to foreclosure because households often cannot manage the high housing costs created by the mortgage obligations of two loans.

The United States has been facing a chronic shortage of affordably priced rental and ownership housing since the 1980s. One response availed by numerous low-income households has been to move into mobile or manufactured homes.[26] In 1999, the median price of a new site–built home was $173,000—more than five times the median price of a new mobile home, which was $33,000.[27] Buying a mobile home provides households with a low-cost option for leaving the rental market (where rent increases have been outpacing income increases for the past three decades); however, mobile homes do not provide the equity-building effect of conventional homes because they depreciate in value over time and many families rent, rather than own, the land on which their mobile home sits. Very little scholarship has examined the financial burdens of households living in mobile homes, even though 7 percent of the U.S. population lived in mobile homes in 1990 and this figure may be even higher today because mobile and manufactured homes accounted for 12 percent of new homes constructed in 2008.[28] As Table 4.1 shows, mobile homes are quite prevalent among bankrupt households, with more than 22 percent of the sample living in mobile or manufactured homes; the 2007 CBP thus provides a good sample for examining the effect of mobile home ownership on housing cost burdens.

Table 4.1 shows the descriptive statistics for loan characteristics of the bankrupt homeowner sample. About 20 percent of households had an adjustable-rate mortgage on their homes and about 16 percent used a piggyback loan when buying their home. Home equity loans were also prevalent, with more than 30 percent of households having borrowed against their homes.

The results of the logistic regression analysis, which included demographic factors as well as the loan characteristics discussed in the preceding paragraphs, suggest that housing cost burdens are not strongly shaped by mortgage lending characteristics. Loan-to-value ratio was the only loan characteristic that was statistically significant. Notably, though, it has the greatest certainty of effect of all factors in the model. Households that have a loan-to-value ratio lower than 100 percent are more than four times more likely than those with loan-to-value ratios higher than 120 percent to have high housing costs relative to incomes. This is a curious finding; one would expect households with higher loan-to-value ratios to be paying a higher proportion of their incomes for housing because the changes in mortgage lending in recent years facilitated the substitution of equity for additional debt. As the traditional boundaries for borrowing were exceeded, housing cost burdens should have grown, especially as real income growth among the middle class was largely stagnant during that period, as described in Chapter 11. This finding on loan-to-value ratio needs corroboration from additional research on a sample of nonbankrupt homeowners. It may be that the nature of bankruptcy relief attracts a peculiar mix of families; those who have relatively low loan-to-value ratios may want to avail themselves of the right to cure defaults on their home loans in bankruptcy to prevent a foreclosure that would strip them of their home equity. At the same time, people in bankruptcy often have experienced significant drops in income before bankruptcy,[29] which could result in dramatically higher housing cost ratios at the time of the bankruptcy filing.

None of the other loan characteristics—adjustable-rate mortgages, piggyback loans, and home equity loans—have statistically significant effects on housing affordability. More than 20 percent of the households had adjustable-rate mortgages, a proportion much higher than in the general population. John Eggum, Katherine Porter, and Tara Twomey provide a detailed illustration of how the sharp uptick in monthly payment from an adjustable-rate mortgage likely propelled a family into bankruptcy.[30] In a separate model of the 2007 CBP data (full results not reported here), I found that bankrupt households with fixed-rate mortgages were more likely to have cost-burden ratios lower than 20 percent. This suggests that adjustable-rate mortgages do relate to moderately higher housing costs. The most likely explanation for the nonsignificant result of the adjustable-rate mortgage variable in the regression analysis is that having this type of loan was highly correlated with other factors in the analysis. For example, households with adjustable-rate mortgages were 3.4 times as likely as those with fixed-rate mortgages to have a piggyback loan.

Finally, the fact that living in a mobile or manufactured home does not seem to have a significant effect on housing cost burden is a novel finding. Researchers have been troubled about whether to treat households living in mobile or manufactured homes as homeowners, because they own their shelter in one sense, or as renters, because mobile homes are not considered real property in many states and many mobile homes sit on rented land. It is well established that renter households are more likely to be housing-cost-burdened than owner households.[31] The finding here suggests that households that own mobile homes should perhaps be treated more like owners than renters in future housing research because they are not particularly apt to have the higher housing cost ratios that characterize renters.

BEHAVIOR OF HOMEOWNERS IN FINANCIAL TROUBLE

Many households arrive in bankruptcy at risk of foreclosure. A little less than half (47 percent) of homeowners had missed at least one mortgage payment (or made at least one late payment) in the two years before they filed for bankruptcy. A little more than a third of bankrupt homeowners (36 percent) were threatened with foreclosure by their lenders before bankruptcy, and about three-fourths of that group actually had foreclosure actions initiated against them. Homeowners often look to bankruptcy to address these problems. As Sullivan, Warren, and Westbrook have explained, families "often want desperately to hold on to their homes, and their bankruptcy filings may be an attempt to clear out other debts so they can pour their often shrinking incomes into their mortgage payments. For many, hanging on to their home is no longer a matter of economic rationality; it has become a struggle to save an important part of their lives, one that a financial advisor might tell them to let go."[32] The CBP data from 2007 corroborate the importance of saving homes as a motivation for filing. More than two-thirds (71 percent) of bankrupt homeowners reported that saving their home was the most important or a very important reason for their bankruptcy.

Because bankruptcy is an effort to save a home, the CBP data are useful for exploring how homeowners and lenders behave when mortgage loans are in default. There are several possible strategies that lenders and homeowners might deploy during default, including negotiation, voluntary surrender, and initiation of a foreclosure. I examine how housing cost ratios and loan characteristics are associated with default behavior. Do housing costs affect whether homeowners state a desire to save their homes as a reason for filing for bankruptcy? Do housing costs affect whether they contact their mortgage companies before bankruptcy or face foreclosure threats before bankruptcy? To shed light on these issues, I conducted difference of means tests (using Levene's test for equality of variances and t-tests for equality of means) between bankrupt households with unaffordable (greater than 30 percent) or affordable (30 percent or less) housing cost ratios. The findings offer insight into how foreclosure prevention programs might be tailored in light of the behavior of homeowners in financial trouble.

During the home foreclosure crisis, many people have lamented that homeowners at risk of foreclosure do not contact their mortgage companies to see whether their payment problems can be worked out. Consider that many families thought to be eligible for loan modifications purportedly do not respond when their mortgage companies contact them.[33] Although the CBP collected its data in 2007 before the foreclosure crisis was fully developed, only 38 percent of the bankrupt households successfully contacted their mortgage companies to even ask for help with their difficulties in making their mortgage payments. This works out to only about half of all homeowners who said that they filed for bankruptcy to save their homes, suggesting that many families turn to bankruptcy without having negotiated with their mortgage companies first. This failure of outreach may stem from homeowners believing that their mortgage companies will not help them, from difficulty in knowing how to contact their mortgage companies, or from an unwillingness to acknowledge the likelihood of home loss until it is too late to negotiate because foreclosure is imminent. This said, mortgage companies are also culpable for this low rate because many of them were unwilling to modify loans and did not respond when distressed homeowners attempted to contact them.

Households that contacted their mortgage companies were more likely to have adjustable-rate mortgages ($p = 0.015$), have home equity loans ($p = 0.018$), and have missed payments before bankruptcy ($p = 0.033$) than households that did not contact their mortgage companies. Somewhat surprisingly, neither housing cost ratios nor loan-to-value ratios differed significantly among households that reached out to their mortgage companies and those that filed for bankruptcy without trying to negotiate. Because both ratios are thought to be predictors of sustainable homeownership, it is notable that they do not seem to be related to homeowners' determination of the potential benefits of negotiation or loan modification. Debtors' propensity to have contacted their mortgage companies also did not differ among households that stated that saving their homes was an important reason for bankruptcy filing and those that did not give such a reason.

I also analyzed lender behavior toward homeowners in financial trouble. Bankrupt homeowners who had received foreclosure notices before bankruptcy had much lower net wealth than those who did not ($p = 0.044$). Lenders were also more likely to initiate actual foreclosure actions against households that had adjustable-rate mortgages ($p = 0.010$), had home equity loans ($p = 0.009$), and had contacted the lender ($p = 0.000$) than those that did not. The latter is particularly interesting because it suggests that mortgage companies may learn information when negotiating with homeowners in trouble that leads them to decide to pursue foreclosure actions. Surprisingly, neither housing cost-burden ratios nor loan-to-value ratios explained whether lenders threatened or initiated foreclosure.

These findings shed light on how homeowners respond to financial trouble and how lenders react to default. While there are differences based on objective loan criteria, such as the presence of adjustable-rate mortgages, home equity loans, and missed or late payments, the standard measure of housing affordability—housing cost ratio—does not seem to inform such decisions. Given that no differences were found based on loan-to-value ratios either, it may be that these two traditional criteria were largely ignored during the early years of the foreclosure crisis. Ultimately, however, both loan-to-value and housing cost ratios may help determine a family's success in saving their homes using bankruptcy relief. Further research on outcomes of bankruptcy for homeowners, such as that of Sarah Carroll and Wenli Li,[34] with the addition of housing cost ratios as an explanatory variable, would be useful in understanding how home affordability affects bankruptcy's efficacy as a home-saving strategy.

POLICY IMPLICATIONS

In scholarly and policy debates about how to regulate mortgage lending to prevent future foreclosure crises, criteria for underwriting loans have taken center stage. In recent federal programs adopted to stem the rising tide of foreclosures, cost-burden ratios have figured prominently, such as in the federal government's HAMP loan modification program.[35] One focus of such discussions and policy efforts needs to be whether a one-size-fits-all housing cost ratio is appropriate. Indeed, when the mortgage industry abandoned the 30 percent standard and replaced it with higher ones, it argued that a one-size-fits-all approach was inappropriate because it did not account for variations among households on important factors such as absolute dollars of income. Moreover, the 30 percent standard that governments have used since the 1960s may no longer be tenable given the high cost of housing (even after the housing bubble) in many areas.

The findings in this chapter show that housing cost ratios clearly vary on the basis of many factors unrelated to loan terms themselves, including demographic characteristics that exist after income and net wealth are controlled. Given the increasing technical sophistication of underwriting models, these factors could perhaps be incorporated into more tailored guidelines for appropriate housing cost ratios. For example, the relationship between the age of the head of household and housing cost burden is linear. Perhaps future loan products should factor age into default risk by attaching an age premium to the interest rate. While discrimination is prohibited in some situations, it is currently lawful to differentially price products that have a clear age-based risk variation, such as health and auto insurance. Similarly, the mortgage industry may be encouraged to adopt a lower cost burden for low-income households than for moderate and higher income households. Perhaps the acceptable ratios could be 25 percent for households lower than 80 percent of area median income, 30 percent for those in the range of 81 to 120 percent, and 40 percent for those higher than 120 percent. If a scaled standard such as this could be enforced, it would prevent low-income households from entering into unsustainable home loans while allowing banks and mortgage companies greater flexibility in lending to higher income households.

Although families in bankruptcy are not representative of all households and caution is warranted in extrapolating these findings, this chapter nonetheless illustrates the relevance of housing affordability in determining successful and failed homeownership. With more than half a million homeowners declaring bankruptcy each year to save their homes, these data on housing cost burdens have policy significance. The high cost of homeownership may hamper the ability of some families to benefit from bankruptcy. The data on demographic variation suggest that the inability to modify most home mortgages in bankruptcy will disproportionately harm certain demographic groups who are more likely to have high housing costs. The bankruptcy data also reveal how homeowners and lenders react to actual or imminent default in ways that seem to ignore housing cost burdens, despite their relationship to sustainable homeownership. Adoption of underwriting standards that prevent families from taking out mortgage loans with high housing cost ratios will reduce may families' foreclosure risk. And recognizing the important of housing cost ratios in modifications of delinquent loans will result in sustainable foreclosure prevention.

CHAPTER FIVE

College Lessons

The Financial Risks of Dropping Out

Katherine Porter

Decades of demographic work have pinpointed the educational attainment of people in bankruptcy.[1] While the overall level of education has crept upward,[2] the largest group of people in bankruptcy remains those with "some college."[3] More than 43 percent of people who filed for bankruptcy in 2007 were in this middle group, having started a postsecondary education but ended it before earning a four-year college degree. People who enroll in college hope to attain middle-class status and to access higher paying jobs. As a policy matter, there is widespread agreement about the value of postsecondary education and expanding access to college.

This push to college reflects robust research showing that higher education has economic benefits. For college graduates, this proposition is true and enduring. The typical worker with a bachelor's degree earns 71 percent more than the worker with only a high school diploma.[4] A college degree also insulates Americans from financial collapse. College graduates and those with advanced degrees are underrepresented in bankruptcy. But the protective benefits of education are not linear, and not every educational effort after college provides a corresponding financial advantage. In fact, Americans who have some college credit but do not earn a bachelor's degree seem vulnerable to financial failure. This group is sharply overrepresented in bankruptcy compared with the general population. The educational demographics of bankruptcy are a reminder that the financial benefits of a four-year degree may obscure the economic risks of failed college attempts.

Using people in bankruptcy as a lens on the hardships of people who attempt but do not complete college, I explore the varied educational experiences that may be categorized as "some college" and profile bankruptcy debtors with some college to show their dire economic circumstances. In the bankrupt population, people with some college have debt-to-income ratios similar to those with only high school educations, suggesting that college attendance without a four-year degree may not have a protective effect against overwhelming debt or produce sufficient income for people to manage debt burdens. I sharpen this finding by focusing on a subgroup of those who enrolled in college: student loan borrowers. Thirty percent of all student loan debtors in bankruptcy are people who dropped out of college, a fact not identified in the debate over whether bankruptcy should discharge student loans. The bankruptcy data show that student loans create identical economic burdens for college dropouts and college graduates. People who attempt college make a financial investment in themselves by taking on debt but then fail to realize college's economic benefits if they do not earn a bachelor's degree.

These findings highlight the risks of advocating "college for all."[5] In efforts to promote college, the consequences of noncompletion are often overlooked. Educational policymakers need to evaluate the costs of college attempts and to pay attention to the graduation rate of educational institutions. The push for a more educated workforce should perhaps be tempered by consideration of whether failed college efforts actually may increase the risk of financial failure. The bankruptcy system could play a modest role in softening the risks of college attempts if the law were amended to permit the discharge of student loan debt owed by people who did not complete their educational programs. This would ease the burdens of student loan borrowers who do not have the benefit of a degree to help them earn their way out of debt. Such a change would reduce the risks of attempting college and increase pressure on colleges to reduce dropout rates.

AIM HIGH, FINISH LOW:
ECONOMIC CONSEQUENCES OF SOME COLLEGE ATTAINMENT

Bankruptcy is a public measure of financial hardship. Yet, the public records contain almost no demographic information about people who seek bankruptcy relief. The data of the 2007 Consumer Bankruptcy Project (CBP) provide a measure of how educational attainment may protect consumers from, or expose them to, economic risks.

The bankrupt population has a different distribution of educational attainment than the general population; people in bankruptcy are more likely to have some postsecondary education (see Figure 2.3 in Chapter 2) than the general population. In 2007, 58.9 percent of bankrupt debtors had attended college. However, three-quarters of these college efforts did not result in a bachelor's degree. Among people in bankruptcy, "some college" is the modal educational attainment. More than four in ten debtors had more education than a high school diploma but less than a bachelor's degree.

People with some college are overrepresented in bankruptcy compared with their presence in the general population. In the U.S. population, only

27.2 percent fall in the some college category; in the bankrupt population, the some college group is 43.4 percent of people. As Elizabeth Warren and Deborah Thorne report in Chapter 2, bankrupt debtors as a group are better educated than the general population, but people with bachelor's degrees or advanced degrees are underrepresented in bankruptcy. The additional education of bankrupt people is in the form of some college coursework, not a four-year degree.

The "some college" category is itself a challenge to define. There is little consensus on how to categorize those who have an intermediate outcome between a high school diploma and a bachelor's degree. The U.S. Census provides three measures: some college, no degree; associate's degree, occupational; and associate's degree, academic.[6] The written questionnaire distributed to bankrupt debtors in the CBP, however, offered three somewhat different categories between a high school diploma and a bachelor's degree: some college credit, but less than one year; one or more years of college, no degree; and associate's degree.

Figure 5.1 shows the percentage of people in bankruptcy with different types of education that can be termed "some college." Only 9.4 percent of people in bankruptcy have an associate's degree. Most bankrupt people with some college have no degree to validate their educational attainment. As a fraction of the some college group, people with no degree outnumber people with an associate's degree by approximately three to one.[7]

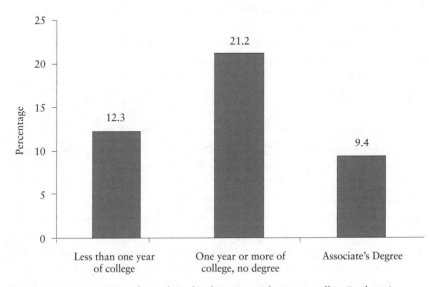

Figure 5.1   Percentage of people in bankruptcy with "some college" education
SOURCE: Consumer Bankruptcy Project 2007.

NOTE: n = 1,456 for groups shown in the figure. Percentages are shown as a fraction of the bankruptcy population.

People in bankruptcy who have some college coursework did make a substantial effort at college, notwithstanding their failure to earn a degree. More than one in five (21.2 percent) of all bankrupt people have spent more than a year in college but have no degree to show for their investment. This group is about half of all those with some college. The large size of this population in bankruptcy is particularly troubling because time spent in college often equates with more debt (both student loans and other consumer debts for living costs) and with reduced years accruing job training, seniority, and retirement savings.

Both types of "some college" people (those with only college coursework and those with an associate's degree) are overrepresented in bankruptcy compared with the general population. The difference is fairly small for associate's degree holders, with 9.4 percent of people in bankruptcy having associate's degrees compared with 8.2 percent of the general population.[8] An associate's degree may have been a student's final aspiration, a first step in a failed effort to earn a four-year degree, or the result of the student giving up on attaining a bachelor's degree. Financial failure seems particularly likely, however, for those who took college courses but have no degree. People who attempted college but earned no degree make up only 19 percent of the general population but 33.5 percent of the bankrupt population. The magnitude of this difference reinforces the importance of earning a degree. Whether the additional education is useful as a signal to employers that unlocks higher wage jobs or because it prepares people to make more prudent financial decisions, a four-year college degree seems to reduce the incidence of bankruptcy.

The economic consequences of college coursework compared with earning an associate's degree are reflected in the relative earning power of these groups. In the general population, those with associate's degrees earn more than those with a high school diploma. In 2007, the real hourly wage for high school graduates was $15.14; it was $17.08 for associate's degree holders.[9] These numbers do not reveal the income effect of college enrollment that does not end in a degree. While the invisibility of the "some college" group makes data scant, research suggests that the incomes of people with associate's degrees and those with only college coursework may be quite similar.[10] Figure 5.2 shows U.S. Census statistics on the incomes of people by type of education. In 2007, the average worker who had some college education but no associate's degree earned $36,989 annually. The average worker who spent the additional time and money, and perhaps incurred the additional student loan debt, to pursue an associate's degree earned $40,226. On a monthly basis, this gives the average associate's degree holder $270 extra dollars per month compared with a peer who has only some college. Although this difference may seem large, much of this additional income

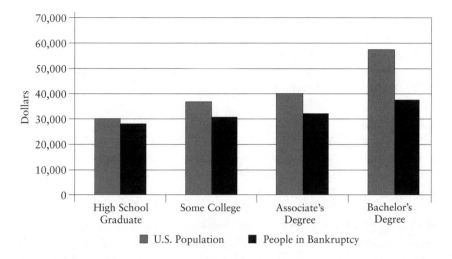

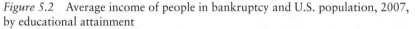

Figure 5.2   Average income of people in bankruptcy and U.S. population, 2007, by educational attainment

SOURCES: Consumer Bankruptcy Project 2007; U.S. Census Bureau.

NOTES: n = 2,242, including those people with less than a high school degree or graduate/professional school, who were excluded from the figure. The "high school graduate" category includes only individuals with a high school degree; it does not include individuals with less than a high school degree. Similarly, the "bachelor's degree" category does not include individuals with a graduate/professional degree.

Outliers were defined as individuals with annual income exceeding $250,000; forty-six observations were dropped on this basis. Income of people in bankruptcy comes from Schedule I of bankruptcy court records. Payroll deductions were added to net income ("monthly total income" on Schedule I) to approximate census gross income. Income data from both the CBP and U.S. Census are for individuals, not households.

could be subsumed by payments on student loans borrowed to finance the additional college.

An analysis of U.S. Census data extrapolates income figures to create synthetic work-life estimates of earnings. A person with a four-year degree is projected to earn one-third more over his or her life than a person without such a degree, a finding that likely prompted the U.S. Census researchers to title their report "The Big Payoff."[11] The payoff from an associate's degree is quite marginal, however, reinforcing the importance of parsing what "college" means. People whose educational attainment is an associate's degree can expect to earn $1.6 million over a lifetime; those who took college coursework but did not earn any degree can expect to earn $1.5 million.[12] This similarity in earnings highlights the modest financial return on investment one makes to obtain an associate's degree. Some college brings with it a much smaller income benefit than a bachelor's degree.

Income may be the single most important factor in keeping families safe from financial failure. Even as debts mount, families with sufficient income can keep up with payments on those debts. Families in bankruptcy have much lower incomes than the general population (see Chapter 2), reflecting the prevalence before bankruptcy of job problems, illness and injury, or family changes that reduce one's ability to work.[13] To understand the economic consequences of a partial college education, I examined the incomes of people in bankruptcy by educational attainment. Figure 5.2 shows that, consistent with data from the general population, there is a notable income difference between people in bankruptcy with only a high school degree and those with a bachelor's degree. But the income effect of "some college" is very small. The mean annual income of a high school graduate at the time of bankruptcy is $28,175, but those who enrolled in college but did not receive a degree earn $30,560. This difference is not statistically significant (Scheffe multiple-comparison test, $p = 0.452$). Importantly, the income benefit of an associate's degree versus college coursework is also very slim. At the time of bankruptcy, the average person with an associate's degree had an income of $32,260, a difference that is not statistically significant from the average income of a bankrupt person with some college but no degree (Scheffe multiple-comparison test, $p = 0.950$). Bankruptcy debtors with some college (coursework or an associate's degree) have incomes close to bankrupt people who did not pursue postsecondary education. College attendance that does not result in a bachelor's degree offers only marginal gains in income, which may partially explain the overrepresentation of the "some college" demographic in bankruptcy.

The income data hint at the difficulty that bankrupt households face in paying off their debts. At the time of bankruptcy, the total debts of bankrupt debtors utterly overwhelm their ability to pay.[14] Average (mean) total debts and unsecured debts generally increase with educational level (Table 5.1). A multiple-comparison test (Scheffe) showed a statistical difference between the debts of the bachelor's degree group and all other education groups

TABLE 5.1

Average debts of people in bankruptcy, by educational attainment

	Less than high school diploma	High school graduate	Some college but no degree	Associate's degree	Bachelor's degree	Graduate or professional degree
Total debt	$82,609	$109,171	$133,466	$144,556	$193,983	$222,029
Unsecured debt	$28,643	$40,086	$48,955	$48,815	$68,464	$85,656

SOURCE: Consumer Bankruptcy Project 2007.

NOTES: n = 2,226 for total debt; n = 2,239 for unsecured debt. One-way ANOVA and multiple-comparison post hoc test (Scheffe) were used to determine statistical differences among educational attainment with a threshold of $p < 0.05$. For total debt, all combinations of educational attainment groups were different with two exceptions: there was no statistical difference between (1) some college but no degree and associate's degree, and (2) bachelor's degree and graduate/professional degree. For unsecured debt, all combinations of educational attainment groups were different with three exceptions: there was no statistical difference between (1) high school graduate and associate's degree, (2) some college but no degree and associate's degree, and (3) bachelor's degree and graduate/professional degree.

($p < 0.05$), with the exception of graduate/professional degree. A bachelor's degree increases income but also debt. Those who attempted college but earned no degree have similar debt to those with an associate's degree. The bankruptcy rate of those with some college does not seem driven by an observable propensity to borrow; the spike in debt comes with a bachelor's degree. The data do not suggest that people who fail at college lack self-control and discipline and therefore borrow with less restraint than people who completed college. Among bankrupt debtors, people who attempt college have not spent themselves into debt as if they had bachelor's degrees.

Another measure of a household's debt burden is the ratio of each bankrupt household's debt to its income. To minimize differences in relative homeownership rates and to recognize that homes are assets (even if highly leveraged), I focus on nonmortgage debt as a fraction of income. This measure reflects the immediate pinch on families in bankruptcy because nonmortgage debt usually is overdue at the time of bankruptcy, such as a defaulted credit card balance, or is short-term debt payable within the next few years, such as a car loan. The median nonmortgage debt-to-income ratio for those with college attendance is 1.75. This number equates to a person needing to devote all income for not quite two years to paying off debt other than any mortgage debt. Again, those with associate's degrees fared only somewhat better, with a ratio of 1.6. There was no statistical difference between those who had only some college coursework and those who earned an associate's degree. As Figure 5.3 illustrates, the typical person in either of the "some college" categories had essentially the same overwhelming combination of high debts and low incomes that pushed high school graduates into bankruptcy.

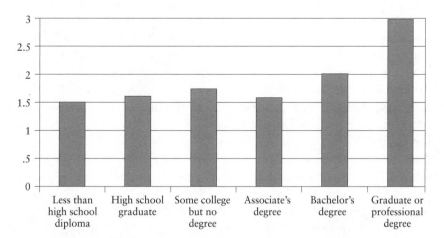

Figure 5.3   Median ratio of nonmortgage debt to annual income of people in bankruptcy, by educational attainment

SOURCE: Consumer Bankruptcy Project 2007.

NOTE: n = 2,171.

The bankruptcy data illustrate that it is a four-year degree rather than merely college attendance that makes an economic difference, both for income and debt. People with some college are similar to high school graduates in terms of the burden that their debts impose on their incomes. Those who attempt but do not complete college seem to be particularly vulnerable to financial collapse and are overrepresented in bankruptcy compared with the general population. As the College Board says in its promotional materials, college may indeed pay,[15] but this phrase needs to carry a definitional caveat that "college" means a four-year degree. The demographics of bankruptcy reveal the fragile economic position of those who make unsuccessful college attempts.

STUDENT LOAN DEBTS OF DROPOUTS

Attempting a college education is costly, and reliance on student loans to finance college is widespread. At least half of all students who start a postsecondary education program receive student loans.[16] The likelihood of borrowing depends on the type of educational program attempted. Students were more likely to borrow if they tried to obtain a bachelor's degree (67 percent) at a four-year institution than if they tried to earn an associate's degree (33 percent) at a public two-year college. Students who attended a for-profit educational program of less than four years were the most likely to borrow (68 percent).[17] Debt and college go hand-in-hand, including for those whose education will not result in a bachelor's degree.

Dropping out is a common educational outcome. Among those who began educational programs in 1995–1996, approximately one-third had not earned a degree and were no longer enrolled six years later.[18] Completion rates are lower at non-four-year institutions. The Department of Education reports a 57.3 percent completion rate for those who seek a four-year degree, but only a 30.9 percent completion rate for those who enroll in associate's degree programs.[19]

People leave college for a variety of reasons, the most common being job or financial demands, followed by family demands, according to a U.S. Department of Education study.[20] Figure 5.4 shows the self-reported reasons that student loan borrowers in bankruptcy did not complete their educations. More than one-fourth of debtors cited a change in family circumstances. These situations typically corresponded to additional caregiving responsibilities, for example due to the birth of a child or a death in the family. Family demands may be particularly likely to derail the education of women. The other leading reasons, such as needing to get a job or becoming unable to afford the costs of education, may be particularly likely to afflict students from economically disadvantaged backgrounds. These students often rely solely on borrowing and their own earnings to pay for college. Some may even contribute income to their families while in school.

The typical dropout is not someone who simply cannot choose a major or who does not like college. As in the general population, the vast majority of people in bankruptcy do not complete their educational programs because of financial or family circumstances, not because of uninterest in education. As shown in Figure 5.4, fewer than 8 percent of student loan debtors in bankruptcy reported that they did not wish to continue with their educational programs.

Bankruptcy exposes the risks of getting student loans to finance failed educational attempts. One in four households in the 2007 CBP sample owed money on student loans when they filed for bankruptcy.[21] In this group of 250 student loan borrowers in bankruptcy, 30.1 percent (seventy-five people) dropped out of college. Although there is a large literature on whether student loans should be dischargeable in bankruptcy, the low rate of college completion among people in bankruptcy has not previously been identified. This is a crucial missing fact from the debate about the appropriate scope of the bankruptcy discharge for educational debt. People who borrowed and dropped out of postsecondary education, and later sought bankruptcy because of financial problems, are a particularly powerful example of the economic risks of college.

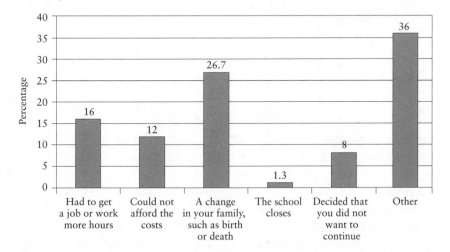

Figure 5.4 Reasons for dropping out of college among student loan borrowers in bankruptcy

SOURCE: Consumer Bankruptcy Project 2007.

NOTE: n = 75. More than half of "Other" answers described a situation that was related to family circumstances or job demands.

Student loan debtors in bankruptcy borrowed for a range of different educational pursuits, from a vocational certificate to a Ph.D. The profile of those who dropped out is very similar to that of all student loan debtors in bankruptcy. Among student loan borrowers in bankruptcy who did not complete their educational programs, more than one in three (34.7 percent) had enrolled in trade school or community college. Another 5.3 percent were not able to identify the type of school, a likely indication of a nondegree program. These data are a reminder that along with fears about the moral hazard of highly educated people filing for bankruptcy because of six-figure student loans, people with only limited educations also come into bankruptcy burdened with student loans. The "some college" group is a sizable fraction of all student loan debtors in bankruptcy.

People who did not complete their educations had nearly identical educational debts to those who did earn their degrees.[22] The student loans of bankrupt people who dropped out of college were substantial: 55 percent owed more than $10,000 in education debt. The median borrower who dropped out of college and had student loans at the time of filing for bankruptcy owed $8,048 in educational debt; the average borrower in this group owed $21,179.[23] Those who owed more than $20,000 in student loans most commonly had dropped out of a four-year institution, which is not surprising given that these schools are often more expensive than community colleges and require more coursework for a degree. Pursuit of a more advanced degree (such as a bachelor's or graduate degree) brings more dollars of student loan debt. However, it is these degrees that enable an individual to achieve the income benefit of the additional education and that provide increased economic security.[24]

The student loan debts of people in bankruptcy are heavy burdens given the relatively low incomes earned at the time of bankruptcy filing. A study of Iowa borrowers offers a useful benchmark that could be applied to future studies of student loan borrowers in bankruptcy. It calculated the proportion of student loan borrowers with "excessive" student loan burdens, defined as obligations that would require a borrower to devote more than 12 percent of income to nonmortgage debt.[25] Even under an assumption that people owed no type of nonmortgage debt other than student loans (such as credit card debt, car loans, or medical bills), 16.1 percent of all borrowers had student loan payments that were excessive. Among those who did not complete their educations, more than one-quarter (approximately 26 percent) had excessive student loan debt burdens.[26] The bankruptcy data do not reveal the monthly payments on debtors' student loans, making it impossible to calculate comparable statistics for people in bankruptcy. However, as Warren and Thorne report in Chapter 2, the typical (median) household earns only

$32,988 at the time of bankruptcy filing. On that gross income, a $10,000 debt would generate a significant repayment obligation.

Student loan debtors in bankruptcy face myriad financial pressures and may well be in default on their student loans. Research has shown that graduation is the most significant factor in predicting default on student loans. Failure to graduate increases the default probability by about 10 percentage points, when other observed characteristics such as race, parental income, and grades in school are held constant.[27] A study of student loan debtors who entered repayment in 2005 found that 33 percent of those who did not earn a credential became delinquent and another 26 percent defaulted.[28] People who drop out of college double their odds of being unemployed six years after taking on the student loan debt.[29]

The correlation between dropping out and student loan default may be mirrored in the bankruptcy population. At present, there are no data on what fraction of people in bankruptcy have defaulted on their student loans, although the 2007 CBP did gather some data that are suggestive on this question. In a written survey completed near the time of their bankruptcies, debtors were asked whether their student loan debts substantially contributed to their need to file for bankruptcy. Not quite one-third (31.8 percent) of student loan debtors answered yes to this question. Among student loan debtors who had dropped out of college, 34.8 percent said student loans were a substantial contributing factor to their bankruptcy. This difference is not statistically significant, suggesting that educational debt does not directly explain the overrepresentation of people with some college in bankruptcy.

Other data are consistent with the conclusion that people in bankruptcy struggle about equally with student loans, regardless of degree completion. In interviews one year after their bankruptcies, debtors were asked how difficult it was to pay their student loans. In nearly all cases student loans were not discharged in bankruptcy. Three-fourths (75.8 percent) of student loan borrowers reported that it was very difficult or somewhat difficult to pay those debts after bankruptcy. This result likely reflects continuing income problems after bankruptcy.[30] Figure 5.5 shows the percentage of student loan borrowers struggling to pay their student loans, broken out by whether the borrower completed college. Although a higher percentage of those who dropped out said it was very difficult to pay their student loan debts, the difference was not statistically significant. Given the similar amounts of student loan debt of those who dropped out and those who completed college, it is perhaps not surprising that all student loan borrowers—degree earners and dropouts—struggle to repay educational debt.

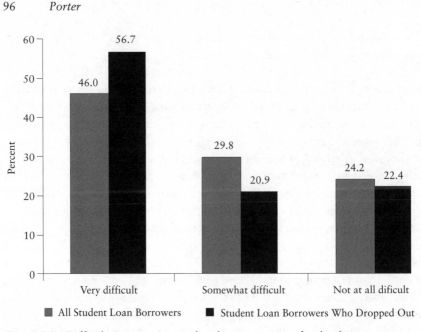

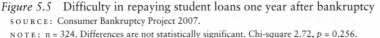

■ All Student Loan Borrowers   ■ Student Loan Borrowers Who Dropped Out

Figure 5.5   Difficulty in repaying student loans one year after bankruptcy
SOURCE: Consumer Bankruptcy Project 2007.
NOTE: n = 324. Differences are not statistically significant. Chi-square 2.72, $p = 0.256$.

RECALIBRATING THE RISKS OF COLLEGE ATTEMPTS

People who attempt college are placing a wager that they will earn a degree and unlock the higher salary and middle-class lifestyle that are associated with a college education. For those who win the bet and earn a bachelor's degree, the financial benefits are real and enduring. The investment of time and money that they made in themselves pays off, as a bachelor's degree increases upward mobility and reduces bankruptcy.

The bet on college is expensive for those who do not finish, however, and can ultimately lead to negative financial consequences, including a higher likelihood of bankruptcy. The earnings increase from college coursework, a certificate, or an associate's degree, as opposed to a four-year degree, is often quite modest. Compounding the income issue are the student loans that many people who attempt college owe. A report from the Education Trust identified the problem: "hundreds of thousands of young people leave our higher education system unsuccessfully, burdened with large student loans that must be repaid, but without the benefit of the wages a college degree provides."[31]

The burdens of student loan debt have consequences for people's financial futures. More than half (51.6 percent) of people in bankruptcy with student loans said education debt caused them to defer contributions for retirement or have a lower rate of savings. Student loans also have an inter-generational effect, retarding opportunity for other family members. More than 17 percent of student loan borrowers in bankruptcy said they did not help a family member attend school because of the burden of their own student loan debts. People who enroll in college take other financial risks in addition to student loans. Students often begin using credit cards during college to pay tuition and buy books or to fund the middle-class lifestyle that they hope they will achieve someday as a college graduate.[32] Yet, those attempting college will have deferred entry into the job market, losing se-niority and reducing the number of working years they have to save for retirement.

A fully developed policy of encouraging postsecondary education re-quires an understanding of the financial risks borne by those who attempt but fail to earn college degrees. Although college debt is often touted as "good" debt, the bankruptcy data caution that such debt perhaps merits that label only if the borrower obtains a four-year degree. The real and significant benefits of bachelor's degrees have distracted scholars and poli-cymakers from the financial hardships that confront those who dropped out of college or perhaps aspired to only certificates or two-year degrees. The logic may be that since obtaining a bachelor's degree pays off, attempting college also should pay off—albeit to a lesser extent for the proportionally shorter time in college. But the bankruptcy data suggest a weakness in this "learn more, earn more" strategy. The financial protection of college does not increase with each dollar borrowed or each course taken.

To date, bankruptcy scholars have used educational attainment data to highlight the economic fragility of the middle class.[33] But bankruptcy law itself can be a tool to reduce the harshest outcome of failing at college and to influence educational policy.[34] In successive revisions of bankruptcy law, policymakers have made it more difficult for student loans to be dis-charged.[35] Today, virtually all student loans are not dischargeable absent exceptional circumstances.[36] Most people who file for bankruptcy do not even attempt to have any student loans discharged because the legal stan-dard in bankruptcy that paying the student loan debt would be an "undue hardship" is very difficult to meet.[37]

The justifications for making student loans nondischargeable have var-ied over time.[38] Many of them, whether framed in economic or fairness terms, focus on the idea that education confers an economic benefit that en-ables and/or obligates borrowers to repay their student loans. This rationale provides only slim support for requiring borrowers who did not complete their educational programs to pay all of their student loan debts. The ratio-nale is especially weak for those in such severe financial distress that they have sought bankruptcy relief. The 1973 Bankruptcy Commission implicitly recognized this problem, even as it supported restricting discharge for student loans. It concluded that "credit extended to finance higher education that enables a person to earn substantially greater income over his working life should not as a matter of policy be dischargeable before he has demonstrated that for any reason he is unable to earn sufficient income to maintain himself and his dependents and to repay the educational debt."[39] This chapter's findings suggest that people with only some college education or those who dropped out of a four-year program will often meet the commission's criteria for discharge of student loans. Given the necessity of a four-year degree for increasing wages, borrowers without bachelor's degrees earn incomes nearly identical to their counterparts who never attempted postsecondary education. Repaying student loan debts is particularly burdensome for those who dropped out of a four-year college because this group has more educational debt.[40]

Under current law, bankruptcy courts do not appear routinely to consider the type of degree and completion of a program in their decisions on whether a bankruptcy debtor would face an undue hardship in repaying student loans. Instead, courts focus on a debtor's overall financial profile and on the precipitating cause of the bankruptcy.[41] This analysis needs to be changed in order to provide meaningful debt relief to those with only some college education. Rather than applying the same undue hardship standard to all student loan debtors, policymakers should recognize the reduced earning power of those with only some college and the injustice and impossibility of asking people to earn their way out of student loan debt without the economic benefits of a completed education. Bankruptcy law should be amended to permit the discharge of student loan debt in bankruptcy if the borrower did not complete a degree.

Concerns about moral hazard accompany any expansion of the bankruptcy discharge. One solution is to create an exception to the general rule of discharge if the student loan lender or the U.S. Trustee, acting as a guardian of the bankruptcy system's integrity, establishes that the borrower is acting in bad faith. Bankruptcy law already contains screens for general bad faith,[42] but indicia for a bad faith effort to discharge student loan debt could include filing for bankruptcy near the completion of a degree or program or attempting to discharge student loans when the debtor dropped out of college for reasons other than an unanticipated family or financial change.[43] The law could prevent fraud by allowing a student loan lender to claw back unexpected income that debtors earn in the five years after their bankruptcy discharge, particularly if that income was the result of a debtor finishing college. The policy behind such a rule is that debtors whose education does pay off or who increase their educational attainment have the ability to repay their student loans.

These bankruptcy reforms could make incremental improvements to educational policies aimed at encouraging college. Although interest rates may increase if student loans are dischargeable in bankruptcy, lenders could reduce this cost with preventative efforts. For example, lenders could pressure institutions to increase graduation rates. Because conferral of a degree would protect student loan debt from being discharged in bankruptcy, lenders also could encourage college completion among borrowers. Such a reform could lead to other desirable changes related to improving graduation rates, such as heightened scrutiny of marketing practices for postsecondary education or innovative tuition structures in which the cost of each year of education is successively higher. This latter practice would lower the initial cost of attempting college but still permit students to finance the costs of their education.

By spreading the risk among lenders, and ultimately among all borrowers, those who are successful in their gamble on college will help subsidize the risks for those who lose the bet and drop out of college. This risk spreading will cushion the consequences of encouraging college for all. Although some may object to a cross-subsidy among those who complete college (but pay slightly higher interest rates for students loans) and those who drop out of college (and can discharge their student loans in bankruptcy), the reform may be desirable as a way to reduce the inequality of educational opportunity. Changing the student loan discharge policy in bankruptcy may particularly encourage those who are most likely to suffer interruptions in their educations, such as women and those from economically disadvantaged backgrounds, to attempt college. Adding a safety valve in bankruptcy for student loans could increase college enrollment. Coupled with improved graduation rates, the result could be a better educated workforce. Such a result inures to the benefit of the entire society, which also bears the costs of families being so mired in student loan debt that they cannot save for retirement, seek additional education, or support their family members' educational efforts.

CONCLUSION

The costs and risks of attempting college have not been well documented, perhaps because the benefits of obtaining a four-year degree distract scholars and policymakers from the consequences of not completing that degree. More than one in four Americans has an educational attainment of "some college," stranding them with the burdens of having pursued college without the economic benefits of a four-year degree. These people are overrepresented in bankruptcy, making up more than 43 percent of all bankrupt debtors. The predominance of those with some college in bank-ruptcy reflects the financial risks of attempting college, including student loan debt and deferred income and savings while enrolled in college. The bankruptcy data highlight the need for paying additional attention to the risks of failed college attempts. The data also are a reminder that bank-ruptcy law itself can have a modest role in addressing the economic risks of dropping out of college. Those who dropped out of college make up 30 percent of the student loan debtors in bankruptcy and struggle as much as degree earners to repay those student loans after bankruptcy. Amending the law to permit the discharge of student loans if borrowers did not com-plete a degree has the potential to improve student loan underwriting, tu-ition structures, college admission procedures, and educational outcomes. Softening the risks of college attempts is a crucial aspect of encouraging a diverse group of Americans to achieve their educational potential. Social aspirations of encouraging widespread college attendance need to be ac-companied by relief from the financial risks of college noncompletion.

CHAPTER SIX

Striking Out on Their Own

The Self-Employed in Bankruptcy

Robert M. Lawless

The stories we hear about business owners and entrepreneurship are the ones that mythologize individuals who started with little, risked it all, and are now leaders of thriving corporations. Such a story is told of Sergey Brin and Larry Page, two Ph.D. students in computer science who started a business that grew into Google. As so many of these tales go, the story emphasizes modest beginnings in a shared campus laboratory before moves to garages, apartments, and eventually a small office space. Early startup financing was nonexistent. Instead, to finance the purchase of desks in one version or computer servers in another version, Brin and Page had to put their own credit on the line.[44] As Page described it, "we had to use all of our credit cards and our friends' credit cards and our parents' credit cards."[45] Google, of course, has become one of the world's most successful corporations, and Brin and Page are among the wealthiest individuals on the planet. The Google startup story is rightfully told as an example of successful entrepreneurship. Brin and Page took a huge gamble that paid off in an incredible way.[46]

But there are different stories of entrepreneurship, too. The 2007 Consumer Bankruptcy Project (CBP) learned the stories of business owners and entrepreneurs who experienced painful failures. After Don Long lost his job of seventeen years driving a delivery truck in a large city, he and his wife, Betsy, moved across the country to the midsized urban community where they had grown up and could count on the support of family and friends.[47] They took half of the money that they received from the sale of their home and invested in two locations offering services for automobiles. After a year of operation, it became apparent that the previous owner had misrepresented the cash flow generated by the two retail locations. Nonetheless, in an attempt to make a go of the business, the Longs borrowed heavily on their credit cards. After three and a half years of running the businesses, the Longs filed for Chapter 7 bankruptcy. In their bankruptcy court documents, they listed more than $40,000 in unpaid credit card bills and more than $1.3 million owed to a bank for a business loan. Although the Longs had incorporated the business to help protect them from personal liability, Don had to personally guarantee the bank debt to get the loan. As assets, they listed a $40,000 house with a mortgage of nearly the same amount, less than $3,500 in retirement savings between the two of them, and two cars, the newest of which was an eight-year-old sedan. Since the businesses had failed, Don had begun working as a sales clerk for a large retail chain. In four years, the Longs went from a six-figure income with steady employment to a $24,000 annual income and virtually no assets. The businesses had failed, and the financial fortunes of the Longs went with them.

The Google creation story is just one example of a narrative that gets repeated as an inspiration to would-be entrepreneurs. Other examples include the successful movie the *Blair Witch Project*, financed on the credit cards of directors Eduardo Sanchez and Daniel Myrick. Famed movie director Spike Lee similarly is said to have financed his first production by maxing out his credit cards.[48] Bruce Kovner, a hedge-fund manager listed in *Forbes* magazine's annual list of the world's wealthiest billionaires, borrowed $3,000 on a credit card to begin his trading career.[49] Often, but not always, these stories are accompanied by cautionary language about the risks of credit-card financing, but in the middle of an exemplary success story, these cautions have all the effect of a sotto voce disclaimer at the end of a high-energy sales pitch.

The stories of the business startups that do not make it, leaving their owners awash in debt, are not told. People like the Longs do not end up in the pages of *Forbes* magazine. The typical startup occurs in ordinary, everyday industries and often begins because the owner is unemployed—as with the Longs. Their story is an example of the hundreds of thousands of Americans each year who find themselves having to file for bankruptcy. This chapter tells the story of the entrepreneurs who fail and must seek bankruptcy to cope with the consequences of having owned a business. In America's capitalist economy, we should care about the self-employed who end up in bankruptcy court because their stories are a powerful reminder of the downside of taking financial risks. Self-employment failures are a part of the reality of self-employment. Scott Shane's book *The Illusions of Entrepreneurship* documents how the reality of small-business ownership varies dramatically from the epic narratives told about entrepreneurial success stories. Shane is sharply critical about the Pollyannaish bromides that government leaders use when promoting entrepreneurship. He aptly observes, "Making policy decisions on the basis of myths about the impact of start-ups leads to a lot of wasted resources and bad incentives."[50] Starting a small business can lead to job creation for some people but to overwhelming debt for others, who are left with failed business enterprises. People contemplating self-employment should have a clear understanding of the potential downside risks.

A more complete narrative about self-employment neither should demonize business ownership nor dismiss the success of those who started small businesses that grew into very large ones. Brin, Page, Kovner, and others took extraordinary risks that paid off for them and are rightly lauded for their success. In a country of more than three hundred million people, however, it is not surprising that a few will find wild success from starting a business. But we must be careful to assess business ownership from a realistic appraisal of the benefits of success, the costs of failure, and the probability of both. In short, we must guard against survivor bias. The bankruptcy data show that many self-employed individuals go broke owing tens of thousands of dollars of unsecured debt and even larger mortgage debts. They are at the bottom of the bottom of the financial heap. Failure and bankruptcy are possible—perhaps even more likely—outcomes, for many would-be entrepreneurs. Telling these stories is important for an understanding of the risks of starting a small business.

We also should care about the stories of the self-employed because they help to change the narrative about why people file for bankruptcy. Overconsumption remains a popular but largely false explanation about U.S. bankruptcy filings. The perils of self-employment are another challenge to the overconsumption myth. As the data in this chapter show, about 14 percent of bankruptcy cases have a filer who reports self-employment at the time of bankruptcy, and for 12 percent of bankruptcy cases, self-employment is reported as a reason for the bankruptcy. These percentages imply that each year hundreds of thousands of people file bankruptcies that are related to self-employment.

This chapter presents data on the self-employed who file for bankruptcy. The first part documents the incidence of self-employment among bankruptcy filers, a rate that is much higher than government data suggest. The self-employment rate in bankruptcy is somewhat higher than the self-employment rate in the general population, suggesting some association (which is not necessarily causation) between self-employment and bankruptcy. The second part of the chapter documents the financial condition of the self-employed in bankruptcy. The self-employed are distinct financially from other bankruptcy debtors; they go broke with more debt and in a deeper financial hole than other Americans who seek bankruptcy relief. Many self-employed have left the ranks of the salaried and wage earners only to strike out financially.

It is important to note what the bankruptcy data cannot tell us. By their nature, the CBP data have no control groups of comparably situated, financially distressed self-employed people who did not file for bankruptcy or of self-employed people who did not experience financial distress. The data in this chapter cannot alone speak to whether self-employment causes an increased risk of bankruptcy. It is possible that the self-employed people who file for bankruptcy are just particularly bad at running a business (although they do not differ from self-employed people in the general population on most demographic characteristics). What the data do accomplish is to round out the narrative about American entrepreneurship, adding information about the failures that complements the more widely known tales of the phenomenal successes.

HOW MANY SELF-EMPLOYED ARE IN BANKRUPTCY?

A casual reading of government statistics might lead one to conclude that very few self-employed people end up in bankruptcy court. The Administrative Office of the U.S. Courts (AO) tracks business filings, and the percentage of cases categorized as a business filing has declined precipitously since the mid-1980s. In reality, a significant portion of bankruptcy cases are filed by people who are self-employed at or near the time of bankruptcy, implying that hundreds of thousands of businesses owned by self-employed people are involved in bankruptcy each year. To explain the discrepancy between official government statistics and the reality of bankruptcy requires an understanding of how the government statistics are collected.

Figure 6.1 shows business cases as a percentage of all bankruptcy filings according to the AO. Before 1979, the AO data explicitly counted bankruptcies by self-employed people as business filings. After that date, the AO started counting business filings on the basis of whether a checkbox on the bankruptcy petition indicated that the case's debts were predominately business in nature. Many self-employed bankruptcy filers should have predominately business debts, and in the years immediately after 1979 the percentage of bankruptcy filings remained similar to what it had been before, even rising a bit. It is unlikely that the decline in the early 1990s in business filings captures a real phenomenon. For the AO's numbers to be right, we would have to believe that "the twelve months ending June 30, 2003, experienced just about the same number of business filings as the same period in 1980, when the population of the United States was 22 percent smaller and inflation-adjusted GDP was 50 percent smaller."[51]

My coauthored previous research suggested that the dramatic decline in business filings reported in the government data most likely was caused by law firms having adopted computer software that helped them complete bankruptcy forms. Although different vendors offer their own versions of software, all of them use a default setting indicating that a bankruptcy filing is a consumer case. The decline in business filings was probably nothing more than an increase in the technological adaptation of law offices throughout the 1990s.[52]

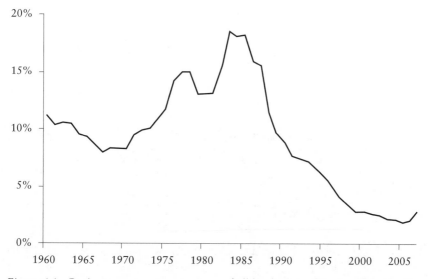

Figure 6.1 Business cases as a percentage of all bankruptcy filings as tabulated in U.S. government data, 1959–2009

SOURCE: Administrative Office of U.S. Courts, 1959–2009.

NOTE: The AO tabulates business filing on the basis of a checkbox on the bankruptcy petition where the debtor indicates the character of the filing.

Using data from bankruptcy cases filed in 2001, this prior research found that 13.5 percent of all bankruptcy filings reported self-employment at the time of or within two years before the bankruptcy filing. Before 1979, the AO data would have shown all of these bankruptcies as business filings, and the 13.5 percent figure is close to the historical mean of the fraction of all bankruptcies that are business failures.[53]

The 2007 CBP allows for more refined counts of how many bankruptcy cases may involve businesses because it disaggregates full- and part-time self-employment. As Table 6.1 shows, 14.0 percent of all cases indicated full-time self-employment (for either self or spouse/partner) at the time of bankruptcy or in the two years before bankruptcy. At the time of bankruptcy, however, only 8.5 percent reported full-time self-employment, and there is a similar relative decline in self-employment during the two-year prebankruptcy period if part-time self-employment is included (20.2 percent to 13.6 percent). Of those reporting full-time self-employment at the time of bankruptcy or in the prior two years, 58.4 percent identified "Financial problems that resulted from being self-employed" as one of the reasons for their bankruptcy on the written questionnaire they completed shortly after filing for bankruptcy. Together, these data suggest that many people lose self-employment during the downward financial spiral into bankruptcy. Because

TABLE 6.1
Self-employment rates of people in bankruptcy

	Nature of self-employment	
	Full time only	Full time or part time
At time of bankruptcy	8.5%	13.6%
At time of bankruptcy or prior two years	14.0%	20.2%

SOURCE: Consumer Bankruptcy Project 2007.

NOTE: n = 976. Cases are counted as involving self-employment if either a person or a person's spouse/partner reported self-employment. Respondents were asked, "At any time during the two years before your bankruptcy, including the day you filed, were you self-employed at a business that you owned or co-owned?" Respondents who answered affirmatively were then asked to characterize the self-employment as full time or part time as well as about self-employment at the moment of bankruptcy. If applicable, similar questions were asked about a spouse or partner's self-employment.

the financial problems that lead to bankruptcy can also lead to a loss of self-employment, it is important to ask about self-employment during the period before the bankruptcy filing so as to capture an accurate count of people with self-employment problems in bankruptcy.

Depending on whether one counts full-time or part-time self-employment and depending on whether one counts at the time of bankruptcy or includes the prior two years, one arrives at different estimates about the level of self-employment in bankruptcy. Excluding debtors who lost self-employment before bankruptcy undercounts the true rate because it excludes people who would be self-employed but for their financial distress. At the same time, including people who had part-time self-employment results in an overcount as it sweeps in people who operated a small business for just a few hours a week or month to supplement income from a full-time job. The estimate that minimizes the risk of undercount or overcount therefore comes from the people who reported full-time self-employment at the time of bankruptcy or within the prior two years. This figure shows a self-employment rate in bankruptcy of 14.0 percent, very close to the previous finding from the 2001 data that 13.5 percent of bankruptcy cases involve a self-employed person. The two findings, coming from databases collected six years apart, suggest constancy over time. With more than 1.5 million bankruptcy filings in 2010, the 14.0 percent rate of self-employment would mean that more than two hundred thousand bankruptcy cases that year involved self-employed people.

SELF-EMPLOYMENT AS A RISK FACTOR FOR BANKRUPTCY

The data in Table 6.1 establish that the self-employed are in bankruptcy at higher rates than government data would suggest, but they do not reveal whether the self-employed appear in bankruptcy at a higher rate than the general population. If there is a higher rate of self-employment among bankruptcy filers, then the data would suggest (but hardly prove) that self-employment could be a risk factor for bankruptcy. The CBP data allow for a comparison of self-employment rates between bankruptcy filers and the general population.

Surprisingly, there is no regular data collection on self-employment rates in the United States. Historically, the Census Bureau's Current Population Survey would not count the owner of an incorporated business as self-employed, reasoning that the owner was an employee of the corporation. This sort of legal formality does not capture the economic reality of small businesses in which the owner's financial destiny is tightly tied to the business. Another possible data source, the Small Business Administration (SBA), has historically tracked business firms, not business owners. Even then, the SBA data distinguished between firms with employees and firms without employees, reporting data separately for both types of firms but not providing a blended estimate. Although the presence of employees might have policy implications for the SBA's work, the existence of employees does not change the owner's characterization as self-employed.

Because there is no consistent measure for counting self-employed people in the population, Table 6.2 uses various sources to estimate the self-employment rate in the United States. These sources show a lower rate of self-employment in the general population than the estimate of a 14.0 percent rate in bankruptcy cases. Making comparisons between the CBP data and the general population data, however, must be done carefully for two reasons. First, the CBP calculation is based on bankruptcy cases, which can

TABLE 6.2
Estimates of the self-employment rate in the U.S. population

Author(s)	Principal findings	Data source
Fairlie and Robb (2008)	9.9% overall	Current Population Survey
Fairlie (2005)	At age 42, 12.1% of men and 9.8% of women	National Longitudinal Survey of Youth
Fairlie (unpublished data)	9.8% overall	Current Population Survey
Ferber and Waldfogel (1998)	8.8% for men, 5.5% for women	National Longitudinal Survey of Youth
Haynes (2007)	12.2% for nonveteran households	Survey of Consumer Finance
Manser and Picot (1999)	10.5% overall	Current Population Survey
Shane (2008)	7.2% overall	Organization for Economic Co-operation and Development (OECD)

NOTE: Dates are dates of publication; full citations appear in the bibliography. Many of the listed studies also report self-employment rates for various demographic characteristics such as race, gender, and age, but these breakdowns are omitted from the table.

sometimes involve two married people, and the estimates from the studies in Table 6.2 are per person. But if reported on a per-person basis, the CBP estimate does not change dramatically, dropping only to 13.5 percent.

The second reason presents more troubling concerns about comparison but does not rule out rough estimates. The CBP figure of 14.0 percent includes cases in which a debtor lost self-employment in the two years before bankruptcy. In contrast, the studies in Table 6.2 measured self-employment at a particular point in time. One would expect these studies to have produced higher numbers if they captured self-employment over a more extended period of time. People move in and out of self-employment for a variety of reasons. The CBP figure of 8.5 percent of cases with a debtor or spouse/partner reporting full-time self-employment at the time of bankruptcy, however, produces too low of an estimate. Of the people who reported losing self-employment during the two years before bankruptcy, 57.4 percent identified self-employment as a reason for the bankruptcy filing even though they were not self-employed at the time of bankruptcy. These people likely would have been self-employed but for the financial distress that led to the bankruptcy filing. In trying to make a comparison about whether self-employment is a risk factor for bankruptcy, one must count the people who lose self-employment because of financial distress in the same way that one must count both ex-smokers and current smokers to get a complete picture of how smoking is a risk factor for various health problems. A rough estimate might be to add together (1) the people who specifically identify self-employment at the time of bankruptcy with (2) the people who lost self-employment during the two years before bankruptcy and who identified self-employment as a reason for the bankruptcy. This calculation produces an estimate of 11.7 percent of people in bankruptcy with problems potentially related to self-employment.

Taking a perfectly accurate measure of who becomes financially distressed because of self-employment requires at least full information and probably also a time machine to rerun the debtor's life to create the conditions for the counterfactual inquiry: "If I had not been self-employed, would I have experienced financial distress?" A range of estimates is the best that can be done with the current data, and this range runs from 8.5 percent to 14.0 percent, with a midrange estimate of 11.7 percent based on assumptions discussed in the previous paragraph about the reasons people lost self-employment. The low end of this range generally corresponds to the rates of self-employment shown in Table 6.2, but we know this figure almost certainly misses many people who lost self-employment as they spiraled into bankruptcy. The middle- and high-end figures of the range are higher than most of the estimates for self-employment in the general population. These higher estimates suggest that self-employment creates a higher risk for bankruptcy, although the increased risk does not appear to be dramatic.

In addition to the caveats already discussed about making comparisons between the self-employment rates in the general population and the CBP data, it also should be noted that the relationship documented here is correlational, not necessarily causal. It could be that the characteristics that determine self-employment—for example, a willingness to take financial gambles or preexisting unemployment—are themselves risk factors for bankruptcy. In other words, some self-employed people in bankruptcy may have experienced financial failure even if they were wage earners and had not been self-employed.

This discussion has analyzed how the CBP data on bankruptcies could be compared with counts of self-employment in the general population. This analysis is not necessary to return to an undisputed fact: 14.0 percent of bankruptcy cases in the CBP sample involve a debtor who reported full-time self-employment at the time of bankruptcy or in the prior two years. More than two hundred thousand of the consumer bankruptcy cases each year seem to be filed by self-employed people. The size of this figure points to the importance of understanding the experiences of the self-employed in bankruptcy as lessons about the risk of entrepreneurship.

THE BOTTOM OF THE BOTTOM

If the 1.5 million bankruptcy cases filed each year come from people at the bottom of the financial heap, the two hundred thousand cases involving the full-time self-employed are at the bottom of the bottom. Even compared with other bankruptcy filers, the self-employed are in a deeper financial hole. They owe more, have pledged a greater percentage of their assets as collateral, and have higher debt-to-income ratios. In the very deepest financial hole are those self-employed who say that their self-employment was a reason for their bankruptcy. These are people who strived for the independence and financial success that is supposed to come from owning a business and consequently took big financial risks to establish their businesses. Instead of living the American Dream, these self-employed people have found themselves declaring bankruptcy.

For most every self-employed person who files for bankruptcy, it makes no sense to talk of a business with a separate existence apart from its owner. Ideas in corporate and partnership law about insulating owners from liability for their businesses have little practical meaning in bankruptcy, where the owner's financial life is the business's financial life and vice versa. Only 36.5 percent of the self-employed in bankruptcy said that they operated their business as a corporation, limited partnership, limited liability company, or similar entity that would protect them from personal liability for the business's debts. Neglecting to incorporate is not necessarily a poor decision for a small-business owner who has to guarantee the business's debts or who has to use his or her own credit card to borrow for the business's needs. (Many so-called business cards require the owner's personal liability.) Moreover, many small-business loans require the owner to guarantee the business's debts. For most small-business owners, incorporation brings added hassle and expense but very little in the way of financial protection.

Having financial responsibility for the business's debts is part of being a small-business owner, at least for the self-employed who filed for bankruptcy. Nearly all (96.0 percent) of self-employed bankruptcy cases reported some use of personal financial resources to support the business, such as (1) using personal earnings or savings, (2) borrowing from a friend or relative, (3) borrowing from a bank, (4) using a credit card for which they had financial responsibility, (5) guaranteeing a business's debts, (6) using a home equity line of credit, or (7) otherwise pledging a house or other personal assets as collateral for a loan intended for the business. Even among those who organized their businesses as a limited liability entity, 95.0 percent reported having undertaken one or more of the above-listed actions that placed at least some of their personal financial resources at risk for the business. Of the 263 business owners who provided detailed financial information about their businesses, 98.9 percent reported personal financial exposure for their business either because they had not incorporated the business or because they used their own financial resources to support the business. When the self-employed enter bankruptcy, they come doubly laden with obligations, unable to pay both their personal debts and their business's debts.

The self-employed have more assets and more income, as Table 6.3 shows, but also more debt than all bankruptcy debtors.[54] In fact, the debt-

TABLE 6.3
Financial conditions, self-employed vs. all other bankruptcy filers

	Self-employed	All other filers	Wilcoxon results
Levels (medians)			
Total assets	$107,914	$39,291	$Z = 5.64$ ($p < 0.001$)
Total debt	$170,288	$78,268	$Z = 8.23$ ($p < 0.001$)
Annual income	$37,242	$26,472	$Z = 5.22$ ($p < 0.001$)
Ratios (medians)			
Debt-to-asset ratio	1.56	1.62	$Z = -0.33$ ($p = 0.755$)
Debt-to-income ratio	4.85	3.22	$Z = 6.36$ ($p < 0.001$)

SOURCE: Consumer Bankruptcy Project 2007.

NOTE: A case was considered to have self-employment if the respondent indicated full-time self-employment for the respondent or a spouse/partner. Total n = 976, of which 137 met the definition for self-employment, with cases missing financial data for each variable excluded from the corresponding analysis. "Wilcoxon results" refers to results of Wilcoxon rank-sum tests and corresponding *p* values.

to-asset ratio is roughly comparable between the groups. The acid test for the ability to service debts, however, is the ratio of debt to income. Many assets are hard to liquidate, and the inability to keep up with ongoing obligations is usually a direct function of income flow. Here, the difference between the groups is most telling. For the median self-employed debtor, it would take almost five years worth of income to retire the outstanding debts. For all other debtors, the figure is only a little more than three years. If the median self-employed person devoted all income to debt repayment—foregoing food, clothing, and all other necessities of life—it still would take that person five years of work before all outstanding debts were repaid. When they arrive in bankruptcy court, the self-employed are in a deep financial hole.

It is possible that this difference is explained by home ownership, as the self-employed have higher rates of home ownership (65.0 percent) than other filers (48.2 percent, Chi-square = 13.22, $p < 0.001$), and home ownership often comes with a mortgage. Even just among homeowners, however, the median debt-to-income ratio for the self-employed debtors (6.11) is much higher than for other debtors (4.67) (Wilcoxon rank-sum $Z = 4.15$, $p < 0.001$).

As dramatic as these differences are, they treat all self-employed filers as a common group, which might not reflect the circumstances. Like any other individual, a self-employed person might file for bankruptcy for a variety of reasons, including ones that are more typically related to consumer bankruptcies such as medical debt or difficulty in supporting a family after divorce or family breakup. These self-employed debtors, therefore, may have bankruptcies that are closer in character to consumer bankruptcies filed by those with regular employment than to those filed by self-employed people. On the written questionnaire, CBP respondents were able to identify their own perceptions about the reasons for their bankruptcy from a list of nineteen possible causes of bankruptcy (plus a residual category for "something else" not specified on the list). One of the listed reasons was problems stemming from self-employment, and positive responses to this choice were used in the previous part to analyze and reconcile the rates of self-employment in bankruptcy and the general population. If the financial stress of self-employment is contributing to the bankruptcy, we are most likely to see that effect among those who specifically identify self-employment as a reason for their bankruptcy.

The data bear out this hypothesis. Medians for various financial characteristics are reported in Table 6.4 and compared on the basis of whether self-employment was given as a reason for bankruptcy. The debt-to-income ratio again reveals the most important information about debtors' financial conditions. Debtors who identify self-employment as a reason for bankruptcy have more debt, more income, and more assets. Yet, they also have a median debt-to-income ratio of 5.84 compared with 3.23 for all other debtors (Wilcoxon rank-sum, $Z = -5.94$, $p < 0.001$). Even among the self-employed, there is

TABLE 6.4
Financial conditions, self-employment identified as reason for bankruptcy

	Self-employed stated as reason for bankruptcy	All other filers	Wilcoxon results
Levels (medians)			
Total assets	$154,062	$45,544	Z = 5.66 (p < 0.001)
Total debt	$194,074	$84,024	Z = 7.88 (p < 0.001)
Annual income	$43,901	$31,157	Z = 5.31 (p < 0.001)
Ratios (medians)			
Debt-to-asset ratio	1.56	1.61	Z = -0.13 (p = 0.897)
Debt-to-income ratio	5.84	3.23	Z = -5.94 (p < 0.001)

SOURCE: Consumer Bankruptcy Project 2007.

NOTE: A case was considered to have self-employment if the respondent indicated full-time self-employment for the respondent or a spouse/partner. Total n = 976, of which 80 met the definition of self-employment and identified self-employment as a reason for bankruptcy. "Wilcoxon results" refers to results of Wilcoxon rank-sum tests and corresponding *p* values.

meaningful difference in the debt-to-income ratios of those who identify self-employment as a reason for bankruptcy (5.84) and those who do not (4.45, Wilcoxon rank-sum, Z = -2.06, *p* = 0.040). If self-employment is a reason for the bankruptcy filing, the financial hole is particularly deep, with almost six years of income needed for debtors to retire all outstanding debt. Those whose business failure pushed them into bankruptcy are in worse financial shape than those without self-employment and those whose self-employment was not a reason for their bankruptcy. The collapse of self-employment leads to particularly grim debt loads.

It is not merely the amount of debt, but the type of debt that distinguishes the self-employed in bankruptcy. Based on interviews he conducted in 1996–1997, Ronald Mann documented a shift toward unsecured lending to small businesses and away from secured lending. Financial institutions were willing to lend to small businesses amounts of up to $100,000 in exchange for the owner's personal guaranty to pay the debt. Mann predicted greater uses of unsecured lending in small-business finance.[55] Multiple data sources show that his prediction has come to pass, with small-business owners increasingly relying on unsecured borrowing to finance operations. The Federal Reserve's Survey of Small Business Finances finds that business owners used personal credit cards at about the same rate, 47 percent, in 1998 and 2003 but that use of business credit cards, for which the owner typically has personal liability, jumped from 34 percent to 48 percent in the same period.[56] Other estimates of credit card use by small businesses also suggest the prominence of capitalization by credit card. The Panel Study on Entrepreneurial Dynamics finds that 28 percent of small-business owners say they used a credit card to get the startup funds for their businesses, and 23 percent used bank loans.[57] In a private survey, 85 percent of small-business owners reported having one or more credit cards that they used for current business purposes.[58]

Medians for total unsecured debt and its components are reported in Table 6.5 and compared on the basis of whether self-employment was given as a reason for bankruptcy. As the table shows, a key characteristic of the people who identified self-employment as a reason for bankruptcy is huge amounts of unsecured debt compared with other bankruptcy filers. The median person who identified problems with self-employment as a reason for bankruptcy had more than twice as much unsecured debt as the median for other filers.

The components of this unsecured debt burden reveal how the self-employed made financial bets that led them to bankruptcy. The CBP coded unsecured debt into five categories based on the name of the creditor to whom the debt was owed. These categories were credit card debt, student loans, utility bills, rent/lease obligations, and medical debt. Debts that could not be coded into one of these categories were placed into a residual category of unclassified debt, which would include personal loans or any unsecured business loan. When self-employment is a reported reason for bankruptcy, credit card and unclassified debt are much higher, as shown in Table 6.5. But the amounts of other unsecured debt are similar to those of other filers. The types of debt that are most likely to have been used to finance a business—credit card debt and other unsecured debt—are two to three times higher at the medians for the self-employed than for other bankruptcy filers. Moreover, the amounts are about $30,000 to $45,000 in 2007 dollars, typical for the initial capital of a business started from scratch or purchased from

TABLE 6.5

Unsecured debts, self-employment identified as reason for bankruptcy

	Self-employed stated as reason for bankruptcy	All other filers	Wilcoxon results
Total unsecured debt (median)	$77,569	$31,982	Z = -7.61, p < 0.001
Components (medians)			
Credit card debt	$49,093	$22,670	Z = -5.17, p < 0.001
Other unsecured debt	$1,643	$1,156	Z = -0.73, p = 0.468
Unclassified unsecured debt	$23,126	$6,199	Z = -4.70, p < 0.001

SOURCE: Consumer Bankruptcy Project 2007.

NOTE: A case was considered to have self-employment if the respondent indicated full-time self-employment for the respondent or a spouse/partner. Total n = 976, of which 80 met the definition of self-employment and identified self-employment as a reason for the bankruptcy. "Wilcoxon results" refers to results of Wilcoxon rank-sum tests and corresponding *p* values.

another.[59] These findings reinforce a study that identified credit card debt as making it less likely for a new firm to survive, with every $1,000 in credit card debt increasing the probability by 2.2 percent that a firm would close.[60] Rather than borrowing their way to a prosperous business, these would-be entrepreneurs borrowed their way to a bankruptcy court.

Although self-employment bankruptcies are notable for their high amounts of outstanding credit card debt, mortgage borrowing (including home equity lines of credit) does not show this pattern. Although the median debtor who identified self-employment as a reason for bankruptcy had higher mortgage debt than other filers ($137,345 versus $101,015), the effect goes away once the value of the home is considered. The median debtor identifying self-employment as a reason for bankruptcy reported a loan-to-value (LTV) ratio on the home of 91.2 percent, slightly lower than the median LTV ratio for other filers (93.1 percent). This small difference is not statistically significant. ($Z = -0.638$, $p = 0.524$).

Findings about the median can tell us about the typical self-employed debtor in bankruptcy but cannot convey the full range of experiences of the self-employed who file for bankruptcy. Although credit card debt and general unsecured borrowing dominate the debt burdens of most self-employed filers while home equity borrowing generally appears in the same amounts as for other filers, individual balance sheets can vary dramatically. Home equity borrowing does play a role for some self-employed bankruptcy filers. One in four debtors who identified self-employment as a reason for bankruptcy reported using a home equity line of credit to finance their business, and more than 30 percent of the same group reported being under water on their home (that is, they had an LTV greater than 1 as measured in 2007 before the collapse of the housing market). Self-employed debtors with high mortgage debt have not merely substituted mortgage borrowing for credit card and general unsecured borrowing. They too reported higher amounts of unsecured borrowing, suggesting that perhaps the self-employed turn to mortgage lending after piling on substantial credit card debts.

Overall, the data show that typical self-employed people whose business problems contributed to their filing for bankruptcy are loaded down with business debts. Nearly all self-employed debtors have taken on some responsibility for the business's debts in one form or another. Limited liability for a business entity is beside the point for these debtors because of contractual guarantees or, as the data show more typically happens, because of credit card or other unsecured borrowing for which they have personal responsibility. When the self-employed collapse into bankruptcy, they arrive in a deeper financial hole than the rest of consumer bankruptcy filers.

As already discussed, heroic tales abound of owners who have taken on huge amounts of personal liability and grown a small business into a multimillion-dollar success. For example, *Entrepreneur* magazine ran a story called "Play Your Cards Right," with the subtitle revealing what budding entrepreneurial success stories need to do: "Financing with Credit Cards Is a Risk—But It Can Pay Off." The U.S. Chamber of Commerce even identified access to high-cost credit such as home equity lines of credit, credit cards, and auto title loans as important to the success of small businesses (and thereby advanced what it saw as a reason not to support the regulation of such high-cost credit).[61] People who borrow heavily to start a business are portrayed as risk takers, and the title "entrepreneur" is given to these bold capitalists, distinguishing them from the mere mortals who scratch out a living running a business. But when the businesses fail, these people get a different label—"bankruptcy debtor." Those sources touting entrepreneurship do not tell the tales of failure. Instead, the stigma and pain of failure leave these stories hidden in the bankruptcy system.

CONCLUSION

One might react to the data about the self-employed in bankruptcy by proposing reforms to the U.S. Bankruptcy Code. At the margins, several useful changes might be made. Chapter 13, which allows debtors to repay a portion of their debts over a period of years, contemplates regular payments, which in turn contemplate a regular income (11 U.S.C. § 109[e]). For most self-employed people, however, income can be highly volatile. Relaxation of the regular income rule, perhaps looking to income over a quarter or a year rather than at the time of bankruptcy filing, would make Chapter 13 a more realistic option for many self-employed debtors. Implementing this change would only require flexibility in administration by bankruptcy trustees and judges.

Also, the self-employed in bankruptcy often are subject to the 2005 amendments to the bankruptcy law that were aimed at allegedly overspending consumer bankruptcy debtors. For example, the Longs filed for bankruptcy owing $1.3 million on a personal guaranty for a business loan, but the bankruptcy system still treated their case as a consumer bankruptcy so they had to go through the usual credit counseling, financial education, and paperwork submissions required of all consumers. But, for example, a consumer credit counseling program designed to help debtors get consumption spending under control makes little sense for a person who took a risk on a business that did not pay off. Paperwork requirements such as pay stubs are largely irrelevant in the context of a failed business owner who likely does not receive a salary. For the hundreds of thousands of self-employed debtors each year, these requirements are just additional hurdles that add to the expense of filing for bankruptcy and only delay the bankruptcy relief that they need. Some of the paperwork requirements already do not apply to debtors who identify as business filers, but the judicial characterization of most any personal obligation as consumer debt leads many filers like the Longs to declare themselves as consumer filers even if they are not. It is important that the bankruptcy law should recognize business failures for what they are and not recharacterize such events as bankruptcies caused by typical consumer debts. Amending portions of the 2005 law so they do not apply to people with a failed business would help cushion the collapse of small businesses.

Tinkering with the bankruptcy law, however, is just playing at the margins of the problem. More importantly, the story about the self-employed in bankruptcy needs to be told to complement the more conventional narrative that talks only of successful entrepreneurs. This chapter has tried to complete this story of small businesses by looking at the self-employed who file for bankruptcy. The findings tell us more not only about small businesses, but also about financial failure.

PART III

HURTING AT HOME

CHAPTER SEVEN

No Forwarding Address

Losing Homes in Bankruptcy

Marianne B. Culhane

The Clark family has lost its piece of the American Dream.[1] In 2001, Mark and Anne Clark, then twenty-nine and twenty-five years old and earning $50,000 a year, bought a modest home in the Midwest for $83,000 with a fixed-rate loan at 6 percent interest. At first they thrived, loving the neighborhood and its good schools for their two young sons. Then the auto industry hit the skids, and Mark lost his steady job. With just a high school education, he turned to self-employment as a truck driver at a lower and less steady income. Anne, who had one year of college, kept working as a payroll clerk, where her salary was low but stable and her benefits included family health insurance. Then $4,000 in unexpected medical expenses hit the Clarks, and their insurer denied coverage. In desperation, Mark and Anne refinanced their mortgage and ended up with a subprime adjustable-rate loan. Their interest rate rose to 11 percent, pushing payments far above their budget. Their lender would not work with them, and other lenders rejected their request to refinance. When their lender started to foreclose in early 2007, Mark and Anne filed for bankruptcy, hoping against hope to save their home.

But even bankruptcy and its legal tools for helping homeowners proved inadequate. Mark and Anne could not make their ongoing house payments each month, so the bankruptcy court soon let foreclosure proceed. Before the year was out, Mark and Anne deeded the only home they had ever owned back to their mortgage lender. Angry, sad, and embarrassed by financial failure, they pulled their sons, then ages eight and ten, out of the school they loved, left their friends and neighborhood behind, and crowded into a small apartment in a nearby town. Odds are that the Clarks will not own another home before their sons are grown and living on their own.[2]

Since 2007, the United States has been in a home foreclosure crisis. Many home mortgages made between 2001 and 2007, either for purchase or refinance, were subprime or nontraditional loans that included features like adjustable interest rates and optional payment amounts.[3] Borrowers such as the Clarks may not have fully understood these complex terms and certainly could not manage the escalating payments in an economy of widespread unemployment and declining home prices. Such loans have caused millions of families to lose their American Dream of homeownership, have cost investors billions of dollars, and have pushed the entire economy into a downward spiral. Experts predict that more than half of all subprime mortgages granted after 2000 will end in foreclosure.[4]

Plummeting home values and rising unemployment have spread the pain beyond subprime borrowers. Many prime borrowers with fixed-rate loans now owe more on their mortgages than their homes are worth and cannot afford the ongoing payments.[5] Estimates near the end of 2010 suggested that more than seven million homes would be lost to foreclosure by the end of 2012 and that only one in seven delinquent borrowers could be helped by current mortgage modification programs.[6] In their first years, such private and government-sponsored programs have helped very few families, and the modifications offered all too often lead to quick redefaults.[7] For example, the Home Affordable Modification Program (HAMP), launched in March 2009 with $75 billion in incentives to lenders, was intended to bring about the modification of three to four million home mortgages. Eighteen months later, only five hundred thousand mortgages had been permanently modified. Even more discouraging were federal government predictions that 40 percent of those modified mortgages would end in renewed default within five years.[8]

The grim reality is that most seriously delinquent homeowners will lose their homes. The policy emphasis on foreclosure prevention has diverted attention from the epidemic of inevitable home loss and involuntary relocation. Scholars and policymakers know very little about home loss, yet millions of families have already lost their homes and millions more will suffer the same fate. Studying the painful process of involuntary home loss is a vital prerequisite to the development of policies intended to ease the transition out of homeownership and soften the financial and emotional consequences of home loss. Any meaningful reformulation of the American Dream of homeownership has to be sensitive to the fallout from the wave of foreclosures that has swept the nation.

This chapter looks at financially distressed homeowners like Mark and Anne Clark who tried, but failed, to save their homes through bankruptcy. It is a picture of loss—not just the loss of the economic benefits of a home, but also of the psychological values and social rewards that lead millions of families to attempt the American Dream of homeownership. First I briefly describe the characteristics of bankrupt homeowners and the limited help that bankruptcy offers in preventing foreclosure. I then look at how many homes are lost despite families' efforts to save them by filing for bankruptcy;

provide insights into where families go after being forced out of their homes; and explore, relying on the words of the debtors themselves, what debtors value and miss most about their lost homes and their lost status as homeowners. Finally, I consider how these findings can help decision makers craft policy responses to the home losses wreaked by the foreclosure crisis.

BANKRUPT HOMEOWNERS

The Sample

This chapter uses a sample from the 2007 Consumer Bankruptcy Project (CBP), which drew a national random sample of more than two thousand Chapter 7 and Chapter 13 bankruptcy cases. All debtors completed a written survey, and data were obtained from their bankruptcy court records. Nine to twelve months later, 1,032 bankrupt households took part in detailed phone interviews; more than half of those interviewed (562, or 54.5 percent) had been homeowners when their bankruptcy cases were filed. While homeowners in bankruptcy are a small and not entirely typical subset of the larger universe of homeowners who lose houses to foreclosure, the wealth of information from the bankruptcy court files and CBP written surveys and phone interviews gives an unusually complete picture of families who lost homes at the outset of the home foreclosure crisis of the late 2000s. The families in this chapter tried to hang on to their houses by filing for bankruptcy; they were not strategic defaulters who walked away simply because their homes were underwater.

When the bankrupt homeowners in the 2007 CBP are compared with U.S. homeowners generally, it is clear that few debtors in bankruptcy are trying to save McMansions. Using the 2007 version of the Federal Reserve's Survey of Consumer Finances (SCF) as a comparison sample, one can see that the homes of bankrupt families are much more modest than those of typical Americans. The median home value of a bankrupt household was only $110,000, just over half of the $200,000 median in the SCF sample of Americans in the general population. However, those modest homes of bankrupt households were saddled with almost as much mortgage debt as those of nonbankrupt households: the median mortgage debt of households in the SCF was $107,000, and the median mortgage debt of a bankrupt household was only $3,000 less, at $104,000. Thus, there were dramatic differences in home equity between the two groups. The median homeowners in bankruptcy had only $14,800 in home equity, a small fraction of the $91,000 in equity of the median homeowner in the United States. And in 2007 when both sets of data were collected, nearly all American homeowners (99 percent) had positive equity, compared with only 69 percent of bankrupt homeowners.[9]

Of course, both home values and home equity have dropped precipitously since 2007. The Case-Shiller index in mid-2009 reported drops of 31 percent in home values across the nation since the 2006 peak and forecasts further declines of at least 8 percent.[10] Losses of this magnitude will have wiped out home equity for many homeowners. This economic decline makes the plight of bankrupt homeowners a useful starting point for understanding the suffering of today's homeowners facing foreclosure.

What Bankruptcy Offers Homeowners in Financial Distress

Interviews with the bankrupt households clearly showed that fear of losing a home is a major driver of families' decisions to file for bankruptcy. Debtors in more than half (54.5 percent) of the 1,032 cases in the CBP sample told interviewers that they had owned their homes when they filed for bankruptcy. Nine out of ten of these homeowners said that keeping their homes had been "very important" when they filed. Only 5 percent of homeowners had already resigned themselves to home loss at the time of filing for bankruptcy, agreeing in their bankruptcy court documents to surrender their homes to mortgage lenders. The vast majority of homeowners enter bankruptcy wanting to fight to keep their homes, looking for help from the law in staving off foreclosure and becoming current on their mortgage obligations.

Homeowners who are and remain current on house payments through a bankruptcy case will not lose the home to their mortgage lender during the case.[11] Before filing for bankruptcy, many households in the 2007 CBP sample had made mortgage payments a top priority, even when they could not pay other debts. Fully 41 percent told phone interviewers that they had never been even one month behind in house payments during the two years before they filed for bankruptcy. As one recently divorced mother of a thirteen-year-old put it: "[My home] was the most important thing out of everything. As bad as things were, I was not going to lose my home and my child's home. I was not going to let that happen. My house payment got paid if I had to beg, borrow, or steal."

Many debtors who file for bankruptcy, however, are behind on their mortgage payments. By the time they file, some are a few months late and others are on the eve of a foreclosure sale. Homeowners desperate to save their homes often seek refuge in bankruptcy court, but they find only limited relief there. Bankruptcy does not reduce the principal or interest on a home mortgage, absent the unusual situation of a lender consenting to a modification of the loan. If homeowners simply cannot make the ongoing payments after the interest rates on their mortgage loans have risen, bankruptcy law does not rewrite those loans to lower the interest rates or to subsidize mortgage payments.

Bankruptcy does, however, offer some specific provisions to help home-owners who are behind on their mortgages and want to catch up on missed payments. Chapter 7, the most common type of consumer bankruptcy, usually delays a creditor from foreclosing for a few months and permits a debtor to discharge credit card and some other debts, freeing up income that can then be used for house payments. When the debtor is in default, the lender usually will wait three to six months for the bankruptcy case to end and foreclose at that point. The lender's more expensive option is to ask the court to permit foreclosure before the bankruptcy case ends, which sometimes will be granted. Chapter 7 also protects the debtor from having to pay a deficiency. Foreclosure sales often net far less than the amount due on the mortgage, and in most states, the debtor owes the lender the difference, called a deficiency. Chapter 7's debt forgiveness would cover that deficiency. Thus, Chapter 7 debtors may lose their homes in bankruptcy, but mortgage lenders normally cannot take other assets or garnish wages to collect a deficiency because bankruptcy discharges that obligation.[12]

Chapter 13, the other common type of consumer bankruptcy, was designed to help debtors keep their homes, but as in Chapter 7, the home mortgage loan cannot be modified.[13] Absent unusual circumstances, the principal of the debt is still owed and interest rates normally cannot be modified.[14] However, Chapter 13 allows debtors to stop a foreclosure and cure a default due to missed payments by repaying the amount in arrears over the next three to five years. Debtors can catch up on these missed payments without creditor consent, but they must get bankruptcy court approval of their repayment plan. To do so, debtors must first persuade the court that they will be able to make each future house payment as it falls due, plus have enough income to cover payments previously missed.[15] Then debtors must make those payments as promised. However, much can go wrong over the three to five years of a Chapter 13 repayment plan. Only one-third of debtors succeed in making all the payments due; most Chapter 13 cases fail within a year or two.[16] For homeowners in default, foreclosure likely will soon follow their missed payments and the dismissal of their bankruptcy case. Thus, although bankruptcy has a home-saving purpose, the outcome can sometimes be home loss.

HOME LOSS IN BANKRUPTCY: THE HIDDEN PHENOMENON

Nine to twelve months after their bankruptcy cases were filed, the CBP homeowners were asked in telephone interviews whether they still lived in the home they had owned and occupied at the time they filed for bankruptcy. Nearly one in five (19 percent, or 107 of 562) said "no." More than a quarter of the Chapter 7 filers (26 percent) had moved out of their former homes. Chapter 13 debtors had fared a bit better because of the additional remedies available to homeowners in Chapter 13, but more than 10 percent of these households no longer lived in the homes they had owned and occupied when they filed for bankruptcy. Table 7.1 shows what happened to these lost homes.

Adding up the first three categories in Table 7.1 shows that more than 65 percent of the homes that debtors vacated after their bankruptcy filing had been sold or surrendered because of financial distress. Foreclosure was the most common reason that debtors moved out of their homes after bankruptcy, explaining more than four in ten changes in residence.

There is every reason to expect that many more bankruptcy debtors have lost their homes since these phone interviews took place in late 2007 and early 2008. First, the time required to complete a foreclosure varies in different states, so some bankrupt families would have been interviewed while still occupying homes in the early stages of foreclosure. Also, even if a debtor has ceased making house payments in bankruptcy, it may take two or three months for a lender to obtain bankruptcy court permission to begin the foreclosure process. Second, some mortgage servicers have been delaying initiation of foreclosure because of low housing prices and huge inventories of unsold homes threatening even further price declines. Third, economic trends in 2008 and 2009 would have pushed many more of these debtors into default. Unemployment rates have continued to rise, hitting millions of Americans with loss of income and of health insurance. Homeowners, especially those whose mortgage debt exceeds their home's value, may suffer prolonged unemployment, as they cannot quickly sell their homes in order to relocate for new jobs.[17]

The statistic reported here, that one in five homeowners who file for bankruptcy loses the home within one year after filing, almost certainly underreports the ultimate rate of home loss from financial pressure. Additional

TABLE 7.1

Fate of homes lost in the first year after bankruptcy filing

	N	%
Lost due to foreclosure	44	41.1
Sold by debtor because of financial pressures	12	11.2
Deeded back or returned to lender	14	13.1
Spouse/ex-spouse has house because of separation/divorce	10	9.3
Other	24	22.4
Don't know	3	2.8
Total	107	99.9

SOURCE: Consumer Bankruptcy Project 2007.

longitudinal study may reveal a much higher rate of home loss, particularly among those Chapter 13 debtors who prove unable to make their mortgage payments for the full three to five years under their repayment plan. The rate of early home loss hints at a vast gulf that may exist between homeowners' hopes when they enter bankruptcy and actual results.

NEXT STOP: WHERE TO GO AFTER HOME LOSS?

Phone interviewers asked the CBP families who had moved out of the homes they owned at the time of filing to describe their current living situations. Debtors were to choose one of four answers: (1) renting, (2) buying another house, (3) living with someone without paying rent, or (4) other. Figure 7.1 summarizes their responses. Few displaced homeowners, only 6 percent, reported buying another home to replace the one they had surrendered or lost via foreclosure. Home loss for financial reasons is almost always about a transition out of homeownership, rather than into a different home as an owner. Far more common was retreat into rented quarters, with 70 percent of the debtors who lost their homes renting one year after filing for bankruptcy. Another 8 percent had moved in with family or friends to whom they were not paying rent.

Who Will Take Them In: Family or Landlords?

Within the categories shown in Figure 7.1, important distinctions could exist that would reveal a great deal about the well-being of former homeowners. Almost nothing is known about those who said "other," except for a few

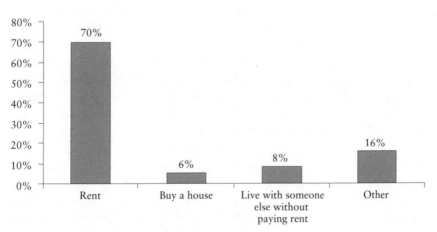

Figure 7.1   Replacement shelter after home loss
SOURCE: Consumer Bankruptcy Project 2007.
NOTE: n = 107.

debtors who spontaneously volunteered additional information on their situations. And the 70 percent of homeowners who rented may have very different situations—renting homes similar to those they lost or living in small apartments or renting from friends or family in a shared living space.

Only those who said they were living with someone but not paying rent were asked to specify with whom they were living. However, the volunteer responses from those who said "renting" or "other" suggest that relatives and friends are often a source of shelter, rather than landlords who are not related to the debtors. At least twenty-one former homeowners said they and their families had moved in with and were paying rent or otherwise contributing to the household expenses of other family members—parents, adult children, nonfiling spouses—or friends.

Further research could explore whether these family/friend living arrangements were made because professional landlords had refused to take in tenants with the black mark of a recent bankruptcy on their credit reports, whether market rents were too high, or whether living with family or friends was simply the best choice among other alternatives. Deborah Thorne, in a 2004 survey of seven hundred debtors who had filed for bankruptcy three years earlier, found that about 17 percent of those who were not homeowners after bankruptcy had been rejected as tenants, often by more than one landlord, because of their bankruptcy. Another 40 percent had eventually rented apartments but reported that their prior bankruptcy had made the process more time-consuming, difficult, and expensive. Landlords, they said, often required double or triple the usual security deposits, payment of several months' rent in advance, and sometimes a cosigner—all because of their bankruptcy.[18]

Many debtors in the 2007 CBP sample may have encountered similar discrimination, so moving in with family or friends may have been their only viable choice. Clearly, some sample debtors expected that trying to rent from landlords unknown to them would be difficult or impossible after bankruptcy. All the CBP homeowners were asked why keeping their homes had been so important when they filed for bankruptcy. A frequent response was fear that their credit report would prevent both renting a future living space and borrowing to buy another home. These comments were typical: "We could not replace it [the home]. . . . We would have been struggling to find a rental and couldn't qualify for any kind of loan to buy something else," and "I knew my credit would be shot [and so] I wouldn't be able to buy another home or even be able to rent."

Family or friends may be an appealing option for recent bankrupt debtors because they do not require a credit check and may offer free or reduced-rent living options. But moving in with family or friends can also have substantial drawbacks. The bankrupt households may simply be adding their financial burdens to those of host families who also struggle to make ends meet. Relatively few families in the United States can easily take on the financial burdens of feeding another family or have enough spare room to accommodate more people for an extended time. Crowding and loss of privacy can quickly raise tensions. As one debtor put it: "I am forty-three years old. I don't want to move back in with my mom. When I did move back in with my mom, she still laid down the law." These newly combined family households may turn out to be stress-filled and unworkable, leading to very temporary shelter options.[19] This could mean another change of schools for children already displaced once, plus the expense of a yet another move for their financially strained parents. A recent study of the effect of the housing crisis on Latino families emphasized overcrowding in combined households and the constant fear that another move would soon be needed.[20]

It seems likely that most of these displaced households would have moved into less desirable quarters, often in more dangerous neighborhoods. Even those with enough income to pay for space in more desirable locales might have found their credit report, with the recent bankruptcy on it, an insuperable barrier. As we see below, this downward mobility was widely feared by the CBP debtors.

Fear of Homelessness

None of the former homeowners told phone interviewers that they had in fact become homeless since their bankruptcy filing, but many expressed fears of homelessness, and some had experienced it before bankruptcy. One mother in the South, who was still in her home at the time, told phone interviewers: "I have been homeless before, and I never want it to happen again. I have been homeless with six children before." However, many debtors in the initial sample of written survey respondents could not be reached for phone interviews nine to twelve months after their bankruptcies were filed. Others declined to take part in the interviews because of illness or reluctance to relive the painful bankruptcy process. Some who were reached refused to disclose their current living situations. If any debtors had become homeless, they also would have been difficult to reach by phone (even if they had a cell phone) and thus would likely have been left out of phone interviews. No news may not mean good news for families whom the interviewers could not reach.

Tenure in Lost Homes

Many sample debtors who lost a home between filing for bankruptcy and the phone interview had owned that home for a relatively short time. Fifty percent were out of their house within six years after purchase. Half of that group were out in three years or fewer. Such short spans of homeowner-ship are not likely to produce the financial gains or social stability that homebuyers seek. Price appreciation to create home equity takes time, es-pecially when one buys near the top of a bubble market with a high loan-to-value mortgage. However, even short-term owners will feel the pain of home loss, including the stress and expense of having to move, usually into more cramped rental or borrowed quarters; the upheaval of changing their children's schools; and the embarrassment of financial failure. Families may also lose confidence in their ability to succeed as homeowners in the future and may choose to rent even after their financial situations stabilize rather than risk another home loss. Lauren Willis suggests that it may be worse to have been a short-time homeowner than never to have owned a home at all, as the pain of home loss will almost certainly exceed any gain in financial or psychological welfare.[21]

On the other hand, 25 percent of those who lost a home in the first year after bankruptcy had owned their home ten years or more. In three sample cases, debtors lost homes they had owned for forty years. For long-term owners, the dislocation may be even more painful. For example, one midwestern woman, a sixty-nine-year-old retired factory worker wid-owed some twenty years, had to surrender the home she had owned since 1966. She had taken out several home equity loans to cover living expenses over the preceding years. When failing health forced her to retire, Social Security did not cover those loan payments. She declined to disclose her current living arrangements, but her distress at the loss of her home was clear. She told the phone interviewer that her home "meant everything" to her. "It was one of the hardest things I ever done," she said. "I haven't gotten over it yet."

Some of these long-term homeowners may have lost substantial equity as well, but many had cashed out their equity before bankruptcy through refinancing and home equity loans. Half of the sample homeowners had re-financed their mortgages at least once. Refinancing, of course, carries trans-action fees, which can be hefty, and borrowers often use the occasion to take out new cash, so the principal balance may increase substantially, whether or not the interest rate changes. Frequent "refi's" or "flips" can be very ex-pensive and put a home at risk. Nearly a quarter of the CBP homeowners who had refinanced three or more times lost their homes soon after filing for bankruptcy. One-third of the CBP homeowners had one or more addi-tional loans: junior loans secured by their homes, home equity lines of credit (HELOC), or home improvement loans. The few CBP debtors with three or more such loans had a home loss rate of 43 percent, more than double the overall rate. When debtors bought their homes, they must have hoped thereby to acquire an asset accumulation tool, but those tools failed them.

The loss of wealth from unmanageable refinancing and junior liens is a major part of the home foreclosure story.

The Hard Road Ahead

Few of the bankruptcy debtors who lost their homes are likely to become homeowners again soon. Their homeownership, now ended by financial failure, most likely will be followed by long-term renting or sharing space with relatives. Donald Haurin and Stuart Rosenthal's longitudinal study of the duration and termination of "spells" of homeownership, renting, and living with family shows that, on average, those who lose homes because of foreclosure or other forced sale will not own a home again for ten years or more.[22] The consequences of home loss are enduring, dragging down households' ability to accumulate wealth and achieve social stability for a decade or more. Jay Zagorsky and Lois Lupica's research shows that the homeownership rate of former bankrupt individuals remains lower than that of people who never filed, even when measured more than ten years after bankruptcy.[23] More longitudinal research on bankruptcy, the effectiveness of the discharge, and the time needed to regain lost status would be helpful.

LOST HOMES, LOST HOPES

Bankrupt debtors who lose their homes suffer immediate hard consequences: they must find somewhere else to live, perhaps persuading someone to take them in despite their recent or ongoing bankruptcy; they must pack up belongings and transport what they can afford to take or sell or abandon items too expensive to move or too large for their new residences; and they must leave friends and neighbors behind and move children away from familiar schools. At each of these turns, they face out-of-pocket expenses and the embarrassment of failure in the eyes of their neighbors, children, families, and others. Losing a home is nearly always a step down the social and economic ladder, and it may even be a tumble into serious hardship, such as renting in a high-crime area or having to endure unfit living conditions.

The consequences of home loss may be suffered for years. Some of the pain is financial, as families may lose current equity in their homes. More likely, however, the family who has lost a home has lost financial hopes for the future from expected price appreciation and the forced savings effect of making mortgage payments. There are also painful psychological losses, for "homeownership is about status, about participation in a community, about school districts and opportunities for children, about family memories and continuity, about emotional as well as financial security."[24] After a real estate bubble burst in Britain, a thirteen-year longitudinal study of home losses found that unsustainable housing debt inflicted as much psychological pain on homeowners as marital dissolution.[25] We do not yet have such data in the United States, but the possibility is very real that the foreclosure epidemic that started in late 2007 will inflict lasting hurt on the well-being of American families.

Homeowners in the 2007 CBP sample were asked by interviewers why keeping their homes had been so important and to describe what they feared to lose in foreclosure. Their brief responses to this query were transcribed in the debtors' own words, providing insights into debtors' thinking on the consequences of home loss. Not surprisingly, many people cited financial considerations; they believed they had equity in their homes. Others were worried about the financial burden of rental payments, which they feared would be more costly than their mortgage payments had been. Most homeowners, however, gave reasons other than dollars and cents for trying so hard to save their homes. Parents emphasized the need to protect children from unsafe neighborhoods and the hardships of school moves. Some older debtors were concerned with preserving family memories, hanging on to a physical space once shared with now deceased parents or spouses and retaining a place where adult children and grandchildren still enjoyed gathering. Others saw home loss as a blow to their self-image and as an end to their middle-class status in the eyes of family and friends. For some, medical problems made the prospect of home loss especially fearsome because of difficulties locating rental housing that could accommodate a disability. Finally, some mourned the loss of homes they had built or extensively remodeled themselves. Some debtors expressed several of these reasons, each in itself a powerful harm from the perspective of the homeowner.

Parents' Hopes to Protect Children

Elizabeth Warren and Amelia Warren Tyagi have studied how the efforts of parents to find good schools and safe environments for their children may lead them to take on mortgage debt beyond their means and to try extremely hard to retain those homes despite the financial pressures they impose.[26] Eric Nguyen recently found that bankrupt parents with young children are more likely than childless debtors "to value the specific location of their home" in order to "keep the children in a particular school district" or to "avoid severing social connections the children have made."[27] Teachers, psychologists, and economists agree that relocation can be traumatic for children, particularly when the changes are involuntary for the parents. Children can sense their parents' loss of control and anxiety. Home loss increases stress on children and often leads to educational regression. And high turnover in schools has negative effects for both new and existing students.[28]

Close to half of the homeowners (48 percent, or 271 of 562 cases) in the phone interview sample had school-age children or grandchildren in their households. Although these parents and grandparents hoped to provide stable homes and schooling for the children, they lost their homes at nearly the same rate as those without school-age children. About 19 percent of both groups had lost their homes within one year after bankruptcy. This near equality of loss rates in the 2007 sample may be yet another indicator of the recent deterioration of homeowners' financial prospects. Nguyen's study of a 2001 sample of bankruptcy debtors found that homeowners with school-age children were more than twice as likely to keep their homes in bankruptcy compared with those without children in school.[29] By 2007, it seems, having children still raised the stakes of losing a home, but parents no longer were more successful than others at avoiding home loss. The consequences of the housing crisis of the late 2000s may be falling equally on parents and non-parents, ratcheting up the pain of this wave of foreclosures compared with home losses in prior years.

Some children of bankrupt families were forced to change schools more than once for financial reasons. Among households that owned their homes at the time of bankruptcy, 11 percent had children who had already quit or changed schools because of money pressures at least once in the two years before their parents' bankruptcy. The fifty families with school-age children who lost their homes in the first year after bankruptcy included at least four families whose children had also suffered a prebankruptcy school change forced by financial problems. For example, an initial reaction to threatened home loss may be to move children from private into public schools, then later—when foreclosure forces the family into an entirely new community—to a different public school.

Some of these school changes may be unnecessary. A federal statute, the McKinney-Vento Homeless Assistance Act, requires public school districts to permit children who become homeless to continue to attend their former school and to provide transportation in many cases. The broad definition of a homeless child under that act extends to those "sharing the housing of other persons due to loss of housing, economic hardship, or a similar reason"—in other words, the common situation of moving in with family or friends after a foreclosure. Even if such a child and his or her family later find more permanent housing in another school district, the child may be entitled to finish out the school year in and have transportation to the original school.[30] However, few parents would know of these rights, and tight school budgets during a recession may make compliance difficult.

The Clark family, whose home loss story opened this chapter, put schools first in their response to the importance of saving their home, saying that they "loved the school and the area." A mother of a ten-year-old said: "I had already moved twice and I didn't want to go through that again. I wanted my son to have a decent place to grow up and I didn't want to do that to him again." After losing her home to foreclosure, a divorced mother of four children aged seven to fourteen said, "I had to find a place that would accommodate four children in the same area so they wouldn't have to change schools." Safety was another major concern for parents. The father of a five-year-old in a large southwestern city said: "To go down from here would really endanger my family. We don't live in the best neighborhood now. If we had to move down, it would be bad." These concerns underscore the risks to children from home loss. Parents may be as fearful of the social harms to their children from forced dislocation as they are of financial losses.

The financial distress that typically precedes bankruptcy can impose a variety of changes on families. They may cut back on vacation time, change what they eat, eliminate expenses for school activities, or cut other discretionary expenses. Such changes can be bewildering for children.[31] The father of two young teens said that he and his wife wanted to keep their home "because we are part of a community here and our children have lived their whole lives in this home. . . . I felt that continuity would be the one thing that would help get us through all this." A recently widowed mother of children aged eleven and fourteen said, "It was important to my kids to have a home and I felt I was letting them down if I had to move them." Yet, only two years after they lost their father, this family also lost their home to foreclosure despite trying bankruptcy relief.

Home as the Family's Center of Memories and Hope

Some debtors had owned their homes for many years, long enough for their children to have grown up and moved away. These debtors saw their houses as the main link to those children. A couple in their early seventies who had owned their home for almost thirty years sounded forlorn as they explained that they wanted a place for their family to come home to: "All the things a family enjoys revolve around a home. If you don't have a home, you don't have a family and that's the most important thing we have to look forward to." Another person who had owned a home for more than a decade before filing for bankruptcy explained why he wanted to keep the family home: "Because we have roots here. We have lived here nearly all our married life, we raised our kids here. We have memories here. When the kids come, they enjoy coming here, they really feel like this is still home to them. . . . All these memories make it hard to think about moving."

For others, the home is a link to loved ones who have died. A middle-aged woman said, "I grew up in this house and I inherited part of it and there are a lot of memories in this house since my mom and dad passed away." A recently widowed woman lamented, "It's all I have . . . also my only connection that I still have with my husband that died." Clearly, homes and homeownership have a psychological importance, providing a sense of stability and continuity and evoking sweet memories of happier times.

Home as a Marker of Financial Success

Homeownership has long been seen as an important indicator of middle-class status and financial prudence (see Chapter 2). Some people in bankruptcy saw the loss of their homes and the transition into renting as a potent sign of failure. A Chapter 13 debtor in Kentucky put it this way: "Just the whole status, just esteem in home ownership, taught from early on that you should own your own home. If you have ever rented before, you are just throwing your money away." A Chapter 7 debtor said, "It was the first house I bought and I didn't want to look like a failure." A man in the upper Midwest lamented: "I felt like I was a failure if I lost it. That I couldn't make a home. For a man, that's a big deal." This perception of a sudden and profound loss of status can cause increased tension between spouses and between parents and children.

Medical Problems Make Moving Difficult

Some debtors and their families had medical problems that made moving particularly difficult, especially if the home they were about to lose was specially adapted to their health needs. One woman, who with her husband had managed to save their home at least in the first year after bankruptcy, said: "I knew that we would have practically no income. My husband was not working and I had just discovered that I had breast cancer. So we had to have our house. No one can kick you out of your house once it's paid for." Another woman noted difficulties "because my husband needed so much special care that my home was equipped for." Medical problems and disability exacerbate the difficulty of seeking new shelter. A person's inability to climb stairs, for example, severely limits the choice of rental housing and may also make it impossible to move in with relatives or friends who do not live at ground level, even if they are willing to share living space.

Home as a Product of Debtors' Own Efforts: Sweat Equity

Debtors who had built or remodeled their homes themselves seemed to feel an extra bond to those homes. As a fifty-year-old man in the South put it: "The house was originally just an old mobile home. I drove every nail, hung every piece of sheet rock, painted every wall. . . . Now we have a nice home." Another debtor said: "I had blood, sweat, and tears in the house. It was a work of love." This do-it-yourself ethic resonates with the idea that Americans are supposed to be self-made successes. The loss of a home, particularly one in which the debtor invested so much hands-on labor, can strip people of pride and hope.

CONCLUSION

A desire to save their homes from foreclosure is a major reason why millions of families file for bankruptcy each year. Yet bankruptcy is only partially effective at helping them in this regard. Just one year after the CBP sample families had declared themselves broke and sought protection in bankruptcy court, nearly 20 percent had already lost their homes. While some of these losses stemmed from divorce or relocation, most were due to financial distress. Bankruptcy fails to help some families avoid surrendering their houses to lenders, selling them to meet debts, or being foreclosed upon by lenders. Home loss is also part of the bankruptcy process, despite its potential for helping families save their homes.

The country's foreclosure crisis began in 2007, and very high rates of foreclosure continue into 2012. Millions of homeowners have been and probably will be forced out of their homes, despite some programs aimed at loan modification or foreclosure prevention. Home loss, forced relocation, and downward mobility of this magnitude are uncharted territory. Scholars and policymakers need to look closely at the process of home loss to find ways to ease the painful path out of homeownership. Melissa Jacoby has suggested that the goals commonly cited to justify governmental promotion of home ownership and mortgage lending, such as wealth building, positive social and psychological states, and community stability, could also be furthered by better exit strategies for homeowners saddled with unsustainable housing debt.[33] Designing these strategies is an urgent task.

Two policies worth considering are providing more affordable rental housing and providing more publicity on available emergency assistance. A possible source of additional rental housing is the ever-growing inventory of foreclosed homes. One promising model would have investors purchase loans from securitized trusts and hire local nonprofit organizations to manage the homes as rental property. Former owners could stay on as renters and avoid the multiple moves that too often follow foreclosure. Some of these renters, those whose long-term financial situation is less dire, might be good candidates for an option to purchase.[34]

People recently forced from their homes because of financial problems may have had little or no prior contact with emergency assistance programs and may not know about public benefits available to them. For example, how many parents now doubling up with relatives would guess that the

McKinney-Vento Act might give their children free rides to their old school even though they now live outside that school's boundaries?[35]

The empirical data on home loss among bankruptcy debtors provide some insights into where homeowners go after foreclosure and the harms that home loss impose on them. The data suggest that home loss will likely continue far into the future, particularly affecting some of America's most vulnerable citizens, such as parents of young children, the disabled, and older citizens. This chapter's findings, combined with further work, could help undergird policy initiatives to soften home loss, one of the harshest consequences of the housing crisis.

CHAPTER EIGHT

Women's Work, Women's Worry?

Debt Management in Financially Distressed Families

Deborah Thorne

Traci and Rick were in their late thirties when they filed for bankruptcy. At the time, they lived in a modestly furnished older home, drove a high-mileage station wagon, and had three children. Rick had spent most of his adult life as a salesman for various auto parts stores; unfortunately, when his most recent employer went bankrupt, he was out of a job. Rick eventually found part-time employment at Costco and also worked nights and weekends out of his garage as a mechanic. Traci had an associate's degree in business from a local community college and worked as an office assistant and delivery driver for an auto parts store.

Traci had always managed the family's bills. Rick would thumb through them when they came in the mail, but figuring out how to pay them and eventually dealing with debt collectors was his wife's job. As they edged toward bankruptcy, the stress of unmanageable debts, collection calls, threats of wage garnishment, and the possibility of losing their home in foreclosure became virtually unbearable for Traci. Her feelings of despair over their financial situation left her wishing for death:

> When I went in for surgery, I prayed to God that I didn't wake up. That I never came out of it. I just didn't want to come home. . . . I wanted to have an easy suicide. I really, I was to that point where I hoped they'd get in there and something bad would go wrong and it would be done. I remember waking up and thinking "Oh shit! I'm still here." . . . I didn't want to live. I didn't want to wake up. . . . I wanted them to wheel me away and I'd never have to come home. And that was a lazy, easy, selfish way out [*she begins crying*], but that was the only way. For me.

Rick acknowledged that he was unfamiliar with their finances: "I guess I just never realized before how much it costs . . . for everyday stuff." Consequently, his emotional distress did not begin until Traci told him that, from her perspective, bankruptcy was their only option. Mostly, he was angry that she had not shared the extent of their financial problems with him sooner. "I never realized how bad it really was, until it was horrible," he said. "All I knew is, I went to work and I was making money working on cars on the side and doing everything I could, and I thought everything was, well, that at least we were staying afloat. And that wasn't the case at all."

Rick and Traci both talked openly about the ways in which the strain of the debts taxed their marriage. "I'd have to say that things were not nice around here at that time," Traci said. "It wasn't fighting, but Rick hid in the garage and I hid in the house and we never talked. It was safer that way. We don't fight, we just suffer." Rick concurred: "Things were horrible. Yeah, oh, there was a lot of times of sleeping on the couch, things like that. It just caused a lot of stress. . . . July was our fifteenth wedding anniversary and we've been through a lot, but that [the bankruptcy] was probably, by far, absolutely the most horrible thing."

Traci and Rick told me their story in 1999, when I interviewed nineteen recently bankrupt couples in Spokane, Washington, to explore whether the experience of bankruptcy was gendered and how it affected marital relationships. Three-quarters of these couples described a gendered division of household financial labor similar to Traci and Rick's: before they filed for bankruptcy, the wives paid the bills and managed the household debts.[1] Furthermore, wives, much more than their husbands, reported that pre-bankruptcy financial difficulties caused them considerable emotional distress. And finally, similar to Traci and Rick, the strain of the debts severely undermined many of the couples' relationships.

In this chapter, I analyze data from the 2007 Consumer Bankruptcy Project (CBP) to determine how accurately these earlier qualitative findings reflect the experiences of the hundreds of thousands of American couples who file for bankruptcy each year.[2] For example, among couples who are on the cusp of consumer bankruptcy, who manages the chore of paying bills? My earlier research suggests that most couples who file for bankruptcy use a wife-only configuration for paying bills, rather than equally sharing this chore or adopting a husband-only configuration. Evidence of a wife-only bill-paying configuration would expand the existing literature that concludes that in lower income households, but not necessarily those that are severely indebted, women are disproportionately responsible for managing the money.[3]

Existing literature also suggests that during financial hardship and when debts are in default, feelings of stress and anxiety are elevated.[4] Findings discussed in this chapter probe whether wives experience emotional distress before bankruptcy more than husbands, and if so, whether greater rates of emotional distress are associated with bill-paying responsibilities. On the one hand, Traci's story, as well as the stories of many of the other women I interviewed in 1999, suggests that unmanageable debt burdens are particularly emotionally distressful for women. Furthermore, women's primary role as bill payers may be associated with their emotional distress. Researchers have found that low-control chores correlate with psychological distress,[5] and paying bills in a severely indebted household is inarguably a low-control activity that permits little discretion or economic empowerment. On the other hand, since bankruptcy remains stigmatized,[6] husbands may feel that the financial failure of bankruptcy implies an inability on their part to provide for their families; thus, husbands may be more likely to experience emotional distress. Another possibility is that among couples who share the bill-paying responsibilities equally, the proverb "many hands make light work" may serve to effectively equalize the emotional distress that wives and husbands experience.

In contexts other than bankruptcy, researchers have documented that financial problems take a considerable toll on marital relationships.[7] Among scholars who study consumer bankruptcy, there is consensus that the financial problems that typically precede bankruptcy correlate with marital discord and divorce.[8] The current study confirms that the pressures of debts that occur before bankruptcy cause extreme marital strain. It also extends these findings to explore whether husbands and wives experience marital strain equally, whether bill-paying responsibilities are correlated with marital satisfaction, and whether marital satisfaction improves with bankruptcy and debt relief. Finally, the results presented in this chapter suggest a causal relationship between prebankruptcy financial pressures and separation and divorce. This chapter's data illuminate the human costs of financial distress on women and men.

BILL PAYING IS WOMEN'S WORK

Over the past two decades, studies on the household division of labor have focused chiefly on the amount of time spent on, and sex-typing of, household chores. Two enduring patterns have emerged. First, although men have slightly increased the amount of time they spend on household chores, women continue to do the lion's share.[9] Second, chores remain doggedly sex-typed.[10] Specifically, women tend to be responsible for low-control chores that have limited discretion or autonomy. Low-control chores must be "performed under the pressure of time and urgency; the evening meal, for example, has to be prepared and cleaned up after work, regardless of how tired one is—it cannot be postponed until the weekend."[11] In contrast, high-control chores, such as home, car, and lawn maintenance, are more discretionary, are performed less frequently and often on weekends, and are generally the domain of men.

Managing the bills, especially in households on the precipice of bankruptcy, exemplifies a low-control chore. Since virtually every dollar is spoken for before it is earned in such households, there is little discretion or autonomy over where and how to spend or invest. Payment due dates are nonnegotiable, as the phone calls and dunning letters from debt collectors remind people. Late or missed payments often result in increased interest rates, fees, wage garnishments, discontinuation of utilities, repossession of property, or foreclosure.

Scholars whose research is not limited to financially distressed families conclude that paying bills is gender neutral and generally equally shared—women and men are similarly likely to have responsibility for this chore.[12] Other scholars suggest that when household income is limited or inadequate, the financial labor becomes gendered and shifts to women.[13] This transition from an equally shared to a wife-only chore configuration is consistent with the expectation that within financially distressed households paying bills is a low-control chore.

Data from the CBP suggest that before bankruptcy, when debts routinely outstrip income, it is overwhelmingly wives who are responsible for the chore of paying the bills: more than half of the respondents (52.0 percent) reported a wife-only configuration. One-quarter (25.1 percent) described a husband-only configuration, while the remaining couples (22.9 percent) reported that they share the bill-paying responsibilities equally. Consequently, women *alone* are twice as likely to shoulder the bill-paying responsibilities during the period before bankruptcy—when debt collectors are calling; income is far short of debt burdens; and couples are at risk of lawsuits, wage garnishments, or repossession of their property. These findings suggest that within these severely financially strained households, the low-control chore of paying bills is *not* gender neutral; instead, it is overwhelmingly women's work.

The data also suggest that the struggle to meet financial obligations is frequently a protracted one—despite (erroneous) assumptions that bankruptcy is a first course of action for indebted households. Seven of ten couples (70.8 percent) seriously struggled with their debts for one year or more before they filed for bankruptcy. The time they spent trying to repay the debts does not differ by bill-paying configuration; women and men who paid the bills alone and couples who shared this chore were equally likely to have worked hard for at least a year to avoid bankruptcy. However, since wives are most often in charge of paying the bills, it is their labor, much more than their husband's, which is exacted in a lengthy, but eventually futile, financial battle.

THE EMOTIONAL DISTRESS OF FINANCIAL PROBLEMS
IS WOMEN'S WORRY

Numerous studies have concluded that unmanageable debt is associated with increased emotional distress. Robert Peirce and colleagues report that financial hardship is a leading source of stress.[14] Patricia Drentea asserts that when payments are in default and debt loads increase, debtors' anxiety is elevated.[15] Still other research concludes that financial strain is positively correlated with depression.[16]

At the time of couples' bankruptcies, their financial circumstances were abysmal. For example, they had a median *unsecured* debt-to-income ratio of 1.27. In other words, these families owed unsecured debts, such as credit card bills and medical bills, equal to approximately sixteen months of their pretax income. The median *total* debt-to-income ratio, which also included secured loans such as mortgages and car loans, was 3.53. Thus, if they put *all* of their pretax income toward repaying their debts, reduced ongoing expenses to zero, and incurred no additional debt whatsoever, it would take three and a half years for these families to repay what they owed. This level of financial hardship suggests that these couples were exceptionally vulnerable to severe emotional distress before bankruptcy.

Results from Traci and Rick's interview, as well as from many of the other interviews in my 1999 study, suggested a trend: women, much more than men, asserted that the couples' financial circumstances caused them substantial emotional distress.[17] The large, national sample of the 2007 CBP allowed for a more rigorous examination of experiences of emotional distress. Since low-control chores generally correlate with psychological distress,[18] I hypothesized that, regardless of gender, the spouse who was responsible for the bills would experience the most emotional distress. Another plausible hypothesis, however, was that the distress affiliated with the financial failure of bankruptcy may be gendered: that is, the norm of male-as-breadwinner may increase the likelihood that husbands felt shame and thus more distress. Finally, I anticipated that couples who shared the financial chores would report the lowest levels of emotional distress because the financial responsibilities and associated strain were diffused between the couple rather than shouldered by only one spouse.

In order to measure emotional distress before bankruptcy, CBP respondents were asked:

- How stressed were you about your household finances immediately before bankruptcy?
- How likely were you to *lie awake at night and worry* about your financial situation immediately before bankruptcy?
- How *depressed* did you feel immediately before bankruptcy?[19]

These questions were asked of all coupled CBP respondents: those who were solely responsible for paying bills (wife-only and husband-only configurations), those who shared the chore equally with their spouses (equally shared configuration), and those who were not at all involved with paying bills because their spouses handled the chore.

Collectively, the findings across all three measures of emotional distress—stress, insomnia, and depression—were unexpected. First, on virtually all of the emotional distress variables, and regardless of sex, levels of emotional distress were not significantly affected by debt-paying configurations. Second, wives, *regardless of their debt-paying configuration*, were significantly more likely than husbands to report that household financial circumstances caused them considerable emotional distress before bankruptcy. Put another way, the distress associated with severe indebtedness is gendered, with wives disproportionately reporting stress, insomnia, and depression.

Stress

Along with shockingly high debt burdens, results suggest that stress is one of the most commonly shared characteristics among people who seek bankruptcy relief, regardless of their sex. Before filing for bankruptcy, 87.4 percent of all coupled respondents reported being very stressed over their finances; another 10.2 percent were somewhat stressed. Only a very small percentage (2.4 percent) reported that their household finances did not cause them any stress at all. Clearly, the year before bankruptcy is highly stressful.

When reports of stress are parsed by bill-paying configuration and sex, significant differences exist only between the sexes. Specifically, 92.9 percent of women, versus 79.4 percent of men, reported being very stressed (see Table 8.1)—a difference of 13.5 percentage points. These results strongly suggest that, among couples, women are considerably more stressed about finances before bankruptcy than are men.

Although stress levels for neither women nor men differed significantly by bill-paying configuration, it is interesting that women who managed the debts with their husbands were the most likely to report being very stressed. This unexpected result challenges the hypothesis that working as a team alleviates the stress of paying bills, especially for women. Among women, those who were not involved with the bills (husband-only configuration) were most likely to report not being stressed at all—although it was only a modest 4.7 percent who were not stressed. With their husbands solely responsible for paying bills, women may be less aware of the severity of their financial problems and therefore less likely to experience stress.

TABLE 8.I
Level of stress over finances before bankruptcy, by sex and
bill-paying configuration

	Very stressed (%)	Somewhat stressed (%)	Not at all stressed (%)
All respondents by sex***			
Women	92.9	5.2	1.9
Men	79.4	17.4	3.2
Bill-paying configuration			
	Female respondents' level of stress		
Wife pays bills	92.9	5.7	1.4
Wife and husband both pay bills	97.0	1.5	1.5
Wife does not pay bills	86.0	9.3	4.7
	Male respondents' level of stress		
Husband pays bills	76.1	20.7	3.3
Husband and wife both pay bills	78.9	17.5	3.5
Husband does not pay bills	84.1	13.0	2.9

SOURCE: Consumer Bankruptcy Project 2007.
NOTE: N = 541.
***$p < 0.001$, ordinal regression.

When asked about their stress levels, many respondents volunteered details of how the stress was manifested in their lives. Some described it as one of the worst things they had ever experienced. For example, a fifty-five-year-old woman compared the stress of her family's financial situation to a death sentence: "I hope I am never put in that position again. . . . It was like I had been handed a death sentence. I don't know if I could pull myself out again. It was like self-destruction. I don't want to ever be there again, or put myself there again. It was the hardest thing I ever went through." For many other people, the stress caused psychological and physical ailments. A small-business owner was prescribed medications and experienced unmanageable psychological problems because of the stress of his financial situation: "I'm on four different medications. I went into deep depression, anxiety attacks, sleeplessness. One month ago I was rushed to the hospital with all kinds of different symptoms . . . they ran all kinds of tests and they all came back negative and it was attributed to stress, worrying about the family and losing the house and what the future might bring and not being able to get a new job, even a minimal retail job."

Several other respondents said that the stress caused their blood pressure to spike to dangerously high levels. A woman whose husband's hours at a beef-processing plant were cut during the mad cow disease scare insisted that the stress of their bills affected her blood pressure: "I normally have high blood pressure, but right before we filed [for bankruptcy] my blood pressure went up from 160 to over 200 and they couldn't get it back down." Other people experienced heart problems that they attributed to the stress of their debts. A man from Ohio, who was otherwise healthy, explained that stress caused him to have a heart attack:

> Well, I was focused on how to get out of the bills. I am a very moral person. That's why I put off declaring bankruptcy. But I was so far down that I could see no way out. I believe filing [for] bankruptcy is morally wrong and I still believe it. But they were going to garnish my wages at sixty-two, and they could garnish my wages for my whole life and I'd never be out of the hole. The stress contributed to my heart attack. I'm not overweight and I exercise regularly.

Although women were significantly more likely than men to experience very high stress because of the worry over finances, the majority of coupled respondents, regardless of sex and bill-paying configuration, were highly stressed. For some, the stress was experienced as an overwhelming emotional burden. For others, the stress took a considerable physical toll.

Insomnia

A 2009 study by the National Sleep Foundation concluded that almost one-third of Americans lose sleep because of worries over "money issues."[20] As a result of this sleeplessness, Americans are "much less likely to work efficiently, exercise, eat healthy, and have sex."[21] People who file for bankruptcy also report that they are losing sleep—but at considerably higher rates. As a group, just over 70 percent (71.7 percent) of coupled respondents said that before their bankruptcies they were very likely to lie awake at night and worry about their finances; only about one in ten (11.7 percent) reported no loss of sleep.

Again, the significant difference is between women and men, rather than between those spouses who pay the bills and those who do not.[22] As shown in Table 8.2, the gender differences for insomnia are even greater than the gender differences for stress. More than three-quarters (78.4 percent) of women were very likely to lose sleep because of worry over the bills, whereas only six in ten men (61.0 percent) reported a similar reaction—a difference of 17 percentage points. A very small percentage of women, about seven out of every one hundred, was not at all likely to lose sleep over the finances. In contrast, men were more than twice as likely to report no lost sleep; seventeen of every one hundred men indicated they did not lie awake at night worrying. These results suggest that before bankruptcy, wives, significantly more than husbands, lie awake at night worrying about the couples' dire financial situation.

TABLE 8.2
Likelihood of lying awake at night worrying about finances,
by sex and bill-paying configuration

	Very likely (%)	Somewhat likely (%)	Not at all likely (%)
All respondents by sex***			
Women	78.4	13.9	7.7
Men	61.0	21.6	17.4
Bill-paying configuration			
	Female respondents' likelihood of lying awake		
Wife pays bills	81.6	12.3	6.1
Wife and husband both pay bills	76.1	17.9	6.0
Wife does not pay bills	65.1	16.3	18.6**
	Male respondents' likelihood of lying awake		
Husband pays bills	56.5	26.1	17.4
Husband and wife both pay bills	64.9	14.0	21.1
Husband does not pay bills	63.8	21.7	14.5

SOURCE: Consumer Bankruptcy Project 2007.
NOTE: N = 541.
**$p < 0.01$, ***$p < 0.001$; ordinal regression.

Again, some respondents were willing to describe the insomnia that resulted from their financial worries. For example, a police officer said: "It was the stress of it all. It really affected me, always thinking about it. I couldn't sleep. I still don't sleep too well because of [the debts and the bankruptcy]." Others described physical effects from the sleep deprivation. A middle-aged woman from Chicago who filed for bankruptcy primarily for medical reasons said: "I lost a lot of weight. My hair fell out. I wasn't sleeping. My nerves. I was so ashamed." A father of five talked about how the lack of sleep made him sick: "When you can't meet your bills and obligations, the stress makes you sick. You can't sleep or eat right." A thirty-two-year-old administrative assistant indicated that insomnia undermined her effectiveness at work, as well as her health: "The stress caused lack of sleep, which caused lack of focus at work. It also caused me not to eat, and when I don't eat then I get sick." Still other respondents said that when the worry about the debts became unbearable, they relied on sleeping pills. Assuming that the medications were effective, the frequency of insomnia might actually be underreported.

Depression

Like stress and insomnia, bankruptcy also appears to be correlated with depression. Half of all coupled respondents indicated that before they filed for bankruptcy they were very depressed; just over one-third (36.5 percent) were somewhat depressed. Only one in eight (12.6 percent) were not at all depressed. Comments from respondents suggest that a sense of failure is often at the heart of their depression, and sometimes that sense of failure stems from an inability to provide for the family. For example, a married woman with two children, one of whom was born with a terminal genetic illness that led to overwhelming medical bills, said: "I felt like I couldn't do the things I was supposed to do, like paying bills and taking care of my family. I wanted to do those things, but I felt like I wasn't. I felt really bad about that." A forty-six-year-old father also believed that he had let his family down: "I had been promising my oldest boy that we would get our own house and nobody would tell us to leave again. But here I was, back under somebody's thumb. Feelings of failure and of letting my family down."

Other comments suggest that feelings of failure result from respondents' inability to repay their debts. A seventy-four-year-old man who filed for bankruptcy because the payment on his adjustable-rate mortgage had doubled said: "I thought I was a man of integrity. And when I couldn't pay my debts and bills, I was very depressed."

Many people described how their depression grew from feelings of despair and the futility of their situations; they concluded that regardless of how long or hard they worked to repay their debts, their efforts would be pointless and they would never regain their financial footing. For example, a college-educated mother of a toddler said that she was depressed because it seemed that she "was never going to get out of the hole." A man from the Midwest who filed primarily because of medical bills associated with his wife's diabetes said: "I felt like I was sinking and there was nothing I could do about it. The income didn't match the debt. I could never level off and reverse the process."

Finally, many people insisted that the shame associated with bankruptcy was central to their depression. A wife and mother in her mid-forties said that she was depressed because she thought that "people were going to think I was a bad person." A retired woman who had worked as a mediator, teacher, and psychotherapist also explained her depression as a result of poor self-esteem because of financial failure: "It was something I didn't want people to know about and it was completely foreign to how I felt about myself and how I had lived my life." A middle-aged man who lived on disability benefits reported being very depressed for similar reasons: "We felt ashamed—and having to have family know [about the bankruptcy] and my wife's family looking down on us." A thirty-two-year-old insurance salesman echoed this connection between depression and shame: "You are ashamed. Again, who do you talk to or lean on? Because there is a stigma with bankruptcy! You feel it's 100 percent your fault. So who do you go to for sympathy?"

TABLE 8.3
Level of depression, by sex and bill-paying configuration

	Very depressed (%)	Somewhat depressed (%)	Not at all depressed (%)
All respondents by sex***			
Women	57.1	33.6	9.3
Men	42.2	40.4	17.4
Bill-paying configuration			
	Female respondents' likelihood of lying awake		
Wife pays bills			
Wife and husband both pay bills	56.7	28.4	14.9
Wife does not pay bills	58.1	27.9	14.0
	Male respondents' likelihood of lying awake		
Husband pays bills	37.0	39.1	23.9
Husband and wife both pay bills	40.4	43.9	15.8
Husband does not pay bills	50.7	39.1	10.1

SOURCE: Consumer Bankruptcy Project 2007.
NOTE: N = 541.
***$p < 0.001$; ordinal regression.

As with the two previous indicators of emotional distress—stress and insomnia—the findings suggest that depression is a strongly gendered response to severe indebtedness. As Table 8.3 illustrates, women, regardless of bill-paying responsibility, were significantly more likely to experience high levels of depression before bankruptcy than were men: 57.1 percent of women, but only 42.2 percent of men, reported being very depressed. Conversely, men (17.4 percent) were almost twice as likely as women (9.3 percent) to say that they did not experience any depression at all. Like women, men's rate of self-reported depression was not associated with bill-paying configuration.

MARITAL STRAIN AND BANKRUPTCY RELIEF

As Rick and Traci's story at the beginning of this chapter illustrates, financial strain can critically undermine marital relationships. Indeed, research over the past thirty years has consistently demonstrated that financial hardship is a powerful destabilizing element in couples' relationships.[23] For example, David Caplovitz reported that the recession and inflation of the 1970s increased marital strain, especially for blue-collar and poor families.[24] Results from the Iowa Youth and Families Project reached a similar conclusion about the detrimental effects of the farm crisis of the 1980s: economic pressures damaged emotional well-being, often resulting in marital instability and dissatisfaction, increased conflict, and deceased warmth and support between couples.[25] More recently, Jeffrey Dew concluded that consumer debt predicts increased marital conflict.[26] Studying marital satisfaction among bankrupt couples provides an unprecedented opportunity to extend our understanding of how extraordinary, but increasingly more common, debt loads can affect couples' relationships.

Increased Tension and More Frequent Arguments

Findings from the 2007 CBP suggest that the period before bankruptcy is exceptionally trying for many marriages, causing elevated tension, increased arguments, and even separation and divorce. Indeed, eight of every ten coupled respondents (80.7 percent) stated that, because of the financial pressures that preceded their bankruptcies, they experienced increased tension and more frequent arguments with their spouses. For example, a wife and mother of a teenaged daughter said that she and her husband "couldn't sleep because we were always arguing and yelling about money. We don't do this in front of our daughter, but it can certainly make you stay awake worrying." A male respondent in his mid-sixties who worked as a newspaper reporter described how the strain of the debts taxed his relationship with his wife: "It was harder for us to talk to each other. We were stressed out. Our fuses were shorter so things bothered us to a greater degree than they normally would have. We ended up being at odds over trivial things."

There were no significant differences between women and men on this measure: both sexes were equally likely to report that the financial distress before their bankruptcies caused increased tension and arguments with their spouses. Consequently, while the *emotional* distress before bankruptcy is unquestionably gendered, men and women experience similar levels of *marital* distress before they file for bankruptcy. For couples, financial distress is undeniably a household event: even if only one spouse suffers emotional distress from the pressure of the debts, the strain spills over into the couple's interactions, potentially threatening marriages.

Marital Satisfaction before and after Bankruptcy

A notable percentage of all coupled respondents reported being dissatisfied with their marriages *before* bankruptcy. Specifically, 41.8 percent were either somewhat or not at all satisfied in their relationships, while fewer than six out of ten (58.2 percent) reported they were very satisfied (see Table 8.4). Not surprisingly, there is a significant negative correlation between marital satisfaction before bankruptcy and the amount of financial stress that respondents reported experiencing; specifically, marital satisfaction decreased as the reported level of stress associated with the debts increased.[27]

Although women and men were similarly likely to report that the debts caused increased tension and arguments with their spouses, levels of mari-

TABLE 8.4

Marital satisfaction before and after bankruptcy for
all respondents combined and by sex

Response in relation to the bankruptcy	Very satisfied (%)	Somewhat satisfied (%)	Not at all satisfied (%)
All respondents			
Before***	58.2	27.4	14.4
After***	78.0	19.0	3.0
Women			
Before***	52.0	29.6	18.4
After*	74.6	23.0	2.4
Men			
Before***	67.0	24.3	8.7
After*	82.8	13.3	3.9

SOURCE: Consumer Bankruptcy Project 2007.

NOTE: N = 522 (before bankruptcy); N = 432 (after bankruptcy).

*$p < 0.05$, **$p < 0.01$, ***$p < 0.001$; ordinal regression.

tal satisfaction before bankruptcy were significantly gendered: women were much less likely to be satisfied with their marriages than men. Specifically, women (18.4 percent) were more than twice as likely as men (8.7 percent) to say that they were not at all satisfied with their marriages. Conversely, whereas more than two-thirds of men (67.0 percent) were very satisfied with their marriages, only about half of women (52.0 percent) were similarly satisfied—a 15 percentage point difference. This gendered difference in marital satisfaction does not appear to be sensitive to bill paying, as bill-paying configuration by sex does not produce significant differences between men and women. Regardless of solo or shared bill-paying responsibility, across the board, women reported lower levels of marital satisfaction before the couple filed for bankruptcy.

On a positive note, however, there appears to be a strong correlation between the debt relief that results from bankruptcy and improved marital satisfaction. Among those respondents who were still living with their spouses approximately a year after bankruptcy, more than three-quarters (78.0 percent) were very satisfied with their marriages, whereas only 3.0 percent were dissatisfied. Inarguably, the most optimistic finding here is that before filing for bankruptcy, 14.4 percent of all respondents reported being not at all satisfied in their marriages; however, after filing, only 3.0 percent were not at all satisfied. Put another way, among couples who are still together a year after bankruptcy, filing reduces the likelihood of being not at all satisfied with one's marriage by more than 400 percent.[28] This would suggest that filing for bankruptcy may indeed provide couples with the dual benefits of both a financial fresh start *and* a marital fresh start.

However, marital satisfaction after bankruptcy is significantly gendered. While both sexes are about equally likely to report being not at all satisfied in their marriages, women are 10 percentage points more likely to be only somewhat satisfied and 8 percentage points less likely to be very satisfied. But again, there is a considerable uptick in respondents' reported marital satisfaction, regardless of sex. It does appear that bankruptcy is highly correlated with improved marital satisfaction for both men and women.

As with marital satisfaction before bankruptcy, bill-paying responsibility does not have a significant relationship in men's and women's reports of marital satisfaction after bankruptcy. These data do not support the hypothesized relationship that those who are solely responsible for bills may be particularly likely to experience improved marital satisfaction when the stress of paying those bills is reduced through debt relief. It may well be that the emotional distress of debt problems overwhelms the additional burdens of paying bills, so that bankruptcy relief provides powerful improvements in quality of life to both men and women.

Financial Strain, Divorce, and Separation: A Causal Relationship?

Marriage is a venerated social institution in the United States. For example, in 2007, there were approximately 2.2 million weddings.[29] That same year, three-quarters (or 56 million) of the 75 million family households were married couple households.[30] Despite the country's zeal for marriage, however, Americans also appear to have an affinity for divorce: Robert Schoen and Vladimir Canudas-Romo state that the rate of divorce in the United States exceeds that of all other Western countries.[31] Today, couples are more than twice as likely to divorce as in the 1950s.[32] Schoen and Nicola Standish conclude that 42 to 44 percent of American marriages end in divorce.[33]

Of course, couples divorce for myriad reasons, but the findings presented in this chapter and elsewhere strongly suggest that the financial struggles that precede personal bankruptcy are highly correlated with marital strain and even divorce. However, the issue of causality remains unclear. For that reason, Jonathan Fisher and Angela Lyons have recently called for more research into the "role that financial distress plays within a marriage and how that affects the decision to divorce."[34]

To explore the causal relationship between bankruptcy and divorce, the CBP asked coupled respondents, all of who were married or permanently partnered in the year before their bankruptcies, whether prebankruptcy financial pressures *caused* them to consider separation or divorce.

A disturbing 36 percent, or more than one-third of coupled respondents, said that the fallout from the financial distress before bankruptcy extended beyond tension and arguments and caused them to consider separation or divorce.

Of course, thinking about leaving one's spouse is considerably different from actually doing it. Of the 541 coupled respondents, 98 (18 percent) said that in the year after their bankruptcies they had either divorced or permanently separated from their original partners. And of these divorces and separations, 68 percent were *explicitly* identified as due to the financial pressures that the couple experienced before bankruptcy. This means that one in eight couples (12.5 percent) in the sample separated or divorced *because of* the financial pressures they experienced before bankruptcy. For these couples, the fresh start of bankruptcy came at a substantial cost—their marriages. They may have discharged many of their debts without substantial repayment, but they paid a very high cost in personal terms to do so.

The survey data reveal that just over half (52 percent) of consumer bankruptcies are filed by married or permanently partnered couples. This suggests that of the approximately 822,000 households that filed for bankruptcy in 2007,[35] roughly 103,000 couples would have divorced or separated primarily because of the stress of the debts. Unfortunately, as the number of consumer bankruptcies continues to climb, surpassing the one million mark in 2009, it is likely that the number of divorces and separations caused by the financial strain that precedes bankruptcy will accelerate at a similar rate.

Comments from respondents describe quite clearly how financial stress undermines and causes irreparable damage to relationships. A woman who worked as a school counselor and was a mother of a four-year-old boy said that because of the strain of the debts, she and her husband separated: "We didn't separate before the bankruptcy, but we did after we filed. It had really damaged our relationship and it could never be the same. I felt I had to move out and take my young son because it was affecting him so much too." A man who worked on an assembly line insisted that his divorce was the direct result of financial strain: "We were not divorced before we filed, but the money pressures caused us to separate and divorce after the bankruptcy was filed." In part because of their financial problems, and despite sharply eroding marital satisfaction, many couples may stay married until after their bankruptcy is filed.

In a nutshell, the findings suggest that, particularly for women, the severe indebtedness that precedes bankruptcy undercuts marital satisfaction. The strain of the debt causes increased tension and arguments and results in more than one in eight couples either divorced or separated in the first year after bankruptcy. However, among couples who remain married, it appears that the debt relief of bankruptcy translates into increased marital satisfaction for both women and men.

DISCUSSION

Data from this study show that among coupled respondents, regardless of sex or bill-paying responsibility, severe financial strain was highly correlated with emotional distress, and the majority of *both* men and women experienced stress, insomnia, and depression before filing for bankruptcy. Virtually all respondents (98 percent) indicated that, because of their dire financial situations, they were very much or somewhat stressed; more than 75 percent reported being very much or somewhat likely to lie awake at night worrying about the bills; and more than 85 percent were very much or somewhat depressed before filing for bankruptcy. The debt problems also negatively affected marriages, with more than eight in ten respondents saying that financial pressures caused increased tension and arguments with their spouses or partners, and one in eight couples divorcing or separating explicitly because of the financial pressures before bankruptcy. When it comes to emotional distress and marital discord before bankruptcy, husbands and wives both suffer.

However, the findings also reveal that personal bankruptcy is a gendered experience. Among the bankrupt couples, women were significantly more likely to be responsible for paying the household bills as the family struggled to make ends meet before bankruptcy, women were significantly more likely to experience emotional distress before bankruptcy, and women were significantly more dissatisfied with their marriages before (and even after) bankruptcy. Elizabeth Warren has argued that bankruptcy is a women's issue; specifically, she asserts that women are overrepresented in consumer bankruptcy as a demographic matter.[36] My findings suggest that the *experience* of financial distress and bankruptcy is itself gendered: not only are women disproportionately more likely to go bankrupt, they appear to be disproportionately more likely to suffer from the experience.

Scholars who study working-class households conclude that when money is limited, the chore of managing the bills is women's work. My results provide additional support for the prevalence of such a relationship. Bankrupt households reported a gendered division of bill-paying responsibilities. Because bankruptcy couples were in extreme financial distress—indeed, they had just declared their situations hopeless and asked for legal relief—some caution is warranted in generalizing the findings to households whose financial distress may be less acute, such as those who live paycheck-to-paycheck or those with low incomes but little or no debt. And while bankrupt house-holds divided the chore of paying bills in a gendered way, there were very few significant associations between bill-paying responsibility and emotional distress or marital satisfaction. Those phenomena were certainly gendered, but bill-paying responsibility did not appear to exacerbate such effects in measurable ways.

In 2005, the bankruptcy laws were amended. As a result of these re-forms, it became more expensive, difficult, and time-consuming to file for bankruptcy. Research suggests that the reforms had several deleterious consequences for consumers, not the least of which were significant in-creases in the amount of debt that households accumulated before seeking bankruptcy relief and increases in the percentage of households that post-poned filing for bankruptcy.[37] Essentially, the reforms created barriers that caused couples to struggle for longer periods of time while trying to repay their debts. Ronald Mann argues that a primary objective of the reforms was to delay filings, thus increasing lenders' profits by trapping borrow-ers in a "sweat box" of debt.[38] Given my findings, however, women and men do not sweat equally—women sweat more. When a family postpones bankruptcy, most often it is women who shoulder the burden of trying to make ends meet. And during this extended period of financial struggle, women are most likely to suffer emotional distress such as stress, insomnia, and depression and experience lower rates of marital satisfaction. These findings highlight the ways in which severe financial strain—the type of financial strain that often precedes bankruptcy—is a women's issue. The bankruptcy reforms may not have intentionally targeted women, but the data suggest it is women who suffer disproportionate harm as a result of the reforms.

This chapter also reports on the ways in which the massive debt often associated with bankruptcy, and the act of filing for bankruptcy, appear to affect marriages. On the one hand, the data strongly suggest that the financial strain experienced by bankrupt households may weaken and even destroy marriages and partnerships. On the other hand, at least among those couples whose relationships can withstand it, filing for bankruptcy may ac-tually improve marital satisfaction and even salvage some marriages that were initially in trouble because of financial distress. Unfortunately, if the bankruptcy reforms do indeed cause couples to postpone filing, one impli-cation may well be delayed relief from marital discord—and an extended period of fighting and tension before bankruptcy may, tragically, exacerbate the connection between financial distress and marital dissolution. Conse-quently, easing access to bankruptcy may actually reduce the number of marriages that are damaged past the point of repair from debt distress.

In many ways, the opening story of Rick and Traci is fairly representative of couples who file for bankruptcy, as measured by the CBP data. Like Traci, women tended to be responsible for managing the bills, and they were also more likely to report emotional distress. And Rick and Traci's marriage, like those of the majority of couples in the study, was assaulted by the strain of their unmanageable debts. For most couples, emotional distress and marital satisfaction improved after bankruptcy—their emotional lives and financial lives moved in tandem. However, Rick and Traci's story is a powerful reminder that for a considerable proportion of bankrupt couples, the fissures in their marriages that resulted from the unmanageable and overwhelming debts often caused irreparable damage. Traci wept when she explained that although she and Rick were still married, their relationship was in tatters, and they could not afford to divorce: "We're stuck. . . . We'll figure out what's left of this marriage and work from there. Because we can't afford to be apart or mean to each other at this point. We can't afford it. . . . Every day, I want out. . . . You're just kind of holding your breath. Status quo. It's not getting worse, but it's not going anywhere."

PART IV

THE HARD ROAD OUT

CHAPTER NINE

The Do-It-Yourself Mirage

Complexity in the Bankruptcy System

Angela Littwin

More than a million families declare bankruptcy each year, making it one of the most commonly used legal processes in the United States. At the same time, debtors who seek bankruptcy relief are, by definition, financially constrained and thus struggle to afford the costs associated with the process. The challenge of operating a high-volume legal system used primarily by people who have difficulty paying for lawyers pervades most areas of law that serve individuals, but the bankruptcy system has always faced an additional problem of its own: complexity. From its inception with the U.S. Bankruptcy Code of 1978, the consumer bankruptcy system had elements that were borrowed from business bankruptcy, rather than being specifically designed for individuals. Reforms to bankruptcy law, none of which were simplification efforts, have been layered on top of this initial complexity. The bankruptcy system reached a new peak in complexity with the 2005 amendments, which added more than a dozen ways for debtors to run afoul of technical requirements and thereby have their cases dismissed.

This increased complexity has put particular pressure on one crucial decision that all consumer bankruptcy filers must make: whether to hire a lawyer. What was always a difficult choice has turned into an excruciating one. On the one hand, lawyers' fees have increased to the point at which, in many cases, legal fees are higher than debtors' monthly incomes. At the same time, a do-it-yourself bankruptcy is risky. Errors can cause families to lose their homes or cars, to be denied a discharge of debt, or even to face criminal or civil investigations. Debtors appear to be balancing cost and risk in a nuanced manner. An analysis of who files for bankruptcy pro se—that is, without a lawyer—suggests that both factors play important roles. As one might expect, people who forego a lawyer have lower incomes. More surprisingly, those who file without a lawyer are much better educated than those who use lawyers. This suggests that rather than merely pricing the poorest debtors out of the market for bankruptcy counsel, the high attorneys' fees may have additionally prompted the best-educated debtors to decide that they can manage on their own.

But the bankruptcy system undermines this decision-making process as it is too complex for even well-educated debtors to succeed without lawyers. Data from the 2007 Consumer Bankruptcy Project (CBP) show that pro se debtors fare significantly worse in bankruptcy than their represented counterparts. For example, 20 percent of unrepresented bankruptcy debtors in Chapter 7—the faster and simpler form of bankruptcy—were unable to discharge their debts, compared with just 2 percent of represented debtors. This disparity held even for people with four-year college degrees.

When faced with rising legal fees, some debtors may want a do-it-yourself bankruptcy, but the system thwarts the attempts of even the most sophisticated. The complexity of the process leaves debtors with two inadequate options: pay $1,000 to $3,000 for a bankruptcy lawyer—on top of courts fees and other administrative costs—or try bankruptcy on their own and face high odds of losing their homes, their cars, or their discharge from debt. Of course, there is always a third option, which is foregoing bankruptcy relief altogether.

This chapter examines the choice of whether to hire a bankruptcy lawyer from two perspectives. First, it uses a demographic analysis of who files for bankruptcy without legal representation to explore the factors debtors appear to be considering when making this decision. Second, it shows how complexity undermines debtors' calculations by making bankruptcy too difficult for even the most sophisticated consumer debtors to reliably succeed pro se. The chapter concludes by mentioning potential reforms that could make this decision less painful and decrease debtors' chances of leaving bankruptcy without relief.

FINANCIAL PRESSURE OR EDUCATED CHOICE?
WHO FILES FOR BANKRUPTCY WITHOUT A LAWYER

Consumer bankruptcy filers are trapped between cost and risk when deciding whether to hire a lawyer because legal representation is expensive. Costs rose precipitously in the wake of the 2005 bankruptcy amendments. By 2007, legal fees in many cases were almost as high as debtors' monthly incomes.[1] This raises a concern that debtors are being priced out of the market for legal representation. Data from the 2007 CBP suggest the legitimacy of these concerns. Among the CBP's national, random sample, 3.5 percent of debtors filed for bankruptcy pro se in 2007. Although this percentage may seem small, it is an increase of 75 percent from 2001, when 2 percent of debtors in the CBP sample were unrepresented.[2] Moreover, there were more than 1.4 million consumer bankruptcies in 2009.[3] If the percentage of debtors without representation holds steady, that would represent approximately 45,500 debtors filing without counsel every year.

This is an access-to-justice issue. If debtors are filing without lawyers because lawyers have become unaffordable, the most economically vulnerable debtors will be entering bankruptcy with the deck stacked against them. It is also suggestive of highly constrained choice. If the main factor differentiating debtors who file without lawyers is income, then one inference is that they would not have filed alone if they could have afforded a lawyer. The issue of affordability also makes the increase in pro se filings additionally problematic because the bankruptcy reform of 2005 was supposed to leave untouched the access of poorer debtors to bankruptcy. The goal of the new statute was to screen out only debtors who might have enough income to repay their debts outside of bankruptcy, not lower income debtors who desperately need relief.[4]

Data from the 2007 CBP show that unrepresented debtors had significantly lower incomes at the time of bankruptcy, despite the previously mentioned finding that they were also better educated. This suggests that they lacked the funds to pay for a lawyer. This finding is presented in Table 9.1.[5] The results are shown as odds ratios, which compare the probabilities of certain events occurring under a given set of circumstances. For example, Table 9.1 shows that the odds of non-Hispanic African American debtors using lawyers were about 43 percent less than the odds for white debtors, and that the odds of homeowners having representation were more than four times as high as those of people who did not own homes. The income results are more difficult to explain in plain English. (Because income distributions do not form a bell curve, I had to convert the income data to logs.) But generally speaking, the more income a household had, the greater its odds of hiring representation. These results were statistically significant. The strong relationship between income and legal representation suggests that affordability plays a major role in the decision to hire or forego a bankruptcy lawyer.

Table 9.1 presents three models that show more precisely the relationship between income and the other factors. The first model is a bivariate analysis that includes only income and legal representation. The second adds controls for basic demographic factors, such as race and ethnicity, education, and age. The third includes the demographic variables and also adds the bankruptcy-specific variables of homeownership, prior bankruptcy, whether the household had any assets at the time of bankruptcy, and bankruptcy chapter.

Other financial variables are important in assessing a debtor's financial health, but measures such as assets and debt loads are less likely to be

TABLE 9.1

Odds ratios of bankruptcy debtor having a lawyer by income (logistic regression)

	Bivariate model	Model with demographic variables	Model with demographic and bankruptcy variables
Income (log)	1.263**(0.065)	1.266** (0.066)	1.198** (0.068)
Race and ethnicity			
Non-Hispanic white (ref.)	--	--	--
Non-Hispanic black		0.445**(0.118)	0.426** (0.118)
Other		1.365 (0.480)	1.500 (0.540)
Education			
No college (ref.)	--	--	--
Some college		0.501* (0.167)	0.449* (0.152)
College degree		0.314** (0.113)	0.250** (0.092)
Household age		1.013 (0.010)	1.008 (0.010)
Home ownership			4.331** (2.331)
Prior bankruptcy			0.573 (0.201)
Assets (any assets other than primary residence)			3.381** (1.407)
Chapter 13 case			0.799 (0.314)
Log likelihood	−482.756	−474.692	−450.703
Pseudo R^2	0.0434	0.0594	0.1069

SOURCE: Consumer Bankruptcy Project 2007.

NOTE: n= 2,438 for each model. Coefficients are odds ratios from a logistic regression with a dependent variable of having legal representation. Standard errors are shown in parentheses. Interaction between homeowner and chapter is not statistically significant. A flag variable was added in the model for missing values. None of the differences between missing values and nonmissing values were statistically significant.

*p < 0.05, **p < 0.01.

indicative of a debtor's ability to obtain money for a lawyer's fee. People in bankruptcy tend to have very few assets besides their homes. Selling the home to pay for a bankruptcy lawyer would be unthinkable for the majority of homeowner-debtors who enter bankruptcy primarily to save their homes, and in the recession of the late 2000s, selling the home often was not a viable alternative anyway. Most debtors are so indebted by the time they reach bankruptcy court that borrowing against their homes—or any other assets, for that matter—is rarely an option. In addition, another recent study suggests that two of the main ways debtors obtain the money to hire bankruptcy lawyers are saving over the course of several months and using immediate cash infusions (such as tax refunds and paychecks).[6] Debtors' ability to use either of these approaches depends highly on their incomes.

Furthermore, if debtors look to assets to pay lawyers' fees, pro se bankruptcy filers are, in fact, worse off along this dimension. They had many fewer assets upon arrival in bankruptcy. The median asset value for unrepresented debtors was $25,578, compared with $52,030 for debt-ors with lawyers. These assets were also canceled out by correspondingly larger debt. Unrepresented debtors had a net worth of negative $35,368, compared with the slightly more modest negative $25,757 for represented debtors. The one area where unrepresented debtors appeared to be in better shape was in the ratio of debt to income, which measures how long it would take a debtor to pay off his or her debts if that person used all income to do so. For both types of debtors, this number was more than three years, but it was slightly higher for represented debtors. This probably does not mean that pro se debtors are meaningfully better off in this way. It is most likely a result of the fact that represented debtors are more likely to be homeowners and therefore have much higher levels of secured debt. Thus, a correlation appears to exist between pro se status and particularly severe financial limitations.

But financial indicators are not the entire story. Despite their lower in-comes and less valuable assets, debtors who filed for bankruptcy on their own were significantly better educated than those who used lawyers. This suggests that filing for bankruptcy without a lawyer may have been more of a conscious decision about resource allocation than a simple inability to afford counsel. All of the lower income filers may have considered a do-it-yourself bankruptcy, but only the most educated thought they could succeed.

As Figure 9.1 shows, the more education debtors had, the greater their odds of filing for bankruptcy without legal representation. To analyze edu-cation, I divided the respondents into three categories: those with no college experience, those who had attended college but did not receive a bachelor's degree, and those who obtained a bachelor's degree or higher. These inter-vals seemed to be the intuitive places that would mark shifts in debtors' comfort levels with the legal system or confidence in their ability to navigate it. For households in which the spouses or partners differed in their levels of educational attainment, I categorized the household on the basis of the highest educational attainment of either person on the theory that this best

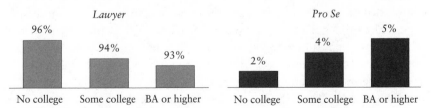

Figure 9.1   Percentage of represented and pro se debtors by educational level
SOURCE: Consumer Bankruptcy Project 2007.

NOTE: n (lawyer) = 2,269; n (pro se) = 81. The difference between "no college" and "BA or higher" for each representation status was significant at $p < 0.001$ (Pearson Chi-square). Totals for each educational category do not equal 100 percent because debtors using nonlawyer petition preparers were excluded.

reflects a household's collective confidence that it can understand the bankruptcy process.[7]

The odds of hiring a lawyer declined with education. Those with college degrees were the most likely to file pro se. Those with no college were the most likely to hire a lawyer. This result remained statistically significant when one controls for demographic and bankruptcy-related variables (see Table 9.1).

That debtors who have pursued more education are more likely to forego legal counsel suggests that it is not simply the lowest-income debtors who are being priced out of this market. Debtors may be weighing the affordability of hiring an attorney against their perceived ability to do the job themselves. Those with more education may have better access to materials such as do-it-yourself books or websites and may have more faith in their ability to use them effectively. Bankruptcy filers are mired in financial distress, and many try to cut any expenses possible during the period before filing. People with college degrees may believe that they can save precious income dollars for food and other necessities by doing the work of filing for bankruptcy themselves.

There is, however, an alternative explanation. It may be the case that, when the lowest-income, least-educated would-be filers learned about the cost and complexity of the bankruptcy process, they decided to forego bankruptcy altogether. Under this hypothesis, if bankruptcy were easier, these lower income would-be filers might have filed pro se. But because this group of debtors was also less educated, they might have been more intimidated by the complexity of the process and thus more likely to decide against bankruptcy instead of risking a pro se filing. With debtors who have lower incomes and lower education not filing, a disproportionate number of higher education debtors are left in the low-income pro se pool.

This possibility, however, seems unlikely to account fully for the inverse relationship between education and pro se status. If lower income, less-educated would-be filers deciding against bankruptcy were driving the education result, we would expect to see a decrease in low-income filers after the 2005 amendments, which dramatically increased the cost and complexity of the process. Instead, the income distribution among bankruptcy filers did not change between 2001 and 2007.[8] In particular, the percentage of bankruptcy filers with lower incomes did not decrease during this period. This suggests that rising attorney's fees, though they may be having other negative effects, are not pushing debtors out of the bankruptcy system altogether. Thus, the hypothesis that increased complexity is driving less-educated, lower income debtors to decline to file for bankruptcy does not seem likely.

The third important factor—homeownership—provides additional support for the idea that, even though financial constraints highly influenced debtors, they still considered factors beyond affordability. As Table 9.1 shows, a household that owned its home was more than three times as likely to hire a lawyer as a non-homeowning household, even when one controls for income, education, and other factors. Owning a home makes a bankruptcy case riskier and more complex. The increase in risk is simply a reflection of the fact that homeowners have more to lose. They rarely arrive in bankruptcy without a mortgage, and many lose their houses to foreclosure despite filing for bankruptcy (see Chapter 7). A debtor worried about losing the family home may be less likely to risk a do-it-yourself bankruptcy. Homeowner bankruptcies also tend to be more complex, requiring more lawyer attention for each case, and are much more likely to be filed under Chapter 13, the more complicated of the two bankruptcy chapters.[9] It is easy to see how debtors with more complex cases might be less confident in their ability to file for bankruptcy themselves.

The final significant variable was race. Even when one controls for the other relevant factors, African American households were more than 50 percent less likely to be represented than households of other races (see Table 9.1). I ran the same regression with Asian American, Hispanic, and multiracial/multiethnic households, but none of these results was significant. The sample of Asian American debtors was probably too small for significant results to be obtained, and the sample of Hispanic debtors may have been too diverse. The potential causes of the lower likelihood of African Americans hiring lawyers are as varied and myriad as they are familiar, including discrimination, geographic disparities in lawyer advertising, social isolation, and distrust of the legal system. Understanding which, if any, of these factors are contributing to the relationship between race and pro se filings would require an in-depth analysis that is beyond the scope of this analysis (see Chapter 10, however, for a discussion of the role of race in consumer bankruptcy).

NEGATIVE OUTCOMES FOR UNREPRESENTED DEBTORS

The complexity of the bankruptcy system undermines debtors' ability to choose successfully between incurring the expense of a lawyer and risking filing for bankruptcy on their own. Pro se debtors have significantly worse case outcomes, and highly educated debtors are no exception. The demographic analysis in the previous section suggests that debtors are weighing the risks of complexity when considering a pro se bankruptcy, but the fact that pro se debtors do so badly in court suggests that they may still be underestimating the difficulty of filing for bankruptcy alone.

The goal of debtors filing for bankruptcy is to obtain a discharge of debt. Once the court grants this discharge, debtors are no longer legally responsible for many of the debts previously acquired. Secured loans such as those on houses and cars must be paid in order to keep the collateral, but most unsecured debts, including credit card debt, are no longer legally binding. Unrepresented debtors were significantly more likely to have their cases dismissed before they received such a discharge or made significant progress toward one.

Since bankruptcy cases proceed differently for Chapter 7 and Chapter 13, the two main consumer bankruptcy chapters, I studied case dispositions separately for each. Chapter 7 is the faster and more commonly used way to discharge debt, although it is usually not recommended for homeowners. The immediate debt relief means that the final outcome for most cases is determined within a few months or a year. Chapter 13 is more homeowner friendly and allows debtors to pay their attorneys in installments, but it requires debtors to repay a substantial portion of their debts over three to five years. Thus, Chapter 13 cases are ongoing for several years after bankruptcy is filed.

In Chapter 7, I coded a debtor receiving a discharge of debts as a positive outcome. If the case was dismissed without a discharge or converted to Chapter 13, I counted it as a negative outcome because the debtor was unable to obtain the debt relief sought. Having a case converted to Chapter 13 means that the debtor would be required to propose a multiyear payment plan and that the bankruptcy discharge would be conditioned on its successful completion. A dismissal without discharge means that the debtor failed to obtain bankruptcy relief altogether. These negative outcomes might occur if, for example, the debtor failed to file the proper documentation or did not meet the eligibility requirements for Chapter 7.

Coding Chapter 13 outcomes was more complicated. Because most Chapter 13 cases take three to five years to complete, final outcomes of these cases were not yet available when data were gathered. There is, however, one earlier important step that can serve as a useful measure of debtor success: the confirmation of a payment plan. Confirmation functions as a gate that screens out a large number of debtors. Without a court-approved plan, a debtor cannot move on to the next phase of Chapter 13 bankruptcy and becomes ineligible for a discharge of debt. So examining which debtors are unable to satisfy this prerequisite allows me to compare debtors who may or may not ultimately reach their final goal with debtors who were unsuccessful early in the case. When the court confirmed a debtor's plan, I recorded that as a positive outcome. If the case was dismissed before a plan could be approved or if the court found the debtor's proposed plan unsatisfactory, I coded this as a negative outcome. There are many other possible results in a Chapter 13 bankruptcy, but I narrowed my analysis to these two because they were the most clearly positive or negative outcomes that happen early in a case.[10]

In Chapter 7 cases, 17.6 percent of unrepresented debtors had their cases dismissed or converted to Chapter 13. In contrast, only 1.9 percent of debtors with lawyers met this fate, a statistically significant difference.[11] A regression analysis estimated that represented debtors were approximately ten times more likely to receive a discharge than their pro se counterparts, even when one controls for other possible contributing factors such as income, education, homeownership, age, race, and prior bankruptcies. Filing pro se dramatically escalated the chance that a Chapter 7 bankruptcy would not provide a person with debt relief. The discharge eluded one in

TABLE 9.2

Odds ratios of positive outcome in Chapter 7 bankruptcy (logistic regression)

	Bivariate model	Model with demographic variables	Model with demographic and bankruptcy variables
Petition preparer	3.830† (3.085)	2.900 (2.378)	2.485 (2.062)
Pro se (ref.)	--	--	--
Lawyer	11.239** (4.463)	8.472** (3.582)	9.540** (4.222)
Race and ethnicity			
Non-Hispanic white (ref.)	--	--	--
Non-Hispanic black		0.566 (0.247)	0.515 (0.231)
Other		0.854 (0.360)	0.820 (0.353)
Education			
No college (ref.)	--	--	--
Some college		0.702 (0.296)	0.677 (0.295)
College degree		0.427† (0.195)	0.413† (0.196)
Income (log)		1.063 (0.093)	1.097 (0.096)
Household age		1.000 (0.013)	1.005 (0.014)
Home ownership			1.265 (1.011)
Prior bankruptcy			0.536 (0.355)
Assets (any assets other than primary residence)			0.753 (0.527)
Forms and schedules			
All missing (ref.)	--	--	--
Some or all completed			29.463** (25.288)
Log likelihood	−173.643	−168.272	−163.211
Pseudo R^2	0.0719	0.1006	0.1277

SOURCE: Consumer Bankruptcy Project 2007.

NOTE: n = 1,602 for each model. Coefficients are odds ratios from a logistic regression with a dependent variable of having a positive outcome in Chapter 7 bankruptcy. Standard errors are in parentheses. Interaction between homeowner and chapter is not statistically significant. A flag variable was added in the model for missing values. None of the differences between missing values and nonmissing values were statistically significant.

† $p < 0.10$, * $p < 0.05$, ** $p < 0.01$.

five people who tried a do-it-yourself Chapter 7 bankruptcy (see Table 9.2). The results for Chapter 13 cases were even more striking. It was nearly impossible for a pro se debtor to confirm a plan; a full 91.3 percent of these cases were dismissed before confirmation. Among debtors with lawyers, the failure rate was only 14.9 percent, a statistically significant difference.[12] When one controls for the same factors as in the Chapter 7 regression, represented Chapter 13 debtors were approximately forty-five times more likely to confirm payment plans than their pro se counterparts (see Table 9.3). Chapter 13, the more complex of the two forms of con-

TABLE 9.3

Odds ratios of posiotive outcome in Chapter 13 bankruptcy (logistic regression)

	Bivariate model	Model with demographic variables	Model with demographic and bankruptcy variables
Petition preparer	13.125** (13.109)	12.251* (13.282)	10.980* (11.875)
Pro se (ref.)	--	--	--
Lawyer	60.187** (44.964)	38.752** (30.202)	44.826** (35.728)
Race and ethnicity			
Non-Hispanic white (ref.)	--	--	--
Non-Hispanic black		0.741 (0.180)	0.807 (0.202)
Other		0.964 (0.278)	0.974 (0.283)
Education			
No college (ref.)	--	--	--
Some college		0.876 (0.219)	0.917 (0.231)
College degree		0.683 (0.208)	0.698 (0.215)
Income (log)		0.989 (0.184)	1.184 (0.253)
Household age		1.001 (0.010)	1.003 (0.010)
Home ownership			0.506 (0.348)
Prior bankruptcy			0.852 (0.195)
Assets (any assets other than primary residence)			1.127 (0.276)
Forms and schedules			
All missing (ref.)	--	--	--
Some or all completed			0.293 (0.440)
Log likelihood	–329.786	–311.437	–305.275
Pseudo R^2	0.0931	0.1435	0.1605

SOURCE: Consumer Bankruptcy Project 2007.

NOTE: n = 786 for each model. Coefficients are odds ratios from a logistic regression with a dependent variable of having a positive outcome in Chapter 13 bankruptcy. Standard errors in parentheses. Interaction between homeowner and chapter is not statistically significant. A flag variable was added in the model for missing values. None of the differences between missing values and nonmissing values were statistically significant.

*$p < 0.05$, **$p < 0.01$.

sumer bankruptcy, correspondingly creates more obstacles for success for people without lawyers.

Having a better education did not protect unrepresented debtors from dismissal. In both bankruptcy chapters, college-educated pro se debtors with four-year degrees did not fare any better than their counterparts with some college or no college. As Table 9.2 shows, education was not a statistically significant predictor of a Chapter 7 debtor receiving a discharge. Similarly, Table 9.3 shows that education did not help pro se debtors avoid preconfirmation dismissal in Chapter 13 either.

Education does not safeguard debtors against a negative outcome in bankruptcy. Well-educated debtors may be more apt to attempt bankruptcy without legal assistance, but they are no more likely to succeed. This is the mirage of do-it-yourself bankruptcy. The system appears to be defeating the efforts even of college graduates, the group of laypeople who should be best equipped to navigate it.

ACCOUNTING FOR THE NEGATIVE OUTCOMES

Filing a bankruptcy case is not easy. It has always been a detail-oriented process, and the 2005 amendments added a number of provisions that require automatic dismissal when the debtor fails to file certain documentation or complete certain procedural steps. The possible mistakes and omissions range from failing to file pay stubs or update tax records to filling out forms incorrectly to missing the deadline for stating whether the debtor intends to surrender his or her house or car.

These procedural hurdles may be more likely to trip up people who do not have lawyers helping them. A related possibility is that while these problems plague all cases about equally, lawyers are easily able to correct such problems and avoid dismissal, whereas the procedural errors prove fatal for pro se cases. When technical deficiencies in a debtor's legal paperwork occur, courts often issue "show cause" orders instructing debtors to explain why their cases should not be dismissed. If the problem is corrected in response to the court's order, the case will not be dismissed. Debtors with lawyers should be better able to respond to these court orders and to correct paperwork problems.

The 2007 CBP court records data allow for a detailed examination of these possibilities. When a party filed a motion arguing that the case should be dismissed because of the debtor's failure to file documentation or meet a procedural requirement, this was coded as a "technical deficiency motion." Pro se debtors were significantly more likely than their represented counterparts to face such motions in both bankruptcy chapters. They were also significantly less likely to correct these deficiencies and avoid dismissal.

In Chapter 7, technical deficiency motions were filed in 43.1 percent of pro se cases but only in 16.7 percent of cases where the debtor had legal representation. In general, technical deficiency motions were significantly more likely to be brought in Chapter 13 cases than Chapter 7 cases, with parties bringing these motions against 32 percent of all Chapter 13 debtors. This is probably because Chapter 13 is more complex and technically demanding. More than half of unrepresented Chapter 13 debtors (54.2 percent) had technical deficiency motions brought against them. This compares with 30.8 percent of represented debtors, a statistically significant difference. Lawyers seem to make a difference in ensuring that a debtor's paperwork is complete, accurate, and well documented.

Lawyers also appeared to have a major effect on whether such deficiencies were corrected. Cases in which a lawyer was retained were much less likely than pro se cases to be dismissed in response to a technical deficiency motion. In Chapter 7, 40 percent of pro se cases that faced technical deficiency motions were dismissed, whereas the rate for represented debtors was only 7.4 percent.[13] In Chapter 13, the difference was even more striking. Every pro se case in which a technical deficiency motion was brought was dismissed, illustrating how staggeringly difficult it is for unrepresented debtors to confirm plans in Chapter 13.[14] In contrast, more than 90 percent of debtors in cases that lawyers filed responded successfully to technical deficiencies.

These differences in outcome suggest that lawyers are able to comply with the onerous paperwork requirements of bankruptcy, even if they occasionally fail to do so at the outset of a case. This is not surprising. Lawyers are more likely to understand the motions and to know how to correct the deficiencies. They also have better access to the other parties to discuss settling matters and, indeed, better access to the courthouse. While bankruptcy lawyers typically file cases and amendments electronically, a pro se debtor may need to take off time from work to address a problem. The poor odds of a pro se debtor in avoiding or correcting technical errors offer a powerful reminder that law is not free.

IMPROVING BANKRUPTCY

Analysis of the 2007 CBP data strongly suggests that the bankruptcy system does not work for people who do not hire lawyers. Approximately 3.5 percent of bankruptcy filers were pro se, and they had significantly higher odds of exiting bankruptcy without any debt relief. And it was not just unsophisticated debtors getting caught. Even pro se debtors with bachelor's degrees had significant difficulty in using bankruptcy to relieve their debt burdens. The pain of foregoing a lawyer was particularly acute in Chapter 13 bankruptcy, where more than 90 percent of unrepresented debtors did not confirm plans—the first step on a long road to debt relief.

At the same time, families considering bankruptcy cannot afford lawyers without difficulty, leaving debtors in a dilemma with no good options. The issues presented by pro se litigants are not unique to bankruptcy, but the bankruptcy system is especially in need of reform. In consumer bankruptcy, the unrepresented party is usually the debtor. Even in the rare case in which a creditor is unrepresented, unsecured creditors always have some protection through the trustee, who has a duty to defend their interests. This imbalance is particularly problematic because the debtor is at the heart of the process. It is the debtor whom the bankruptcy system seeks to provide with a fresh start or to rehabilitate, and these goals suffer when debtors run afoul of the procedural requirements and are not heard on the merits of the case.

Moreover, the problems presented by filers with no representation are only the tip of the iceberg. The cost of legal services means that even debtors with lawyers are often effectively pro se for many purposes. Because all consumer bankruptcy debtors are, by definition, struggling financially, cost almost always constrains the legal services provided. Consumer bankruptcy attorneys have adapted to this reality by providing basic bankruptcy services for a flat fee.[15] As discussed above, obtaining representation enables debtors to avoid many of the procedural obstacles the bankruptcy process poses, but the flat-fee system leaves them highly vulnerable to other difficulties. This is because the flat fee typically does not include payment for the attorney to bring or defend against litigation within the bankruptcy case. When a creditor, for example, threatens to contest a discharge, a flat-fee debtor is unlikely to be able to afford the costs of opposing the motion and is much more likely to settle, regardless of the merits. This, in turn, give a creditor incentives to bring unmeritorious motions in hopes of forcing the debtor to settle and give the creditor more favorable treatment. This is precisely the sort of problem pro se litigants generally face.

In addition, even the relatively modest legal fees for basic bankruptcy services constrict consumer debtors' access to the system. A large portion of consumer debtors delay bankruptcy for several months in order to save money for the attorney's fees.[16] This delay can significantly increase debtors' financial distress.[17] In addition, many debtors who initially contact attorneys may never successfully save for the fee and end up filing pro se or foregoing bankruptcy relief altogether.

The matter is made more complex by the fact that these very cost-saving measures, which are fairly controversial within the bankruptcy community,

are being urged as "best practice" innovations in the general pro se literature. For example, the newest trend in legal-cost reform is the promotion of
"unbundled" legal services.[18] Unbundling refers to encouraging attorneys
to offer discrete services rather than always handling the representation of
an entire case. This enables lawyers to charge less and provide some services
to clients who otherwise might not be able to afford any representation.
Previously, lawyers have been reluctant to engage in unbundling for fear
that they would be held responsible for errors made at any point in the case,
not just in the parts on which they worked. Many states are amending their
malpractice laws and ethical rules to enable attorneys to offer this lower
cost alternative.[19]

Consumer bankruptcy lawyers, however, already provide unbundled
representation. As noted, the bankruptcy system's experience with unbundling has been mixed. Many commentators are concerned that unbundling
leaves clients effectively pro se for the resolution of matters crucial to their
cases. Policymakers considering unbundling as part of an access-to-justice
reform package should look to the experience of the bankruptcy system to
understand the trade-offs.

Similarly, the bankruptcy system already makes extensive use of paralegals and lay advocates, which is another reform suggested in the pro se literature.[20] The idea is to encourage legal service providers who cater to low- and
moderate-income clients to use paralegals and others to handle many functions that lawyers would handle absent the need for cost-effectiveness. For
example, a high-profile report published by the Harvard Law School argues
that legal services providers should adopt a pyramid structure, in which the
lowest-cost service alternative that can solve a client's problem effectively
is employed—be that alternative a lawyer, a lay advocate, a hotline volunteer, or even an informational website.[21] This is how the typical consumer
bankruptcy lawyer already operates. Clients spend a significant amount of
time with paralegals who help them gather documents and prepare their
petitions. They spend much less time with the lawyers, who supervise the
petition-preparation process and handle tasks such as court appearances.
This system has been largely successful. Despite their extreme financial distress, the vast majority of consumer bankruptcy filers have a lawyer, an
outcome that would be impossible if lawyers performed and charged for all
the tasks that paralegals currently complete.

The bankruptcy system has also experimented with lay petition preparers. These are separate organizations run by laypeople who help debtors file
for bankruptcy without legal advice. Among other actors in the bankruptcy
system, lay petition preparers have a reputation for low-quality work and
for making mistakes that do the debtor more harm than good.[22] The analyses presented in Tables 9.2 and 9.3, however, show that outcomes for debt-

ors filing with petition preparers are significantly better than those of pro se filers, although they are worse than those of represented debtors. Using lay advocates in this way is a partial solution at best. Again, legal service providers in other areas seeking to implement these reforms should look to the bankruptcy experience when making changes.

Despite being on the cutting edge in some respects, the bankruptcy system can do much more. There are two main ways to make bankruptcy more affordable: making it easier and providing more help.

Simplification is particularly appealing because it would not only improve outcomes for pro se filers, but would also enable more debtors to hire attorneys and drive down attorneys' fees for all filers. Chapter 7 is the easier chapter to simplify. Analysis of 2001 CBP data suggests that pro se debtors successfully discharged their debts in Chapter 7 before the 2005 amendments added major technical hurdles to the process.[23] The solution here may be as simple as repealing the additional paperwork and documentation requirements imposed in 2005.

On the other hand, more improvements could be made. Even before 2005, Chapter 7 debtors were probably spending enough on lawyers that the expense interfered with the prompt and effective resolution of their cases.[24] A comprehensive solution would involve evaluating the paperwork and documentation requirements in light of how much value each one generates for creditors and its function in preventing fraud or abuse. Forms and schedules that are not significantly contributing to either goal should be pared down or eliminated. Those that remain should then be simplified and made more user friendly. Currently, consumer debtors must complete more than ten forms, the same forms used in business bankruptcies with the same instructions. An obvious first step would be to create separate forms with instructions relevant to consumer debtors. The Federal Judicial Conference has embarked on an effort to make the forms for individual bankruptcies more user friendly.[25] Readable forms will also benefit represented clients, who must sign off on the accuracy of their bankruptcy court documents even though those documents were completed by lawyers.

The overall point is that Chapter 7 does not need to be difficult, especially because in the vast majority of cases, creditors will not recover anything from the estate.[26]

Simplifying Chapter 13 requires a more difficult set of trade-offs. Under the existing system, it is nearly impossible for pro se debtors to confirm Chapter 13 plans, and this effect cannot be attributed primarily to the 2005 bankruptcy reforms. Data from the 2001 CBP show similarly dire outcomes in Chapter 13 before the new law. Chapter 13 requires debtors to repay their available income to creditors, and much of the detailed documentation is directly relevant to the question of what the debtor can pay. The very premise of Chapter 13, repayment over time and retention of a debtor's assets, may always require a high level of complexity that will thwart do-it-yourself efforts.

All the assistance debtors need does not necessarily have to come from attorneys, however. The bankruptcy system could provide debtors with more help meeting technical requirements. There are many options for approaching this challenge. The goal should be to enable pro se filers to complete their cases successfully as well as to enable all debtors to reduce their legal expenses by handling more of the administrative aspects of their cases without lawyers.

State family courts have been the leaders in this area by necessity; a majority of domestic-relations litigants are pro se.[27] Many of their programs could be adapted to the bankruptcy context. An effective but resource-intensive option that several courts have adopted is to establish a pro se clerk, an attorney with expertise in helping unrepresented people. Pro se clerks do not actually represent pro se individuals but instead provide resources, answer questions, help with paperwork, and generally point unrepresented people in the right direction. They can also provide referrals to low-cost or pro bono attorneys. Some bankruptcy courts have established these programs, but they represent a small minority, and the federal judicial system does not fund pro se clerks for bankruptcy courts.[28] Other federal courts already have pro se clerks, even though many receive fewer pro se filings than the bankruptcy system.

A less expensive way to provide in-person assistance may be to establish bankruptcy clinics staffed by law students and pro bono attorneys, who could be encouraged to provide supervision in a variety of ways. The Massachusetts state court system, for example, takes an original approach. The state's judges provide free educational programs to attorneys who agree to volunteer pro bono hours.[29] Bankruptcy judges are highly active in bankruptcy continuing legal education programs, making this an attractive possibility.

Another more cost-effective option may be to bring petition preparers in-house. Lay petition preparers are used in other courts, such as the New York City family court system.[30] This idea would encounter some resistance in the bankruptcy community, since the current lay petition preparation companies do not have a strong reputation for effectiveness now. The data presented above, however, show that debtors who use petition preparers are faring significantly better than their pro se counterparts on several measures, even though they are faring significantly worse than debtors who retain lawyers. In addition, a court-based program would provide supervision and have the potential to improve these services.

There are also a variety of alternatives for courts without the resources to hire dedicated pro se staff. Bankruptcy courts could, for example, offer group classes that teach debtors how to file a bankruptcy petition, and more generally, how to navigate the system. Similarly, the role of credit counselors could be expanded to include bankruptcy instruction.

Several courts, both inside and outside the bankruptcy system, have begun using the Internet to assist individuals in court. Maricopa County, in Arizona, has taken the lead on this with its interactive eCourt program that helps users prepare court documents by taking part in an online "interview" about their legal situations. The Florida state court system has taken a similar path with its "Statewide Electronic Courthouse."[31] Most court systems have some Internet information available to prospective pro se petitioners, but the degree of helpfulness varies. Bankruptcy courts can do more. Computer-based programs are a particularly good fit for pro se bankruptcy filers because so many of them are well educated. In addition to providing much-needed information, court websites can reduce the number of filers obtaining inaccurate or incomplete information elsewhere on the web.[32] Courts should aim for readable websites written in plain English and take advantage of interactivity as a way to guide users through the bankruptcy process. The Internet offers the further advantage of providing an inexpensive way to present materials in a number of languages. Courts should also continue the trend of working with public libraries and providing computer stations at the courthouse to make this information accessible to individuals without home computers.

As courts continue to experiment with these services, more data will become available about which approaches are the most effective. Any of the above ideas would take some of the administrative burden off of the debtors' lawyers and allow those lawyers to concentrate on their legal functions, such as explaining to debtors their rights, advising them in negotiations with creditors, and litigating contested issues—and to enable them to reduce their fees when these services are not required.

CONCLUSION

Conditioning effective bankruptcy relief on hiring an attorney leaves all debtors with an untenable choice and many of them mired in debt. A small but important minority of debtors attempt unsuccessfully to represent themselves, and an unknown number of others almost certainly forego bankruptcy altogether because of legal costs. Even represented debtors delay bankruptcy for this reason and pay attorneys more than they can afford.

There is an irony here. The point of bankruptcy is to enable the financially distressed to resolve their affairs, but legal fees make bankruptcy inaccessible or difficult for the financially distressed. The $1,000 to $3,000 that the average consumer debtor spends on attorneys may seem small compared with the large sums at stake in corporate bankruptcies, but it can be critical in the consumer context. An additional $2,000 can make or break a debtor's attempt to pay a child-support claim, to save a home, or simply to begin a new financial chapter in life.

A redesigned system that reduces complexity and increases assistance could drive down those fees and give people a realistic chance of debt relief without an attorney. The relief offered by the current system, with its elaborate documentation requirements and automatic dismissals, can be a cruel mirage for the many debtors who cannot afford the help they need to obtain it.

CHAPTER TEN

Less Forgiven

Race and Chapter 13 Bankruptcy

Dov Cohen and Robert M. Lawless

The U.S. bankruptcy system furthers several ideals. First, it provides restitution to creditors by maximizing their collective recovery in a way that would not occur if they each separately pursued the debtor. Second, it offers forgiveness and debt relief to the "honest but unfortunate" debtor.[1] Third, it offers these debtors a chance at reform by making different purchasing and borrowing decisions in the future, the so-called fresh start. Of course, these ideals are often in conflict. For example, a more robust fresh start for a debtor often means less recovery for creditors.

Before filing for bankruptcy, every debtor must choose a chapter of the U.S. Bankruptcy Code under which to seek relief; for almost all individuals, the choice is between Chapter 7 and Chapter 13. The two chapters have very different consequences for the debtor and strike different balances among the often competing ideals of the bankruptcy system. Generally speaking, Chapter 7 stresses forgiveness of debt, and Chapter 13 stresses reform of the debtor and repayment to creditors. Indeed, a debtor cannot file for Chapter 13 unless his or her *creditors* would be at least as well off under a Chapter 13 filing as a Chapter 7 filing.

In Chapter 7, a debtor turns over all nonexempt assets to a bankruptcy trustee who then sells the assets and distributes the proceeds to creditors. (Exempt assets are typically such things as a certain amount of equity in a home, a modest automobile, and retirement savings.) A Chapter 7 debtor must continue to pay the debt on any assets that are collateral for a loan— often a home or an automobile—or risk losing the asset in a foreclosure sale as would happen outside of bankruptcy if the debtor missed payments. Although the formal rules call for liquidation of the debtor's nonexempt assets, this is actually relatively rare. In more than 90 percent of Chapter 7 bankruptcy cases, there are no nonexempt assets to liquidate.[2] Most Chapter 7 debtors do not see the inside of a bankruptcy courtroom and receive a discharge of debt about four months after filing for bankruptcy.

In contrast, a Chapter 13 bankruptcy involves a three- to five-year payment plan under which the debtor must devote all of his or her disposable income to repaying unsecured creditors (that is, those creditors whose loans are not secured by collateral). As in Chapter 7, a Chapter 13 debtor must pay the debt for which there is collateral or risk losing the collateral. Only after making all payments under the repayment plan for three to five years does a Chapter 13 debtor receive a discharge. Studies using data from before the 2005 changes to the U.S. bankruptcy law found that only approximately one in three debtors completed all payments called for by a Chapter 13 plan and received a discharge of eligible debts.[3]

From the debtor's perspective, Chapter 7 requires no repayment to unsecured creditors (in more than 90 percent of the cases), and it generally is faster, more likely to result in a discharge of the debtor's obligations, and costs much less to file than a Chapter 13 plan. For example, the 2007 Consumer Bankruptcy Project (CBP) data show that the median Chapter 13 debtor paid $2,500 in attorneys' fees compared with $1,000 in fees for the median Chapter 7 debtor. Given that Chapter 7 seems more beneficial for debtors, why do some people choose Chapter 13? First, Chapter 13 gives debtors some advantages when they are behind on their mortgage payments, and for this reason, Chapter 13 will often be advantageous for those trying to save a house from foreclosure. Similar rules in Chapter 13 help debtors needing to restructure certain types of other secured loans on personal property, including automobile loans. Second, formal legal rules give a bankruptcy judge the power to dismiss a Chapter 7 case (or give the debtor the opportunity to instead convert the case to Chapter 13) whenever use of Chapter 7 would be an "abuse" of the bankruptcy system. The 2005 changes to the bankruptcy law added a means test for evaluating Chapter 7 cases for abuse. The test screens debtors' incomes against the median income for a household of their size in their state of residence and incorporates a schedule of allowed expenses for above-median-income debtors. Third, although Chapter 13 is more expensive than Chapter 7, debtors can pay their attorneys over the life of the Chapter 13 plan. In contrast, Chapter 7 debtors have to come up with attorneys' fee before a bankruptcy filing. Fourth, Chapter 13 is a procedural device for allowing debtors who feel a moral obligation to make partial repayment to creditors to do so. Among bankruptcy professionals, the desire to save a home is believed to be the overriding motive for debtors who choose to file Chapter 13, though very little formal data exist on this point.[4]

Most debtors filing for bankruptcy know little about the intricacies of bankruptcy law and depend on their attorneys for guidance. And, as noted, there are legitimate reasons why an attorney might steer a client toward

Chapter 13. However, there are also illegitimate reasons why a debtor may be guided toward Chapter 13 instead of Chapter 7. This chapter explores the possibility that race is one reason that people are guided into Chapter 13 bankruptcy instead of Chapter 7 bankruptcy. It reports data that African Americans in bankruptcy are more likely to file Chapter 13 and to make at least partial restitution to creditors compared with debtors of other races. The racial differences are large. For a typical debtor measured by median characteristics, an African American is more than twice as likely to file Chapter 13 than Chapter 7, even after one controls for other factors believed to drive chapter choice such as homeownership, pending foreclosure, income, assets, debts, and other financial and socioeconomic factors. Compared with other debtors, African Americans are more likely to have to earn their discharge by making payments into a Chapter 13 plan to repay their debt. Thus, African Americans end up less forgiven than debtors of other races.

Correlation, of course, is not causation. In this chapter, we document a phenomenon but not the reasons for it. Further scrutiny is clearly needed. One conclusion consistent with our data certainly is that African Americans are being discriminated against through systematic guidance into repayment plans rather than being forgiven. But our data also cannot rule out a different conclusion, namely, that African Americans choose Chapter 13 plans out of a sense of honor, duty, or a moral obligation to repay. And we cannot rule out the possibility that perhaps some other unmeasured economic or cultural factor explains the racial disparity in chapter choice. In the final part of this chapter, we discuss some difficulties inherent in the interpretation of our data.

We first explore the great disparity in Chapter 7 and Chapter 13 rates around the United States and review the previous literature explaining the reasons for this disparity. The most prominent theory is that local legal culture drives chapter choice. We then discuss the methodology of the present study and review the results of our data analysis showing the racial disparity in chapter choice. Finally, we consider the policy implications of what we can say from the data.

CHAPTER 13 RATES AND THE PRIOR LITERATURE

The U.S. Bankruptcy Code is a creature of federal law; thus, one would expect there to be only minor variations across the country in its application. In fact, however, a large variance exists across the United States in the percentage of bankruptcy cases filed as Chapter 13s. At the time the sample was drawn for the 2007 CBP study, Chapter 13s were 38.7 percent of all bankruptcies across the country.[5] Table 10.1 shows how the overall rate of Chapter 13 filings masks huge differences among the federal judicial districts. Clearly, something other than uniform federal law is driving chapter choice in bankruptcy.

In a series of studies, scholars have labeled that "something else" as local legal culture. The substantial variation in Chapter 13 rates was first noted in the seminal Brookings Institution report on the state of the bankruptcy system as it existed in the early 1970s. Then known as Chapter XIII and governed by the predecessor to today's bankruptcy law, Chapter XIII rates varied in the seven districts in the Brookings study from 4 percent to 76 percent.[6] The difference was attributed primarily to differences in attorney attitudes and, to a lesser extent, to the attitudes of local bankruptcy judges toward Chapter XIII.[7]

Later, Gary Neustadter summarized his experience of observing client interviews with six bankruptcy attorneys in two states (which were not disclosed to preserve anonymity). Although not the primary focus of the article, Neustadter describes client-attorney interactions in which the attorney was the guiding force in deciding whether the client would file Chapter 7 or Chapter 13.[8] One attorney believed that debtors should pay what they could to creditors and therefore guided debtors toward Chapter 13. A different attorney's law practice "implement[ed] his philosophical commitment to socialism," and this attorney tended to guide clients toward Chapter 7.[9] Another attorney started with Chapter 13 and turned

TABLE 10.1

Chapter 13 as a percentage of all bankruptcy filings

Lowest percentage of Chapter 13 filings	Highest percentage of Chapter 13 filings
Iowa, northern: 8.4%	Texas, southern: 57.4%
North Dakota: 11.0%	Texas, northern: 57.9%
West Virginia, northern: 11.1%	Georgia, middle: 58.2%
West Virginia, southern: 11.1%	North Carolina, eastern: 58.9%
New Mexico: 12.5%	South Carolina: 65.5%
Oklahoma, northern: 14.3%	Alabama, middle: 70.8%
Hawaii: 14.8%	Louisiana, western: 71.8%
Iowa, southern: 15.0%	Alabama, southern: 72.4%
Alaska: 15.4%	Tennessee, western: 74.8%
South Dakota: 15.7%	Georgia, southern: 77.4%

SOURCE: Bankruptcy Data Project at Harvard (http://bdp.law.harvard.edu/index.cfm), January–April 2007.

NOTE: Table shows the percentage of Chapter 13 filings of all bankruptcy filings for the ten lowest and highest federal judicial districts in the fifty states and the District of Columbia.

to Chapter 7 only when the client interview got to a point at which it was apparent that the client's income was not sufficient to fund a Chapter 13 plan. The dynamic of chapter choice that Neustadter described was decidedly attorney-centered.

Jean Braucher used the term "local legal culture" to describe the results of fifty-seven interviews with consumer bankruptcy attorneys and bankruptcy trustees in Austin and San Antonio (Texas) and Dayton and Cincinnati (Ohio). She concluded that, in addition to furthering their clients' and their own financial interests, lawyers "also attempted to fulfill some version of appropriate social role playing on the part of their clients and themselves."[10] She summarized the attorneys' attitudes toward the choice of Chapter 7 versus Chapter 13 as follows:

> One difference among the lawyers is in the degree to which they encourage clients' desires to do "the right thing" for reasons of morality and self-esteem as opposed to focusing more on obtaining the best financial deal for clients. Not surprisingly, Chapter 7 lawyers see their role as purely or predominantly to get the best financial deal for clients. On the other hand, lawyers who do the most Chapter 13 cases, especially high percentage plans, are more likely to emphasize their clients' need for self-esteem and desire to do what they consider morally right.[11]

Braucher again described a chapter choice dominated by attorneys but especially dominated by attorneys' values. The attorneys in Braucher's study did not consider the client's needs irrelevant. Indeed, many tried to implement what they saw as the client's needs, but what the client "needed" was often seen through the lens of the attorney's values.

On the heels of Braucher's study was the article by Teresa Sullivan, Elizabeth Warren, and Jay Westbrook that found similar dynamics using an earlier wave of the CBP.[12] The article emphasized the persistence of local legal culture, using bankruptcy court data going back twenty years and showing wide disparities in both choice of chapter and case outcomes in Chapter 13 cases from district to district. The authors modeled different structures that would affect chapter choice at critical decision-making junctures for attorneys, judges, or other actors such as bankruptcy trustees. The article helped firmly entrench the idea that local legal culture explained a wide disparity in chapter choice in a bankruptcy system with uniform federal law.

The idea of local legal culture developed in these articles has become an acknowledged factor at work in the consumer bankruptcy system. Of course, the phrase "local legal culture" can be interpreted many ways. It has generally been defined as the practices adopted in a local legal community. For the present purposes, this definition has at least three problems and one virtue. "Local" is a problem because it is generally taken to mean areas defined by political boundaries (judicial districts in our study, for example) rather than boundaries that are psychologically meaningful to people. "Legal" is a problem because the cultural values we discuss may be a product of broad community sentiment, rather than ones unique to the local legal community. "Culture" is a problem because in the present case we have no measures of the attitudes, values, and beliefs of professionals in the legal system. On the other hand, the advantage of the present definition is that it fits with a common conception of the term that many people have—local legal culture is what the people in a local legal community "do"; it is their practices that define them.

METHODOLOGY

Public bankruptcy court records do not include information on the race of bankruptcy filers. For this chapter, we used data from the court records and survey questionnaire in the 2007 CBP sample (see the appendix for more details). This chapter does not make use of any of the telephone interview data from that study.

On the CBP survey, respondents could self-identify as belonging to one or more racial groups defined as "African-American or Black," "Asian-American," "Hispanic or Latino/a," "White or Caucasian," and "Other." The number of survey respondents in the 2007 CBP was 2,438. In 173 cases, one or both members of a household did not provide their racial self-identification. In this chapter's analyses, some observations were dropped because of missing survey answers. The total number of cases available for any particular analysis is reported in the tables.

For people cohabitating with a spouse or partner, the CBP survey asked for demographic information for both people. For our analysis, we considered a household to be African American if either person in a two-person household (or the sole person in a one-person household) self-identified as African American, regardless of whether they also identified another ethnicity. The results are qualitatively similar if an African American household is defined only to include those households in which all people identified as African American.

There is no way of knowing whether the racial demographics for people completing the survey are truly representative of the universe of bankruptcy filers. A check of a random sample of court records from nonrespondents to the CBP study revealed that respondents and nonrespondents did not differ on most every *financial* characteristic, such as income, assets, or debts.[13] Nonetheless, the race of respondents in our sample may still be different from the universe of bankruptcy filers, and this limitation represents a weakness of our study. The issue of racial bias in bankruptcy requires further scrutiny with additional data. Adding demographic questions to the bankruptcy court records would facilitate such research.

RESULTS

African Americans in bankruptcy filed Chapter 13 at about twice the rate of other racial groups. Of the 511 people who identified as African American in the sample, more than half, 54.6 percent, filed Chapter 13, compared with only 28.2 percent of the 1,754 people who listed a different race (Chi-square = 122.40, $p < 0.001$). The disparities remain dramatically different regardless of whether one aggregates all other racial categories or uses separate racial categories. Our data show that African Americans were the only racial category that had a higher Chapter 13 rate than whites (28.8 percent) and that filed at a rate above the national average of all races combined at the time of our sample (approximately 39 percent).

Because saving a home is often considered to be an important motive in filing for Chapter 13, it is important to control for homeownership in any study assessing chapter choice. Among both homeowners and nonhomeowners, however, the African American Chapter 13 rate was about twice as high as that of people from all other races. Among homeowners, 74 percent of African American households filed Chapter 13, compared with 39 percent of households of all other races (Chi-square = 98.62, $p < 0.001$; see Fig. 10.1). Among nonhomeowners, 33 percent of African Americans filed for Chapter 13, compared with 17 percent of those of all other races (Chi-square = 29.22, $p < 0.001$). Again, the differences remain large even when the "all other races" category is divided into its component parts.

These univariate differences, of course, do not control for other factors that may be affecting chapter choice. In the 2007 CBP sample that we used, African American debtors lived in federal judicial districts with higher rates of Chapter 13 filings generally. That is, the average Chapter 13 filing rate for the judicial districts where African Americans lived was 46 percent compared with an average Chapter 13 filing rate of 36 percent for judicial districts where non–African Americans lived ($t = 13.76$, $p < 0.001$). What this means is unclear.

Among other possibilities, the connection could be either tautological or causal: (1) The tautological connection could be thus: African Americans are more likely to file Chapter 13 bankruptcy than Chapter 7 bankruptcy and thus African Americans are likely to inflate the Chapter 13 rate of any district in which they live. That is, the high proportion of

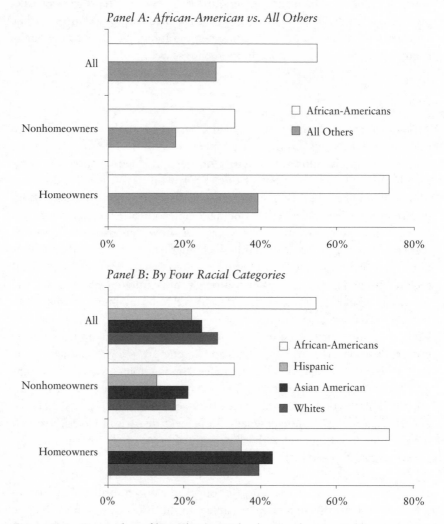

Figure 10.1   Respondents filing Chapter 13 bankruptcy by race and home ownership

s o u r c e : Consumer Bankruptcy Project 2007.

n o t e : The figure reports the proportion of Chapter 13 cases for all respondents (N = 2,264), for those who are not homeowners (N = 1,121) and for those who are homeowners (N = 1,143) (numbers do not sum to 2,265 because one case contained missing data for homeownership). For unmarried or married couples living in one household, race is classified on the basis of either person identifying as the race in question. For married or unmarried couples, the methodology surveys both people if only one person filed for bankruptcy. Respondents could identify as belonging to more than one race.

Chapter 13 bankruptcies by African Americans leads to a high proportion of Chapter 13 bankruptcies in the district as a whole. (2) The connection also could be causal, as follows: because there *historically* have been a lot of African American debtors in a given district, a local legal culture might have developed that favors restitution or reform, rather than immediate and full forgiveness. Thus, having a large number of African American debtors has historically created a culture that favors Chapter 13, and this may lead to high Chapter 13 filing rates for people of all races at the current time. (3) A different explanation entirely could hold. It may be that the race effect is purely an artifact of local legal culture. African Americans may just happen to live in districts that have a culture favoring Chapter 13 (for reasons having nothing to do with race), and thus African Americans simply end up being disproportionately overrepresented in Chapter 13 when compared with debtors of other races.

The second and third explanations would suggest that the *proximal* cause of high African American Chapter 13 rates is local legal culture, not active racial discrimination at the current time. (The second and third explanations differ in that the second supposes that race has played a *distal* role historically in shaping local legal culture, whereas the third posits no distal role of race in shaping culture. In other work, with a more sociological focus, we are exploring these possibilities.)

For the present purposes, it would be important to show that the race effect in the 2007 CBP dataset cannot be explained by the role of local legal culture (whatever the historical reasons for the culture's existence). That is, it is important to rule out the possibility that the race effect is simply an artifact of African Americans just happening to live in districts where the Chapter 13 rate is high *for everybody*.

To examine this possibility, we controlled for the percentage of non–African Americans in a given state who filed Chapter 13 (versus Chapter 7). If the race effect is really an artifact of local legal culture favoring Chapter 13 for people of all races (whether African American or not), then once we control for the effect of non–African American Chapter 13 filing rates, we will have pulled out this local culture effect, and the race disparity should disappear. If there *is* a race effect once we control for non–African American Chapter 13 filing rates, then this implies that African Americans are more likely than those of other races to end up filing under Chapter 13, over and above any effect of local legal culture.

We estimated a logistic regression model of Chapter 13 filing that controlled for the non–African American Chapter 13 rate as well as other factors that might affect chapter choice. The dependent variable was the type of bankruptcy, with Chapter 13 scored as a "1" and Chapter 7 as a "0." The independent dichotomous variables also were scored as "1" if the debtor was positive for the characteristic and "0" otherwise. The main independent variable of interest was a debtor's self-identification as African American. The regression also controlled for homeownership as well as a pending foreclosure as a reason for the bankruptcy as stated by the debtor in the CBP survey. We would expect both homeownership and pending foreclosure to be positively associated with a Chapter 13 filing because of the legal rules in Chapter 13 that are favorable to homeowners.

The regression also controlled for two legal institutional factors that might affect chapter choice. First, we expected that the debtor having legal representation would be positively associated with Chapter 13 filing. Because of the complexity of Chapter 13 compared with Chapter 7, fewer debtors are able to navigate it without legal representation (see Chapter 9). Second, we controlled for whether the debtor filed for bankruptcy between 1999 and 2005. Because a Chapter 7 discharge within the previous eight years makes a new Chapter 7 discharge unavailable, we expected prior bankruptcy to be positively associated with the decision to file Chapter 13.[14]

The regression also controlled for financial factors that might affect chapter choice. Because Chapter 13 requires a regular income, we expected income to be positively associated with Chapter 13 filings. There is probably some curb on this positive association, however: higher incomes allow one to pay the up-front fees attorneys charge in Chapter 7 cases, obviating the need to choose Chapter 13 in order to spread out attorney payments. Because we expected Chapter 13 to be associated with homeownership and with having more nonexempt assets, we also expected asset levels to be positively associated with the choice of Chapter 13. Total debt we expected to be positively associated with Chapter 7 (and therefore negatively associated with Chapter 13) because more debt means that the faster and easier-to-obtain Chapter 7 discharge will be of more benefit. We expected Chapter 13 filing rates to be positively associated with "priority debts" (such as taxes) because Chapter 13 provides some advantages relative to Chapter 7 in dealing with such debts. The regression also controlled for the fraction of all debt that is secured debt and credit card debt. The financial variables were all log transformed (with "1" added to all values to prevent undefined transformations) or represented as percentages to eliminate skewness in the underlying distributions. Finally, we entered into the regression a number of socioeconomic and demographic variables usually associated with race, including education level, occupational prestige score, whether the household was headed by a single woman, and the number of dependents.

Table 10.2 presents the results of the logistic regression predicting that a bankruptcy will be a Chapter 13 filing. The total number of observations was 1,981. For two-person households, educational level and occupational prestige scores were averaged across both respondents. Cases from judicial districts with fewer than five cases of non–African Americans were excluded. The table reports coefficients and robust clustered standard errors clustered on federal judicial districts.[15]

The logistic regression shows that, even after one controls for these other variables, African Americans in bankruptcy are more likely to file under Chapter 13. Doing the mathematical calculation to reverse the transformations of the logistic regression shows the magnitude of the ef-

TABLE 10.2
Logistic regression of Chapter 13 bankruptcy

	Chapter 13 filing	
	Coefficient	Standard error
Either household member is African American	0.97*	0.20
Non–African American Chapter 13 rate for district[a]	4.68*	0.49
Homeowner	0.23	0.21
Identified pending foreclosure as reason for bankruptcy	1.43*	0.13
Filed prior bankruptcy between 1999 and 2005	2.28*	0.31
Log of monthly income	1.65*	0.29
Log of total assets	0.42*	0.17
Log of total debt	−0.99*	0.23
Log of priority debt	0.08*	0.02
Secured debt as percentage of total debt	1.18*	0.41
Credit card debt as percentage of total debt	−0.45	0.45
Represented by attorney during bankruptcy	0.53	0.44
Earned bachelor's degree or higher	0.28	0.23
Occupational prestige score	−0.02*	0.01
Number of dependents in household	−0.18*	0.05
Live with a spouse or partner	−0.24	0.21
Single female head of household	−0.28	0.24
Constant	−9.28*	2.26

SOURCE: Consumer Bankruptcy Project 2007.

NOTE: N = 1,981. The overall model has a Wald Chi-square statistic of 533.45, which, with seventeen degrees of freedom, is statistically significant at $p < 0.05$. The pseudo R^2 is 0.41. With the use of a 50 percent threshold, the model correctly classifies 83.19 percent of the cases.

[a]The non–African American Chapter 13 rate in the district is computed as the percentage of Chapter 13s filed by non–African American debtors in the CBP sample and from the same judicial district. Observations from judicial districts with fewer than five non–African Americans in the sample are excluded from the analysis, resulting in twenty-nine dropped observations. The results are qualitatively similar if these cases are included.

*$p < 0.05$.

fects. An African American homeowner who is at the median for all homeowners for the other variables and characteristics in the regression has a 25.6 percent probability of filing Chapter 13, compared with only an 11.6 percent probability for comparable debtors from all other races. For nonhomeowners, an African American at the median characteristics for nonhomeowners has a 6.5 percent probability of filing Chapter 13, compared with a 2.6 percent probability for a debtor of all other races. Because these probabilities are calculated using median figures, they result in very low probabilities of a Chapter 13 filing because debtors at the median figures do not usually file Chapter 13. (Recall that in general about two in three cases are Chapter 7 bankruptcies.) The point is not the absolute probability but the relative differences by race. Not only does the regression show that race is associated with chapter choice, but it also suggests that even after one controls for other legal, economic, and socioeconomic factors that might affect the decision, African Americans are much more likely than debtors of other races to file Chapter 13.

Almost all the control variables in the logistic regression show the expected effects. Homeownership shows the expected positive relationship with Chapter 13 although it is not statistically significant. The lack of significance may be surprising given the association of Chapter 13 with home ownership, but the result is probably explained by having control variables for assets, debts, and, especially, whether a pending foreclosure was a reason for the bankruptcy filing. Indeed, if a pending foreclosure is eliminated from the regression as an independent variable, homeownership then has a statistically significant positive relationship with Chapter 13 filing, although the overall regression results do not qualitatively differ.

Disaggregating the data geographically leads to a final statistical analysis that provides still more evidence against the hypothesis that the race effect is an artifact of local legal culture that favors Chapter 13 generally. If there is no actual race effect and differences are entirely attributable to variations in local legal culture, then we should find that, *within a given locale*, African Americans and debtors of other races file Chapter 13 at similar rates. To disaggregate the data geographically, we looked at all states where there were at least ten African American filers and ten filers from other races. Table 10.3 reports the correlation between racial identification as African American and filing Chapter 13. The correlations can be considered effect sizes that measure the effect of race on the probability of filing Chapter 13. As shown in Table 10.3, the hypothesis that there are no differences in treatment by race appears unlikely to be correct. Among the nineteen states with ten or more cases as defined above, African Americans have higher Chapter 13 rates in eighteen of them. In the one state where African

Americans have lower Chapter 13 filing rates, the difference is neither large ($r = -0.11$) nor statistically significant (sign test on the eighteen positive to one negative correlations, $p < 0.0001$). We also did a parallel analysis at the level of judicial district. Among the thirty-eight districts with at least five African American and five non–African American filers, African American filers have higher Chapter 13 rates in thirty-three of them (sign test on the thirty-three positive to five negative correlations, $p < 0.0001$). Thus, the disaggregated geographic data add to the logistic regression analyses and provide further evidence of the disproportionate representation of African Americans among Chapter 13 filers.

The interpretation of racial difference would be more ambiguous if African Americans were more likely to file Chapter 13 but also more likely to have either more lenient Chapter 13 plans or better legal outcomes as a result. For example, some Chapter 13 plans involve no actual repayment of

TABLE 10.3
Correlations between race and chapter
bankruptcies for selected states

State	r value
Virginia (N = 49)	0.56*
Louisiana (N = 29)	0.50*
Mississippi (N = 40)	0.37*
Alabama (N = 69)	0.36*
Illinois (N = 122)	0.33*
Missouri (N = 63)	0.33*
Texas (N = 130)	0.30*
Tennessee (N = 131)	0.29*
Maryland (N = 23)	0.27
Georgia (N = 118)	0.26*
California (N = 126)	0.23*
Ohio (N = 142)	0.23*
Pennsylvania (N = 88)	0.16
New Jersey (N = 33)	0.14
New York (N = 76)	0.14
Michigan (N = 164)	0.07
North Carolina (N = 50)	0.07
Florida (N = 86)	0.02
Indiana (N = 89)	–0.11

SOURCE: Consumer Bankruptcy Project 2007.
NOTE: Table includes only the nineteen states with at least ten African American respondents and ten non–African American respondents.
*$p < 0.05$.

debt and thus may resemble a Chapter 7 case in terms of actual outcome. If African Americans make low payments or fare particularly well in Chapter 13, then their overrepresentation may not be a cause for concern about fair and just treatment of indebtedness. However, it does not appear that African Americans have Chapter 13 plans that are any more lenient than those for debtors from other races. Chapter 13 plans for African Americans in the sample proposed an average percentage payment to unsecured creditors (known as the dividend) of 30.9 percent compared with 26.1 percent for all other races ($t = 1.48$, $p = 0.14$). Another measure of leniency also found no significant difference between African Americans and people of other races: the Chapter 13 plans for African Americans proposed zero payment to unsecured creditors at virtually the same rate (34.2 percent) as all other races (34.1 percent) (Chi-square = 0.002, $p = 0.965$). Furthermore, the Chapter 13 plans of African Americans had worse outcomes than those of debtors from other races. Data collected approximately ten to fourteen months after the filing showed that Chapter 13s for African Americans were dismissed or converted to Chapter 7 at higher rates than those of other races—36.2 percent versus 25.5 percent, respectively (Chi-square = 9.45, $p = 0.002$). Neither of these outcomes is particularly desirable. A dismissed case throws the debtor out of the bankruptcy system entirely, and the debtor is back at the mercy of creditors. A converted case at least offers the prospect of a discharge under Chapter 7, but the debtor first will have paid the much higher attorneys' fees of a Chapter 13 case and sometimes will face further fees for legal services arising during the conversion. Thus, African Americans are overrepresented in Chapter 13 compared with Chapter 7 and do not appear to be gaining better results from that chapter choice.

IMPLICATIONS AND CONCLUSION

This chapter has tried to demonstrate the importance of race in understanding chapter choice in bankruptcy. Although chapter choice seems like an arcane topic only of interest to bankruptcy specialists, it has profound effects for the people who file for bankruptcy. In 2010, there were 1.56 million bankruptcies, with just over 435,000 of these being Chapter 13s.[16] For sure, Chapter 13 has its advantages, but those advantages come with monetary and personal costs. Chapter 13 filers typically pay their attorneys two to three times as much as they would for a Chapter 7 filing and then submit to a three- to five-year plan during which they must devote all their disposable income to repayment of creditors. Only after making all the plan payments over these years does a Chapter 13 debtor receive a discharge, and estimates are that two of every three debtors do not make it that far.[17] In comparison, only a few Chapter 7 debtors have to pay their creditors anything at all. Chapter 7 typically results in a discharge within months of filing, and the proceeding has more the feel of an administrative agency action than a court case. Most Chapter 7 debtors never appear in the courtroom or see a bankruptcy judge, instead attending only a meeting with a bankruptcy trustee at which creditors can theoretically appear but in practice rarely do. Overall, Chapter 13 debtors find themselves less forgiven than their compatriots who file Chapter 7.

We have demonstrated that African Americans are much more likely to file Chapter 13 than bankruptcy filers from other races. We tried to carefully rule out other possible explanations for the effect of race, whether these explanations involved factors related to the rational costs and benefits of filing Chapter 7 versus 13 (such as income, debts, assets, homeownership, and so on) or whether these explanations were demographic factors (education, occupational prestige, and so on) that are usually correlated with race. We also found that the race effect could not be accounted for by local legal culture: controlling for the percentage of debtors from other races who filed Chapter 13 within a state or judicial district changed the effect of the race variable only slightly. Even after implementing a number of statistical controls, we could not eliminate the race disparity in Chapter 13 filings.

The present research offers only a first take on these issues. It has many problems and limitations, three of which we describe in more detail. The first has to do with all of the data being correlational, and correlation cannot prove causation. Attitudes in the local legal culture about race may be partly responsible for the differential Chapter 13 filing rates of African Americans, but this hypothesis represents a *residual explanation.* That is, we attribute the gap to attitudes about race only because the racial effect cannot be explained away by any of the other factors we controlled for. We have no independently constructed measure of attitudes about race; and even if we did have such a measure, the correlation between that measure and Chapter 13 filing rates would be just that—correlational. There is always the possibility of an omitted variable lurking underneath any correlation.

The second problem is related to the first in that we know little about the causal actors that are influencing chapter choice. Perhaps Chapter 13 filings relate to stern attitudes about debt and restitution. But that observation invites the question, *whose* attitudes are at work in the system? Does the disparity in chapter choice reflect the attitudes of African Americans, who feel honor-bound to pay back a portion of their debts? Or does the selection of bankruptcy chapter primarily reflect the attitudes of attorneys, trustees, or judges, who feel obliged to make *other* people—particularly African American people—pay back their debts? The chapter choice is probably influenced by many different causal actors, and we have glimpsed only the end of the process in examining whether a person ultimately filed Chapter 7 or Chapter 13. Prior literature has suggested that attorneys often have a dramatic influence on chapter choice, sometimes subtly guiding the process by how they frame the different types of bankruptcy and consequences of the choice, sometimes making overt recommendations, and sometimes simply making decisions for clients without sufficiently explaining the options to them.

Even if one supposes that African Americans are disproportionately guided toward Chapter 13 by their attorneys, however, it is still unclear at what level the effect is operating. There are at least two possibilities. One is that the effect is driven by individual attorneys who are relatively more likely to nudge their African American clients toward Chapter 13, compared with clients from other races who they are relatively more likely to nudge toward Chapter 7. Another possibility involves market segmentation. Under this possibility, no individual attorney may be giving differential treatment to African Americans; it may be simply that attorneys specializing in Chapter 13 are relatively more likely to market themselves to, or be found by, African American debtors, whereas attorneys specializing in Chapter 7 are relatively more likely to market themselves to, or be found by, debtors from other races. It is unclear whether either or both of these possibilities are true. If the market segmentation hypothesis is true, it is still unclear how much this effect would be driven by the preferences of clientele or by the supply and marketing strategies of attorneys.

The third problem is a serious one but it is tractable. In the 2007 CBP study used here, we have no idea how much of our results are driven by self-selection bias, with some people choosing to simply not take part in the survey. We have no idea what proportion of those who did not respond to the survey are African American or how nonrespondents might differ from those who did respond to the survey. Although a limitation of the present survey, this problem can be fixed in the future by bankruptcy courts. Mandatory reporting of the respondent's race on the bankruptcy petition would permit further scrutiny of the racial gap. Data on the race of debtors would allow the justice system to keep track of racial disparities and highlight any locales where further scrutiny might be required.

Given our data and its limitations, we advocate additional study of the system to examine the issue of racial bias. At this point, the data cannot justify a repeal of Chapter 13 on the grounds of discrimination or disparate effect on African Americans. We are also cognizant of the many benefits of Chapter 13, which allows many people to save their houses, express their values about restitution to creditors, file for bankruptcy without the up-front money for attorneys' fees, or achieve other goals. Furthermore, a high frequency of Chapter 13s in a given place may represent a legitimate expression of local cultural norms. If the values of reform and repayment embodied in those norms are legitimate, the expression of those norms in policy may be legitimate, too.

We do believe that the present data are consistent with the idea that at least one illegitimate factor—race—is presently influencing the outcomes of people in the bankruptcy process. The current data have their weaknesses, but they are consistent with the argument that there is a serious bias in the workings of the bankruptcy system, one of the most frequently used systems of justice in the country. For the sake of the integrity of the bankruptcy system and of confidence in the operation of law in the United States, we suggest that race effects in the bankruptcy system merit further scrutiny.

CHAPTER ELEVEN

Borrowing to the Brink

Consumer Debt in America

Kevin T. Leicht

This book has highlighted the ways in which unmanageable debt threatens the well-being of the American middle class. The chapters have described the harms of financial failure from several perspectives. Some authors have explored the experiences in bankruptcy of certain groups, such as homeowners, African Americans, and married couples. Others have chronicled the ways in which unprecedented debt burdens limit mobility and opportunity for groups such as college students and entrepreneurs, and ultimately, for America's middle class.

I now turn to arguing that wealth and debt are significant forces in creating and perpetuating social inequality in the United States. To understand this phenomenon, the social scientific study of wealth, consumption, and debt needs sustained academic and policy attention. This task is urgent. The country is suffering from a deep recession driven by unsustainable levels of household borrowing, and Americans today face increased job and income volatility. These forces have put the prosperity of the middle class at grave risk. Yet wealth and debt are notoriously difficult to measure in conventional social science research, and consumer debt burden as a significant new dimension of social inequality is only now being studied and understood. In America's capitalist economy, borrowing can be a path to prosperity. The bankruptcy data are a powerful reminder, however, that borrowing also can be a path to poverty. The data in this book from the 2007 Consumer Bankruptcy Project (CBP) are an important lens on how household debt crushes the aspirations of some families for middle-class stability and success.

I offer two additional views on debt and the plight of the middle class. These are big-picture observations that situate the somber findings of the preceding chapters in social and historical contexts. First, I document how the rise of easily available consumer credit occurred simultaneously with the stagnation of middle-class incomes. Families today are in a double bind; they earn fewer dollars and are trying to pay more debt. Second, I examine how the crushing debt burdens of families in bankruptcy are related to the deregulation of the credit markets in the past two decades. I conduct a simple simulation that exposes households that filed for bankruptcy in 2007 to the regulated credit market of the 1970s, a world with hard credit limits, usury laws that capped interest rates, and tighter credit underwriting standards. The results are sobering. Families in bankruptcy today struggle with hundreds of dollars more in monthly payments than the prior generation could ever have borrowed. The findings suggest the potential of regulatory reform of consumer credit markets to reduce the risk and pain that debt imposes on America's middle class.

BORROWING TO FINANCE THE AMERICAN DREAM

As Chapter 1 of this book describes, the American middle class is laden with unprecedented levels of debt. These obligations powerfully shape the prospects of families, but of course, consumer indebtedness occurs in the context of other economic and social forces. My exploration of the relationship between debt and middle-class prosperity focuses on the relationship between declining household wages and growing household debt burdens. I argue that in recent decades the middle class has been loaned money as a substitute for being paid an appropriate, productivity-enhanced wage. The American Dream is no longer just about hard work—about getting an honest day's pay for an honest day's work and enjoying the fruits of one's labor. In recent years, the pursuit of the American Dream has been financed with borrowed money. A middle-class lifestyle is now about unregulated interest rates, complex loan products, student loans, and multiple credit card debts. The middle class has been squeezed on both ends; today's working families earn lower wages and must try to service higher debts.

To illustrate the current plight of the American middle class, I provide a simple historical simulation that highlights the dramatic growth in debt burdens of the middle class in the past twenty-five years. In my rudimentary statistical simulation, families who filed for bankruptcy in 2007 are "moved" to a mid-1970s world of regulated credit and are subjected to a regime of credit limits that reflects traditional underwriting standards based on ability to pay. This analysis is designed to provide estimates for two key measures of interest. First, how much of the crushing debt loads accumulated by families in bankruptcy could not have been accumulated in the regulated consumer credit markets of the 1970s? And second, how many families could probably have avoided bankruptcy if the United States returned to traditional lending standards and a regulated consumer credit market? This simple simulation does not address the opportunity costs of borrowing less money (would people in a world of regulated credit pursue less education? buy fewer homes? or consume less overall?), but it erases consumer debt that exceeds 1970s regulated thresholds to reveal what household wealth would look like with a return to credit regulation.

The simulation analysis is inspired by a multifaceted argument with five major components:

1. The U.S. middle class has experienced unprecedented declines in real purchasing power since the mid-1970s.

2. Gaps between stagnant incomes and conventional consumption needs have been filled by easily available credit.

3. This influx of consumer credit appeared around the time that middle-class incomes stagnated.

4. Because the United States has experienced very real productivity gains over the past twenty-five years, and middle-class incomes have stagnated, borrowing money substituted for actually getting paid a productivity-enhanced wage.

5. The result of these changes is a middle class that is struggling to maintain financial stability in the face of unprecedented levels of household debt.

The historical and statistical analyses in this chapter help provide a context for the role that the widespread availability of credit has really played in helping families maintain or simulate a social class position.[1] This simulation of social class is one of many forces that have postponed a day of reckoning about the failure of the postindustrial economy to deliver its economic prosperity to large swaths of working Americans. This problem is at the heart of the pain that is confronting the contemporary middle class. An elucidation of the relationship between wages and debts is crucial to helping Americans see that the proud tradition of middle-class prosperity is at grave risk of disappearing.

THE BOUNDARIES OF MIDDLE-CLASS STATUS

As Elizabeth Warren and Deborah Thorne describe in Chapter 2, most Americans define themselves as middle class. Despite the disagreements found in popular and academic discourse, Warren and Thorne focus on income, education, occupational prestige, and homeownership as major defining characteristics of the middle class. Sociologists often combine the first three characteristics and collectively label them as contributors to *socioeconomic status*. As in prior work,[2] I define the middle class as households with incomes derived primarily from salaries and wages;[3] with adults who work in jobs such as lower level managers, nurses and teachers, and small-scale self-employed people running businesses such as car washes and day care centers; who attended or graduated from a four-year college; and whose primary source of wealth is homeownership. While defining the American middle class is a bit elusive, the economic changes in the middle class can be easily seen in hard data.

DECLINES IN REAL INCOME DOLLARS FOR THE MIDDLE CLASS

The U.S. economy depends on the purchasing power of the middle class to fuel economic growth; that is, middle-class families buy the goods and services that are the bulwark of the country's economic output. Yet, during the past few decades middle-class incomes have not risen. Since the 1970s, there have been major downward shifts in the real purchasing power of middle-class wages when adjusted for inflation. These wages have declined despite real gains in productivity that we would expect would increase the pay of workers who create that productivity. The remarkable ability of the economy to grow while middle-class wages stagnated came from the widespread expansion of consumer credit during the same period. The purchasing power of the middle class was widely heralded as a public good. Until that pattern hit the breaking point with the financial crisis that began in 2007, middle-class consumption buoyed up the collective economy and produced seemingly relentless upward prosperity in living standards. But in the margins some people were pinched hard, and many, many more were set up for future pain. This era was marked by rising inequality in wealth, a large increase in the numbers of families in bankruptcy, and increased job insecurity. The root of the recession was seeded by the "income/credit squeeze" that characterized household balance sheets in recent decades.

The clearest evidence of the downward pressure in real purchasing power is the change in real median family earnings (Figure 11.1). Median pretax family income (the figure that separates the top half of the income distribution from the bottom half) actually declined slightly between 1971 and 1983 (by $1,500), grew by $6,200 (12 percent) during the economic recovery of the late 1980s (1989), and then stagnated. Real median family income in 1998 (the height of the late 1990s economic recovery) was only $2,400 (4 percent) higher than in 1989. And between 1998 and 2007, the income of the typical family hardly grew at all. By 2007, real median family income was only $8,700 (16 percent) higher than three decades before in 1971, an average growth rate of 0.4 percent yearly. And almost all of this real family income gain was produced by increased working hours and labor force participation of women.[4]

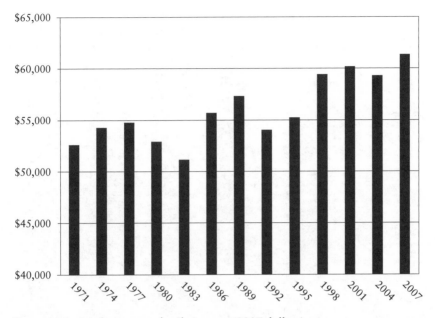

Figure 11.1   Median pretax family income (2007 dollars)
SOURCE: DeNavas-Walt, Proctor, and Smith, U.S. Census Bureau, *Income, Poverty and Health Insurance Coverage.*

The stagnating income and earnings at the middle of the distribution mask the steady trend toward greater income inequality. Figure 11.2 shows that income inequality rose substantially from 1970 to 2006. The top quintile of all families in 1970 received 43.3 percent of aggregate household income. By 2006, the share of that group had grown to 50.5 percent. The pressure on the middle class is revealed by the change in the relative size of the third fifth of the income distribution—those households that made between $41,000 and $62,500 in 2006. This middle group's relative share of the aggregate income dropped from 17 percent to 15 percent over the past thirty years. In fact, the shares for all families in the bottom four-fifths of the income distribution have declined relative to the top. During the past three decades, the nation's most well-off families (the top 20 percent) got a bigger slice of the income pie, while the bulk of families (the remaining 80 percent) were served up steadily smaller servings of income to live on.

Despite minimal growth and a decreasing share, middle-class incomes have been strained further by increased expenses for the mainstays of middle-class life—single-family homes, health-care premiums and out-of-pocket costs, child care, and higher education. Adjusted for inflation, the median sale price of a single-family home rose from $129,000 in 1971 to $247,900 in 2007 (in 2007 dollars).[5] Even in the midst of the so-called hous-

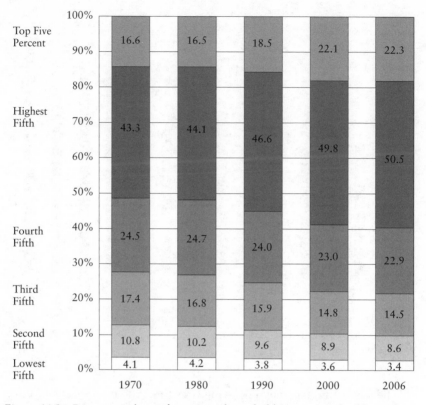

Figure 11.2   Percentage share of aggregate household income received by each fifth and top 5 percent of all households

S O U R C E : DeNavas-Walt, Proctor, and Smith, U.S. Census Bureau, *Income, Poverty and Health Insurance Coverage.*

ing collapse, the median home price in 2009 was $216,000, a huge uptick from the early 1970s that is completely disproportional to the few thousand dollars in increased income during the same period. Undoubtedly, rising home prices were driven by new methods of mortgage financing that were possible only because of the deregulation of consumer credit markets. The effect was to artificially prop up demand for new single-family homes.[6] Family health insurance premiums and out-of-pocket expenses (copayments and deductibles) have risen at a rate twice that of family income since 1996.[7] Today, 22 percent of all American families spend more than 10 percent of their incomes on health care.[8] The costs of children have also skyrocketed. The U.S. Department of Agriculture estimates that middle-income families with children spent 22 percent more in real dollars raising a child from birth to age eighteen in 2009 ($222,360) than in 1960 ($182,857 in 2009 dollars). Much of this difference is due to increases in child care and education expenses. Middle-income families in 2009 spent $37,740 on child care and education before age eighteen, up from just $3,657 (2009 dollars) in 1960. The costs of attending a four-year public college or university rose by 43 percent from 2001 ($8,839) to 2006 ($12,657). All of these price changes far outstrip the meager 16 percent rise in real median family income from 1971 to 2007.

The squeeze on middle-class incomes during the past several decades is not the result of declines in America's economic capacity. In fact, corporate profits soared to unprecedented heights during the same period that incomes stagnated. Throughout the 1990s and early years of the 2000s, companies were making record profits and corporate CEOs were being well compensated. But the economic return to average workers was stagnating, and their relative economic standing was slipping compared with the wealthiest Americans. Corporate profits rose by 8 percent between 1977 and 1987 while median family income rose only 3 percent. In the 1990s and 2000s, profits moved dramatically higher and median incomes flattened further. From 1987 to 1997, corporate profits rose from $432 billion to $826 billion (90 percent) while median family incomes rose from $56,500 to $57,500 (1.8 percent) (in 2007 dollars). The trend continued even in the face of the 2001–2002 recession and beyond; corporate profits from 1997 to 2007 rose 32 percent while median family incomes rose 6 percent.[9]

Families were also buffeted by greater job instability in the 1990s and 2000s,[10] which translated into more volatility in household balance sheets. Political scientist Jacob Hacker has documented this trend, writing: "Family finances have become much more insecure. Although insecurity dropped in the booms of the late 1980s and late 1990s, the long-term trend is sharply upward. In fact, instability in family incomes was roughly five times greater at its peak in the 1990s than in 1972."[11]

There are numerous and heated public and academic debates regarding the causes of these relative trends,[12] but the trends themselves are not in dispute. In the 1990s and 2000s, middle-class families lost economic ground. The simplest explanations point to the role of globalization and the changing role of international competition.[13] Others point to the massive reorganization of the workplace and the enormous drive of employers to cut employee costs to increase profit margins.[14]

MIDDLE-CLASS FAMILIES WERE NOT PAID FROM PRODUCTIVITY GAINS THEY HELPED TO PRODUCE

An alternate explanation for the increased financial pressures on the middle class could be a decline in the overall U.S. economy, but there is strong evidence that the economy generally boosted its productivity during the past two decades. Although productivity lagged for most of the 1970s and 1980s, it rebounded in the 1990s, and despite a modest dip in the 2001 recession, it rebounded thereafter and remained strong until the recession began in late 2007. These patterns hold true across different sectors of the economy. But the productivity gains were not used to improve the lot of the average worker. Instead, the wealth from the dramatic boost in productivity went to those at the very top of the income distribution, or corporations used it to engage in activities designed to bolster increases in productivity and profits still further.[15] A simulation powerfully demonstrates this phenomenon.

What would the distribution of earnings for typical workers look like if some of the productivity gains had been distributed to middle-class families rather than given to the wealthiest Americans or diverted back into corporate activities? Two major complications are involved in answering this question. First, there are several ways workers could be rewarded for increased productivity. For example, they could work fewer hours and take some of the compensation as increased leisure time. The data on work hours suggests this did not happen.[16] Americans now work more hours than all others in the industrialized world except for the Japanese. Companies could also have used the productivity gains to hire more workers. In this scenario, the productivity gains would result in more jobs and lower unemployment. Indeed, in the 1990s the United States saw an impressive trend in job growth.[17] But if the number of available jobs was growing at a fast pace, and the workforce was not growing at the same pace, then there should have been pressure for upward wage movement, and this did not occur. In fact, productivity growth eased pressure on employer hiring because fewer workers could do the work that more workers used to do.

The other option for rewarding workers for productivity improvements is to raise wages. Since it is virtually impossible to make anything other than an arbitrary judgment about the extent to which productivity gains should be divided between average workers and corporations and their owners, I present the simulation results under a series of assumptions, showing how earnings would change in different scenarios.

Radically oriented economists and social scientists might argue that wages should rise in direct proportion to productivity. This is not the same as saying that *all* productivity gains should be redistributed entirely to workers. Instead, workers' earnings should rise in equal proportion to productivity increases. I call this the "100 percent solution." A second approach would be to permit companies to retain most productivity gains for investment in the technological changes needed to remain competitive. Under this assumption, the harm of workers not receiving any wage increase should be compensated for in the long run because the increased investment in equipment, technology, and organizational improvements will yield still more employment growth and higher wages in the future. But most would concede that even in this scenario, the workers who produced those productivity gains should receive some compensation improvement. As a minimum threshold, I allow workers' wages to rise at a rate that reflects 25 percent of the total gains in productivity and refer to this as the "25 percent solution." A third argument would be that productivity gains are equally the product of labor and capital and accordingly should be shared in half. This "50 percent solution" increases wages at one-half the rate that overall productivity rose.

Figure 11.3 shows the dramatic results of the simulations. Real median wages for nonfarm, nonsupervisory workers rose hardly at all between 1988 and 2007 ($11.37 to $11.75 in 1992 dollars). If median wages had risen in lock step with productivity gains, workers' hourly wage would have increased from $11.37 to $16.51, a gain of almost 45 percent. Even the 25 percent solution would have produced a 9 percent increase in real mean hourly

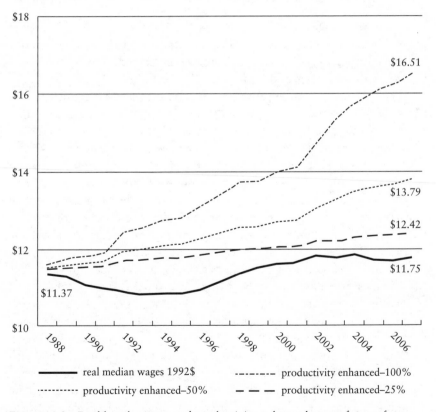

Figure 11.3   Real hourly wages and productivity-enhanced wages for nonfarm, nonsupervisory workers

SOURCE: Author's calculations based on Bureau of Labor Statistics, "National Employment, Hours and Earnings."

wages for nonfarm, nonsupervisory workers over twenty years. That $1.05 hour would amount to an extra $2,100 per year in 1992 real dollars. Depriving workers of productivity gains, as corporations did in the 1990s and 2000s, created serious income problems for workers and the middle-class families they support.

Taken together, the data suggest that in the past two decades the story of the financial well-being of middle-class families is one of economic stagnation, or even economic suffering because of growing wealth inequality and income instability. In the face of these hardships, how have middle-class families maintained their lifestyles? How did the United States become increasingly reliant on consumer spending as its economic engine during the exact same period that most Americans had fewer real dollars to support their families?

WHAT FUELED ALL THAT CONSUMPTION?: CONSUMER CREDIT

A number of changes contributed to or enhanced the purchasing power of the middle class even though their incomes stagnated in real terms. Among the adjustments workers made were to (1) increase their working hours, (2) reduce their savings, and (3) increase their debt load.

The evidence shows that American workers are supplementing their incomes both by working more hours themselves and by bringing a second wage earner into the family, usually a spouse.[18] From 1970 to 1997 the average number of paid hours of work for married couples rose from 52.5 to 62.8 per week. During this same period, the percentage of families in which both husband and wife worked for pay rose from 35.9 percent to 59.5 percent.[19] In addition, the number of married couples who worked more than one hundred hours a week increased dramatically. These trends are depressing in light of the stagnation of earnings among the middle class over the past three decades. Americans today seem to be working more hours just to keep their heads above water and to stave off any decline in real income.

Families also have coped by living from paycheck to paycheck and eliminating savings, something that Elizabeth Warren and Amelia Warren Tyagi point out leaves people with little or no buffer against the whims of misfortune.[20] According to the Panel Study of Income Dynamics, 25 percent of American families could not sustain a poverty-level standard of living for three months if they were forced to live on their accumulated wealth.[21] Since the early 1970s the personal savings rate has plummeted from around a tenth of income to around zero. If you combine job instability with the lack of savings, many Americans are just a few missed paychecks away from financial ruin or bankruptcy.[22]

To make ends meet, Americans have dramatically expanded their use of consumer credit during the past two decades.[23] Although the recession that began in 2007 had seen some very modest deleveraging by 2010 (U.S. savings rates were near 3.6 percent as of April 2010, and consumer spending had slowed as consumers focused on paying off debt),[24] families still carried very high debt burdens into the second decade of the twenty-first century—a legacy of two decades of stagnant wages that is likely to endure into the future.

Credit card debt is a particularly useful substitute for wages because it can be used to meet everyday or large-ticket expenses. Beginning in the 1980s, the number of credit card users and the levels of debt carried on credit cards began to climb. Average credit card debt per household rose from just over $3,000 in 1989 to $7,300 in 2007 (in 2007 dollars). By 2007 a majority of American households were carrying credit card debt from month to month.[25]

Until the credit crunch began in 2008, mortgage lending also skyrocketed in the past two decades. This explosion in mortgage debt was fueled by "innovation" (not to be confused with improvement) in mortgage loan products. Adjustable-rate mortgages, particularly those with low "teaser" rates that adjusted upward dramatically after the first two or three years of the loan, accounted for 31 percent of mortgage originations in 2005.[26] Approximately another 30 percent of originations in 2004 were interest-only loans.[27] By 2005, subprime mortgages represented 20 percent of the mortgage market.[28] Loan-to-value ratios (reflecting the amount of money borrowed relative to the value of the house) averaged around 80 percent for the 1973–2006 period, but the percentage of loans making up more than 90 percent of the house's value peaked above 25 percent in 1995 and remained above 20 percent until 2007.[29] Increasingly, potential homebuyers were hit with a bewildering array of choices that allowed them to buy houses that they could not afford on their stagnant incomes.

The deregulation of the banking industry during the 1980s set the stage for the transformation of the consumer credit landscape. A Supreme Court ruling removed the limits on the maximum interest rates that lenders could charge, constraints on securities dealings were lifted, and interstate branch banking was allowed.[30] These changes facilitated a dramatic rise in the credit available to consumers and the profitability of lending. Investors have fueled the lending industry by purchasing asset-backed securities that help lenders spread their risk and further maximize profits.

These structural changes in consumer credit coincided with stagnant incomes for the average American worker, producing a situation in which families were trapped in a "work and spend" cycle that grew for years and years.[31] American families were offered more ways to borrow money, and more dollars of credit, against their future earnings. And borrow they did. The percentage growth in consumer credit debt saddled Americans with unprecedented levels of household debt. The ratio of debts to personal income grew modestly from 1960 (55 percent) to the mid-1980s (65 percent) and then skyrocketed to 133 percent in 2007.[32] Household debt growth has far outpaced growth in real incomes or real household wealth. By 2007, just before the recession hit, 15 percent of U.S. families had debt exceeding 40 percent of their income.[33]

The expansion of credit made possible by deregulation enabled families to "maintain the image of middle-class respectability and the material accoutrements of economic success even as they struggled simply to stay afloat."[34] Because middle-class families used credit in order to maintain a middle-class lifestyle, any middle-class prosperity observed in the past two decades may be just a debt-driven illusion.

THE CREDIT EXPLOSION AT THE HOUSEHOLD LEVEL: 2007 CONSUMERS IN A 1970S WORLD

The overall story of this chapter is of two opposing forces reshaping the American middle class: incomes have stagnated and debt has increased. Taken together, these trends suggest that the American Dream of the 1990s and 2000s was purchased with borrowed money. To see the effects of this situation, I use the 2007 CBP data on families in bankruptcy to roughly assess how much of the heavy borrowing of middle-class families could have been avoided if the United States had not deregulated its credit markets.

Families in bankruptcy epitomize the harms of debt growth as a substitute for real wage growth. As Brian Bucks describes in Chapter 3, these families enter bankruptcy suffering under staggering debt-to-income ratios, despite being largely middle class by sociological characteristics.[35] The CBP reports that debt-to-income ratios of bankruptcy filers rose from 1.4 in 1981 to 3.4 in 2007, and the unsecured debt-to-income ratio rose from 0.5 in 1981 (half of reported income was owed in unsecured debt) to 1.2 in 2007.[36] My simple simulation takes families that filed for bankruptcy in 2007 and examines how much of their debt would be erased in a 1970s world of regulated credit and traditional standards of underwriting. To simulate this 1970s regulated credit regime, I imposed the following conditions typical of 1970s credit constraints on the households that filed for bankruptcy in 2007:

1. A household would have one credit card with a spending limit of $1,000.
2. A household would have a single mortgage with a payment that did not exceed 30 percent of its monthly income.
3. A household would have car loan payments that did not exceed 10 percent of its monthly income.

My analysis presents a few basic data points to illustrate the growth in consumer debt relative to income. First, I determined how many families who filed for bankruptcy in 2007 had debts that exceeded the 1970s limits set forth above. Second, I examined the characteristics and circumstances of the bankrupt households that exceeded these 1970s credit limits. Third, I calculated how much the debt of the bankrupt households would decline if credit regulation and underwriting returned to the 1970s standards. These data provide a rough estimate for how many of the millions of households that have filed for bankruptcy in recent years could have avoided financial failure if credit use had not ballooned. As I argue above, this use of credit may have been a necessary substitute for families trying to hang on to middle-class amenities in the face of stagnant wages. The simulation provides a way to assess the extent to which the heavy reliance on credit set middle-class families up for financial failure.

As reported in preceding chapters, families who file for bankruptcy are in severe financial distress. Table 11.1 shows the key descriptive statistics for respondents to the 2007 CBP. The average household had $103,000 in assets and $148,000 in debts. Given the importance of wealth to life chances,[37] the negative net worth of these households is a grim reminder of the depth of their financial problems. A staggering amount of this debt was unsecured, much of it owed on credit cards. The average household owed more than $59,000 in unsecured debt; nearly half of their total assets would have to be liquidated just to pay credit card and other unsecured obligations such as medical bills.

Given my hypothesis that credit substituted for wages, the key data are the amounts of debt relative to income. Table 11.1 shows that average

TABLE 11.1
Descriptive statistics of bankrupt households in 2007

	Mean	Standard deviation	Median
Total assets	103,468	150,359	51,580
Total debts	148,225	327,318	87,343
Total unsecured debt	59,653	246,668	33,387
Monthly income	2,603	1,825	2,266
Monthly expenses	2,582	1,817	2,246
Definite medical debt	3,110	16,897	3,110
Definite credit card debt[a]	20,165	30,688	10,004
Rent/mortgage payment	687	643	583
Auto loan payment	160	231	0

SOURCE: Consumer Bankruptcy Project 2007.

NOTE: N = 2432. Values are in dollars.

[a]"Definite credit card debt" is a lower-bound estimate from court records, reflecting specific mention of credit cards, charge accounts, or brand names such as Visa, Discover, etc.

total monthly expenses almost equaled average total monthly income. It is important to remember that these monthly expenses, as reported on the bankruptcy schedules, do not include the debt service payments for dischargeable obligations in bankruptcy, such as credit card debts and other bills. Even with bankruptcy relief, these families barely had enough to make ends meet just trying to make house and car payments and pay other day-to-day expenses such as clothing, medical expenses, and utility bills. Given the lack of disposable income, the average family in bankruptcy clearly has no leftover dollars from its income to pay off its debts.

A closer look at these debt burdens is illustrative. At the mean the mortgage and car payments seem to be well within the 1970s credit cutoffs set forth above; the average household in bankruptcy was spending 26 percent of its income on mortgage or rent payments and 6 percent of its monthly income on auto installment loan payments, and the median auto installment payment was zero. Outstanding medical debts averaged $3,100, but this was dwarfed by the amount of definite credit card debt ($20,165). Fully 73 percent of the 2007 CBP sample had credit card debt beyond the $1,000 1970s "hard line" credit limit (Table 11.2), and 26 percent of bankrupt families had credit card debt that exceeded their yearly incomes.

The situation is less severe with regard to mortgage debt and auto loan payments. Thirty-seven percent of the 2007 CBP respondents had mortgage payments over the conventional 1970s limit of 30 percent of household income, and 27 percent had auto loan payments above the conventional 1970s limit of 10 percent of household income (Table 11.2). The frequency of housing and auto debt problems is less than credit card debt, but suggests that about one in three bankrupt households in 2007 had collateralized loan payments that would have been impossible under the lending standards of the 1970s.

One of the most telling statistics comes from all three debt measures combined. Only 12 percent of the bankrupt households in 2007 did not exceed one of the three thresholds (credit card, mortgage, or auto). More

TABLE 11.2

Percentage of bankrupt households in 2007 beyond
1970s credit thresholds

Excessive debt measure	Percentage
Definite credit card debt > $1,000	73
Mortgage/rent payments > 30% of income	37
Auto installment loan payments > 10% of income	27
All three debt measures exceed 1970s thresholds	9

SOURCE: Consumer Bankruptcy Project 2007.

than one third (36 percent) exceeded two thresholds, and 9 percent exceeded all three thresholds.

I next examined the demographic characteristics of the bankrupt households that had debt burdens that would have been impossible just thirty years ago. How have different households responded to the expansion of credit? Table 11.3 shows the results of logistic regression used to predict the demographic characteristics that make it more likely that households in bankruptcy will have credit card debts greater than $1,000, mortgage payments in excess of 30 percent of monthly income, and auto loan payments in excess of 10 percent of monthly income.

The regression results show that the lack of credit regulation, and the concomitant expansion of credit, had a more pronounced effect on some types of households. Credit card debt patterns are particularly interesting because these debt burdens were so dramatically lower in the 1970s than in the 2000s. The first column of Table 11.3 shows that credit card debt that exceeds $1,000 is more likely among whites than Hispanic or African American bankruptcy filers. Excessive credit card debt is also more likely among the elderly (those older than sixty-five years). And despite fears about youth addicted to plastic,[38] excessive credit card debt is less likely among those aged twenty-five to thirty-four years. Excessive credit card debt is more likely among all income groups above the bottom quintile.

Table 11.3 also shows how excessive mortgage debt is a particular problem for certain demographic groups. Hispanics seem particularly likely to be bearing heavy mortgage burdens relative to their incomes. College-educated households are also affected by this problem. These findings are consistent with the expansion of subprime lending to individuals who likely would have been excluded from the mortgage market in the 1970s. The fact that these families are in bankruptcy is a reminder that the so-called democratization of credit did not always lead to improved financial health.

The third column of Table 11.3 examines differences in circumstances associated with excessive auto loan payments. African Americans are less likely than whites to have big auto loans; this may reveal the continued existence of discrimination in auto lending, which is very likely to be an in-person transaction, unlike credit card or mortgage lending. The fourth column examines the characteristics of the worst-off households—those that exceed all three debt thresholds. African Americans are significantly less likely to fall into this severely indebted group. This latter finding suggests that racial differences in credit patterns persist, despite ideas that subprime lending ended redlining practices.[39] People in bankruptcy with bachelor's degrees are twice as likely to be in the severely indebted group as those with high school diplomas. This finding is notable given the belief in the United

TABLE II.3
Logistic regression of demographic characteristics associated with exceeding 1970s debt thresholds

	Excessive credit card debt (=1)	Excessive mortgage debt (=1)	Excessive auto loan debt (=1)	All three excessive debts combined (=1)
	Exp (B)	Exp (B)	Exp (B)	Exp (B)
Gender				
Male (ref.)	--	--	--	--
Female (=1)	0.99	1.07	0.90	0.97
Marital status				
Married (ref.)	--	--	--	--
Never married	1.27	1.27	0.83	0.76
Separated	0.87	0.91	0.78	0.73
Divorced	1.24	1.14	0.88	0.93
Widowed	1.32	0.97	1.04	0.54
Age (years)				
<25	0.66	0.48**	1.20	0.46
25–34	0.64**	0.82	0.96	0.78
35–44	0.83	0.98	1.02	1.07
45–54 (ref.)	--	--	--	--
55–64	0.87	1.01	0.94	0.85
65+	1.63**	0.88	0.77	0.98
Education				
< High school diploma	--	--	--	--
High school diploma (ref.)	0.67*	0.68*	0.94	0.79
Some college	1.17	1.27*	1.10	1.13
BA	1.34	1.69***	1.49*	2.09***
More than BA	1.09	1.64**	1.14	0.97
Income quintile				
First quintile (ref.)	--	--	--	--
Second quintile $	1.83***	1.02	1.72***	1.43
Third quintile $	1.44*	0.82	1.79***	1.16
Fourth quintile $	1.49**	0.67**	1.63**	1.06
Highest quintile $	2.42***	0.61***	0.90	0.57*
Ethnicity				
White (ref.)	--	--	--	--
African American	0.44***	0.87	0.71**	0.67*
Hispanic	0.55**	2.33***	1.33	1.52
Constant	2.21***	0.61**	0.32***	0.12***

SOURCE: Consumer Bankruptcy Project 2007.
NOTE: N = 2,432.
*$p < 0.05$, **$p < 0.01$, ***$p < 0.001$ (two-tailed tests).

States that a college degree guards against financial problems (see Chapter 5). One possibility is that increases in student loan burdens, or students using credit cards during college, may be forcing more families to turn to borrowing to make ends meet when it comes time to buy a house or car.

THE 1970S WORLD: HOW MUCH DEBT WOULDN'T BE THERE?

The final question I addressed is how much debt of the bankrupt households would be erased if 1970s credit regulations had been in place in 2007 and the preceding years. To answer this, I made artificial changes to the balance sheets of the 2007 bankrupt families to simulate credit markets in the 1970s. I systematically erased credit card debt in excess of $1,000, reduced mortgage payments to 30 percent of income threshold, and reduced car installment loan payments to 10 percent of income threshold. The results are presented in Table 11.4 and graphically in Figures 11.4 and 11.5.

Overall, a regulated credit market would have made a big difference in the well-being of the families who had to seek relief in bankruptcy in 2007. With less debt, these families would have had hundreds of extra dollars freed for current consumption (see Table 11.4). Eliminating credit card debt in excess of the $1,000 1970s limit on unsecured debt would lower the average bankrupt household's minimum monthly payments by $383 and the median household's minimum payment by $180. Cutting mortgage debt to the longstanding 30 percent of income ratio would lower the average bankrupt household's expense by $235 monthly and median household's payment by $80. Lowering car payments would save another $49. All told, returning to the regulated 1970s credit markets would save 2007 bankruptcy filers an average of $667 a month, $260 a month for the median household. This works out to a little more than $8,000 per year on average and $3,120 at the median, representing 26 percent of reported average monthly household income and 11 percent of median income, respectively.

Looking at the relationship between the total debt of bankrupt families in 2007 and a 1970s modified debt level for each decile of debt highlights the way in which traditional credit underwriting would reshape families' balance sheets (see Figure 11.4). At the lowest debt levels, eliminating excessive debt above 1970s regulated credit levels reduces overall consumer debt by 62 percent, from $20,166 to $7,672. The amount of debt relief decreases considerably for those with the highest debt burdens in 2007 because a smaller percentage of the debt owed comes from credit cards. At the median (50th percentile) of debt, placing respondents in a regulated 1970s credit market would reduce total debt by 33 percent. For families whose debt burdens have pushed them to admit financial failure by filing for bankruptcy, these lower debt levels may have allowed them to keep making ends meet.

TABLE II.4
*Debts of families in bankruptcy before and after simulation of
1970s credit markets*

	Mean	Standard deviation	Median
Credit card debt			
Current debt	$20,165	$30,689	$10,004
Average debt erased per household at 1970s threshold	–$19,165	$30,402	–$9,004
Minimum monthly payment on average debt	$403	--	$201
Minimum monthly payment on debt at 1970s threshold	$20	--	$20
Monthly savings under 1970s thresholds	**$383**	--	**$180**
Mortgage/rent payments			
Current payment	$687	$643	$583
Average payment erased per household at 1970s threshold	–$235	$423	–$80
New average payment at 1970s threshold	$452	--	$503
Monthly savings under 1970s thresholds	**$235**	--	**$80**
Auto loan payments			
Current payment	$160	$231	0
Average payment erased per household at 1970s threshold	–$49	$121	0
New average payment at 1970s threshold	$111	--	$0
Monthly savings under 1970s threshold	**$49**	--	**$0**
Total monthly savings under 1970s thresholds	**$667**		**$260**
Average monthly household income	$2,603		$2,266
Monthly savings as % of monthly household income	**26%**		**11%**
Increased available income per year	**$8,004**		**$3,120**

SOURCE: Consumer Bankruptcy Project 2007.

NOTE: Minimum monthly payment on average credit card debt is calculated at 2 percent of the outstanding balance.

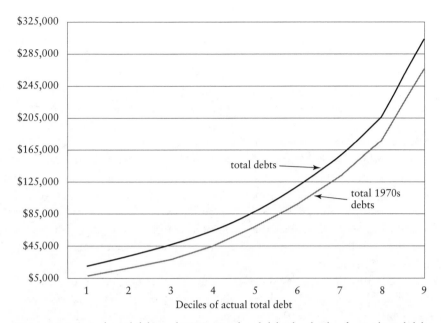

Figure 11.4 Actual total debt and 1970s simulated debt, by decile of actual total debt
SOURCE: Consumer Bankruptcy Project 2007.

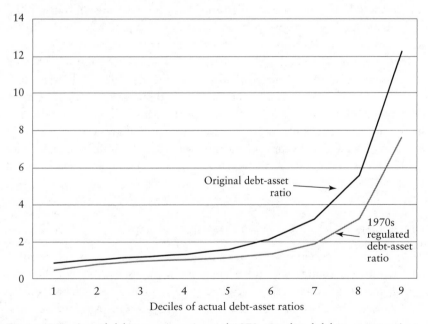

Figure 11.5 Actual debt-to-asset ratios and 1970s simulated debt-to-asset ratios, by decile of actual debt-to-asset ratio
SOURCE: Consumer Bankruptcy Project 2007.

Figure 11.5 shows households' ratio of debts to assets in the simulated 1970s credit market for each decile of actual debt-to-asset ratio. If we take negative net worth (debts greater than assets) as a signal of financial distress, the 1970s credit market would give a positive net worth to 30 percent of families in the 2007 CBP. For many of these families, such assets could be a sufficient resource to keep them out of bankruptcy. The differences in debts incurred relative to assets are dramatic at all decile levels. At the median (50th percentile), debt-to-asset ratios are reduced from 1.59 to 1.17, a substantial reduction of 26 percent in debts relative to assets. Although these families would still have negative net worth, their situation would be much improved and they may have been able to weather the financial adversity without bankruptcy. At the 80th percentile (which includes the outward bound of catastrophic cases that either have no assets at all or have very high debt levels), the debt-to-asset ratio would be reduced from 5.6 to 3.2, a drop of 43 percent.

The simulation results show that the debts of families in bankruptcy would have been dramatically reduced had they lived during the regulated credit market of the 1970s. Given such reductions, some of these households probably could have retained their middle-class lifestyles without the expense and stigma of bankruptcy. However, even with reduced debts, some families would still likely have filed for bankruptcy because job instability and drastic medical bills or other financial shocks would have caused them to fall into financial distress and to borrow to make ends meet.[40] The simulation also does not answer the question of how actual consumers would have behaved under a reduced ability to accumulate debt. There are opportunity costs associated with the lack of available credit—college classes not taken, homes not owned, cars not purchased, and consumption that would not happen. However, these results do show that, even with current incomes that have not kept up with inflation, today's families struggle with debt burdens that are seriously higher than families could have accumulated in the 1970s.

DISCUSSION AND POLICY RECOMMENDATIONS

The modest analysis in this chapter adds some information to the considerable work of the authors in other chapters of this book. My contribution is to highlight the connection between wage stagnation and debt burdens. Middle-class incomes have experienced no real growth in recent decades, and during this same period easily available credit has been used to prop up middle-class purchasing power. The precarious position of the middle class has been fueled by a deregulated credit market that allowed borrowing to substitute for earning. Although the United States made dramatic productivity gains in recent years, that wealth went to people near the top of the U.S. income distribution. Middle-class workers have not received those productivity gains in the form of increased wages, and as a partial result, incomes have stagnated. If even part of the productivity increases had been allotted to wage growth, families could have reduced reliance on borrowing or at least could have managed the very high debt loads that now characterize the middle class.

The chapters in this book paint a grim picture of the middle class. No longer a refuge of stability or prosperity, no longer the beneficiary of growth in the overall U.S. economy, the contemporary middle class is struggling. Its families are stressed by debt burdens that would have been unthinkable, not to mention illegal, under regulations that existed just three decades ago. The credit explosion has put the American Dream under intense pressure. The experiences of the bankrupt families described in this book illustrate the hardships and consequences of borrowing to make ends meet. If this situation is untenable, and unacceptable to our social mores about the role of the middle class in American life, what are the lessons for the future?

First, scholars need to continue to emphasize what is at the heart of three decades of CBP research: Americans in bankruptcy are a typical cross section of the middle class, not a deviant group of chronic failures. People in bankruptcy made the decisions that used to lead to middle-class prosperity—they own homes, have a college education, and are employed. We should turn a deaf ear to policymakers who cite a lack of personal responsibility or moral failure for families' credit problems; they should note that the families in bankruptcy are actually similar to their typical constituents. Families in bankruptcy may have failed not because they made different decisions from their nonbankrupt counterparts, but instead because their borrowing gamble to buy a house or finance college or pay for medical care simply did not pay off. Ill health, layoffs at work, or a need to help out family members may have strained their finances past the breaking point. But the key point is that these bets were placed when the family earned much lower wages (in real dollars) than in prior decades. Without wage growth, these households could not keep up with middle-class lifestyles, ultimately turning to borrowing as a supplement for wages.

Second, many people in bankruptcy are there because they have attempted to engage in activities that American society and culture value, such as pursuing higher education, starting a small business, and owning a single-family home. If we value these activities as the core of what it means to be in the middle class, then we should consider how to ease the consequences of failure from the pursuit of the American Dream. Legislative reforms to make student loan debt dischargeable in bankruptcy, for example, would be a significant step forward in this regard. Another example is to devote policy attention to the way in which the lure of entrepreneurialism will result in a certain amount of small-business failure. Instead of tightening bankruptcy laws for self-employed people as it did in 2005, Congress could recognize that increased employment volatility and the decline in stable manufacturing jobs mean that more Americans will be their own employer—an act that comes with high debt burdens and a risk of financial failure (see Chapter 6). The painful reality exposed in this book is that decisions to pursue the American Dream can themselves push families into bankruptcy. To the extent that middle-class lifestyles are funded by debt and not income, the risks have become greater in recent decades. The families in bankruptcy are a powerful reminder that failure is an outcome for some who pursue the American Dream.

Third, housing affordability played a major role in the financial meltdown that began in 2007. In an environment where average wages have stagnated and an increasing amount of wealth winds up in the hands of very few Americans, buying a house requires a level of borrowing that was not contemplated when a policy of encouraging homeownership was formulated more than fifty years ago. Deceptive mortgage practices and weak underwriting are part of this problem, but basic inflation in the housing market caused by the credit-fueled "housing bubble" is another source of this crisis. Loaning people money for homes they probably cannot afford on their incomes affects the price that all buyers must pay and inflates the housing market. The recession triggered by unsustainable mortgage debt has made plain that too much reliance on consumer debt imposes grave risks on our entire economy.

The question remains, however, whether the United States is going to extrapolate this lesson beyond housing, given the fact that overreliance on credit now pervades nearly all middle-class activities, including attending college, buying a car, and starting a business. Regulation of lending provides some insulation from these risks, and the creation of a Consumer Financial Protection Bureau seems likely to change the regulatory framework for consumer credit. A reduction in household borrowing, however, ultimately will force society to contemplate the need to achieve middle-class prosperity. For example, if student loan debt is hampering the well-being of young Americans for decades in the future, the answer might be a reinvestment in public education. But the United States continues to move in the opposite direction, requiring families to borrow for education, rather than spreading such costs throughout society. The effect of such decisions is to concentrate risks in ordinary Americans; this book suggests that the result will be years in the future in which millions of middle-class families will face financial failure and declare bankruptcy.

Finally, as my historical analysis shows, society has lost sight of the primary engine through which a consumer-driven economy grows and prospers: steady, good-paying jobs. These jobs need to limit families' exposure to income volatility and to produce increases in income over time as productivity expands. The implicit model that built the post–World War II consumer economy was that one accumulated debts when one was young (through education, marriage, and homeownership), but that one gradually paid off those debts over the working years while saving money for retirement. This pattern of credit-fueled consumption only functioned, however, when subjected to two conditions. First, credit was limited in ways that were tied to income, and lending decisions were guided by underwriting standards with a record of success. Second, borrowing to fund consumer consumption was an acceptable risk because America's economy continued to expand—with the gains in productivity leading to wage increases for all U.S. workers. The combination of these features allowed the middle-class families of prior generations to pay off their long-term debts with inflation-discounted dollars. During the past thirty years, however, American workers have been starved of the large productivity gains that their hard work generated. Yet consumer aspirations have not changed as incomes stagnated. When society did not downsize the American Dream, a deregulated credit market stepped in to permit consumption to continue and even flourish. The recession of the late 2000s exposes the costs of this pattern. As of 2011, the bills have come due for the consumer debt that defines the modern middle class. How we rebuild and regulate the consumer credit system will play a big role in determining whether the American Dream will remain only a dream in the next decade.

CHAPTER TWELVE

The Middle Class at Risk

Jacob S. Hacker

"Middle class" is more than an income category. It is an image of a certain kind of society—a society in which those who work hard share in the gains of economic growth, have a good shot at upward mobility, and enjoy the security of a basic safety net.

As the chapters in this book show, that image does not always match reality. Stories of families in bankruptcy are a particularly grim reminder that downward mobility and insecurity are a major part of contemporary middle-class life. Americans do not, it seems, need to be reminded. In a September 2010 poll, only half of Americans agreed that "the American Dream—that if you work hard you'll get ahead—still holds true"; more than four in ten said it no longer did.[1]

It is tempting to attribute this pessimism to hard economic times. Yet middle-class discontent runs much deeper than the current downturn. Over the past generation, economic risk has increasingly shifted from the broad shoulders of government and corporations onto the backs of American workers and their families. The grave and worsening problem of families in bankruptcy is only the most visible tip of a larger iceberg of economic insecurity. To reclaim the ideal of a secure and prosperous middle class, we need to understand what has gone wrong and how we can fix it.

THE GREAT RISK SHIFT

The shift of economic risk onto middle-class families has occurred in nearly every area of Americans' finances: their jobs, their retirement pensions, their homes and savings, their health care, their strategies for balancing work and family. But until the economic collapse that began at the end of 2007, the extent of this shift was largely missed and its causes were largely unexplored.

Even now, the focus remains on the immediate economic crisis and the major financial players who are deemed "too big to fail." But the economic crisis facing working families emerged well before the market crash, and tracing *its* roots is at least as crucial as examining the meltdown at the top of the economic pyramid. For it is at the heart of American family finances that we find the clearest evidence of what I have called the "Great Risk Shift," the massive downward transfer of economic risk and responsibility that has reshaped the financial lives of so many Americans.[2]

The Great Risk Shift is rooted in the erosion of America's distinctive framework of economic security. This framework differs from the frameworks found in other nations less in terms of total *size* and more in the *form* that social protections take. Responsibilities that in other nations the government handles, perhaps with the cooperation of nonprofit mutual insurers, became in the United States the responsibility of employers and for-profit providers. Government policies that promoted and regulated these private benefits to encourage their broad distribution and stability were at the core of America's uniquely "divided welfare state."[3] Yet this distinctive framework has crumbled over the past generation in the face of growing economic pressures on employers, as well as increasing political resistance to the ideal of economic security itself.

To be sure, the two years after President Barack Obama's inauguration in January 2009 witnessed the passage of a number of reforms designed to improve economic security. The biggest by far was the Affordable Care Act, passed in March 2010—a landmark health-care bill that is predicted to newly insure more than thirty million Americans by 2019. But the health-care bill was only one of several major steps taken to improve economic security amid the deepest economic downturn since the Great Depression. In addition, Congress passed a financial reform bill that will provide greater consumer protections for homebuyers and borrowers, enacted (as part of the health-care bill) a new long-term care insurance program, substantially expanded direct government student lending, and passed an economic stimulus package that included a major modernization of unemployment insurance.

Even after the passage of these measures, however, the United States still badly needs a twenty-first-century social contract that protects families against the most severe risks they face, including the financial problems that push families into overwhelming debt and bankruptcy. Forging such a contract will require recognizing and responding to the most fundamental source of U.S. economic insecurity: the deep mismatch between today's economic and social realities and America's strained framework for providing economic security. It will also require recognizing that economic security and economic opportunity are not antithetical, but go hand in hand. Just as investors and entrepreneurs need basic protections to encourage them to take economic risks, so too do ordinary workers and their families require a foundation of economic security to confidently invest in their futures and seize the risky opportunities before them.

AMERICA'S FRAGILE SAFETY NET

We often assume that the United States does little to provide economic security compared with other rich capitalist democracies. This is only partly true. The United States does spend less on government benefits as a share of its economy, but it also relies far more on private workplace benefits, such as health care and retirement pensions. Indeed, when these private benefits are factored into the mix, the U.S. framework of economic security is not smaller than the average system in other rich democracies—it is actually slightly larger.[4] With the help of hundreds of billions of dollars in tax breaks, American employers serve as the first line of defense for millions of workers buffeted by the winds of economic change.

The problem is that this unique employment-based system is coming undone, and in the process, risk is shifting back onto workers and their families. Employers want out of the social contract forged during the more stable economy of the past. And with labor unions weakened and workers worried about just holding onto their jobs, they are largely getting what they want. Meanwhile, America's framework of government support is also strained. Social security is declining in generosity, even as guaranteed private pensions evaporate. Medicare, while ever more costly, has not kept pace with skyrocketing health-care expenses and changing medical practices. Although the share of unemployed workers receiving unemployment benefits has risen in recent years, the long-term trend is one of declining support for Americans out of work, even as unemployment has shifted from cyclical job losses to permanent job displacements. And because the automatic-extension provisions of unemployment insurance have weakened, its ability to provide security depends heavily on the willingness of federal policymakers to extend benefits during downturns—a willingness that has been tested over and over again in recent recessions, leaving unemployed workers at the mercy of fierce partisan fights.

The history of American health insurance tells the story in miniature. Since the late 1970s, employers and insurers have steadily retreated from broad risk pooling in health care, and the number of Americans who lack health coverage has increased with little interruption. In 2007, more than three in five consumer bankruptcy filings (and probably a similar proportion of mortgage foreclosures) were related to medical costs and lost income due to illness or injury.[5] Most who end up facing these economic calamities have health insurance. Most are working. But insurance and work are not always enough.

In the twelve months before May 2007, for example, around three in ten nonelderly adults who had health insurance lacked adequate coverage, according to a survey by *Consumer Reports*.[6] The median family income of these "underinsured" Americans is nearly $60,000—almost exactly the same as the median income of those with adequate coverage. The underinsured are as likely to be white as the well insured, nearly as well educated, and as likely to work full time and in large- or medium-sized companies. The only consistent way in which they differ from those who are better protected is that they are at grave risk of financial collapse in the event of serious illness or injury.

Of course, the underinsured *have* coverage, however inadequate. Millions more lack even this basic protection. Everyone has heard the numbers: more than fifty million Americans do not have health insurance (compared with fewer than thirty million in 1980), the vast majority of them in working families. But the uninsured are a constantly shifting group that includes many more people than that. In the two years beginning in 2007, nearly eighty-seven million people—one out of three nonelderly Americans—went without health insurance at some point. Almost two-thirds were uninsured for at least half a year; more than half were uninsured for at least nine months. Even those whose spells without insurance are short may find themselves overwhelmed with medical bills.

Employment-based health insurance has not been the only casualty of the Great Risk Shift. Companies have also raced away from the promise of guaranteed retirement benefits. In 1985, 62 percent of medium and large firms offered traditional "defined-benefit" pensions that provided a fixed benefit for life; today, the share is less than one-fifth.[7] Instead, companies that provide pensions mostly offer "defined-contribution" plans like the 401(k), in which returns are neither predictable nor assured. Moreover, despite the expansion of 401(k) plans, the share of workers with access to a pension at their current job—either a defined-benefit plan or a 401(k) plan—has fallen from just more than half in 1979 to less than 43 percent in 2009.[8]

Defined-contribution plans are not properly seen as pensions, at least as that term has been traditionally understood. They are essentially private investment accounts sponsored by employers that can be used for building up a tax-free estate as well as for retirement savings. As a result, they greatly increase the degree of risk and responsibility placed on individual workers in retirement planning. Traditional defined-benefit plans are generally mandatory and paid for largely by employers (in lieu of cash wages). They thus represent a form of forced savings. Defined-benefit plans are also insured by the federal government and heavily regulated to protect participants against mismanagement. Perhaps most important, their fixed benefits protect workers against the risk of stock market downturns (asset risk) and the possibility of living longer than expected (longevity risk).

None of this is true of defined-contribution plans. Participation is voluntary, and because of the lack of generous employer contributions, many workers choose not to participate or they contribute inadequate sums.[9] Plans are not adequately regulated to protect against poor asset allocations or corporate or personal mismanagement. The federal government does not insure defined-contribution plans. And defined-contribution accounts provide no inherent protection against asset or longevity risks. Indeed, some features of defined-contribution plans—namely, the ability to borrow against their assets and the distribution of their accumulated savings as lump-sum payments that must be rolled over into new accounts when workers change jobs—exacerbate the risk that workers will prematurely use retirement savings, leaving inadequate income upon retirement. And, perversely, this risk falls most heavily on younger and less highly paid workers, the very workers most in need of secure retirement protection.[10]

We do not yet know how severely the market crisis that began in 2008 will reduce private pension wealth, but the signs are deeply worrisome. Just between mid-2007 and October 2008, an estimated $2 trillion in retirement wealth was lost in 401(k) and individual retirement accounts.[11] The decline in home values stripped families of wealth as well. By the end of 2008, home equity had declined 43 percent from its 2005 level.[12] Because housing wealth represented roughly half of total wealth for the vast majority of families in 2007,[13] the decline in home values also weakens the retirement security of families.

But although we cannot yet know how sustained these losses will be, we do know they come after a generation of decline in the retirement preparedness of Americans. According to researchers at Boston College, the share of working-age households that are at risk of being financially unprepared for retirement at age sixty-five rose from 31 percent in 1983 to 43 percent in 2004 and was projected to be 51 percent in 2009.[14] Younger Americans are far more likely to be at risk than older Americans: roughly half of those born from the mid-1960s through the early 1970s are at risk of being financially unprepared, compared with 35 percent of those born in the decade after World War II.[15] In every age group, low-income Americans are the least financially prepared.[16]

In sum, as private and public economic support has eroded, workers and their families have been forced to bear a greater burden. This is the essence of the Great Risk Shift. Rather than enjoying the protections of insurance that pools risk broadly, Americans are increasingly facing economic risks on their own—and often at their peril.

The erosion of America's distinctive framework of economic protection might be less worrisome if work and family were stable sources of security themselves. Unfortunately, they are not. The job market has grown more uncertain and risky, especially for those who were once best protected from its vagaries. Workers and their families now invest more in education to earn a middle-class living. Yet in today's postindustrial economy, these costly investments are no guarantee of a high, stable, or upward-sloping path, as evidenced by the increased risk for bankruptcy among people with some college education reported in Chapter 5. For displaced workers, the prospect of gaining new jobs with relatively similar pay and benefits has fallen, and the ranks of the long-term unemployed and "shadow unemployed" (workers who have given up looking for jobs altogether) have grown.[17]

Meanwhile, the family, a sphere that was once seen as a refuge from economic risk, has increasingly become a source of risk of its own. According to calculations by Jared Bernstein and Karen Kornbluh, more than three-quarters of the modest 24 percent rise in real income experienced by families in the middle of the income spectrum between 1979 and 2000 was due to increased work hours (primarily the addition of a second earner) rather than rising wages.[18]

With families needing two earners to maintain a middle-class standard of living, their economic calculus has changed in ways that accentuate many of the risks they face. What happens when a woman leaves the workforce to have children, when a child is chronically ill, when one spouse loses his or her job, or when an elderly parent needs assistance? Precisely because it takes more work and more income to maintain a middle-class standard of living, events that require the care and time of family members produce special demands and strains on two-earner families that traditional one-earner families generally did not face.

INCOME INSTABILITY HEIGHTENS ECONOMIC RISK

The new world of work and family has ushered in a new crop of highly leveraged investors—middle-class families. One sign of the change is the rising instability of family incomes. Although the precise magnitude of the increase depends on how the income variance is measured, my own research using the Panel Study of Income Dynamics (PSID) suggests that short-term family income variance essentially doubled from 1969 to 2004. Much of the rise in income volatility occurred before 1985, and volatility dropped substantially in the late 1990s. In recent years, however, income volatility has risen to exceed its 1980s peak. The proportion of working-age individuals experiencing a 50 percent or greater drop in their family incomes has climbed from less than 4 percent in the early 1970s to nearly 10 percent in the early 2000s. And while less-educated and poorer Americans have less stable family incomes than their better-educated and wealthier peers, the increase in family income volatility affects all major demographic and economic groups. Indeed, Americans with at least four years of college experienced a larger increase in family income instability than those with only a high school education over the past generation, with most of the rise occurring in the past fifteen years.[19]

Family income instability is only one aspect of Americans' growing economic insecurity. Along with a team of researchers (and with funding from the Rockefeller Foundation), I have developed the Economic Security Index (ESI).[20] The ESI adds to the research on income instability by looking at economic instability caused by out-of-pocket medical spending as well as by income fluctuations. It also considers whether families have adequate financial safety nets to cushion these economic shocks. In a nutshell, the ESI represents the share of Americans who experience at least a 25 percent decline in their inflation-adjusted "available household income" from one year to the next and who lack an adequate financial safety net to replace this lost income until it has returned to its original level. "Available household income" is income that is reduced by nondiscretionary spending, including, most substantially, the amount of a household's out-of-pocket medical spending (the other main form of nondiscretionary spending the ESI considers is the cost of servicing the household's debts). Thus, Americans may experience income losses of 25 percent or greater due to a decline in income, an increase in medical spending, or a combination of the two.

The ESI, available from 1985 through 2007 (with projections for 2008 and 2009) shows that economic insecurity has increased substantially over the past quarter century (see Figure 12.1). In 1985, 12 percent of Americans experienced a major economic loss sufficient to classify them as insecure in the ESI. During the recession of the early 2000s, this had risen to 17 percent, and projections suggest that in 2009 the level of economic insecurity experienced by Americans was greater than at any time over the past quarter century, with approximately one in five Americans experiencing a decline in available household income of 25 percent or greater without an adequate financial safety net.

This is not just a reflection of the steep economic downturn of recent years. Rather, economic security has been gradually declining since the early 1980s. Seeing beyond short-term economic fluctuations requires statistically calculating the longer term trend in the ESI, which is shown in Figure 12.1. This analysis shows that the ESI has increased by approximately one-third from 1985 to 2007. If the projections to 2009 are included, the ESI increased by almost half (49.9 percent) since 1985. To state this trend in terms of

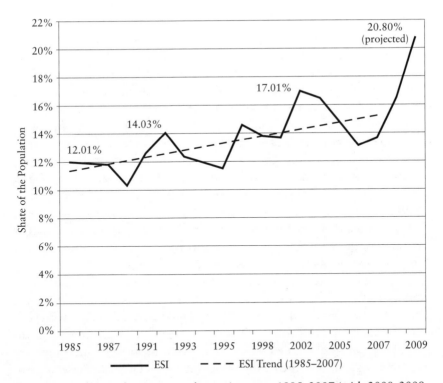

Figure 12.1 Share of Americans who are insecure, 1985–2007 (with 2008–2009 projections)

SOURCE: Hacker et al., Economic Security at Risk.

NOTE: The "insecure" are those whose available household income declines by at least 25 percent from one year to the next as a result of a decline in household income and/or an increase in out-of-pocket medical spending *and* who lack an adequate financial safety net (with "adequate" defined as enough liquid wealth to compensate for the lost income until typical recovery to predrop income or for six years, whatever comes first). See source for additional details.

population, approximately forty-six million Americans were counted as insecure in 2007, up from twenty-eight million in 1985. Moreover, the share of Americans experiencing large drops in available household income has increased even more since the 1960s. A less complete form of the ESI available back to the late 1960s shows that large (25 percent or greater) income losses—the core component of the complete ESI—had already risen by about one-third from the 1960s to the 1980s, making subsequent increases over the past quarter century even more noteworthy.

THE INDEBTED AMERICAN FAMILY

The rising instability of family incomes would be less troubling if families had substantial liquid savings to tide them over during periods with reduced income. Yet, as the ESI suggests and this book documents in great depth, very few families have even modest holdings of wealth besides their house. Instead, Americans are often deeply indebted, especially families with children. According to a 2007 analysis of families with incomes between two and six times the federal poverty level and headed by working-age adults, more than half of middle-class families have no net financial assets (excluding home equity), and nearly four in five middle-class families do not have sufficient assets to cover three-quarters of essential living expenses for even three months should their incomes disappear.[21] And, of course, the economic crisis of the late 2000s only exacerbated the problem, causing a loss of $15 trillion in private family assets and wealth between June 2007 and December 2008.[22]

With debt levels rising, bankruptcy has gone from a rare occurrence to a relatively common one among American families. This book shows that there are few more potent signs of the Great Risk Shift than the steep climb in bankruptcy filings. It also shows that, as bankruptcy rates have risen, the financial characteristics of the bankrupt have grown worse and worse, contrary to the claim that bankruptcy is increasingly being used by people with only mild financial difficulties.[23] Strikingly, married couples with children are much more likely to file for bankruptcy than are couples without children or single individuals.[24] Otherwise, people in bankruptcy are pretty much like other Americans before they file: slightly better educated, roughly as likely to have had a good job, and modestly less likely to own a home. As Elizabeth Warren and Deborah Thorne set out in Chapter 2, the bankrupt are not the persistently poor or the downtrodden looking for relief; they are refugees of the middle class, frequently wondering how they fell so far so fast.

Americans are also losing their homes at record rates. Even before the housing market collapsed in 2008, there had been a fivefold increase since the 1970s in the share of households that fall into foreclosure[25]—a process that begins when homeowners default on their mortgages and can end with homes being auctioned to the highest bidder in local courthouses. The run-up of housing prices before the economic downturn had much less of a positive effect on Americans' net worth than might be supposed. Even as home prices rose, Americans held less and less equity in their homes. As recently as the early 1980s, home equity was around 70 percent of home value on average; in 2007, it was 43 percent—the lowest level on record.[26] In the downturn of the late 2000s, approximately 20 percent of homeowners owed more on their homes than those homes were worth.[27] For scores of ordinary homeowners facing foreclosure—roughly one in twenty-five mortgage-owning households in the past few years, a level not seen since the Great Depression—the American Dream has mutated into the American Nightmare.

THE AMERICAN DREAM OF ECONOMIC SECURITY

No message of this book is clearer than this: economic insecurity is not just a problem of the poor and disadvantaged. It affects solidly middle-class Americans—men and women who thought they had bought the ticket to upward mobility and economic stability by staying in school, buying a home, and investing in their 401(k) accounts. Insecurity today reaches across the income spectrum, the racial divide, and lines of geography and gender. Increasingly, all Americans are riding the economic rollercoaster once reserved for the working poor and, thus, are at risk of losing the secure financial foundation they need to reach for and achieve the American Dream.

Economic security matters deeply to people. When most of us contemplate the financial risks in our lives, we do not concern ourselves all that much with the upside risks—the chance we will receive an unexpected bonus, for example. We worry about the downside risks, and worry about them intensely. In the 1970s, psychologists Amos Tversky and Daniel Kahneman gave a name to this bias: "loss aversion."[28] Most people, it turns out, are not just highly risk-averse—they prefer a bird in the hand to even a very good chance of two in the bush. They are also far more cautious when it comes to bad outcomes than when it comes to good outcomes of exactly the same magnitude. The search for economic security is, in large part, a reflection of a basic human desire for protection against losing what one already has.

This desire is surprisingly strong. Americans are famously opportunity loving, but when asked in 2005 whether they were "more concerned with the opportunity to make money in the future, or the stability of knowing that your present sources of income are protected," 62 percent favored stability and just 29 percent favored opportunity.[29]

It should not be surprising, therefore, that recent polling shows extremely high levels of economic anxiety among all but the richest Americans. In April 2009, two in three adults said that the current economy presented them with more risks than their parents confronted—six times as many as the 11 percent who said they faced fewer risks than their parents.[30] A comprehensive poll concerning economic risk that I helped design—fielded as part of the American National Election Studies—asked Americans about fifteen different sources of economic risk in employment, medical care, wealth, and family relations. More than three-quarters of all Americans reported that they were very or fairly worried about at least one of these economic risks. As Figure 12.2 shows, worries about wealth were the most frequent cause of economic unease, though concerns about medical costs were a close second.[31]

These are not idle worries. Households that experienced these economic risks between March 2008 and September 2009—especially risks that per-

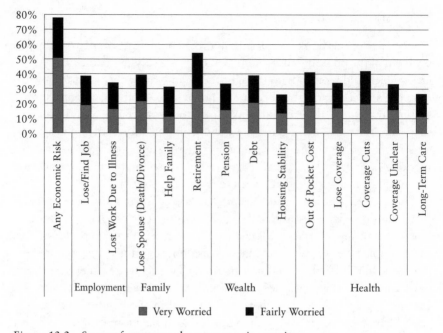

Figure 12.2   Scope of concerns about economic security
SOURCE: Hacker, Rehm, and Schlesinger, "Standing on Shaky Ground."
NOTE: The SERPI was collected in two waves as part of the panel survey of the 2008–2009 American National Election Study (ANES); the spring 2009 wave had just under twenty-five hundred respondents. All results are weighted to account for sample attrition and to be representative of the U.S. population.

sisted for six months or more—reported much higher levels of unmet basic needs: going without food because of the cost, losing one's house or rental, or going without health care because of the expense. This was particularly true of employment and medical risks: households experiencing employment and medical spending risks were three times as likely as unaffected households to report any unmet needs and seven times as likely to report multiple unmet needs. Strikingly, even among families in the third quartile of household income (annual income between $60,000 and $100,000), the same association between economic risks and unmet basic needs held true. More than half of families with income between $60,000 and $100,000 who experienced employment or medical disruptions reported being unable to meet at least one basic economic need.

Yet even before the economic crisis, people were already extremely worried about their economic security. In a February 2007 survey, for example, 63 percent of Americans declared that the economy had become less secure in the past decade, compared with 18 percent who felt the economy had become more secure.[32] The strongest sense of rising insecurity was felt among those with family incomes between $36,000 and $92,000; respondents in this income bracket reported feeling that the economy had grown less secure rather than more secure by a margin greater than four to one (67 percent versus 17 percent, respectively).[33] In the same 2007 poll, a majority of Americans also expected things to get less secure over the next twenty years.

It would be one thing if all this risk came with great reward for the middle class. After all, people will sometimes trade higher risks—a greater chance of losing their job, for example—for higher rewards. Yet the increased economic rewards for middle-class families have been decidedly modest during the era of rising economic insecurity. Although overall economic productivity has risen handsomely, and incomes at the very top of the economic ladder have shot upward, median incomes have grown relatively slowly since the 1970s. As Kevin Leicht explains in Chapter 11, the result has been a growing gulf between productivity growth and the economic fate of the middle class. This divorce is all the more striking in light of the reality that most of the income gains of middle-class families were due to the fact that family members were working more hours, not that they were receiving higher pay. The risk-reward trade-off looks more like a risk-reward rip-off.

REDUCING RISK, ENHANCING OPPORTUNITY

Who killed the old social contract that emphasized shared risk and shared reward? To some, the culprit is the unstoppable forces of technology and globalization. Computers and automation have reduced the rewards for routine skills and encouraged outsourcing and offshoring. The entry of hundreds of millions of literate low-wage workers into the global workforce has undermined the earning power of middle-class Americans. Compared with these vast tides, the conventional wisdom suggests, American politics and policy have played only a bit role—and can do only a limited amount to reclaim the American Dream.

Technological change and globalization matter immensely. But all rich countries have experienced their effects—most more so than the United States—and yet few have seen anything like America's sharp upward shift of economic rewards, erosion of economic security, or breakdown of social benefits. Moreover, in many nations where inequality and insecurity have risen, policymakers have pushed back through active labor market policies, taxes, and public spending. Not so in the United States. Despite the Earned Income Tax Credit and expansion of Medicaid, low-wage workers have continued to fall behind. According to the Congressional Budget Office, even after all public and private benefits and federal taxes are taken into account, almost 40 percent of all household income gains between 1979 and 2007 accrued to the richest 1 percent of Americans—more than received by the bottom 90 percent *combined*.

The recent string of large tax cuts for the richest of Americans has highlighted the long-term role of our tax system in abetting inequality. Far more important and less recognized have been ways in which public policies have remade markets to advantage the top. Failure to enforce the National Labor Relations Act (the Wagner Act) has undermined labor unions as a force for good pay and benefits. Corporate governance rules all but asked top executives to drive up their own earnings. Financial deregulation brought great riches for some while pushing many ordinary families into unaffordable loans, and ultimately crashing the economy.

Perhaps the least visible policy changes were passive-aggressive in nature—deliberate failures to address changing economic and social conditions, such as the need for families to balance work and family. Entire categories of support that have become essential to middle-class life, such as good child care, are simply not a public responsibility. Meanwhile, as we have seen, responsibilities that corporations once shouldered are shifting back onto families. Uniquely among industrial nations, the United States came to rely on employers as miniwelfare states, providing health insurance, pensions, and other benefits that elsewhere enjoyed state sponsorship. But as employers have pulled back, government has not filled the gap, leaving families more vulnerable.

Perhaps it is not surprising then that so many middle-class Americans feel abandoned. Asked in mid-2010 whom government had helped "a great deal" during the downturn, 53 percent of Americans said banks and financial institutions; 44 percent fingered large corporations. Just 2 percent thought economic policies had helped the middle class a great deal.

Of course, we cannot turn back the clock on many of the changes that have swept through our economy and society. Nor would we always want to. Accepting our new economic and social realities does not, however, mean accepting the new economic insecurity, much less accepting the assumptions that lie behind the current assault on the ideal of security. Americans will need to do much on their own initiatives to secure themselves in the new world of work and family, but they should be protected by an improved safety net that fills the most glaring gaps in present protections. This safety net should provide all Americans with the basic security they need to reach for the future as workers, as parents, and as citizens.

The first priority for restoring security should be Hippocrates's injunction to "do no harm." Undoing what risk pooling remains in the private sector without putting something better in place is harmful. Piling tax break upon tax break to allow wealthy and healthy Americans to opt out of our tattered institutions of social insurance is harmful. And though simplifying our tax code makes eminent sense, making it markedly less progressive through a flat tax or national sales tax would also be harmful. A progressive income tax, after all, is effectively a form of insurance, reducing our contribution to public goods when income falls and raising it when income rises. State and local taxes are generally regressive: according to a 2009 analysis, the richest 1 percent of households paid an effective state and local tax rate of just over 5 percent of income (after the federal tax deduction for state and local taxes is taken into account), the middle fifth of households paid 9.4 percent, and the bottom fifth paid 10.9 percent.[34] Although the federal income tax has become less progressive (especially when it comes to the taxation of very high incomes), it remains the last major bulwark against rising economic inequality.

Figure 12.3 shows that the ESI is higher (meaning greater insecurity) for less affluent families than for more affluent ones. Lower income families generally have little or no wealth to protect their standards of living when income declines, and they are least likely to have access to workplace health or disability insurance. Not surprisingly, therefore, unemployment has a much larger effect on the consumption patterns of lower income families than it has on those of higher income families.

Yet although we should work to preserve the best elements of existing policies, we should also recognize that the nature and causes of insecurity,

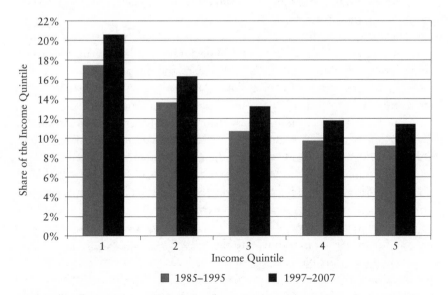

Figure 12.3 Share of Americans who are insecure, 1985–1995, 1997–2007, by income quintile
SOURCE: Hacker et al., Economic Security at Risk.

as well as our understanding of how to best address them, have evolved considerably. During the New Deal, economic insecurity was largely seen as a problem of drops or interruptions in male earnings, whether due to unemployment, retirement, or other costly events. Even as working women became the norm, our programs failed to address the special economic strains that two-earner families face. So too did they fail to address the distinctive unemployment patterns that became increasingly prevalent as industrial employment gave way to service work—for example, the rising prevalence of long-term unemployment (in 2010, it took an average of more than twenty weeks for a person to find a new job, double the amount of time in the 1982–1983 recession)[35] and the shift of workers from one economic sector to another that often leads to large cuts in pay and the need for specialized retraining.

Flaws in existing policies of risk protection have also become apparent. Our framework of social protection is overwhelmingly focused on the aged, even though young adults and families with children face the greatest economic strains. It emphasizes short-term exits from the workforce, even though long-term job losses and the displacement and obsolescence of skills have become more severe. In many ways, it embodies the antiquated notion that family strains can be dealt with by a second earner—usually a woman—who can easily enter or leave the workforce as necessary. Above all, it is based on the idea that job-based private insurance can easily fill the gaps left by public programs, even though it is ever clearer that job-based private insurance is not enough.

These shortcomings suggest that an improved safety net should emphasize portable insurance to help families deal with major interruptions to income and big blows to wealth. They also mean that these promises should be mostly separate from work for a particular employer: the safety net should move from job to job. If this sometimes means corporations are off the hook, so be it. In time, they will pay their workers more to compensate for fewer benefits, and there are plenty of ways to encourage their contributions without having them decide who gets benefits and who does not.

By the same token, however, we should not force massive social risks onto institutions incapable of effectively carrying them. Bankruptcy should not be a backdoor social insurance system, private charity care should not be our main medical safety net, and credit cards should not be supplemental income for families when times are tight. To be sure, when nothing better is possible, the principle "do no harm" may dictate protecting even incomplete and inadequate safety nets. The ultimate goal, however, should be a new framework of social insurance that revitalizes the best elements of the present system, while replacing those parts that work less effectively with stronger alternatives geared toward today's economy and society.

Which brings us to the final principle: measures to enhance economic security should be designed to enhance economic opportunity. Most of us think of our nation's safety net as a way of helping those who have had bad fortune or have fallen on hard times. Yet providing economic security has far broader benefits for our economy and our society. Corporate law has long recognized the need to limit the downside of economic risk taking as a way of encouraging entrepreneurs and investors to make the risky investments necessary to advance in a capitalist economy. The law of bankruptcy and the principle of limited liability—the notion that those who run a firm are not personally liable if the firm fails—allow entrepreneurs to innovate with the security of knowing that they will not be financially destroyed if their risky bets fail.[36]

Just as entrepreneurs need basic protections to foster risk taking, families also need a basic foundation of financial security if they are to feel confident in making the investments required to advance in a dynamic economy. All of the major wellsprings of economic opportunity in the United States—including assets, workplace skills, education, and investments in children—are costly and risky for families to cultivate. Providing security can encourage families to make these investments, aiding not just their own advancement but improving the economy as a whole. Bankruptcy can be a backstop for the worst financial collapses, but it was never intended as a replacement for a well-designed and robust social safety net.

The challenge, then, is to construct a twenty-first-century social contract that protects families against the most severe risks they face, without clamping down on the potentially beneficial processes of change and adjustment that produce some of these risks. Three areas of economic risk in particular cry out for attention: employment risks, retirement income risks, and health-care risks. But it would be a mistake to design economic protections only narrowly around specific economic concerns. Another priority is to create new measures that provide protection across multiple economic risks, such as flexible leave and income-maintenance policies that people can use to deal with taking care of personal sickness, raising children, caring for aging parents, retraining for a job, and other interruptions of earnings. As this book illustrates, failing to provide a sufficient cushion against these adverse financial shocks can leave families borrowing to try to make ends meet. Some of these families will go bankrupt, experiencing threatened and actual home loss (Chapter 4) and increased family stress (Chapter 8) and making reduced investments in education (Chapter 5) and small businesses (Chapter 6). Until comprehensive policies reduce the risks that families face from job loss, medical problems, and family events, more than a million families who experience financial collapse each year will seek aid in the bankruptcy courts.

All these changes, of course, will not come without costs, and they certainly will not come without political struggle. Yet against the costs, one must balance the savings. Billions of dollars in hidden taxes are currently imposed by laws that increase the bankruptcy rate, mandate emergency room care, and bail out the politically sympathetic when things go bad. The elimination of these expenses must be accounted for when tallying up the bill, as should the huge drain that our current system imposes when people do not change jobs, do not have children, or do not invest in new skills because they fear the downside risks. Bankruptcy relief for approximately 1.5 million middle-class families each year is ultimately an enormously wasteful, inefficient, and incapable means of providing economic security to those who most need it.

As this book illustrates, American families can, and do, fail at achieving and maintaining the American Dream of economic security and opportunity. The stories of the bankrupt are powerful evidence of the harms that the existing allocation of risk imposes on families, private industry, and the government in the United States. Left on their own to cope with economic risks, hardworking families will continue to be overwhelmed, and the American middle class will continue to be threatened. New policies are needed to share the risks of the twenty-first-century economy broadly—to help guard people against financial ruin from job loss, illness or injury, family breakup, or small-business collapse. It is time to retool and rebuild America's crumbling framework of economic security to put the American middle class back on a stable path.

Methodology of the
2007 Consumer Bankruptcy Project

Katherine Porter

OVERVIEW

This appendix provides a detailed methodology for the 2007 Consumer Bankruptcy Project (CBP) and an important context for understanding the findings and implications of the chapters of this book. The CBP is an iterative, interdisciplinary study of households that file consumer bankruptcy cases. To date, there have been four studies, which have normally been identified by the year in which the sample of debtors filed for bankruptcy (1981, 1991, 2001, and 2007). Each iteration of the CBP was slightly different in its approach, but all studies collected data on the demographic and economic characteristics of people in bankruptcy.

The principal investigators for both the 1981 and 1991 CBP studies were Teresa Sullivan, Elizabeth Warren, and Jay Lawrence Westbrook. The 1981 CBP used only data from bankruptcy court records. It sampled fifteen hundred cases in Illinois, Pennsylvania, and Texas. The main findings of the 1981 CBP, including a detailed methodology, are presented in Sullivan, Warren, and Westbrook, *As We Forgive Our Debtors*. The 1991 CBP also used data from bankruptcy court records but also included demographic data using a written questionnaire distributed to debtors. The main findings of the 1991 CBP, including a detailed methodology, are provided in Sullivan, Warren, and Westbrook, *The Fragile Middle Class*.

The 2001 CBP featured both an expanded research team and the addition of a new instrument: telephone interviews.[1] The 2001 sample consisted of 1,250 cases from five judicial districts. In addition to data from the bankruptcy court records and a four-page written questionnaire, some respondents participated in telephone interviews one year and three years after bankruptcy. An extended methodology of the 2001 CBP is presented in the appendix of Warren and Tyagi, *The Two-Income Trap*.

The 2007 CBP was a collaborative research endeavor. See the acknowl-edgments to this book for a list of the principal investigators and funders. The analysis and views expressed in this book are those of the authors, not the funders.

SAMPLE

The CBP sample consisted only of cases filed under Chapter 7 or Chapter 13 of the U.S. Bankruptcy Code. Individual (nonentity) debtors can file bankruptcy under other chapters of the Bankruptcy Code, but these cases are very rare and were excluded.[2] The CBP sample excluded cases filed by businesses and included only consumer bankruptcy cases. There is no single, perfect standard for classifying a case as a consumer case, rather than a business case.[3] If the debtor's name on the bankruptcy petition was not that of an individual person (that is, it was a legal entity such as a corporation or a partnership), those cases were eliminated as business cases.

Beginning the last week in January 2007, and continuing for five consecutive weeks, the CBP collected the following information from every bankruptcy petition filed in the United States during that week: debtors' names, debtors' addresses, and chapter filed. Approximately 12,500 to 18,000 cases were filed each week. The 2007 national filing data were supplied by the help of Mike Bickford and his colleagues at AACER (Automated Access to Court Electronic Records), a bankruptcy data company.

From the weekly data of all cases, the following cases were deleted: (1) cases that were not Chapter 7 or Chapter 13 cases, (2) cases that were not personal bankruptcies (there was no person's name listed as a petitioner, only the name of a legal entity such as a corporation or partnership), (3) cases filed outside the fifty states and the District of Columbia (for example, cases filed in Guam and Puerto Rico), and (4) cases that did not have an address listed for the debtor. From the remaining cases, a weekly sample of one thousand was randomly selected for a total of five thousand cases during the sample period.

Although the CBP attempted to contact petitioners immediately following the bankruptcy filing, some addresses were not valid, and correspondence was returned as undeliverable. To replace those cases, an additional random sample of 255 "replacement" cases was drawn. The same procedures were used to contact these debtors as described below.

To study more closely the bankruptcies of older Americans, the CBP collected data from a supplemental sample of bankruptcy cases filed by people who some external validation suggested were likely to be sixty-five years or older. No chapter in this book uses data from the supplemental sample of older Americans.

CONSENT PROCESS

Immediately after each week's random sample was identified, the CBP mailed debtors a letter that briefly described the study and explained that they could expect to receive a questionnaire in the mail in a few days. This letter included a brief note in Spanish, explaining that if debtors needed a Spanish version of the questionnaire, they should call the CBP's toll-free number. The questionnaire itself was translated into Spanish by one person and back-translated into English by another person to check the quality of the translation.

Approximately a week after the initial letter, questionnaires were mailed to the debtors. The questionnaire packet included a cover letter, a questionnaire, a stamped return envelope, and $2 in cash as a token of appreciation.

One week after the questionnaires were mailed, thank you/reminder letters were sent. Research assistants also attempted to contact respondents by phone to remind them to return the questionnaires. Some petitions (usually those of pro se debtors) provided phone numbers; for the remainder, the CBP used an online search engine to locate phone numbers.

Approximately one month after initial questionnaires were mailed, replacement questionnaires, along with another $2 in cash, were mailed to those households that had not yet responded. Included in these mailings was a flyer that informed respondents that they could also complete the questionnaire by either (1) calling a toll-free number and talking with a research assistant, or (2) visiting an online secure site.

Beginning the first of July 2007 (four to six months after the first mailing), the CBP sent a final letter to debtors who had not returned questionnaires and offered them $50 to complete the questionnaire over the phone or online.

RESPONSE RATE

A total of 5,251 questionnaires were mailed to Chapter 7 or Chapter 13 debtors. Even after the replacement process described above, a total of 275 cases (5.2 percent) were returned undeliverable and not replaced. The total number of debtors who were assumed to have received the consent letter and questionnaire is thus 4,976 (5,251 less 275) cases. Table A.1 details the response rate from the 4,976 households.

Of the 2,438 returned questionnaires (complete or incomplete), 70.1 percent of the debtors were single filings (only one person was listed as a bankruptcy debtor in the case). The remaining 29.9 percent of the debtors filed joint cases. All of the joint cases were filed by married couples, but some of the single cases were filed by married people with only one spouse seeking bankruptcy relief.

TABLE A.I
Response rate to written questionnaire mailings

Response type	Number of cases	Percentage of sample
Not returned	2,455	49.3
Refused to participate	83	1.7
Returned completed	2,314	46.5
Returned incomplete	124	2.5
Total of all cases	4,976	100
Total responses received	2,521	50.7
Total returned questionnaires	2,438	49.3

SOURCE: Consumer Bankruptcy Project 2007.

Two-thirds (66 percent) of the debtors who returned questionnaires filed Chapter 7 cases and one-third (34 percent) of the debtors filed Chapter 13 cases. During roughly the same period as the CBP mailings, Chapter 7 cases were 62.3 percent and Chapter 13 cases were 37.7 percent of the total number of Chapter 7 and Chapter 13 nonbusiness bankruptcy cases.[4] This suggests that the sample overrepresents Chapter 7 debtors and underrepresents Chapter 13 debtors.

WRITTEN QUESTIONNAIRE

The questionnaire asked debtors to provide detailed demographic information, including age, marital status, and race. In addition, the questionnaire asked about student loans, homeownership, medical debts, self-employment, and the effects of debts on relationships with children and partners. Respondents were also asked to choose from closed-ended lists to indicate what they did in order to cope financially before they filed for bankruptcy and what the reasons were that contributed to their filing for bankruptcy. The last page of the questionnaire asked whether the debtor was willing to complete a telephone interview, for which they would receive $50 in compensation. The questionnaire also contained a blank space for debtors to share the story of their bankruptcy in their own words.

Questionnaires were coded into a specially designed database by trained research assistants. The coding assistants began their training by coding six practice questionnaires that were intentionally complicated and ambiguous and therefore prone to coding errors. Their coding was reviewed, and they received feedback and further instruction on any errors. The first dozen questionnaires completed by each coder also were reviewed for any errors. Furthermore, if a coder suspected any errors in the questionnaire (for example, inconsistencies in the respondent's answers or problems that the coder could not address), the coder selected a dropdown box that indicated a potential error. Deborah Thorne, a principal investigator, reviewed each of these cases individually. She also responded to all questions from coders.

The questionnaire data were cleaned of obvious errors and inconsistencies. For example, spouses were not to be coded as dependents. If a case had been incorrectly coded this way, Deborah Thorne recoded it, removing the spouse as a dependent. Then, a test of intercoder reliability was conducted. A random sample of 10 percent of questionnaires (approximately 250 questionnaires) was blind coded a second time by a different coder. A research assistant flagged all inconsistencies between each pair of cases. For every 100 cases, there were approximately 10,400 data points and 19 errors. This translates to 1.8 errors per every 1,000 data points, an error rate of less than 0.2 percent.

COURT RECORDS

Once a debtor responded to the researchers, either by returning a completed or blank questionnaire or by refusing to participate, the debtor's court records were collected from the federal court's electronic filing system, Public Access to Court Electronic Records (PACER). For every case, the docket sheet, petition, financial schedules, Statement of Financial Affairs (Form 8), and Statement of Intention (Form 7) were downloaded. If the debtor had filed amendments to any of these documents, the research assistants downloaded the amendments for coding. If applicable in the case, research assistants also downloaded reaffirmation agreements and certain motions (for example, dismissal of the case), as well as any corresponding orders on those motions.

Research assistants coded the files into a specially designed database. Coders received training that covered the basic principles of bankruptcy law, described the purpose and format of the court records, and explained how to code the data from the cases. The coders then completed at least two practice cases: a Chapter 7 case and a Chapter 13 case. The sample cases were reviewed and any errors were discussed with the coder. Some court record coding occurred as part of research seminars at the University of Michigan Law School and Harvard Law School. Jeff Paulsen, a law student with prior bankruptcy training and experience in bankruptcy data software, helped supervise the court record coding process.

The coding process collected the same selected information from each of the court files with the obvious caveat that information inapplicable to a case could not be collected. For example, the information about a Chapter 13 plan could not be collected for the Chapter 7 cases. Overall, the variables collected from the court records fell into two broad groups: 71 variables of identifying information about the debtor, the court, or the court proceedings; and 120 variables of financial information about the debtor.

Slight variations in court forms, local legal culture, and even attorney idiosyncrasies in completing the forms meant that the same information might be presented differently in two different court files. All inquiries were centralized so that coders would receive consistent answers to their questions. Additionally, an "error" variable was used in a manner similar to that variable for the written questionnaires.

For testing of intercoder reliability, a random sample of 10 percent of the court records was blind coded a second time by a different coder. Individual coders were not aware of whether a particular case would be selected for blind recoding or whether the case they were coding was a second coding of a previously coded case. Jeff Paulsen reviewed the first batch of recoded files, approximately 20 court records, and contacted the coders to correct any mistakes that had been made. Once the court record coding was complete, the data from the 258 double-coded cases were compared with that from the original coding of these cases. Melissa Jacoby, a principal investigator, checked any discrepancies in the two codings, examining 132 discrete variables in each case.[5] In the original coding, 297 errors were identified among the 34,056 variable entries, for an error rate of 0.009.[6]

To test for response bias, the CBP drew a random sample of one hundred cases from the population of cases that met the sample criteria. Court records were coded for those cases and then compared with the court records of those debtors who returned questionnaires. Robert Lawless, a principal investigator, performed checks to analyze the existence of bias in key variables. Analysis showed few concerns for response bias: the debtors who returned written questionnaires had similar characteristics to the random sample of all eligible debtors. Table A.2 shows the results of the bias checks. The exceptions of note are that Chapter 13 filers are underrepresented among respondents and that nonrespondents had lower unsecured debt than respondents.

In the first half of 2008, the CBP coded additional variables from the court records. The purpose of this coding was to capture significant information about the progress or outcome of each case, including whether the case had been dismissed or converted and whether certain motions and corresponding orders were filed in the case since the time of the initial coding. To gather these data, CBP researchers downloaded and coded a new version of each debtor's court records. The coding protocols for the 2008 Update Coding, including code training and error checks, were similar to those used in the initial coding. Melissa Jacoby supervised this process.

TABLE A.2
Differences between nonrespondents and respondents

	Nonrespondents	Respondents
Joint filing status	21.2%	29.8%
Chapter 13 case	49.5%	33.9%
Consumer (nonbusiness) debt	98.0%	98.1%
Prior bankruptcy	13.5%	20.4%
Total paid attorney	$1,766 ($1,500)	$1,572 ($1,200)
Home market value[a]	$156,050 ($118,500)	$147,861 ($111,435)
Total real property	$83,870 ($27,240)	$82,216 ($20,000)
Total personal property	$19,970 ($14,082)	$21,692 ($12,443)
Total assets	$103,840 ($56,101)	$103,934 ($50,309)
Total secured debt	$86,783 ($35,701)	$87,353 ($31,079)
Total priority debt	$3,212 ($0)	$2,535 ($0)
Total unsecured debt	$35,247 ($23,924)	$56,999 ($32,807)
Total debts	$125,242 ($84,436)	$146,848 ($86,533)
Combined monthly income	$2,972 ($2,290)	$2,630 ($2,266)
Total expenses	$2,787 ($2,099)	$2,606 ($2,263)

SOURCE: Consumer Bankruptcy Project 2007.

NOTE: Values for continuous variables are means. Medians are reported in parentheses.

[a]Value of the home only for those who owned a home.

TELEPHONE INTERVIEWS

The questionnaire offered respondents the opportunity to volunteer for a telephone interview for which they would be paid $50. Of the 2,314 completed questionnaires that were returned from the sample, 2,007 respondents (86.7 percent) indicated an interest in a telephone interview. Over the course of the interviewing process, 69 of these respondents stated that they no longer wanted to participate.[7] Interviews were completed with 1,032 respondents, which is 51.4 percent of those who indicated that they wanted to be interviewed. All telephone interviews were conducted between September 4, 2007, and February 7, 2008. The median time for completing the interview was one hour, fifteen minutes.

Both money and time helped determine the total number of completed telephone interviews. The CBP had adequate funding for approximately one thousand telephone interviews and agreed that the data collection should end by early February 2008, which was approximately one year after the beginning of the study. At the beginning of the telephone interview process, each interviewer received a unique list of names of respondents who had indicated that they were willing to be interviewed. Before concluding the interviews, interviewers had attempted to contact all respondents who indicated on their questionnaires that they wanted an interview. To accommodate the wide range of respondents' work schedules, the interviewers conducted interviews as early as 6:00 a.m. and as late as midnight. When interviewers were unable to reach a respondent by phone, they left messages with other individuals who answered the phone, left messages on answering machines (out of respect for the respondents, we left no more than three messages, either with the person who answered the phone or on the machine), sent e-mail messages (if the respondent had provided an e-mail address on the questionnaire), and mailed short reminder letters. Interviewers were instructed to work diligently to contact and complete interviews with everyone on their lists, not only those respondents who responded promptly and were immediately available for an interview. To ensure that interviewers did not interview only the most available respondents, interviewers received fresh lists only after they had attempted to contact each respondent on their previous list three times.

The telephone interview comprised five sections: general, medical, housing, small business, and military. The general section addressed employment, credit cards, student loans, psychological and familial effects of indebtedness, privations before bankruptcy, general health and insurance issues, and financial circumstances after bankruptcy. All respondents were asked the general questions. If applicable to their circumstances, debtors were asked questions in the four specialty sections. For example, if the respondent or a spouse was self-employed or owned a small business at any time during the two years before the bankruptcy, they were asked questions from the small-business schedule. The questions in the medical section were asked of debtors who indicated that medical events had contributed to their bankruptcies. Questions in the housing section were asked of debtors who owned their homes at the time of bankruptcy or lost homes shortly before bankruptcy. Military questions were asked if the debtor or spouse currently or had previously served in the armed forces. Of the 1,032 telephone respondents who completed the general telephone interview, 485 also completed the medical section, 658 the housing section, 206 the small-business section, and 219 the military section.

All interviews were completed using a computer-assisted telephone interviewing (CATI) program. Mock interviews pretested the questions and the database. Deborah Thorne trained interviewers to use the CATI program and introduced them to every question in the interview. Using fictitious scenarios, interviewers completed at least two mock interviews with one another, and one mock interview with Thorne. After the interviewers

TABLE A.3

Differences between questionnaire respondents who completed the phone interview and those who did not

	Among those who volunteered for telephone interview	
	Completed phone interview	Did not complete phone interview
Joint filing	53.7%	46.3%
Chapter 13	49.3%	50.7%
Total assets (excludes outliers >$1 million)	$98,608 ($47,755)	$98,267 ($48,106)
Total real property (excludes outliers >$1 million)	$77,154 ($12,175)	$80,095 ($19,150)
Total personal property (excludes outliers >$500,000)	$20,990 ($11,686)	$19,240 ($11,775)
Home market value (excludes outliers >$1 million)	$141,507 ($110,715)	$150,201 ($111,720)
Total secured debt	$81,235 ($27,754)	$85,934 ($28,304)
Total priority debt (excludes outliers >$100,000)	$1,779 ($0)	$1,641 (0)
Total unsecured debt (excludes outliers >$1 million)	$50,660 ($34,137)	$47,237 ($30,575)
Total debts (excludes outliers >$1 million)	$132,284 ($85,954)	$134,983 ($86,642)
Average monthly income (excludes outliers >$10,000)	$2,017 ($1,823)	$2,024 ($1,846)
Spouse average monthly income	$1,542 ($1,352)	$1,517 ($1,378)
Combined monthly income (excludes outliers >$10,000)	$2,570 ($2,273)	$2,498 ($2,194)
Total expenses (excludes outliers >$10,000)	$2,540 ($2,243)	$2,513 ($2,220)

SOURCE: Consumer Bankruptcy Project 2007.

NOTE: Values for continuous variables are means. Medians are reported in parentheses. On none of the variables is there a statistically significant difference between those who completed the phone interviews and those who did not.

completed their first actual interview, Thorne reviewed the data and talked with them about the interview. Throughout the process, Thorne closely supervised the interviewers with frequent e-mail and telephone contact. All interviewers were women, ranging in age from their mid-twenties to late-fifties. All interviewers were provided with toll-free lines so that respondents could call them without charge.

Thorne completed logic tests to clean the telephone data. When there were obvious errors, she compared responses to the telephone interview with responses to the questionnaire and made appropriate corrections.

An analysis for bias was conducted to see whether those who completed interviews were different along observable characteristics from those who did not. Table A.3 shows the analysis, which did not reveal any significant differences.

ACKNOWLEDGMENTS

This book is the product of a grant from the Obermann Center for Advanced Studies at the University of Iowa. The center provided financial and organizational support for a summer seminar at the University of Iowa where participants met to work on these chapters and discuss this volume. That time together greatly improved this book and created new intellectual connections—and friendships—among the authors. Steffie Woolhandler and Ronald Mann joined us for the seminar and added useful insights on the authors' early work.

I thank Jay Semel, former director of the Obermann Center, for his guidance and confidence in this project, and Neda Barrett, the program assistant at the Obermann Center, for her organizational efforts. Ryan Andersen, J.D. 2010, Iowa College of Law, was a truly remarkable research assistant for the Obermann seminar, giving authors everything from written comments on their chapters to transportation to the airport. He and Khanh Andersen, who pitched in to help him, brought laughter and fun to the seminar, and I am grateful to them. Kati Jumper, my assistant at the University of Iowa, is a true collaborator in my research generally; her work on this book was no exception.

Molly Eskridge, my assistant during the 2010–2011 academic year while I visited at Harvard Law School, cheerfully helped with manuscript preparation and final details. Amy Beier, J.D. Class of 2012, University of Iowa College of Law, and Marianna Jackson, J.D. Class of 2011, Harvard Law School, provided careful and timely research assistance. I appreciate their hard work. Parina Patel, lecturer on law at Harvard Law School, improved this book with her review of its many figures and tables. I am grateful for her keen eye and ready offers to help.

The data on bankrupt families reported in this book come from the 2007 Consumer Bankruptcy Project (CBP). The principal investigators for the CBP are David U. Himmelstein, Associate Professor of Medicine, Harvard Medical School; Melissa B. Jacoby, George R. Ward Professor of Law,

University of North Carolina School of Law; Robert M. Lawless, Professor of Law, University of Illinois College of Law; Angela K. Littwin, Assistant Professor of Law, University of Texas School of Law; Katherine Porter, Professor of Law, University of California Irvine School of Law; John A. E. Pottow, Professor of Law, University of Michigan Law School; Teresa A. Sullivan, President, University of Virginia; Deborah K. Thorne, Assistant Professor of Sociology and Wagner Teaching Fellow, Ohio University; Elizabeth Warren, Leo Gottlieb Professor of Law, Harvard Law School, and Steffie Woolhandler, Professor of Medicine, Harvard Medical School. I thank my coinvestigators for allowing the authors to use the data. Funding for the CBP was provided in part through grants from the American Association of Retired Persons, the Harvard Law School, the Robert Wood Johnson Foundation, the University of Michigan Office of the Vice President for Research, and the University of Michigan Law School. Mike Bickford and his team at AACER (Automated Access to Court Electronic Records), Carol Bateson, Denise McDaniel, Jeff Paulsen, Mark Thorne, and Alex Warren made important contributions to data collection for the CBP.

This book's authors grasped that this was a truly collaborative endeavor, and each person made unique contributions. In particular, I thank Brian Bucks for the winning combination of being a fun guy and an economist, Jacob Hacker for a great birthday gift, Bob Lawless for his early commitment to the idea of this book, Kevin Leicht for his knack in writing titles and his help marketing the book, Deborah Thorne for always seeing the connection between being my friend and being my professional collaborator, and Elizabeth Warren for making time out of thin air on several occasions.

Kate Wahl, Judith Hibbard, and Joa Suorez at Stanford University Press were excellent editors. I am fortunate to have had their help.

Many other people contributed to this book, in ways large and small. Ann O'Leary and Elizabeth Porter helped me move this book to completion with encouragement at crucial moments. I thank them, along with others who I hope will forgive me for remaining unnamed.

My final thank you is to my husband, Matt Hoffman. He always believes in me and he supports my work in numerous ways, including being a true partner in raising our beautiful boys.

Chapter One

1. "Downward mobility has virtually no ritual face. It is not captured in myths or ceremonies that might help individuals in its grip to make the transition from a higher to a lower social status"; Newman, *Falling from Grace*, 9.

2. Lawless, "July Bankruptcy Filings Rise."

3. In November 2008, a little fewer than half of the people in a RAND survey said that they were worse off than they were one year earlier. Chakrabarti, Lee, van der Klaauw, and Zafar, "Household Debt," 8.

4. Hurd and Rohwedder, "Effects of the Financial Crisis," 27.

5. Schwartz, "Jobless and Staying That Way," WK1.

6. Kharas, "The Emerging Middle Class," 7.

7. The White House, "White House Announces Middle Class Task Force."

8. The White House, "Remarks by the President and Vice President."

9. Biden, *Annual Report of the White House Task Force on the Middle Class*.

10. Glick and Lansing, "U.S. Household Deleveraging," 1.

11. Mian and Sufi, "Household Leverage and the Recession," 1.

12. Wolff, "Recent Trends in Household Wealth," 34.

13. Ibid., 47, Table 5.

14. Ibid., 50, Table 8.

15. Bucks et al., "Changes in U.S. Family Finances," A37, Table 12.

16. Wolff, "Recent Trends in Household Wealth," 26.

17. Bucks et al., "Changes in U.S. Family Finances," A42.

18. Ibid., A37.

19. In 2007, the U.S. homeownership rate was 68.1 percent; U.S. Census Bureau, "Housing Vacancies and Homeownership." As of 2007, 54.7 percent of American men and 51.2 percent of American women were married; U.S. Census Bureau, "America's Families and Living Arrangements: 2007." In 2007, 27 percent of adults aged twenty-five or older reported having at least a bachelor's degree; Crissey, *Educational Attainment in the United States: 2007*. A 2007 Gallup survey found that more than 40 percent of Americans claimed to attend church or synagogue regularly; Newport, "Just Why Do Americans Attend Church?"

20. Lawless, "The Paradox of Consumer Credit," 361–62.

21. Stolberg and Baker, "Obama's Measures for Middle Class."

22. Federal Reserve Bank of New York, "U.S. Credit Conditions.".

23. Elmer and Seelig, "The Rising Long-Term Trend," 25, Figure 1.

24. Slaughter, "Foreclosures Hit Record."

25. Federal Trade Commission, *Federal Trade Commission Annual Report 2010.*

26. New York Times, *Class Matters*, 248.

27. Pew Social Trends Staff, *Inside the Middle Class.*

28. "Religious views, politics, age, weight and even health problems are more palatable topics of conversation than credit card debt," according to a poll by GK Roper Public Affairs and Media; Prater, "Poll: Credit Card Debt."

29. As examples, compare the media coverage and energetic work of the Congressional Oversight Panel on the Troubled Asset Relief Program (TARP) and the appointment of a special inspector general for TARP with the relatively lax oversight of the government's federal loan modification programs or the largely ignored reports of the White House Task Force on the Middle Class.

30. Braucher, "Humpty Dumpty and the Foreclosure Crisis." Fuller, "U.S. Effort Aids Only 9% of Eligible Homeowners," B8. Simon, "Grave Errors as Undead Rework Loans."

31. "Greenspan puzzled over one piece of data that a Fed employee showed him in his final weeks. A trade publication reported that subprime mortgages had ballooned to 20 percent of all loans, triple the level of a few years earlier. 'I looked at the numbers . . . and said, Where did they get these numbers from?' Greenspan recalled in a recent interview. He was skeptical that such loans had grown in a short period 'to such gargantuan proportions'"; Klein and Goldfarb, "The Bubble," A1.

32. "The so-called 'Credit Cardholders' Bill of Rights' (H.R. 5244), while well-intentioned, will increase the cost of credit for consumers and small businesses across the country, result in less access to credit for consumers and businesses alike, and may further roil the securities markets—all at a time when our economy can least afford it"; Yingling, "ABA Statement on House Passage of H.R. 5244." "The consequence of so sweeping a bill would be to force the industry to raise the cost of credit for everyone, including those who present less risk of default to the lender, and reduce the availability of credit for those customers who present a greater risk of default"; *Credit Cardholders' Bill of Rights Act of 2008* (Finneran).

33. Federal Reserve Bank of New York, *Quarterly Report on Household Debt and Credit.* Another Federal Reserve research report finds that as of early 2010 total household debt had decreased by 7.4 percent from its peak in 2008; Brown et al., "The Financial Crisis at the Kitchen Table," 4.

34. Mian and Sufi, "Household Leverage and the Recession," 28.

35. Luhby, "Americans' Wealth Drops $1.3 Trillion."

36. Lusardi, Schneider, and Tufano, "Financially Fragile Households," 9.

37. Brown et al., "The Financial Crisis at the Kitchen Table," 11. The authors conclude: "while household debt paydown has helped improve household balance sheets, it has also likely contributed to slow consumption growth since the beginning of the recession. Thus the trajectory for consumer indebtedness has important implications for consumption and economic growth going forward."

38. See, for example, Stanley and Girth, *Bankruptcy.*

39. A copy of the survey is reproduced in the appendix of Lawless et al., "Did Bankruptcy Reform Fail?," 362–63.

40. See, for example, Himmelstein et al., "Medical Bankruptcy." Jiménez, "Distribution of Assets," 797. Lawless et al., "Did Bankruptcy Reform Fail?"

41. Newman, *Falling from Grace*, 7.

42. Warren and Tyagi, *The Two-Income Trap*, 81. Sullivan, Warren, and Westbrook, *The Fragile Middle Class*, 14–22.

43. Elmer and Seelig, "The Rising Long-Term Trend," 1.

44. U.S. Census Bureau, "U.S. Census Bureau Reports on Residential Vacancies and Homeownership."

45. Cooper, "Governments Go to Extremes," A1.

46. Tennessee Student Assistance Corporation, "College Pays." College Board, "Education Pays Update: 2005."

47. Center for Responsible Lending, *Snapshot of a Foreclosure Crisis*.

48. This is not to say that bankruptcy law does not reflect latent assumptions about who will or should use the system; Dickerson, "Race Matters in Bankruptcy."

49. Dodd-Frank Wall Street Reform and Consumer Protection Act.

50. Theil, "The Urge to Splurge," 28.

51. Glick and Lansing, "U.S. Household Deleveraging," 3.

52. Mann and Porter, "Saving Up for Bankruptcy," 310, 313.

53. Debtors theoretically choose to file under Chapter 7 or Chapter 13, but research suggests that this decision is usually made by attorneys or by debtors after the strong advice of their attorneys; Braucher, "Lawyers and Consumer Bankruptcy," 526–39.

54. U.S. Courts, "Bankruptcy Statistics: Filings." In recent years, the share of Chapter 13 cases has declined. In 2009, about 25 percent of all consumer cases were Chapter 13 filings; Porter, "Today's Consumers Prefer Chapter 7 Bankruptcy."

55. In 2007, 93 percent of bankruptcy cases filed by individuals were no-asset cases; Jiménez, "Distribution of Assets," 797.

56. Porter and Thorne, "The Failure of Bankruptcy's Fresh Start," 91, 94, Figure 6.

57. A multidistrict study of the Chapter 13 system found that about 19 percent of all filings were dismissed before confirmation; Norberg and Velkey, "Debtor Discharge and Creditor Repayment," 505–06.

58. Ibid., 505, note 70. Bermant and Flynn, "Measuring Projected Performance in Chapter 13," 22.

59. U.S. Courts, "Bankruptcy Forms."

60. Credit agencies may choose to report bankruptcy for fewer years; reportedly, seven years is typical current practice; Porter, "Life after Debt," 30. The bankruptcy filing also affects debtors' credit scores and the availability of credit; Cohen-Cole, Duygan-Bump, and Montoriol-Garriga, "Forgive and Forget," 3. Debtors have ample opportunity to borrow after bankruptcy, however, especially from creditors who issue low-limit, high-fee credit cards; Porter, "Bankrupt Profits," 1369.

61. 2007 Consumer Bankruptcy Project.

62. U.S. Const. art. I, § 8, cl. 4.

63. Sullivan, Warren, and Westbrook, "The Persistence of Local Legal Culture." Braucher, "Lawyers and Consumer Bankruptcy."

64. Golmant and Ulrich, "Bankruptcy Repeat Filings," 169.

65. Lawless et al., "Did Bankruptcy Reform Fail?," 362–63.

Chapter Two
Data described in this chapter are from the CBP studies of 1991, 2001, and 2007. The authors thank Danielle D'Onfro, Harvard Law School class of 2011, for her very able research assistance.

1. The proportion of filers with higher educational accomplishments, more prestigious occupations, or homeownership increased from 1991 to 2001; Warren, "Financial Collapse and Class Status," 115. Using all three criteria to measure class status, we conclude in this chapter that the proportion of filers who would be classified as middle class rose again from 2001 (91.8 percent) to 2007 (95 percent) (see Figure 2.7).

2. Many scholars identify middle-class status by reference to income, often with acknowledgement that other measures add additional insight; see Gilbert, *American Class Structure*, 12, 259; Cannon, "On the Absolute or Relative Basis of Perception," 348, 350; and Kolko, "Economic Mobility and Social Stratification," 38.

3. Cohn includes in the middle class those with an annual income of $50,000–70,000; Cohn, "Middle Class Blues." Gary Burtless of the Brookings Institute defined the middle class as having incomes in the range of $24,000–96,000, while MIT economist Frank Levy explained that the middle class had incomes between $30,000 and $90,000 annually; Vigeland, "What Is the Middle Class."

4. Unless otherwise indicated, all income data for bankrupt respondents are in 2007 dollars. Lawless et al. present more data on the income, debts, and assets of bankrupt households in "Did Bankruptcy Reform Fail?," 404. The income figures in this chapter differ from those reported in Lawless et al. Although both figures come from Schedule I of debtors' bankruptcy court records, this chapter reports a figure that approximates gross income—"combined monthly income" (bottom line figure on Schedule I) plus the households' payroll deductions—whereas Lawless et al. use only "combined monthly income." This chapter uses approximate gross income to increase comparability with the census data on the general population. The choice of Lawless et al. to use an alternate income calculation was to facilitate comparison with bankruptcy data from prior CBP studies in 1981, 1991, and 2001.

5. DeNavas-Walt, Proctor, and Smith, *Income, Poverty, and Health Insurance*, 7, Table 1.

6. In 2007, the year these data were drawn, the U.S. Department of Health and Human Services published the following poverty guidelines: a single person with annual income less than $10,210 is defined as living in poverty; the same is true for a two-person household with annual income of $13,690 or less, a three-person household with annual income of $17,170 or less, and a four-person household with annual income of $20,650 or less; U.S. Department of Health and Human Services, "2007 HHS Poverty Guidelines." And although the majority of the bankruptcy households were not officially "in poverty," their household incomes were low enough that one financial stumble could quickly land them there.

7. Mental Health Counseling Degree, "Masters Mental Health Counseling Salary."

8. PayScale, "Salary Survey."

9. If a respondent or a respondent's spouse answered yes to any of the following on a written questionnaire administered near the time of their bankruptcy filing, they were defined as having experienced a job problem: (1) they had, during the two years before the bankruptcy, lost two weeks or more of income because

they were (a) laid off or fired, (b) ill or injured, (c) took time off to care for a sick family member, or (d) any other reason; OR (2) their employment status at the time of the bankruptcy was (a) not employed, seeking work, or (b) not employed, unable to work for medical reasons; OR (3) they indicated as a reason for filing for bankruptcy any of the following: (a) decline in income, (b) financial problems that resulted from being self-employed, or (c) illness or injury that caused them, or their spouse or partner, to miss two weeks or more of work.

10. Bureau of Labor Statistics, "Employment Status of the Civilian Noninstitutional Population."

11. Scholars have discussed the relationship between loss of income and bankruptcy filings using data from the 1981, 1991, and 2001 CBPs; Sullivan, Warren, and Westbrook, *As We Forgive Our Debtors*, 95–102 (1981 CBP); Sullivan, Warren, and Westbrook, *The Fragile Middle Class*, 15–18 (1991 CBP); Warren and Tyagi, *The Two-Income Trap*, 81, 106 (2001 CBP).

12. Marger, *Social Inequality*, 58–61.

13. Marger provides additional discussion of the differences among the three categories of middle class; ibid., 59–61 and 111–114. Table 2.1 shows the characteristics of Marger's three levels of the middle class.

TABLE 2.1
Characteristics of the three levels of middle class

Upper-middle class	Income: $75,000–$1 million
	Occupations: Upper-level managers, professional, some business owners
	Education: At least four years of college; postgraduate training for many
	Percentage of families in this category: 18–20
Lower-middle class	Income: $35,000–$75,000
	Occupations: Lower-level managers, semiprofessionals, craftspeople
	Education: At least high school graduate; often some college
	Percentage of families in this category: 25–30
Working class	Income: $25,000–$40,000
	Occupations: Operatives, clerical, retail sales workers
	Education: High school graduate
	Percentage of families in this category: 25–30

SOURCE: Marger, *Social Inequality*, 58. Courtesy of The McGraw-Hill Companies, Inc.

14. Oliver and Shapiro, *Black Wealth/White Wealth*, 6, 17–23. Keister describes how for the bottom 80 percent of Americans, 66 percent of their wealth is in their primary residence; Keister, *Wealth in America*, 122. Williams, Nesiba, and Diaz McConnell, "Changing Face of Inequality," 181–208.

15. Featherman and Hauser, *Opportunity and Change*, 266–68, 282.

16. Marger, *Social Inequality*, 197.

17. U.S. Census Bureau, *Statistical Abstract: 2009*, 146, Table 224.

18. Table 2.2 shows 1991, 2001, and 2007 data on educational attainment.

TABLE 2.2

Educational levels of U.S. population and people in bankruptcy, 1991, 2001, and 2007

	No high school (%)	High school diploma only (%)	Some college (%)	College diploma (%)	Advanced degree (%)
1991					
U.S. population	21.6	39.1	19.7	11.8	7.7
People in bankruptcy	21.8	31.7	35.1	8.6	2.8
2001					
U.S. population	16.9	32.8	27.1	15.7	7.5
People in bankruptcy	19.1	28.8	38.6	9.6	3.9
2007					
U.S. population	15.1	31.5	27.2	17.5	8.7
People in bankruptcy	10.5	30.6	43.4	11.4	4.1

SOURCES: U.S. Census Bureau; Consumer Bankruptcy Projects 1991, 2001, and 2007.

19. We recognize that there has been debate over the usefulness of occupational prestige scoring and the meaning of prestige; Goldthorpe and Hope, "Occupational Grading and Occupational Prestige," 23–26, 33–37. The authors assert that prestige is primarily an indication of one's ability to demand and receive deference and opportunities over the life course, and as such one's occupation is key to the lived experience of social class.

20. Donald Treiman's classic work concludes that as occupational prestige scores increase, so too do the authority, autonomy, and power that employees enjoy at their jobs; Treiman, "Standard Occupational Prestige Scale," 285–290.

21. As with previous CBP studies, occupations were coded using the 1970 Occupational Classification codes available from the Interuniversity Consortium for Political and Social Research. The 1970 codes are still widely in use as the last "pure" occupational codes used by the U.S. Census Bureau and have been used in major studies such as the General Social Survey. Since the 1970 Census, the bureau has moved to sets of codes that incorporate industry as well as occupation, but there are available several "walkovers" that permit correspondence from one set of codes to another.

In the 2007 CBP study, occupational descriptions of homemaker, housewife, and stay-at-home parent were scored at 51; Dworkin, "Prestige Ranking," 59–63. In 1991 and 2001 CBPs, however, homemakers were not assigned a score. When the 2007 occupation data were scored both ways—with and without a score for homemakers—there was no significant difference in outcomes. For consistency with our earlier studies, the data reported in this chapter do not reflect a score for homemakers. Respondents who indicated that they were retired, disabled, unemployed, or students were not assigned a score. Occupations that were otherwise unclassifiable were also not coded. If respondents listed more than one occupation, the occupation listed first was coded. If they wrote that they were currently unemployed but indicated that they used to work in a specific occupation, that occupation was coded.

22. Table 2.3 shows the occupational prestige scores for CBP respondents and the U.S. population in 1991 and 2001.

TABLE 2.3

Occupational prestige scores of U.S. population and people in bankruptcy, 1991 and 2001

	1991		2001	
Decile	U.S. population	People in bankruptcy	U.S. population	People in bankruptcy
10	27.5	22.0	27.5	17.0
20	30.0	29.0	31.0	25.0
30	34.0	32.0	34.0	31.0
40	38.0	36.0	39.0	34.0
50	41.5	37.0	43.0	36.0
60	45.5	42.0	46.0	42.0
70	48.5	47.0	50.0	46.0
80	51.0	48.0	56.0	50.0
90	63.4	50.0	64.5	51.0

SOURCES: National Opinion Research Center, *General Social Surveys, 1972–2006*; Consumer Bankruptcy Project, 1991 and 2001.

23. This analysis represents the scores for each individual debtor who filed for bankruptcy, including husbands and wives separately if they filed joint petitions. In the summary section ("Adding the Ways to the Middle Class"), we recombine the joint debtors to determine the class status of the household as a whole.

24. Oliver and Shapiro, *Black Wealth/White Wealth*, passim.

25. The 43.9 percent reported in 1991 may be artificially low, an artifact of sampling that inadvertently produced a disproportionately high response rate among those receiving legal advice from Community Legal Service in Philadelphia—a group that was unlikely to own homes; Warren, "Financial Collapse and Class Status," 137–38. Even so, the jump from 2001 to 2007 is remarkable.

26. RealtyTrac, "More than 430,000 Foreclosure Filings Reported." RealtyTrac, "Record 2.9 Million U.S. Properties Receive Foreclosure Filings in 2010."

27. U.S. Census Bureau, *Statistical Abstract: 1993*, 734, Table 1247.

28. Sullivan, Warren, and Westbrook, *The Fragile Middle Class*, 208–09. Warren and Tyagi, *The Two-Income Trap*, 127. These scholars discuss in more detail the extensive financial scrutiny that homeowners once had to endure in order to qualify for a mortgage.

29. "Text: President Bush's Acceptance Speech."

30. Hughes, Jr., and Perry-Jenkins, "Social Class Issues," 175–82. Hughes and Perry-Jenkins discuss the situations in which household class status is best determined by the characteristics of a single adult in the household (individual as unit of analysis) or adults' combined characteristics (household as unit of analysis). They stress that ultimately both measures have their strengths and that the "research question and the family outcomes of interest" should dictate the choice of whether to use data from one or both adults (176).

31. Cf. Ramsay and Sim, "Personal Insolvency in Australia," 12–18.

32. Data for 2000–2008 was from the U.S. Courts, "Bankruptcy Statistics."

Numbers of bankruptcy filings for 2009 came from Lawless, "Guesstimate of 2010 Bankruptcy Filings."

33. Kreider and Elliott, *America's Families*, 2.

34. Rates of bankruptcy filings in 2007 were abnormally low as they continued to rebound from the amendments to bankruptcy law in 2005. To put this in context, over the preceding decade, the United States averaged 1.37 million filings annually, or almost double the number that were filed in 2007. Thus, if the number of filings in 2007 had been typical, the percentage of households filing for bankruptcy would have instead been 1.2 percent, rather than 0.7 percent. In 2010, as families struggled with an economy that had not yet emerged from a severe recession, the number of families filing for bankruptcy was approximately 1.56 million, which was nearly double the number in 2007.

Chapter Three

The views expressed in this chapter are those of the author alone and are not necessarily those of the Board of Governors of the Federal Reserve System or its staff. The views expressed elsewhere in this volume are not necessarily the views of the author or the views of the Board of Governors of the Federal Reserve System or its staff. I thank colleagues at the Federal Reserve Board and participants at the University of Iowa Obermann Center Seminar "Borrowing to the Brink: Consumer Debt in America" for thoughtful comments. I am especially grateful to Arthur Kennickell and Katie Porter for many helpful discussions and comprehensive comments.

1. For instance, the Bankruptcy Database Project at Harvard estimates that 1.44 million individuals (with joint petitions counted as two people) filed for bankruptcy in 2008 compared with 230.12 million adults aged eighteen or older (U.S. Census Bureau, *Statistical Abstract: 2010*," Table 7), which implies a filing rate of 0.6 percent.

2. Dawsey and Ausubel, "Informal Bankruptcy"; Hynes, "Broke but Not Bankrupt," "Bankruptcy and State Collections," 606.

3. The percentages of filings by bankruptcy chapter and region were constructed from judicial district-level administrative data available through the Bankruptcy Database Project at Harvard. Weights might be designed to additionally account for the week of the filing, as would be appropriate if there were substantial differences in filings over the time period the data were collected. In fact, though, this timing appears relatively unimportant.

4. See Bucks et al., "Changes in U.S. Family Finances," for a general overview of the SCF, and Kennickell, "List Sample Design," "Modeling Wealth," "Darkness Made Visible," for details of the list sample design.

5. The weights account for differences across households in the probability of selection due to the sample design, differences in response rates that are correlated with observable characteristics, and deviations of the sample relative to the population of all U.S. households for key characteristics such as region, age, and homeownership.

6. As a means of organizing the data consistently, the head of household in the SCF is designated to be the male in a mixed-sex couple or the older person in a same-sex couple.

7. The SCF question would not identify households in which someone other than the head or that person's spouse or partner filed for bankruptcy. In the case

of couples, the SCF also does not identify which member of the couple had filed or whether the couple filed jointly.

8. Porter and Thorne find that a quarter of filers interviewed in the 2001 wave of the CBP reported difficulties in paying debts one year after filing for Chapter 7 bankruptcy; "The Failure of Bankruptcy's Fresh Start," 83–84. Using SCF data, Han and Li conclude that families who filed for bankruptcy are more likely than comparable families who never filed to report having missed a debt payment in the prior year even more than nine years after the filing. They report similar results for the likelihood of falling behind on a payment by sixty days or more and find that the difference in this likelihood is most pronounced for those who had filed six to nine years earlier; "Household Borrowing," 22–24, Table 7.

9. The definition of those who were turned down or received less credit excludes families who received the full amount after reapplying to the same institution or elsewhere.

10. Jappelli, "Who is Credit Constrained?"; Duca and Rosenthal, "Borrowing Constraints"; Gropp, Scholz, and White, "Personal Bankruptcy."

11. Roughly 11 percent had applied but been turned down for credit, 15 percent had chosen not to apply for a loan because they anticipated the application would be denied, and 4 percent met both criteria.

12. Bucks et al., "Changes in U.S. Family Finances," A49.

13. Families with high debt payments relative to income may not be the same as those with high levels of debt relative to income as payments depend not only on the outstanding balance, but also on the interest rate, term of the loan, and sometimes other factors.

14. Households with a high payment-to-income ratio (PIR) when mortgage debt is included have higher median assets, median debt, and homeownership rates than do filers in the CBP and families in each of the SCF subgroups (see online appendix Table A2: www.sup.org/broke). Even so, more than 60 percent of households with a nonmortgage PIR greater than 25 percent have a total PIR greater than 40 percent, the threshold used by Bucks et al. to characterize high-PIR households ("Changes in U.S. Family Finances"). Excluding payments on mortgage debt also treats the housing costs of renters and homeowners comparably, as rent payments are not included in the debt PIR.

15. Johnson and Li find that households with high ratios of debt payments to income are more likely to be turned down for credit and that, together with a family's liquid assets-to-income ratio, the PIR is useful in identifying households that appear to be constrained in their ability to smooth consumption over time; "The Debt-Payment-to-Income Ratio".

16. Kennickell and Lusardi, "Disentangling the Importance."

17. Ibid., 4–5.

18. This measure is similar to Kennickell and Lusardi's measure of available assets. One notable difference is the treatment of debt: Kennickell and Lusardi subtract six months of payments on loans and 20 percent of outstanding credit card balances from the assets included in their savings measure; ibid., 16.

19. If "savings" were alternatively defined as total financial assets or as net worth, 27 percent and 14 percent of families, respectively, would be classified as having insufficient savings.

20. Those who have previously filed are also more likely to meet each of the individual financial-distress criteria as well.

21. Sullivan, Warren, and Westbrook, *The Fragile Middle Class*.

22. The potential scope for differences in definitions or in respondents' under-standing to contribute to discrepancies in measures is apparent even within surveys. The CBP data include instances in which the value of the petitioner's home, for instance, does not match in two parts of the bankruptcy court records where the value is reported. These discrepancies may reflect errors by debtors or may indicate nuanced differences in these measures.

23. Details of the SCF imputation procedure are described in Kennickell, "Imputation of the 1989 Survey of Consumer Finances," "Multiple Imputation." Estimated standard errors for the SCF estimates cited below are available online in the supplementary appendix Table A3: www.sup.org/broke. These estimates account for imputation and sampling variance. The latter are calculated using the 999 SCF bootstrap replicates and sample weights generated in accordance with the sample design. See Kennickell, "Revisions to the Variance Estimation Procedure," for details of variance estimation procedures in the SCF, and Montalto and Sung, "Multiple Imputation," for a discussion of estimation and inference in the SCF.

24. This assumption may be more palatable for the CBP court record data used in this chapter because the shares of missing values for these variables are comparatively low, ranging between 2 and 4 percent. By comparison, 6 to 10 percent of values for demographic characteristics such as age, education, and race or ethnicity are missing. These data were collected on the initial written questionnaire. Moreover, only 42 percent of the households that returned the initial questionnaire completed the follow-up telephone interview, so that more than half of the filers in the sample of filers considered in this chapter have missing values for all of the variables reported in the follow-up survey. The appendix to this volume provides useful details on the possible extent of response bias in completing the written questionnaire and the telephone interview.

25. Details of the definition of each of the SCF and CBP variables are available online in the supplementary appendix Table A1: www.sup.org/broke. Most balance sheet components for SCF households are defined as in Bucks et al., "Changes in U.S. Family Finances." For the CBP, in instances where the value of an asset or debt is reported or can be readily calculated in more than one place in the bankruptcy court record, I generally draw on multiple sources to construct the CBP measure. I define mortgage debt in the CBP, for instance, as the maximum of the value of voluntary home-secured liens reported on Schedule A and Schedule D because many differences between these amounts are due to missing or zero values.

26. Moreover, reported income during the prior calendar year is generally considered less precise than the six-month income reported for the purposes of the means-test calculation because debtors are not asked to break down the prior calendar year's income into component parts and because that information is not heavily scrutinized by the trustee. Because the prior year income data have been ignored in favor of other income data, to date the CBP has not yet reviewed the data on income in the prior calendar year as extensively as the other income measures.

27. White, "Abuse or Protection?," details bankruptcy filers' incentives before and after the Bankruptcy Abuse Prevention and Consumer Protection Act.

28. The median ratio for all filers with both income amounts available from court records was 0.99. The income measures are also generally similar for filers who might be considered more likely to adjust earnings in anticipation of a filing. The median ratio was 1.03 for filers with income in the prior calendar year that was

100 to 125 percent of the applicable state median income (the key threshold for the means test) is 1.03, and the median ratio for filers whose income over the six-month period preceding the filing was 75 to 100 percent of this threshold is 0.96.

29. Although some of the card issuers may also have made a signature loan to a debtor, in most cases these obligations are for bank-issued credit cards.

30. Specifically, the SCF asks "Do you have any other loans?," and, at the interviewer's discretion, this question is followed up with, "These may be loans for household appliances, furniture, hobby or recreational equipment, medical bills, loans from friends or relatives, loans for a business or investment, or other loans." The latter portion is optional but reportedly is generally read by interviewers.

31. Based on their analysis of the follow-up phone survey component of the CBP 2007, Jacoby and Holman find that 26 percent of those who reported medical expenses not covered by insurance in the two years before filing reported that they had paid for at least a portion of these expenses with a credit card; "Managing Medical Bills," 274–75.

32. For most balance sheet components, ownership is defined as having a nonzero amount; however, net worth, income, the leverage ratio (the ratio of debt to assets), and the debt-to-income ratio are calculated for all households, so "ownership" is 100 percent. Home equity is calculated over all homeowners and may be zero or negative.

33. An extreme hypothetical illustrates this point: imagine that 99 percent of bankruptcy filers have student loans, but only 1 percent of credit-constrained households have them. In this scenario, a bankruptcy filer with education debt equal to the conditional median, on the one hand, is just slightly above the median (50.5th percentile) in the overall, unconditional distribution of education debt for this group. The conditional median among credit-constrained households, on the other hand, corresponds to the 99.5th percentile of the overall distribution of education debt for credit constrained families.

34. The fact that not all filers in the CBP reported debt may reflect the fact that some bankruptcy filing schedules were incomplete.

35. The predicted values are estimated based on median regressions of $\ln([\text{debt}/1000] + 1)$ on $\ln([\text{assets}/1000] + 1)$ and its square. Results are similar for alternative transformations of debt and assets. In contrast to least-squares regression, which estimates the mean of the dependent variable as a function of covariates, median regression estimates the analogous function for the median. Koenker, *Quantile Regression*, provides a comprehensive treatment of quantile regression, of which median regression is a special case.

36. In line with this conjecture, Corradin et al. find that, as homestead exemptions increase, households with low net worth hold a greater share of their wealth as home equity; "Who Invests in Home Equity?" They further find that this effect is stronger for households headed by a person who is in poor health, which they note may reflect a higher probability of bankruptcy.

37. Li and White offer empirical evidence that homeowners who have defaulted on their mortgage or who face foreclosure are more likely to file for bankruptcy and vice versa; "Mortgage Default".

38. The homeownership rate in the CBP shown in Table 3.2 is the share of filers who owned their home at the time of filing. As Warren and Thorne discuss in Chapter 2, some families may have lost their homes before filing bankruptcy. The homeownership rate for families with a PIR including mortgage debt that is greater than

40 percent is 90 percent, and 86 percent of families with a high PIR by this alternative definition have a mortgage (see online appendix Table A2: www.sup.org/broke.

39. A more complete assessment of the effects of these incentives on filers' decisions would, for example, likely control for differences in the financial and demographic characteristics of filers and nonbankrupt households and account for variation in homestead and other exemptions across states.

40. One percent of all homeowners; roughly 3 to 4 percent of homeowners in the late-payments, high-PIR, and credit-constrained SCF subgroups; and 11 percent of homeowners with low savings have negative home equity.

41. Hynes, for instance, concludes that consumers sued by creditors are more likely to be economically disadvantaged than bankruptcy filers; "Broke but Not Bankrupt," 37–61.

42. See, in particular, Keys, "The Credit Market Consequences," who provides theoretical arguments and empirical evidence that both strategic motives and adverse shocks as well as their interaction are critical determinants of people's decisions to file for bankruptcy. For discussions of these two perspectives, see also Fay, Hurst, and White, "The Household Bankruptcy Decision"; White, "Why It Pays to File for Bankruptcy" and "Bankruptcy and Consumer Behavior"; Sullivan, Warren, and Westbrook, *The Fragile Middle Class* and "Less Stigma"; and Hynes, "Bankruptcy and State Collections."

Chapter Four
1. Stone, *Shelter Poverty*, 35.
2. Hays, *The Federal Government and Urban Housing*, 61.
3. Stone, *Shelter Poverty*, 350.
4. Joint Center for Housing Studies, *The State of the Nation's Housing 2009*, 27.
5. Stone, *Shelter Poverty*, 24. Anthony, "The Effects of Florida's Growth Management Act."
6. Belsky and Prakken, *Housing Wealth Effects*, 5.
7. Joint Center for Housing Studies, *The State of the Nation's Housing 2009*, 14.
8. Charles, "Can We Live Together?," 64. Turner and Ross, "How Racial Discrimination Affects the Search for Housing," 92. Apgar and Calder, "The Dual Mortgage Market," 7–8.
9. U.S. Census Bureau, "Homeownership Rates."
10. Farley, "Racial Differences." Massey and Denton, *American Apartheid*, 106. Ross and Yinger, *The Color of Credit*. Yinger, "Cash in Your Face," 352, and *Closed Doors*, 105–08.
11. Apgar and Calder, "The Dual Mortgage Market," 2.
12. Bostic and Surette, "Have the Doors Opened Wider?," 413.
13. Modigliani, "Utility Analysis," 47; Friedman, *A Theory of the Consumption Function*, 92.
14. Warren and Tyagi, *The Two-Income Trap*, 78.
15. Sullivan, Warren, and Westbrook, *The Fragile Middle Class*, 71.
16. Bostic and Surette, "Have the Doors Opened Wider?," 29, Table 3.
17. Calder, *Financing the American Dream*. Bosworth, Burtless, and Sabelhaus, "The Decline in Savings."
18. Lawless et al., "Did Bankruptcy Reform Fail?," 382.

19. Leicht and Fitzgerald, *Post-Industrial Peasants*, 37.

20. Bosworth, Burtless, and Sabelhaus, "The Decline in Savings"; Dynan, Skinner, and Zeldes, "Do the Rich Save More?," 414.

21. 11 U.S.C. § 1322(b)(2).

22. Story, "Home Equity Frenzy."

23. Canner, Fergus, and Luckett, "Home Equity Lines of Credit," 363.

24. Greenspan and Kennedy, "Estimates of Home Mortgage Originations," 14, Figure 3.

25. Renaud and Kim, "The Global Housing Price Boom," 7.

26. O'Hare and O'Hare, "Upward Mobility," 29.

27. U.S. Department of Housing and Urban Development, *American Housing Survey: 1999*.

28. Hart, Rhodes, and Morgan, *The Unknown World*, 1–2; Fannie Mae, *Manufactured Housing*, 4.

29. Warren, "Financial Collapse," 122–28.

30. Eggum, Porter, and Twomey, "Saving Homes in Bankruptcy," 1129.

31. CFED, "Assets & Opportunity Scorecard," 2.

32. Sullivan, Warren, and Westbrook, *The Fragile Middle Class*, 21.

33. Braucher, "Humpty Dumpty."

34. Carroll and Li, "The Homeownership Experience," 9.

35. Congressional Oversight Panel, *Evaluating Progress on TARP*, 43, 177–92.

Chapter Five

I thank Ryan Andersen, Brian Locke, and Parina Patel for research assistance.

1. The CBP first collected such data in 1991 when it surveyed debtors. In *The Fragile Middle Class*, Sullivan, Warren, and Westbrook show the educational attainment of bankruptcy debtors and report that the modal category was some college, without a bachelor's degree (53–54, Figure 2.3).

2. "The conclusion is that as Americans at large are becoming better educated, debtors filing for bankruptcy are not slipping into an underclass; indeed, their educational achievements seem to be keeping pace with those of Americans generally"; Warren, "Financial Collapse and Class Status," 128.

3. "Some college" is the modal category of educational attainment in the 2007 CBP sample. In another study, the 2007 Survey of Consumer Finances (SCF) a high school education is apparently the most common educational level of bankruptcy debtors, with 39.5 percent of respondents in that group. Han and Li report that 25.8 percent of bankruptcy debtors have some college; "Household Borrowing," 33, Table 2. This difference could be the result of a different definition of "some college" (for example, as requiring the completion of a degree or certificate, rather than as some college coursework). Another explanation is that the 2007 SCF asked whether a respondent had *ever* filed for bankruptcy, thereby perhaps making its sample of bankruptcy debtors older, and less educated, than a sample of people who filed for bankruptcy *in* 2007.

4. See Crissey, *Educational Attainment in the United States: 2007*, 9, Table 3. This calculation is based on the median earnings of full-time, year-round workers, which normalizes demographic differences in part-time work patterns.

5. For a critical discussion of this policy, see Rosenbaum, *Beyond College for All*.

6. U.S. Census Bureau, *Current Population Survey: 2007*, Table 1.

7. Associate's degree holders are 21.5 percent of the "some college" group; those with no degree but some college coursework make up the remaining 78.5 percent of the group.

8. U.S. Census Bureau, *Current Population Survey: 2007*, Table 1. This group is split about equally between occupational (4.3 percent) and academic (3.9 percent) associate's degrees.

9. Bernstein and Mishel, "Economy's Gains," Table 4. The big jump in economic prosperity comes with a bachelor's degree; this group earned $26.46 per hour in real wages. Bernstein and Mishel also report that wages for those with associate's degrees had less growth (1.7 percent) than wages for either high school graduates (2.5 percent) or four-year college graduates (2.6 percent).

10. Gladieux and Perna report that for student loan borrowers, while median salaries were higher for those who completed an associate's degree than for those who dropped out with only some college coursework, there was no statistically significant difference among mean salaries for the two groups; *Borrowers Who Drop Out*, 19, note 9. But Murray reports that unemployment rates in March 2009 were dramatically lower for those with an associate's degree (6.9 percent) than for high school graduates (11.4 percent). It is unknown what difference, if any, some college coursework makes over a high school diploma alone; "Community College Pays Off."

11. Day and Newburger, *The Big Payoff*, 3.

12. Ibid., 3, Figure 3.

13. Job problems such as unemployment or a cutback in the number of hours or wages is the leading self-reported reason for bankruptcy. In 2001, 71.5 percent of bankrupt families experienced a job loss, a reduction of income, or other job-related problem that contributed to their bankruptcy filing; Warren and Tyagi, *The Two-Income Trap*, 8, note 31.

14. Lawless et al., "Did Bankruptcy Reform Fail?," 371. The authors report that the median bankruptcy debtor owed total debts of more than three times his or her income.

15. College Board, "Parent-Educator Modules." Another example is the subheading "It pays to go to school" in a report that explains that "while some college is better than none, students are financially better off achieving an associate's degree . . . than dropping out of a four-year college"; Lawson and Semaya, *Learn More, Earn More*, 13.

16. Gladieux and Perna, *Borrowers Who Drop Out*, 3. The article reports data collected in 2001 from the entire population of students (more than three million) who started postsecondary education in 1995–1996. That number may have increased. The 2002 National Student Loan Survey reported that 70 percent of students stated that they would not have been able to pursue education after high school without student loans; see Baum and O'Malley, *College on Credit*.

17. Gladieux and Perna, *Borrowers Who Drop Out*, 3, Figure 1.

18. Ibid., 34, Table 1. The dropout rates vary tremendously across institutions. A 2009 study found that on average, four-year colleges graduate fewer than 60 percent of freshmen within six years of their enrollment; Hess et al., *Diplomas and Dropouts*, 8.

19. Knapp et al., *Enrollment in Postsecondary Institutions*. Another study followed people who graduated from high school in 1982 for ten years and found that only 18.7 percent of seniors who planned to earn an associate's degree

achieved or exceeded that educational attainment; Rosenbaum, *Beyond College for All*, 66–67.

20. U.S. Department of Education, *Students Entering and Leaving*, 46–48.

21. The 2007 CBP conducted a telephone survey with 1,032 people who filed for bankruptcy and asked, "At the time you filed for bankruptcy, did you still owe money on any of those educational debts?"

22. Indeed, the student loan burdens of bankruptcy debtors and the general population seem quite similar. In a longitudinal study of student loan borrowers, the median debt for those who had not completed their educational program after six years was $7,000; Gladieux and Perna, *Borrowers Who Drop Out*, 7.

23. These data are self-reported by people in bankruptcy on a written questionnaire that was distributed by mail shortly after the bankruptcy filing. Although the bankruptcy court records ask for all debts in exact amounts, some debtors do not disclose their student loan debt. These debtors may reason that if they cannot discharge student loans in bankruptcy, there is no reason to mention those debts. The bankruptcy court records also may understate student loan debt in that some people list student loan debts as debts entitled to priority payment, although they do not qualify as such. The coding protocols for the 2007 CBP did not recategorize these obligations as nonpriority unsecured debt, which means that they are not reflected as student loan debt in the data.

24. A recent report from the public policy research and advocacy organization Demos that argues that one- and two-year credentials can lead students to economic prosperity concludes that degree completion may be just as important as the type of degree pursued; Wheary and Orozco, *Graduated Success*, 1.

25. The 12 percent of income allocated to nonmortgage debt is the standard set by the U.S. Department of Housing and Urban Development as the criterion to be used in determining the affordability of a mortgage loan; Greiner, "How Much Student Loan Debt Is Too Much?," 10.

26. Ibid., 11, Table 3.

27. Knapp and Seaks, "An Analysis of the Probability of Default." Greene, "An Economic Analysis of Student Loan Default."

28. Cunningham and Kienzl, *Delinquency*, 5.

29. Gladieux and Perna, *Borrowers Who Drop Out*, 8.

30. Porter and Thorne, "The Failure of Bankruptcy's Fresh Start," 112–17.

31. Carey, *A Matter of Degrees*, 5.

32. Manning, *Credit Card Nation*, 15.

33. "Perhaps the high rates of attending college suggest that bankrupt debtors are more likely to be ambitious or risk takers than the population generally, or perhaps the low completion rates signal earlier financial troubles or people who cannot stick to a difficult task"; Warren, "Financial Collapse and Class Status," 130–31.

34. Few people working on the problems of student loan debt consider bankruptcy. "One area that needs further exploration is treatment of student loans under bankruptcy. . . . These provisions should be evaluated to assess whether they treat student loan repayment appropriately"; Project on Student Debt, *White Paper*, 22.

35. The Bankruptcy Abuse Prevention and Consumer Protection Act of 2005 amended section 523(a)(8) to make private students loans also subject to the presumption against dischargeability.

36. 11 U.S.C. § 523(a)(8).

37. Ibid. See also Pardo and Lacey, "Undue Hardship," 419–29.

38. Pottow, "The Nondischargeability of Student Loans," 247–50.

39. Commission on the Bankruptcy Laws of the United States, "Report of the Commission," 2.

40. Given the modest increase in lifetime earnings between those who attain associate's degrees and those who have only some college coursework, another possible approach would be to permit the discharge of any student loan debts of people without bachelor's degrees. This proposal is quite sweeping and would almost certainly curtail or sharply increase the costs of borrowing for certificate programs and at community colleges. Yet, if these programs do not pay off, their benefits may be questionable.

41. Pardo and Lacey, "Undue Hardship," 490–94.

42. See 11 U.S.C. §§ 727 and 1328.

43. The bad faith indicia could be set forth in the law, with a bright-line test, such as completion of 75 percent of the required course hours for a degree. Alternatively, judges could be allowed to exercise their judgment, weighing the current financial situations of debtors and their testimony under oath as to why they dropped out of their educational programs and their future plans for employment or education. Given the situations of most bankruptcy debtors, which often include earning a very low income, chronic health problems, or family interruptions such as divorce, it may be years, if not decades, if they can contemplate returning to college.

Chapter Six

1. Brin, interview by Terry Gross.

2. Kharif, "Google's Larry Page."

3. Vise and Malseed, *The Google Story*.

4. These are not their real names.

5. Manning, *Credit Card Nation*, 227.

6. Schwager, *Stock Market Wizards*, 187–88. "The Forbes 400," 348.

7. Shane, *The Illusions of Entrepreneurship*, 8.

8. Lawless and Warren, "The Myth of the Disappearing Business Bankruptcy," 752.

9. Ibid., 757–68.

10. Ibid., 782–83.

11. The financial data all display substantial skewness, making the means poor measures of central tendency. Consequently, this chapter reports median figures in the tables and text.

12. Mann, "The Role of Secured Credit," 36–40.

13. Mach and Wolken, "Financial Services Used by Small Businesses," A181.

14. Stouder and Kirchoff, "Funding the First Year of Business," 361.

15. National Federation of Independent Business, *Access to Credit*, 24.

16. Shane, *The Illusions of Entrepreneurship*, 80.

17. Scott, *The Use of Credit Card Debt*, 4.

18. Durkin, *The Impact of the Consumer Financial Protection Agency*, 23–25.

Chapter Seven

1. Names and ages have been slightly altered to protect the debtors' privacy.

2. Zagorsky and Lupica, "A Study of Consumers' Post-Discharge Finances," 303. Haurin and Rosenthal, *The Sustainability of Homeownership*, 50.

3. *Home Mortgages* (Shear), 2–4. Eggum, Porter, and Twomey, "Saving Homes in Bankruptcy," 1159–60.

4. Willis, "Will the Mortgage Market Correct?," 1195.

5. Simon and Hagerty, "One in Four Borrowers," 4.

6. As of November 30, 2010, seven million U.S. homeowners were either delinquent or in foreclosure; Gittleson, "Mortgage Modifications." Shenn, "Housing Crash."

7. Armour, "Many Mortgage Modifications."

8. Braucher, "Humpty Dumpty and the Foreclosure Crisis." Adelino, Gerardi, and Willen, "Why Don't Lenders Renegotiate More Home Mortgages?"

9. Bucks et al., "Changes in U.S. Family Finances," A33–A34, A41.

10. Shenn, "Housing Crash."

11. If a bankrupt homeowner has sufficient equity in the home, however, in some states a bankruptcy trustee may force a sale of the home and use some of the proceeds to repay the mortgagee and other creditors. See 11 U.S.C. §§ 522, 704(a).

12. Jacoby, "Home Ownership Risk," 2272.

13. Surprisingly, Chapter 13 bankruptcy allows reduction of the principal and interest rate for mortgages on real estate other than the debtor's principal residence. For example, in Chapter 13 cases, loans on vacation homes and income-producing rental property can be modified. See 11 U.S.C. §§ 1322(b)(2), 1322(c).

14. Eggum, Porter, and Twomey, "Saving Homes in Bankruptcy," 1129–31.

15. 11 U.S.C. § 1322(b)(5).

16. Norberg and Velkey, "Debtor Discharge and Creditor Repayment," 475.

17. Surowiecki, "Home Economics," 62.

18. Thorne, "Personal Bankruptcy and the Credit Report," 33–34.

19. Michael Luo details the tension and strains of overcrowding that result from the return of adult children and their own offspring to their parents' homes after job losses; "'Doubling Up' in Recession-Strained Quarters." He notes that Census Bureau data released in September 2010 show a 12 percent increase in total multifamily households between 2008 and 2010. Such households made up 13.2 percent of all households, the highest percentage since 1968.

20. Bowdler, Quercia, and Smith, *The Foreclosure Generation*, 3–5.

21. Willis, "Will the Mortgage Market Correct?," 1193.

22. Haurin and Rosenthal, *The Sustainability of Homeownership*, 50.

23. Zagorsky and Lupica, "A Study of Consumers' Post-Discharge Finances," 303–04.

24. Sullivan, Warren, and Westbrook, *The Fragile Middle Class*, 200.

25. Taylor, Pevalin, and Todd, "The Psychological Costs," 1032.

26. Warren and Tyagi, *The Two-Income Trap*, 22–23.

27. Nguyen, "Parents in Financial Crisis," 232.

28. Willis, "Will the Mortgage Market Correct?," 1192. Pribesh and Downey, "Why Are Residential and School Moves," 531. Armour, "Foreclosure's Financial Strains."

29. Nguyen, "Parents in Financial Crisis," 238–41.

30. 42 U.S.C. § 11431 et seq., Title VII-B.

31. Shellenbarger, "Break It to 'em Gently" and "When Tough Times Weigh on the Kids."

Chapter Eight

1. Thorne, "Extreme Financial Strain," 188.

2. Of the 1,032 telephone interviews conducted during the 2007 CBP, 541 (52 percent) were completed by respondents who lived with a spouse or permanent partner in the year before their bankruptcies. All data in this chapter are from this subsample of *coupled* respondents who completed a telephone interview. (Not all coupled respondents were married, but for ease of discussion I use the terms "wife" and "husband" throughout the chapter.) Wives were more likely to complete the phone interview: 59 percent of the interviews were completed by women. Based on the most relevant financial measures and type of bankruptcy, the subsample of couples who completed telephone interviews appears to be similar to all couples in the CBP sample (see Table 8.5). Thus there does not appear to be any detectable response bias.

TABLE 8.5

Comparison of relevant financial measures and bankruptcy type of all couples in the 2007 CBP sample and those couples who completed the telephone interview

Parameter	All couples (n = 1,185)	Couples who completed the interview (n = 541)
Median annual income	$35,724	$36,228
Median total assets	$91,368	$89,878
Median unsecured debt	$38,557	$41,411
Median total debt	$121,367	$123,595
Median unsecured debt-to-income ratio	1.12:1	1.27:1
Median total debt-to-income ratio	3.48:1	3.53:1
Percentage who filed Chapter 7	62%	63%

SOURCE: Consumer Bankruptcy Project (CBP) 2007.

NOTE: Difference between "all couples surveyed" and "couples who completed the interview" was not found for any of the above variables ($p > 0.05$).

3. Komarovsky, *Blue-Collar Marriage*, 222. Komter, "Hidden Power in Marriage," 201. Rubin, *Worlds of Pain*, 106–13. Vogler, "Money in the Household," 692. Vogler and Pahl, "Money, Power and Inequality," 283.

4. Peirce et al., "Financial Stress, Social Support," 45 ("during financial hardship"). Drentea, "Age, Debt and Anxiety," 445 ("when debts are in default").

5. Barnett and Shen, "Gender, High- and Low-Schedule-Control Housework Tasks," 419, 422.

6. Thorne and Anderson, "Managing the Stigma," 82–83.

7. Albrecht, Bahr, and Goodman, *Divorce and Remarriage*, 54–55, 148–49. Conger, Rueter, and Elder, Jr., "Couple Resilience," 68. Conger et al., "Linking Economic Hardship," 652–55. Dew, "Two Sides of the Same Coin?," 100. Gudmunson et al., "Linking Financial Strain," 371–74.

8. Sullivan, Warren, and Westbrook, "Bankruptcy and the Family," 209–13. Sullivan, Warren, and Westbrook, *The Fragile Middle Class*, 172–98.

9. Blair and Lichter, "Measuring the Division of Household Labor," 109. Coltrane, "Research on Household Labor," 1208.

10. Blair and Lichter, "Measuring the Division of Household Labor," 98–101. Coltrane, "Research on Household Labor," 1208–33. Twiggs, McQuillan, and Ferree, "Meaning and Measurement," 722.

11. Barnett and Shen, "Gender, High- and Low-Schedule-Control Housework Tasks," 422, 423.

12. Coltrane, "Research on Household Labor," 1210. Estes, Noonan, and Maume, "Is Work-Family Policy," 533. Noonan, "The Impact of Domestic Work," 1137.

13. Komarovsky, *Blue-Collar Marriage,* 222. Komter, "Hidden Power in Marriage," 201. Morris, "Redundancy and Patterns of Household Finance," 492. Pahl, "Household Spending, Personal Spending," 123–24. Thorne, "Extreme Financial Strain," 188. Vogler and Pahl, "Money, Power and Inequality," 283.

14. Peirce et al., "Financial Stress, Social Support," 45.

15. Drentea, "Age, Debt and Anxiety," 445.

16. Conger, Rueter, and Elder, Jr., "Couple Resilience," 68. Gerson, "Severe Debt Can Cause Depression."

17. Thorne, "Extreme Financial Strain," 185.

18. Barnett and Shen, "Gender, High- and Low-Schedule-Control Housework Tasks," 422.

19. Analysis of qualitative data collected during earlier CBP studies generated the three variables used to measure emotional distress.

20. National Sleep Foundation, "2009 Sleep in America Poll."

21. Reinberg, "With the Economy Down."

22. There was one interaction effect between sex and paying bills. Specifically, ordinal regression analysis suggested that women who had no bill-paying responsibilities (husband-only configuration) were three times more likely to report no sleep deprivation (see Table 8.2). This result was statistically significant ($p < 0.01$), offering more support for the hypothesis that women who are not involved with bills may be partially sheltered from emotional harms.

23. Albrecht, Bahr, and Goodman, *Divorce and Remarriage,* 54–55, 148–49. Conger, Rueter, and Elder, Jr., "Couple Resilience," 68. Conger et al., "Linking Economic Hardship," 652–55. Dew, "Two Sides of the Same Coin?," 99–100. Gudmunson et al., "Linking Financial Strain," 371–74.

24. Caplovitz, *Making Ends Meet,* 126.

25. Conger, Rueter, and Elder, Jr. "Couple Resilience," 54 (marital instability and dissatisfaction). Conger, Ge, and Lorenz, "Economic Stress and Marital Relations," 201–03 (increased conflict). Conger et al., "Linking Economic Hardship," 652–54 (decreased warmth).

26. Dew, "Two Sides of the Same Coin?," 100.

27. Because directionality was hypothesized, a one-tailed test for correlation was conducted. Furthermore, because the data are ordinal, and thus nonparametric, a Spearman's Rho rather than a Pearson's test was used to analyze the data. Results were significant with $p < 0.018$.

28. Among only the respondents who were still married at the time of the interview (n = 432), their marital satisfaction before bankruptcy was as follows: 66.4 percent were very satisfied; 26.3 percent were somewhat satisfied; and 7.3 percent were not at all satisfied. Thus, these respondents were half as likely as all respondents to indicate that before bankruptcy they were not at all satisfied with their marriages (7.3 percent and 14.4 percent, respectively), suggesting that the people who divorced

before the interview were generally less satisfied in their marriages. However, even among respondents who remained married, after filing for bankruptcy the percentage who were not at all satisfied declined by more than half, and those who reported being very satisfied increased by 12 percentage points. Thus, the trend is consistent: filing for bankruptcy appears to be correlated with increased marital satisfaction.

29. Tejada-Vera and Sutton, *Births, Marriages.*

30. Kreider and Elliott, *America's Families*, 3, Table 1.

31. Schoen and Canudas-Romo, "Timing Effects on Divorce," 749.

32. Williams, Sawyer, and Wahlstrom, *Marriages, Families & Intimate Relationships*, 504.

33. Schoen and Standish, "The Retrenchment of Marriage," 557.

34. Fisher and Lyons, "Till Debt Do Us Part," 37.

35. U.S. Courts, "Business and Nonbusiness Bankruptcy Cases Commenced."

36. Warren, "What Is a Women's Issue?," 24–31.

37. Lawless et al., "Did Bankruptcy Reform Fail?," 365–75, 381. The percentage of respondents who reported that they seriously struggled to repay their bills for "more than two years" increased significantly, from 32.6 percent in 2001 to 43.8 percent in 2007.

38. Mann, *Charging Ahead*, 205.

Chapter Nine

I thank Jennifer Beardsley, Mechele Dickerson, Justin Driver, William Forbath, Mary Fox, Mira Ganor, Robert Gavin, Jennifer Laurin, Tamiko Overton, Judge Elizabeth Stong, Jay Westbrook, and Sean Williams for assistance and comments on earlier drafts of this chapter. Thanks also to Kimberly Huyser and Yujin Kim for excellent research assistance.

1. For Chapter 7 bankruptcy, the median legal fee was $1,000, and the median family income was $1,939. For Chapter 13, the median legal fee was $2,500, and the median income, $3,069.50. Data from the 2007 Consumer Bankruptcy Project.

2. Although the 2001 data were drawn from only five judicial districts and the 2007 CBP was a national random sample, when I limited the 2007 data to districts included in the 2001 study, the effect was even stronger. A fuller analysis of this data, including a discussion of other studies that have reached contrary results, is available in Littwin, "The Affordability Paradox."

3. Rochelle, "Business Bankruptcies Rise."

4. Lawless et al., "Did Bankruptcy Reform Fail?," 352.

5. Not all debtors use a lawyer or file pro se. A third category of debtors use paid, nonlawyer petition preparers to help them complete their bankruptcy paperwork. These are front-end services that aid debtors with the initial paperwork and then have no further involvement in the case. Petition-preparer cases are excluded from Table 9.1 because of the type of regression used. (I originally ran a multinomial regression, but the preparer category was so small that the result did not show any difference.) Thus, I did not analyze represented debtors, pro se debtors, and debtors using petition preparers separately (as I did in Tables 9.2 and 9.3). Excluding the preparer cases from the Table 9.1 analysis generated similar results as either adding those cases to the pro se category or adding them to the lawyer category. In each case, the same variables were statistically significant in the same direction. The only differences were the size of the effects and, to a lesser extent, the degree of statistical significance. The alternate regressions are available upon request. Throughout this

chapter, data from the preparer cases are excluded from the analyses unless otherwise noted and treated separately.

6. Mann and Porter, "Saving Up for Bankruptcy," 318.

7. Averaging the two educational levels resulted in the same trend.

8. Lawless et al., "Did Bankruptcy Reform Fail?," 360, Figure 2. All amounts are calculated in constant 2007 dollars.

9. As Table 9.1 shows, filing under Chapter 13 did not, however, increase the likelihood that a debtor would hire a lawyer beyond the homeownership effect. Owning a home and filing under Chapter 13 were highly correlated.

10. This choice resulted in the exclusion of 137 cases from this analysis, 105 of which were dismissed after confirmation.

11. Pearson Chi-square = 48.645, $p < 0.001$.

12. Yeats's Chi-square = 72.506, $p < 0.001$.

13. From the CBP data, one cannot tell whether the case was dismissed as a result of a technical deficiency motion or for another reason, but the fact that both occur in a disproportionate number of pro se cases suggests that there is a relationship.

14. Again, it was not possible to be sure from the CBP data that the dismissals were in response to the technical deficiency motions.

15. Block-Lieb, "A Comparison of Pro Bono Representation Programs," 41–42, citing Baillie, "Bankruptcy Lawyers, Bankruptcy Judges," 7–28: "Moreover, even in those districts where pro se filings are low there are many pro se appearances in relief from the stay motions and other motions and in adversary proceedings. That occurs because the attorney who handles the Chapter 7 or 13 filing usually does so for a flat fee and is often unwilling to perform further services without additional payments, which the client is often unable to supply having, by definition, no remaining non-exempt assets. In these cases presumably the lawyer who filed the case simply does not appear in the adversary proceeding or makes a motion to withdraw and the motion is granted."

16. Mann and Porter, "Saving Up for Bankruptcy," 318.

17. Mann, "Bankruptcy Reform," 392–93.

18. Charn and Zorza, *Civil Legal Assistance*, 22–23. Broderick and George, "A Nation of Do-It-Yourself Lawyers," A21.

19. Conference of Chief Justices, *Report of Joint Task Force*, 7.

20. Charn and Zorza, *Civil Legal Assistance*, 32–33.

21. Ibid., 41.

22. Tedesco, "In Forma Pauperis in Bankruptcy," 100, note 63. Testerman, "Paralegal Regulation," 37.

23. In 2001, all thirteen pro se debtors who filed Chapter 7 bankruptcy in the CBP sample received discharges. Dismissal was rare in Chapter 7 generally. Only 0.7 percent (3 of 450) of represented debtors failed to obtain a discharge.

24. Mann and Porter, "Saving Up for Bankruptcy," 318. They present a comprehensive empirical analysis of this issue and do not suggest that this difficulty increased after the amendments took effect.

25. Wedoff, *Report of the Advisory Committee*, 339–40.

26. LoPucki and Warren, *Secured Credit*, 118. They provide a nice summary of the research on payouts in consumer bankruptcy cases, which is unlikely to change. Low payouts have been the norm since at least the late 1960s. Stanley and Girth, *Bankruptcy*, 87.

27. Berenson, "Family Law Residency Program?," 109.

28. Robert A. Gavin, Jr., clerk of court, U.S. Bankruptcy Court Eastern District of New York, conversation with author, January 13, 2010.

29. Farrell-Willoughby and Brundage, "Pro Bono Representation ," 44–45.

30. Goldschmidt et al., *Meeting the Challenge of Pro Se Litigation*, 112.

31. Ibid., 102.

32. The following are samples of inaccurate advice found on the Internet: "The thing to remember out here is that your income should be higher than the median of the state. If it is lower then, [*sic*] you do not qualify for the Chapter 7 personal bankruptcies. If it is higher, then you will probably do so even if the rules have changed" ("Declaring Personal Bankruptcy," http://www.declaringpersonalbank ruptcy.net). "The bankrupt person can avail limited credit only as the legal system and his financial statement will not allow him to enjoy credits beyond a certain limit [after discharge]" (Mansi Aggarwal, "Personal Bankruptcy Advice Guide 101," http://ezinearticles.com/?Personal-Bankruptcy-Advice-Guide-101&id=240041).

Chapter Ten

1. *Local Loan Co. v. Hunt*, 292 U.S. 234, 244 (1934).

2. Jiménez, "Distribution of Assets," 797.

3. Norberg and Velkey, "Debtor Discharges and Creditor Repayment," 476. Whitford, "The Ideal of Individualized Justice," 411. Data for cases filed after the reform of bankruptcy law in 2005 are not yet available.

4. Braucher, "Lawyers and Consumer Bankruptcy," 529–30.

5. These statistics were calculated from the data from the Bankruptcy Data Project at Harvard (http://bdp.law.harvard.edu/index.cfm). By February 2011, the rate had fallen to below 28.8 percent.

6. Stanley and Girth, *Bankruptcy*, 74.

7. Ibid., 75.

8. Neustadter, "When Lawyer and Client Meet," 204–07.

9. Ibid., 209.

10. Braucher, "Lawyers and Consumer Bankruptcy," 503.

11. Ibid., 562.

12. Sullivan, Warren, and Westbrook, "The Persistence of Local Legal Culture."

13. The one financial variable in which there was a difference between respondents and nonrespondents was unsecured debt among Chapter 13 filers. Respondents reported a median figure for unsecured debt in Chapter 13 of $23,661, compared with a median of $16,306 for a random sample of nonrespondents; a Wilcoxon rank-sum test produces a Z-statistic of 2.08 ($p = 0.038$). The means for Chapter 13 filers are similarly disparate ($36,056 for respondents versus $24,963 for nonrespondents), although a t-test suggested only marginal statistical significance ($p = 0.089$). Because respondents versus nonrespondents were compared across thirteen financial characteristics and within two different subgroups (Chapter 7 filers and Chapter 13 filers), it is possible that this difference in unsecured debt amounts is due to chance alone. (With twenty-six statistical tests, one would expect to find at least one significant difference by chance alone.) At the same time, we cannot rule out the possibility that the difference reflects some real unrevealed distinction between respondents and nonrespondents.

14. 11 U.S.C. § 727(a)(8). Because a discharge in 2006 eliminated the debtor's eligibility for a new discharge under either Chapter 7 or Chapter 13 during the

time period of the study, we controlled only for bankruptcy filings that occurred before 2006.

15. Separate logistic regressions, not reported here, were run to check the robustness of the specification of the model. These regressions included different independent variables such as the percentage of all cases filed as Chapter 13s during the time of the sample (in lieu of using the cases only in the sample), as well as using different cutoffs or no cutoffs for the number of non–African Americans in the judicial district. Other logistic regressions aggregated data at the state rather than the district level as well as controlling for fixed effects in the judicial districts. Across all these regressions, the results are qualitatively similar. All variables retain the same sign, and the same variables are statistically significant.

16. These statistics were calculated from the data from the Bankruptcy Data Project at Harvard (http://bdp.law.harvard.edu/index.cfm).

17. Norberg and Velkey, "Debtor Discharge and Creditor Repayment," 476. Whitford, "The Ideal of Individualized Justice," 411.

Chapter Eleven

1. Sullivan, "Debt and the Simulation of Social Class."

2. Leicht and Fitzgerald, *Post-Industrial Peasants*, 5.

3. The median family income in the United States in 2007 was $61,355 (in 2007 dollars). U.S. Census Bureau, *Statistical Abstract: 2010*, Table 690.

4. Bradbury and Katz, "Women's Work and Family Income Mobility," 23. Warren and Tyagi, *The Two-Income Trap*, 29–31.

5. U.S. Census Bureau, "Median and Average Sale Prices."

6. Fernandez, Kaboub, and Todorova, "On Democratizing Financial Turmoil," 13. Anderson, Capozza, and Van Order, *Deconstructing the Subprime Debacle*, 17–18.

7. Merlis, Gould, and Mahato, *Rising Out-of-Pocket Spending*. Halle and Seshamani, "Hidden Costs of Healthcare."

8. Halle and Seshamani, "Hidden Costs of Healthcare."

9. U.S. Census Bureau, *Statistical Abstract: 2010*, Table 786.

10. Kim, "An Up and Down Week." PBS, "Changing Face of Unemployment." Castells, *The Rise of the Network Society*, 296. Carnoy, *Sustaining the New Economy*, 73, 109. Uchitelle, *The Disposable American*.

11. Hacker, "Call It the Family Risk Factor."

12. Compare the following authorities: Krugman, *The Great Unraveling*; Stiglitz, *The Roaring Nineties*; Gordon, *Fat and Mean*; Galbraith, *Created Unequal*.

13. Mandel, *The High-Risk Society*, 53.

14. Most notably Gordon, *Fat and Mean*, and Leicht and Fennell, *Professional Work*.

15. Leicht and Fitzgerald, *Post-Industrial Peasants*, 62–79.

16. Schor, *The Overspent American*, 20. Jacobs and Gerson, "Overworked Individuals."

17. Bureau of Labor Statistics, "Labor Productivity and Costs Index."

18. Warren and Tyagi, *The Two-Income Trap*, 55–71. Bradbury and Katz, "Women's Work and Family Income Mobility."

19. Jacobs and Gerson, "Overworked Individuals," 43.

20. Warren and Tyagi, *The Two-Income Trap*, 55–71. Hacker, *The Great Risk Shift*, 11–34.

21. Hacker, *The Great Risk Shift*, 95.

22. Schor, *The Overspent American*, 22.

23. Fernandez, Kaboub, and Todorova, "On Democratizing Financial Turmoil," 5. Kregel, "Minsky's Cushions of Safety," 13. Wray, "Lessons from the Subprime Meltdown," 10.

24. Kim, "An Up and Down Week."

25. Bucks et al., "Changes in U.S. Family Finances," Table 13.

26. Freddie Mac, "Freddie Mac Releases Results of Its 22nd Annual Arm Survey," January 5, 2006, http://www.freddiemac.com/news/archives/rates/2006/20060105_05armsurvey.html.

27. McCoy, "A Growing Tide of Risky Mortgages."

28. Avery, Brevoort, and Carter, "Higher-Priced Home Lending."

29. Anderson, Capozza, and Van Order, *Deconstructing the Subprime Debacle*, 8.

30. Sullivan, "Debt and the Simulation of Social Class," 22. Hacker, *The Great Risk Shift*, 1–9.

31. Schor, *The Overspent American*, 20. Warren and Tyagi, *The Two-Income Trap*, 73–75.

32. Glick and Lansing, "U.S. Household Deleveraging," 1.

33. Joint Economic Committee, *Vicious Cycle*, 2.

34. Manning, *Credit Card Nation*, 22–23.

35. Prior work by CBP researchers provides more detail on the financial characteristics of bankrupt households. Lawless et al., "Did Bankruptcy Reform Fail?," 8–29.

36. Ibid.

37. Keister, *Wealth in America*, 78. Keister, *Getting Rich*, 99. Conley, *Being Black*, 55–108. Conley, *Elsewhere, U.S.A.*, 3–18. Shapiro, *The Hidden Cost of Being African American*, 1–20. Oliver and Shapiro, *Black Wealth/White Wealth*, 35–54.

38. Manning, *Credit Card Nation*, 159–94. Mann, "Bankruptcy Reform," 6–8. Arano and Parker, "Modeling Credit Card Borrowing." Lyons, "Credit Practices and Financial Education Needs."

39. Oliver and Shapiro, *Black Wealth/White Wealth*, 19–21. Shapiro, *The Hidden Cost of Being African American*, 105–10.

40. Compare with Hacker, *The Great Risk Shift*, 61–85, 137–64.

Chapter Twelve

Portions of this chapter are reprinted or adapted from the following sources: (1) Hacker, Jacob S. "Sharing Risk and Responsibility in a New Economic Era." In *Shared Responsibility, Shared Risk: Government, Markets and Social Policy in the Twenty-First Century*, edited by Jacob S. Hacker and Ann O'Leary. New York: Oxford University Press, 2011. By permission of Oxford University Press, Inc. (2) Hacker, Jacob S. "Reclaiming Middle-Class America." *American Prospect* 22, no. 2 (2011). Reprinted with permission of *The American Prospect*. (3) Hacker, Jacob S. *The Great Risk Shift: The New Economic Insecurity and the Decline of the American Dream*. Rev. and exp. ed. New York: Oxford University Press, 2008. By permission of Oxford University Press, Inc. (4) Hacker, Jacob S. "The Real Dangers to the American Middle Class." *Challenge* 50 (2007): 3. Used by permission of M. E. Sharpe.

1. Bailey, "ABC News/Yahoo! News Poll."

2. Hacker, *The Great Risk Shift*, xv–xvi.

3. Hacker, *The Divided Welfare State*, 7–8.

4. Ibid., 13–16.

5. Himmelstein et al., "Medical Bankruptcy," 743–44.

6. Institute for America's Future, "Are You Really Covered?"

7. Economic Policy Institute, "Can't Depend on a Solid Pension."

8. Economic Policy Institute, "The State of Working America."

9. Munnell and Sundén, *401(k) Plans Are Still Coming Up Short*, 3.

10. Ibid., 5.

11. *The Effects of Recent Market Turmoil* (Orszag).

12. Joint Center for Housing Studies, *The State of the Nation's Housing 2009*, 9.

13. Bucks et al., "Changes in U.S. Family Finances," A33, Table 9.1. The top 10 percent of households by wealth hold only 19 percent of their wealth in homes.

14. Munnell, Webb, and Golub-Sass, *The National Retirement Risk Index*, 4, Figure 2.

15. Ibid., 7, Table 3.

16. Ibid., 4, Table 1.

17. Stettner and Allegretto, *The Rising Stakes of Job Loss*, 8–9.

18. Bernstein and Kornbluh, *Running Faster to Stay in Place*, 6, Figure 4.

19. Hacker and Jacobs, *The Rising Instability of American Family Incomes*, 2; 5, Figure A; 8; 13.

20. Hacker et al., *Economic Security at Risk*, 2–3.

21. Wheary, Shapiro, and Draut, *By a Thread*, 2.

22. Weller and Lynch, *Household Wealth in Freefall*, 9.

23. Lawless et al., "Did Bankruptcy Reform Fail?," 353, 384–85.

24. Warren and Tyagi, *The Two-Income Trap*, 6.

25. Elmer and Seelig, "The Rising Long-Term Trend," 36, Figure 11.

26. Weller and Lynch, *Household Wealth in Freefall*, 7, Figure 6.

27. Simon and Hagerty, "House-Price Drops Leave More Underwater."

28. Kahneman and Tversy, "Prospect Theory," 263–91.

29. The Tarrance Group and Lake Snell Perry Mermin and Associates, *Battleground XXVII*, 29.

30. Brownstein, "Financial Risk Cuts Deeper."

31. Hacker, Rehm, and Schlesinger, *Standing on Shaky Ground*, 15.

32. Rockefeller Foundation, *American Worker Survey*, 25.

33. Ibid.

34. Davis et al., *Who Pays?*, 118.

35. Scherer, "Number of Long-Term Unemployed."

36. Moss, *When All Else Fails*, 83.

Appendix

1. The principal investigators in the 2001 CBP were (in alphabetical order) David Himmelstein, Robert Lawless, Bruce Markell, Katherine Porter, John Pottow, Michael Schill, Teresa A. Sullivan, Deborah Thorne, Susan Wachter, Elizabeth Warren, Jay Lawrence Westbrook, and Steffie Woolhandler.

2. Chapter 11 bankruptcy is primarily used by businesses that wish to reorganize; Chapter 12 is for family farmers or fishermen.

3. Lawless and Warren, "The Myth of the Disappearing Business Bankruptcy."

4. The population data come from the Administrative Office of the U.S. Courts. To calculate comparable percentages of filings in the population, the CBP used the number of nonbusiness bankruptcy filings under either Chapter 7 or Chapter 13 (excluding any nonbusiness filings under other chapters) for the months of February 2007 and March 2007. Administrative Office of the U.S. Courts, Bankruptcy Statistics, at http://www.uscourts.gov/Statistics/BankruptcyStatistics.aspx (last visited August 3, 2010) (click on twelve-month period ending in June and then select 2007).

5. One set of variables was excluded from the error check because by necessity and design, they required coders to exercise some discretion in coding the variables. These variables categorized unsecured debts by type, such as medical, rent, definitely credit card, probably credit card, etc.

6. For three variables relating to tallies of creditors, a greater margin of error was used to determine whether an error existed. Many court records contain debts listed for "notice only" or are duplicates that are listed separately to give notice to a collection agency or law firm. Thus, some discretion had to be exercised in tallying the number of different creditors. For these variables, a recheck was performed only if the original coding and recoding differed by more than a few creditors (three to five, depending on the type of debt).

7. Respondents provided a variety of reasons for refusing to complete the phone interview. For example, some debtors with cell phones did not want to use their minutes for the interview, which could take an hour; others said that the bankruptcy process had been too emotional and they did not want to relive the experience; some said they were now to ill to participate (for example, bladder cancer or emphysema); and a few had died.

Adelino, Manuel, Kristopher Gerardi, and Paul S. Willen. "Why Don't Lenders Renegotiate More Home Mortgages? Redefaults, Self-Cures, and Securitization."
Public Policy Discussion Paper no. 09-4, Federal Reserve Bank of Boston,
2009. http://www.bos.frb.org/economic/ppdp/2009/ppdp0904.pdf.

Albrecht, Stan L., Howard M. Bahr, and Kristen L. Goodman. *Divorce and Remarriage: Problems, Adaptations, and Adjustments, Volume 42*. Westport, CT:
Greenwood, 1983.

Anderson, Charles D., Dennis R. Capozza, and Robert Van Order. *Deconstructing
the Subprime Debacle Using New Indices of Underwriting Quality and Economic Conditions: A First Look*. Ann Arbor, MI: University Financial Associates, 2008. http://www.ufanet.com/DeconstructingSubprimeJuly2008.pdf.

Anthony, Jerry. "The Effects of Florida's Growth Management Act on Housing Affordability." *Journal of the American Planning Association* 69, no. 3 (2003):
282–95.

Apgar, William, and Allegra Calder. "The Dual Mortgage Market: The Persistence
of Discrimination in Mortgage Lending." In *The Geography of Opportunity*,
edited by Xavier De Souza Briggs, 101–27. Washington, DC: Brookings Institution Press, 2005.

Arano, Katherine G., and Carl Parker. "Modeling Credit Card Borrowing by Students." *Southwestern Economic Review* 34, no. 1 (2007): 27–40.

Armour, Stephanie. "Foreclosures' Financial Strains Take Toll on Kids." *USA
Today*, July 8, 2008. Accessed February 4, 2011. http://www.usatoday.com/
money/economy/housing/2008-07-08-children-foreclosure-homeless_N.htm.

———. "Many Mortgage Modifications Push Payments . . . Higher." *USA Today*,
September 14, 2009. Accessed February 4, 2011. http://www.usatoday.com/
money/economy/housing/2009-09-14-mortgage-modifications-not-helping_N
.htm.

Avery, Robert B., Kenneth P. Brevoort, and Glenn B. Carter. "Higher-Priced Home
Lending and the 2005 HMDA Data." *Federal Reserve Bulletin* 92 (September
2006): A123–66. Online at Federal Reserve Board, http://www.federalreserve
.gov/pubs/bulletin/2006/hmda/default.htm.

Bailey, Holly. "ABC News/Yahoo! News Poll: People Are Losing Faith in the American Dream." Yahoo! News, September 21, 2010. Accessed January 30, 2011. http://news.yahoo.com/s/yblog_upshot/abc-newsyahoo-news-poll-people -are-losing-faith-in-the-american-dream.

Baillie, James L. "Bankruptcy Lawyers, Bankruptcy Judges and Public Service." In *67th Annual Meeting of the National Conference of Bankruptcy Judges*, 7–27. 1993.

Bankruptcy Abuse Prevention and Consumer Protection Act of 2005, Pub. L. no. 109-8, 119 Stat. 23 (2005).

Bankruptcy Data Project at Harvard. Accessed August 22, 2011. http://bdp.law .harvard.edu

Barnett, Rosalind C., and Yu-Chu Shen. "Gender, High- and Low-Schedule-Control Housework Tasks, and Psychological Distress: A Study of Dual-Earner Couples." *Journal of Family Issues* 18, no. 4 (1997): 403–28.

Baum, Sandy, and Marie O'Malley. *College on Credit: How Borrowers Perceive Their Education Debt; Results of the 2002 National Student Loan Survey.* Reston, VA: Nellie Mae, 2003. Accessed January 30, 2011. http://www.nellie mae.com/pdf/nasls_2002.pdf.

Belsky, Eric, and Joel Prakken. *Housing Wealth Effects: Housing's Impact on Wealth Accumulation, Wealth Distribution and Consumer Spending.* Cambridge, MA: Joint Center for Housing Studies of Harvard University, 2004. Accessed January 30, 2011. http://www.jchs.harvard.edu/publications/finance/w04-13.pdf.

Berenson, Steven K. "A Family Law Residency Program?: A Modest Proposal in Response to the Burdens Created by Self-Represented Litigants in Family Court." *Rutgers Law Journal* 33, no. 1 (2001): 105–64.

Bermant, Gordon, and Ed Flynn. "Measuring Projected Performance in Chapter 13: Comparisons across the States." *American Bankruptcy Institute Journal* 19 (July/August 2000): 22, 34–35.

Bernstein, Jared, and Karen Kornbluh. *Running Faster to Stay in Place: The Growth of Family Work Hours and Incomes.* Washington, DC: New America Foundation, 2005. Accessed January 24, 2011. http://www.newamerica.net/ files/nafmigration/archive/Doc_File_2437_1.pdf.

Bernstein, Jared, and Lawrence Mishel. "Economy's Gains Fail to Reach Most Worker's Paychecks." Economic Policy Institute, August 30, 2007. Accessed January 31, 2011. http://www.epi.org/publications/entry/bp195/.

Biden, Joseph I. *Annual Report of the White House Task Force on the Middle Class.* Washington, DC: Office of the Vice President of the United States, 2010. Accessed August 16, 2010. http://www.whitehouse.gov/sites/default/files/micro sites/100226-annual-report-middle-class.pdf.

Blair, Sampson Lee, and Daniel T. Lichter. "Measuring the Division of Household Labor: Gender Segregation of Housework among American Couples." *Journal of Family Issues* 12, no. 1 (1991): 91–113.

Block-Lieb, Susan. "A Comparison of Pro Bono Representation Programs for Consumer Debtors." *American Bankruptcy Institute Law Review* 2, no. 1 (1994): 37–56.

Bostic, Raphael W., and Brian J. Surette. "Have the Doors Opened Wider? Trends in Homeownership Rates by Race and Income." *Journal of Real Estate Economics and Finance* 23, no. 3 (2001): 411–34.

Bosworth, Barry, Gary Burtless, and Jerry Sabelhaus. "The Decline in Savings: Evidence from Household Surveys." *Brookings Papers on Economic Activity* 1991, no. 1 (1991): 183–256.

Bowdler, Janis, Roberto Quercia, and David Andrew Smith. *The Foreclosure Generation: The Long-Term Impact of the Housing Crisis on Latino Children and Families.* Washington, DC: National Council of La Raza, 2010. Accessed January 31, 2011. http://www.nclr.org/images/uploads/publications/file_Fore closures_final2010.pdf.

Bradbury, Katharine, and Jane Katz. "Women's Work and Family Income Mobility." Public Policy Discussion Paper no. 04-03, Federal Reserve Bank of Boston, 2005. http://www.bos.frb.org/economic/ppdp/2004/ppdp0403.pdf.

Braucher, Jean. "Humpty Dumpty and the Foreclosure Crisis: Lessons from the Lackluster First Year of the Home Affordable Modification Program (HAMP)." *Arizona Law Review* 52, no. 3 (2010): 727–88.

———. "Lawyers and Consumer Bankruptcy: One Code, Many Cultures." *American Bankruptcy Law Journal* 67, no. 4 (1993): 501–83.

Brin, Sergey. Interview by Terry Gross. *Fresh Air*, NPR, October 14, 2003.

Broderick, Jr., John T., and Ronald M. George. "A Nation of Do-It-Yourself Lawyers." *New York Times*, January 1, 2010. Accessed February 4, 2011. http://www.nytimes.com/2010/01/02/opinion/02broderick.html.

Brown, Meta, Andrew Haughwout, Donghoon Lee, and Wilbert van der Klaauw. "The Financial Crisis at the Kitchen Table: Trends in Household Debt and Credit." Staff Report no. 480, Federal Reserve Bank of New York, 2010. http://www.ny.frb.org/research/staff_reports/sr480.pdf.

Brownstein, Ronald. "Financial Risk Cuts Deeper, Poll Finds." *National Journal*, April 25, 2009. Accessed January 24, 2011. http://www.nationaljournal.com/njmagazine/cs_20090425_8127.php.

Bucks, Brian K., Arthur B. Kennickell, Traci L. Mach, and Kevin B. Moore. "Changes in U.S. Family Finances from 2004 to 2007: Evidence from the Survey of Consumer Finances." *Federal Reserve Bulletin* 95 (February 2009): A1–A56.

Bureau of Labor Statistics. "Employment Status of the Civilian Noninstitutional Population by Sex and Age, Seasonally Adjusted." (Household Data Seasonally Adjusted Quarterly Averages.) Accessed July 13, 2009. http://www.bls.gov/web/cpseed1.pdf.

———. "Labor Productivity and Costs." Accessed January 31, 2011. http://www.bls.gov/lpc/.

Calder, Lendol. *Financing the American Dream: A Cultural History of Consumer Credit.* Princeton, NJ: Princeton University Press, 1999.

Canner, Glenn B., James T. Fergus, and Charles A. Luckett. "Home Equity Lines of Credit." *Federal Reserve Bulletin* 74 (June 1988): 361–73.

Cannon, Lyn Weber. "On the Absolute or Relative Basis of Perception: The Case for Middle Class Identification." *Social Indicators Research* 8, no. 3 (1980): 347–63.

Caplovitz, David. *Making Ends Meet: How Families Cope with Inflation and Recession*. Beverly Hills, CA: Sage, 1979.

Carey, Kevin. *A Matter of Degrees: Improving Graduation Rates in Four-Year Colleges and Universities*. Washington, DC: Education Trust, 2004. Accessed January 31, 2011. http://planning.ucsc.edu/retention/Docs/a_matter_of_degrees.pdf.

Carnoy, Martin. *Sustaining the New Economy: Work, Family, and Community in the Information Age*. New York: Russell Sage Foundation, 2000.

Carroll, Sarah W., and Wenli Li. "The Homeownership Experience of Households in Bankruptcy." *Cityscape* 13, no. 1 (2011): 113–34.

Castells, Manuel. *The Rise of the Network Society. The Information Age: Economy, Society, and Culture, Volume 1*. Malden, MA: Blackwell, 1996.

Center for Responsible Lending. *Snapshot of a Foreclosure Crisis*. Durham, NC: Center for Responsible Lending, 2010. Accessed January 2, 2011. http://www.responsiblelending.org/mortgage-lending/research-analysis/snapshot-of-a-foreclosure-crisis.html.

———. "Yield Spread Premiums: A Powerful Incentive for Equity Theft." Issue Brief no. 11, Center for Responsible Lending, Durham, NC, 2004. http://www.responsiblelending.org/mortgage-lending/tools-resources/ib011-YSP_Equity_Theft-0604.pdf.

CFED. "Assets & Opportunity Scorecard 2009–2010." Accessed February 1, 2011. http://scorecard.cfed.org/.

Chakrabarti, Rajashri, Donghoon Lee, Wilburt van der Klaauw, and Basit Zafar. "Household Debt and Saving during the 2007 Recession." Working Paper no. 16999, National Bureau of Economic Research Working Paper. Cambridge, MA. 2011. Accessed May 31, 2011. http://www.nber.org/papers/w16999.

Charles, Camille Zubrinsky. "Can We Live Together? Racial Preferences and Neighborhood Choices." In *The Geography of Opportunity*, edited by Xavier De Souza Briggs, 45–80. Washington, DC: Brookings Institution Press, 2005.

Charn, Jeanne, and Richard Zorza. *Civil Legal Assistance for All Americans: The Bellow-Sacks Access to Civil Legal Services Project*. Cambridge, MA: Harvard Law School, 2005.

Cohen-Cole, Ethan, Burcu Duygan-Bump, and Judit Montoriol-Garriga. "Forgive and Forget: Who Gets Credit after Bankruptcy and Why?" Working Paper, 36th European Finance Association Annual Meeting, Bergen, Norway, 2009. http://papers.ssrn.com/sol3/papers.cfm?abstract_id=1341856##.

Cohn, D'Vera. "The Middle Class Blues." Pew Research Center Social and Demographic Trends, May 29, 2008. Accessed February 1, 2011. http://pewsocial-trends.org/pubs/711/middle-class-blues.

College Board. "Education Pays Update: 2005." Accessed August 16, 2010. http://www.collegeboard.com/prod_downloads/press/cost05/education_pays_05.pdf.

————. "Parent-Educator Modules." Accessed January 28, 2011. http://www
.collegeboundfoundation.org/parents/educator/modules/Module%202/
Module%202.pdf.

Coltrane, Scott. "Research on Household Labor: Modeling and Measuring the
Social Embeddedness of Routine Family Work." *Journal of Marriage and the
Family* 62, no. 4 (2000): 1208–33.

Commission on the Bankruptcy Laws of the United States. "Report of the Com-
mission on the Bankruptcy Laws of the United States: H.R. Doc. 137, 93rd
Cong. 1st Sess. 256 (1973)." In *Collier on Bankruptcy*, 15th ed., edited by
Lawrence P. King, Appendix Part 2(c). Albany, NY: Matthew Bender, 1996.

Conference of Chief Justices. *Report of Joint Task Force on Pro Se Litigation of
the Conference of Chief Justices and Conference of State Court Administrators
2002*. Williamsburg, VA: Conference of Chief Justices, 2002. Accessed January 16, 2011. http://ccj.ncsc.dni.us/TaskForceReportJuly2002.pdf.

Congressional Oversight Panel. *Evaluating Progress on TARP Foreclosure Mitigation
Programs*. Washington, DC: Congressional Oversight Panel, 2010. Accessed
January 31, 2011. http://cop.senate.gov/documents/cop-041410-report.pdf.

Conger, Rand D., Glen H. Elder, Jr., Frederick O. Lorenz, Katherine J. Conger,
Ronald L. Simons, Lee B. Whitbeck, Shirley Huck, and Janet N. Melby. "Linking Economic Hardship to Marital Quality and Instability." *Journal of Marriage and Family* 52, no. 3 (1990): 643–56.

Conger, Rand D., Xiao-Jia Ge, and Frederick O. Lorenz. "Economic Stress and
Marital Relations." In *Families in Troubled Times: Adapting to Change in
Rural America*, edited by Rand D. Conger and Glen H. Elder, Jr., 187–203.
Hawthorne, NY: Aldine de Gruyter, 1994.

Conger, Rand D., Martha A. Rueter, and Glen H. Elder, Jr. "Couple Resilience to
Economic Pressure." *Journal of Personality and Social Psychology* 76, no. 1
(1999): 54–71.

Conley, Dalton. *Being Black, Living in the Red: Race, Wealth and Social Policy in
America*. Berkeley: University of California Press, 1999.

————. *Elsewhere, U.S.A.* New York: Pantheon Books, 2008.

Cooper, Michael. "Governments Go to Extremes as the Downturn Wears On." *New
York Times*, August 7, 2010. Accessed August 16, 2010. http://www.nytimes
.com/2010/08/07/us/07cutbacksWEB.html.

Corradin, Stefano, Reint Gropp, Harry Huizinga, and Luc Laeven. "Who Invests in
Home Equity to Exempt Wealth from Bankruptcy?" Discussion Paper no. 2010-
29, European Banking Center, Tilburg University, Tilburg, Netherlands, 2010.
http://arno.uvt.nl/show.cgi?fid=113204.

*Credit Cardholders' Bill of Rights Act of 2008: Hearings on H.R. 5244, before the
U.S. House Subcommittee on Financial Institutions*. 110th Cong. (2008) (statement of John G. Finneran, Jr., general counsel, Capital One Financial Corporation). Accessed August 16, 2010. http://financialservices.house.gov/hearing110/
finneran031308.pdf.

Crissey, Sarah R. *Educational Attainment in the United States: 2007*. Washington, DC: U.S. Census Bureau, 2009. Accessed August 16, 2010. http://www.census .gov/prod/2009pubs/p20-560.pdf.

Cunningham, Alisa F., and Gregory S. Kienzl. *Delinquency: The Untold Story of Student Loan Borrowing*. Washington, DC: Institute for Higher Education Policy, 2011. Accessed May 31, 2011. http://www.ihep.org/assets/files/ publications/a-f/Delinquency-The_Untold_Story_FINAL_March_2011.pdf.

Davis, Carl, Kelly Davis, Matthew Gardner, Robert S. McIntyre, Jeff McLynch, and Alla Sapozhnikova. *Who Pays?: A Distributional Analysis of the Tax Systems in All 50 States*. 3rd ed. Washington, DC: Institute on Taxation and Economic Policy, 2009. Accessed February 1, 2011. http://www.itepnet.org/whopays3.pdf.

Dawsey, Amanda E., and Lawrence M. Ausubel. "Informal Bankruptcy." Working Paper, Department of Economics, University of Maryland, College Park, 2004. http://www.ausubel.com/creditcard-papers/informal-bankruptcy.pdf.

Day, Jennifer Cheeseman, and Eric C. Newburger. *The Big Payoff: Educational Attainment and Synthetic Estimates of Work-Life Earnings*. Current Population Reports P23-210. Washington, DC: U.S. Census Bureau, 2002. Accessed February 1, 2011. http://www.census.gov/prod/2002pubs/p23-210.pdf.

DeNavas-Walt, Carmen, Bernadette D. Proctor, and Jessica C. Smith. *Income, Poverty, and Health Insurance Coverage in the United States: 2007*. Current Population Reports P60-235. Washington, DC: U.S. Census Bureau, 2008. Accessed January 24, 2011. http://www.census.gov/prod/2008pubs/p60-235.pdf.

Dew, Jeffrey. "Two Sides of the Same Coin? The Differing Roles of Assets and Consumer Debt in Marriage." *Journal of Family and Economic Issues* 28, no. 1 (2007): 89–104.

Dickerson, A. Mechele. "Race Matters in Bankruptcy." *Washington and Lee Law Review* 61, no. 4 (2004): 1725–76.

Dodd-Frank Wall Street Reform and Consumer Protection Act. 2010. Pub. L. no. 111-203, § 1001 et seq. (2010).

Drentea, Patricia. "Age, Debt and Anxiety." *Journal of Health and Social Behavior* 41, no. 4 (2000): 437–50.

Duca, John V., and Stuart S. Rosenthal. "Borrowing Constraints, Household Debt, and Racial Discrimination in Loan Markets." *Journal of Financial Intermediation* 3, no. 1 (1993): 77–103.

Durkin, Thomas A. *The Impact of the Consumer Financial Protection Agency on Small Business*. Washington, DC: Center for Capital Markets Competitiveness, 2009. Accessed February 2, 2011. http://www.uschamber.com/sites/default/ files/reports/090923cfpastudy.pdf.

Dworkin, R. J. "Prestige Ranking of the Housewife Occupation." *Sex Roles* 7, no. 1 (1981): 59–63.

Dynan, Karen, Jonathan Skinner, and Stephen Zeldes. "Do the Rich Save More?" *Journal of Political Economy* 112, no. 2 (2004): 397–444.

Economic Policy Institute. *The State of Working America*. "Can't Depend on a Solid Pension." Accessed February 2, 2011. http://www.stateofworkingamerica.org/ charts/view/191.

———.*The State of Working America.* "Retirement Security Eroding." Accessed January 30, 2011. http://www.stateofworkingamerica.org/charts/view/202.

The Effects of Recent Market Turmoil in Financial Markets on Retirement Security: Hearing, before the U.S. House Committee on Education and Labor. 110th Cong. (2008) (statement of Peter R. Orszag, director, Congressional Budget Office). Accessed January 30, 2011. http://www.cbo.gov/ftpdocs/98xx/doc9864/10-07-RetirementSecurity_Testimony.1.1.shtml.

Eggum, John, Katherine Porter, and Tara Twomey. "Saving Homes in Bankruptcy: Housing Affordability and Loan Modification." *Utah Law Review* 2008, no. 3 (2008): 1123–68.

Elmer, Peter J., and Steven A. Seelig. "The Rising Long-Term Trend of Single-Family Mortgage Foreclosure Rates." Working Paper 98-2, Federal Deposit Insurance Corporation, Washington, DC, 1998. http://www.fdic.gov/bank/analytical/working/98-2.pdf.

Estes, Sarah Beth, Mary C. Noonan, and David J. Maume. "Is Work-Family Policy Use Related to the Gendered Division of Housework?" *Journal of Family and Economic Issues* 28, no. 4 (2007): 527–45.

Fairlie, Robert W. "Current Trends in Self-Employed Business Owners by Race." University of California Santa Cruz, 2004. Accessed February 1, 2011. http://people.ucsc.edu/rfairlie/serates.

———. "Self-employment, Entrepreneurship, and the NLSY79." *Monthly Labor Review* 128, no. 5 (2005): 40–47.

Fairlie, Robert W., and Alicia M. Robb. *Race and Entrepreneurial Success: Black-, Asian-, and White-Owned Businesses in the United States.* Cambridge, MA: MIT Press, 2008.

Fannie Mae. *Manufactured Housing: Standard and MH Select.* Washington, DC: Fannie Mae, 2009. Accessed May 20, 2010. https://www.efanniemae.com/sf/guides/ssg/relatedsellinginfo/manufachousing/pdf/mhmhselectfacts.pdf.

———. *A Statistical Summary of Housing and Mortgage Financing Activities.* Washington, DC: Fannie Mae, 2006. Accessed February 4, 2011. http://web.archive.org/web/20061031005433/http://www.fanniemae.com/ir/pdf/resources/housingmortgage.pdf.

Farley, Reynolds. "Racial Differences in the Search for Housing: Do Whites and Blacks Use the Same Techniques to Find Housing?" *Housing Policy Debate* 7, no. 2 (1996): 367–85.

Farrell-Willoughby, Kathleen, and Laura Brundage. "Pro Bono Representation Helps Meet Needs of Pro Se Filers." *American Bankruptcy Institute Journal* 25, no. 7 (2006): 44–45.

Fay, Scott, Eric Hurst, and Michelle J. White. "The Household Bankruptcy Decision." *American Economic Review* 92, no. 3 (2002): 706–18.

Featherman, David L., and Robert M. Hauser. *Opportunity and Change.* New York: Academic Press, 1978.

Federal Reserve Bank of New York. *Quarterly Report on Household Debt and Credit.* New York: Federal Reserve Bank, 2010. Accessed January 2, 2011.

http://www.newyorkfed.org/research/national_economy/householdcredit/Dis-trictReport_Q22010.pdf.

———. "U.S. Credit Conditions: Foreclosures, Bankruptcies, and Collections." Accessed August 16, 2010. http://www.newyorkfed.org/creditconditions/.

Federal Trade Commission. *Federal Trade Commission Annual Report 2010: Fair Debt Collection Practices Act*. Washington, DC: Federal Trade Commission, 2010. Accessed January 2, 2011. http://www.ftc.gov/os/2010/04/P104802fd cpa2010annrpt.pdf.

Ferber, Marianne A., and Jane Waldfogel. "The Long-Term Consequence of Non-traditional Employment." *Monthly Labor Review* 121, no. 5 (1998): 3–12.

Fernandez, Luisa, Fadhel Kaboub, and Zdravka Todorova. "On Democratizing Financial Turmoil: A Minskian Analysis of the Subprime Crisis." Working Paper no. 548, Levy Economics Institute, Bard College, Annandale-on-Hudson, NY, 2008. http://www.levyinstitute.org/pubs/wp_548.pdf.

Fisher, Jonathan D., and Angela C. Lyons. "Till Debt Do Us Part: A Model of Divorce and Personal Bankruptcy." *Review of Economics of the Household* 4, no. 1 (2006): 35–52.

"The Forbes 400: America's Richest People." *Forbes*, October 11, 1999. Accessed February 4, 2011. http://www.forbes.com/lists/home.jhtml?passListId=54&pass Year=1999&passListType=Person.

Friedman, Milton. *A Theory of the Consumption Function*. Princeton, NJ: Princeton University Press, 1957.

Fuller, Andrea. "U.S. Effort Aids Only 9% of Eligible Homeowners." *New York Times*, August 4, 2009. Accessed February 4, 2011. http://www.nytimes.com/2009/08/05/business/05treasury.html.

Galbraith, James K. *Created Unequal: The Crisis in American Pay*. New York: Free Press, 1998.

———. *The Predator State: How Conservatives Abandoned the Free Market and Why Liberals Should Too*. New York: Free Press, 2008.

Gerson, Emily Starbuck. "Severe Debt Can Cause Depression and Even Suicide." CreditCards.com, September 8, 2008. Accessed January 24, 2011. http://www.creditcards.com/credit-card-news/debt-depression-and-suicide-1264.php.

Gilbert, Dennis. *The American Class Structure: In an Age of Growing Inequality*. 6th ed. Belmont, CA: Wadsworth, 2003.

Gittleson, John. "Mortgage Modifications in U.S. Decline as Fewer People Qualify for Program." *Bloomberg*, December 29, 2010. Accessed February 1, 2011. http://www.bloomberg.com/news/print/2010-12-29/mortgage-modifications-in-u-s-decline-as-fewer-people-qualify-for-program.html.

Gladieux, Lawrence, and Laura Perna. *Borrowers Who Drop Out: A Neglected Aspect of the College Student Loan Trend*. National Center Report no. 05-2. San Jose, CA: National Center for Public Policy and Higher Education, 2005. Accessed February 1, 2011. http://www.highereducation.org/reports/borrowing/borrowers.pdf.

Glick, Reuven, and Kevin J. Lansing. "U.S. Household Deleveraging and Future Consumption Growth." *FRBSF Economic Letter* (San Francisco), May 15,

2009. Accessed February 1, 2011. http://www.frbsf.org/publications/economics/letter/2009/el2009-16.pdf.

Goldschmidt, Jona, Barry Mahoney, Harvey Solomon, and Joan Green. *Meeting the Challenge of Pro Se Litigation: A Report and Guidebook for Judges and Court Managers*. Chicago: American Judicature Society, 1998.

Goldthorpe, John H., and Keith Hope. "Occupational Grading and Occupational Prestige." In *The Analysis of Social Mobility: Methods and Approaches*, edited by Keith Hope, 19–79. Gloucestershire, UK: Clarendon Press, 1972.

Golmant, John, and Tom Ulrich. "Bankruptcy Repeat Filings." *American Bankruptcy Institute Law Review* 14, no. 1 (2006): 169–99.

Gordon, David M. *Fat and Mean: The Corporate Squeeze of Working Americans and the Myth of Managerial Downsizing*. New York: Martin Kessler Books, 1996.

Greene, Laura L. "An Economic Analysis of Student Loan Default." *Educational Evaluation and Policy Analysis* 11, no. 1 (1989): 61–68.

Greenspan, Alan, and James Kennedy. "Estimates of Home Mortgage Originations, Repayments, and Debt on One-to-Four-Family Residences." Working Paper 2005-41, Finance and Economics Discussion Series, Divisions of Research and Statistics and Monetary Affairs, Federal Reserve Board, Washington, DC, 2005. http://www.federalreserve.gov/pubs/feds/2005/200541/200541pap.pdf.

Greiner, Keith. "How Much Student Loan Debt Is Too Much?" *Journal of Student Financial Aid* 26, no. 1 (1996): 7–16.

Gropp, Reint, John Karl Scholz, and Michelle J. White. "Personal Bankruptcy and Credit Supply and Demand." *Quarterly Journal of Economics* 112, no. 1 (1997): 217–51.

Gudmunson, Clinton G., Ivan F. Beutler, Craig L. Israelsen, J. Kelly McCoy, and E. Jeffrey Hill. "Linking Financial Strain to Marital Instability: Examining the Roles of Emotional Distress and Marital Interaction." *Journal of Family and Economic Issues* 28, no. 3 (2007): 357–76.

Hacker, Jacob S. "Call It the Family Risk Factor." *New York Times*, January 11, 2004. Accessed February 4, 2011. http://www.nytimes.com/2004/01/11/opinion/call-it -the-family-risk-factor.html?src=pm.

———. *The Divided Welfare State: The Battle over Public and Private Social Benefits in the United States*. New York: Cambridge University Press, 2002.

———. *The Great Risk Shift: The New Economic Insecurity and the Decline of the American Dream*. Rev. and exp. ed. New York: Oxford University Press, 2008.

Hacker, Jacob S., Gregory Huber, Philipp Rehm, Mark Schlesinger, and Rob Valletta. *Economic Security at Risk: Findings from the Economic Security Index*. New Haven, CT: Economic Security Index and the Rockefeller Foundation, 2010. Accessed January 30, 2011. http://economicsecurityindex.org/assets/Economic%20Security%20Index%20Full%20Report.pdf.

Hacker, Jacob S., and Elisabeth Jacobs. *The Rising Instability of American Family Incomes, 1969–2004: Evidence from the Panel Study of Income Dynamics*. EPI Briefing Paper no. 213. Washington, DC: Economic Policy Institute, 2008.

Accessed January 30, 2011. http://epi.3cdn.net/2a30240ab82efa693b_8tm6i2 z3t.pdf.

Hacker, Jacob S., Philipp Rehm, and Mark Schlesinger. *Standing on Shaky Ground: Americans' Experiences with Economic Insecurity.* New Haven, CT: Economic Security Index and the Rockefeller Foundation, 2010. Accessed January 30, 2011. http://www.economicsecurityindex.org/upload/media/ESI%20 report%20final_12%2013.pdf.

Halle, Michael, and Meena Seshamani. "Hidden Costs of Healthcare: Why Americans Are Paying More but Getting Less." Healthreform.gov. Accessed February 1, 2011. http://www.healthreform.gov/reports/hiddencosts/hiddencosts.pdf.

Han, Song, and Geng Li. "Household Borrowing after Filing for Personal Bankruptcy." *Journal of Money, Credit and Banking* 43, nos. 2–3 (2011): 491–517.

Hart, John, Michelle Rhodes, and John Morgan. *The Unknown World of the Mobile Home.* Baltimore, MD: John Hopkins University Press, 2002.

Haurin, Donald R., and Stuart S. Rosenthal. *The Sustainability of Homeownership: Factors Affecting the Duration of Homeownership and Rental Spells.* Washington, DC: U.S. Department of Housing and Urban Development, 2004. Accessed February 1, 2011. http://www.huduser.org/Publications/pdf/home ownsustainability.pdf.

Haynes, George W. *Income and Wealth of Veteran Business Owners, 1989–2004.* Washington, DC: Small Business Administration, 2007. Accessed January 20, 2011. http://archive.sba.gov/advo/research/rs310tot.pdf.

Hays, R. Allen. *The Federal Government and Urban Housing.* Albany, NY: SUNY Press, 1993.

Hess, Frederick M., Mark Schneider, Kevin Carey, and Andrew P. Kelly. *Diplomas and Dropouts: Which Colleges Actually Graduate Their Students (and Which Don't).* Washington, DC: American Enterprise Institute, 2009. Accessed February 1, 2011. http://www.aei.org/docLib/Diplomas%20and%20Dropouts%20 final.pdf.

Himmelstein, David, Deborah Thorne, Elizabeth Warren, and Steffie Woolhandler. "Medical Bankruptcy in the United States, 2007: Results of a National Study." *American Journal of Medicine* 122, no. 8 (2009): 741–46.

Home Mortgages: Recent Performance of Nonprime Loans Highlights the Potential for Additional Foreclosures; Testimony, before the Joint Economic Committee of the U.S. Congress. 111th Cong. (2009) (statement of William B. Shear, director, Financial Markets and Community Investment, Government Accountability Office). Accessed February 1, 2011. http://www.gao.gov/new.items/ d09922t.pdf.

Hughes, Jr., Robert, and Maureen Perry-Jenkins. "Social Class Issues in Family Life Education." *Family Relations* 45, no. 2 (1996): 175–82.

Hurd, Michael, and Susan Rohwedder. "Effects of the Financial Crisis and Great Recession on American Households." Working Paper WR-810, RAND Corporation, Santa Monica, CA, 2010. http://www.rand.org/pubs/working_ papers/WR810.html.

Hynes, Richard M. "Bankruptcy and State Collections: The Case of the Missing Garnishments." *Cornell Law Review* 91, no. 3 (2006): 603–52.

———. "Broke but Not Bankrupt: Consumer Debt Collection in State Courts." *Florida Law Review* 60, no. 1 (2008): 1–62.

Institute for America's Future. "Are You Really Covered? Why 4 in 10 Americans Can't Depend on Their Health Insurance." Accessed February 2, 2011. http://institute.ourfuture.org/biblio/2009020923/are-you-really-covered-why-4-10-americans-cant-depend-their-health-insurance.

Jacobs, Jerry A., and Kathleen Gerson. "Overworked Individuals or Overworked Families? Explaining Trends in Work, Leisure, and Family Time." *Work and Occupations* 28, no. 1 (2001): 40–63.

Jacoby, Melissa B. "Home Ownership Risk beyond a Subprime Crisis: The Role of Delinquency Management." *Fordham Law Review* 76, no. 5 (2008): 2261–96.

Jacoby, Melissa B., and Mirya R. Holman. "Managing Medical Bills on the Brink of Bankruptcy." *Yale Journal of Health Policy, Law, and Ethics* 10, no. 2 (2010): 239–98.

Jappelli, Tullio. "Who Is Credit Constrained in the U.S. Economy?" *Quarterly Journal of Economics* 105, no. 1 (1990): 219–34.

Jiménez, Dalie. "The Distribution of Assets in Consumer Chapter 7 Bankruptcy Cases." *American Bankruptcy Law Journal* 83, no. 4 (2009): 795–822.

Johnson, Kathleen W., and Geng Li. "The Debt-Payment-to-Income Ratio as an Indicator of Borrowing Constraints: Evidence from Two Household Surveys." *Journal of Money, Credit and Banking* 42, no. 7 (2010): 1373–90.

Joint Center for Housing Studies. *The State of the Nation's Housing 2009*. Cambridge, MA: Harvard University, 2009. Accessed January 24, 2011. http://www.jchs.harvard.edu/publications/markets/son2009/son2009.pdf.

Joint Economic Committee of the United States Congress. *Vicious Cycle: How Unfair Credit Card Company Practices Are Squeezing Consumers and Undermining the Recovery*. Washington, DC: Joint Economic Committee of the U.S. Congress, 2009. Accessed February 1, 2011. http://jec.senate.gov/public/?a=Files.Serve&File_id=42840b23-fed8-447b-a029-e977c0a25544.

Kahneman, Daniel, and Amos Tversy. "Prospect Theory: An Analysis of Decisions under Risk." *Econometrica* 47, no. 2 (1979): 263–91.

Keister, Lisa A. *Getting Rich: America's Rich and How They Got That Way*. New York: Cambridge University Press, 2005.

———. *Wealth in America: Trends in Wealth Inequality*. New York: Cambridge University Press, 2000.

Kennickell, Arthur B. "Darkness Made Visible: Field Management and Nonresponse in the 2004 SCF." Paper presented at the Annual Joint Statistical Meetings, Minneapolis, MN, August 2005. Accessed February 6, 2011. http://www.federalreserve.gov/pubs/oss/oss2/papers/asa2005.5.pdf.

———. "Imputation of the 1989 Survey of Consumer Finances: Stochastic Relaxation and Multiple Imputation." Paper presented at the Annual Meetings of the American Statistical Association, Atlanta, GA, August 1991. Accessed February 1, 2011. http://www.federalreserve.gov/Pubs/OSS/oss3/ssbf98/imp89.pdf.

———. "List Sample Design for 1998 Survey of Consumer Finances." Working Paper, Survey of Consumer Finances, Federal Reserve Board, Washington, DC, 1998. http://www.federalreserve.gov/pubs/oss/oss2/papers/listsample.pdf.

———. "Modeling Wealth with Multiple Observations of Income: Redesign of the Sample for the 2001 Survey of Consumer Finances." Paper presented at the Joint Statistical Meeting, Atlanta, GA, August 2001. Accessed January 20, 2011. http://www.federalreserve.gov/pubs/oss/oss2/papers/scf2001.list.sample.redesign.9.pdf.

———. *"Multiple Imputation in the Survey of Consumer Finances."* Paper presented at the Joint Statistical Meeting, Atlanta, GA, August 1998. Accessed January 20, 2011. http://www.federalreserve.gov/Pubs/OSS/oss2/papers/impute98.pdf.

———. "Revisions to the Variance Estimation Procedure for the SCF." Working Paper, Survey of Consumer Finances, Federal Reserve Board, Washington, DC, 2000. http://www.federalreserve.gov/pubs/oss/oss2/papers/variance.pdf.

Kennickell, Arthur B., and Annamaria Lusardi. "Disentangling the Importance of the Precautionary Saving Motive." Working Paper, Survey of Consumer Finances, Federal Reserve Board, Washington, DC, 2005. http://www.federal reserve.gov/pubs/oss/oss2/papers/precautionary.nov05.2.pdf.

Keys, Benjamin J. "The Credit Market Consequences of Job Displacement." Working Paper 2010-24, Finance and Economics Discussion Series, Divisions of Research and Statistics and Monetary Affairs, Federal Reserve Board, Washington, DC, 2010. http://www.federalreserve.gov/pubs/feds/2010/201024/201024pap.pdf.

Kharas, Homi. "The Emerging Middle Class in Developing Countries." Working Paper no. 285, Organisation for Economic Co-operation and Development Centre, Washington, DC, 2010. http://www.oecd.org/dataoecd/12/52/44457738.pdf.

Kharif, Olga. "Google's Larry Page: Good Ideas Still Get Funded." *Business Week*, March 13, 2001. Accessed February 4, 2011. http://www.businessweek.com/bwdaily/dnflash/mar2001/nf20010313_831.htm.

Kim, Susanna G. "An Up and Down Week Ends on a Positive Note." *New York Times*, June 11, 2010. Accessed February 4, 2011. http://www.nytimes.com/2010/06/11/business/11markets.html?_r=1&scp=1&sq=susanna%20g.%20kim&st=cse.

Klein, Alec, and Zachary Goldfarb. "The Bubble: How Homeowners, Speculators and Wall Street Dealmakers Rode a Wave of Easy Money with Crippling Consequences." *Washington Post*, June 15, 2008. Accessed February 4, 2011. http://www.washingtonpost.com/wp-dyn/content/article/2008/06/14/AR2008061401479.html.

Knapp, Laura G., Janice E. Kelly-Reid, Scott A. Ginder, and Elise S. Miller. *Enrollment in Postsecondary Institutions, Fall 2006; Graduation Rates, 2000 and 2003 Cohorts; and Financial Statistics, Fiscal Year 2006: First Look*. NCES 2008-173. Washington, DC: U.S. Department of Education, 2008. Accessed February 4, 2011. http://nces.ed.gov/pubs2008/2008173.pdf.

Knapp, Laura Greene, and Terry G. Seaks. "An Analysis of the Probability of Default on Federally Guaranteed Student Loans." *Review of Economics and Statistics* 74, no. 3 (1992): 404–11.

Koenker, Roger. *Quantile Regression*. New York: Cambridge University Press, 2005.

Kolko, Gabriel. "Economic Mobility and Social Stratification." *American Journal of Sociology* 63, no. 1 (1957): 30–38.

Komarovsky, Mirra. *Blue-Collar Marriage*. New York: Vintage, 1962.

Komter, Aafke. "Hidden Power in Marriage." *Gender & Society* 3, no. 2 (1989): 187–216.

Kregel, Jan. "Minsky's Cushions of Safety: Systemic Risk and the Crisis in the U.S. Subprime Mortgage Market." Public Policy Brief 93. Annandale-on-Hudson, NY: Levy Economics Institute of Bard College, 2007. Accessed February 1, 2011. http://www.levyinstitute.org/pubs/rpt_18_2.pdf.

Kreider, Rose M., and Diana B. Elliott. *America's Families and Living Arrangements: 2007*. Current Population Reports P20-561. Washington, DC: U.S. Census Bureau, 2009. Accessed January 2, 2011. http://www.census.gov/prod /2009pubs/p20-561.pdf.

Krugman, Paul. *The Great Unraveling: Losing Our Way in the New Century*. New York: W. W. Norton, 2004.

Lawless, Robert. "Guesstimate of 2010 Bankruptcy Filings." Credit Slips: A Discussion on Credit, Finance, and Bankruptcy (blog), December 14, 2009. http:// www.creditslips.org/creditslips/2009/12/guesstimate-of-2010-bankruptcy-filings .html#more.

———. "July Bankruptcy Filings Rise, But Look at the Big Picture." Credit Slips: A Discussion on Credit, Finance, and Bankruptcy (blog), August 3, 2010. http:// www.creditslips.org/creditslips/2010/08/july-bankruptcy-filings-rise-but-look -at-the-big-picture.html#tp.

Lawless, Robert M. "The Paradox of Consumer Credit." *University of Illinois Law Review* 2007, no. 1 (2007): 347–74.

Lawless, Robert M., Angela K. Littwin, Katherine M. Porter, John A. E. Pottow, Deborah K. Thorne, and Elizabeth Warren. "Did Bankruptcy Reform Fail? An Empirical Study of Consumer Debtors." *American Bankruptcy Law Journal* 82, no. 3 (2008): 349–406.

Lawless, Robert M., and Elizabeth Warren. "The Myth of the Disappearing Business Bankruptcy." *California Law Review* 93, no. 3 (2005): 745–95.

Lawson, Sandra, and Amy C. Semaya. *Learn More, Earn More: Getting Ahead in America*. New York: Goldman Sachs, 2009. Accessed February 1, 2011. http://www2.goldmansachs.com/ideas/global-markets-institute/past-research -and-conferences/past-research/more/learn-more-earn-more-doc.pdf.

Leicht, Kevin T., and Mary L. Fennell. *Professional Work: A Sociological Approach*. Hoboken, NJ: Blackwell, 2001.

Leicht, Kevin T., and Scott T. Fitzgerald. *Post-Industrial Peasants: The Illusion of Middle Class Prosperity*. New York: Worth Publishers, 2007.

Li, Wenli, and Michelle White. "Mortgage Default, Foreclosures and Bankruptcy." Working Paper 15472, National Bureau of Economic Research, Cambridge, MA, 2009. http://www.econ.ucsd.edu/miwhite/li-white-nber.pdf.

Littwin, Angela. "The Affordability Paradox: How Consumer Bankruptcy's Great-est Weakness May Account for Its Surprising Success." *William and Mary Law Review* 52, no. 6 (2011): 1933–2023.

LoPucki, Lynn, and Elizabeth Warren. *Secured Credit: A Systems Approach.* 6th ed. New York: Wolters Kluwer, 2009.

Luhby, Tami. "Americans' Wealth Drops $1.3 Trillion." *CNNMoney,* June 11, 2009. Accessed January 1, 2011. http://money.cnn.com/2009/06/11/news/economy/Americans_wealth_drops.

Luo, Michael. "'Doubling Up' in Recession-Strained Quarters." *New York Times,* December 28, 2010. Accessed February 4, 2011. http://www.nytimes.com/2010/12/29/us/29families.html.

Lusardi, Annamaria, Daniel Schneider, and Peter Tufano, "Financially Fragile Households: Evidence and Implications." Netspar Discussion Paper no. 03/2011-013. 2011. http://ssrn.com/abstract=1809708.

Lyons, Angela C. "Credit Practices and Financial Education Needs of Midwest Col-lege Students." Working Paper no. 2007-WP-23, Networks Financial Institute, Indiana State University, Terre Haute, 2007. http://www.networksfinancial institute.org/Lists/Publication%20Library/Attachments/92/2007-WP-23_Lyons.pdf.

Mach, Traci L., and John D. Wolken, "Financial Services Used by Small Businesses: Evidence from the 2003 Survey of Small Business Finances." *Federal Reserve Bulletin* 92 (October 2006): A167–95.

Mandel, Michael. *The High-Risk Society: Peril and Promise in the New Economy.* New York: Times Business, 1996.

Mann, Ronald J. "Bankruptcy Reform and the 'Sweat Box' of Credit Card Debt." *University of Illinois Law Review* 2007, no. 1 (2007): 375–404.

———. *Charging Ahead: The Growth and Regulation of Payment Card Markets.* New York: Cambridge University Press, 2006.

———. "The Role of Secured Credit in Small-Business Lending." *Georgetown Law Journal* 86, no. 1 (1997): 1–44.

Mann, Ronald J., and Katherine Porter. "Saving Up for Bankruptcy." *Georgetown Law Journal* 98, no. 2 (2010): 289–339.

Manning, Robert. *Credit Card Nation: The Consequences of America's Addiction to Credit.* New York: Basic Books, 2000.

Manser, Marilyn E., and Garnett Picot. "The Role of Self-Employment in U.S. and Canadian Job Growth." *Monthly Labor Review* 122, no. 4 (1999): 10–25.

Marger, Martin N. *Social Inequality: Patterns and Processes.* 4th ed. Boston: McGraw-Hill, 2008.

Massey, Douglas S., and Nancy Denton. *American Apartheid: Segregation and the Making of the Underclass.* Cambridge, MA: Harvard University Press, 1993.

McCoy, Peter. "A Growing Tide of Risky Mortgages." *BusinessWeek,* May 18, 2005. Accessed February 4, 2011. http://www.businessweek.com/bwdaily/dnflash/may2005/nf20050518_4924_db016.htm.

Mental Health Counseling Degree. "Masters Mental Health Counseling Salary." Last updated February 19, 2010. http://www.mentalhealthcounselingdegree .com/masters-mental-health-counseling-salary.html.

Merlis, Mark, Douglas Gould, and Bisundev Mahato. *Rising Out-of-Pocket Spending for Medical Care: A Growing Strain on Family Budgets*. New York: The Commonwealth Fund, 2006. Accessed February 1, 2011. http://www.common wealthfund.org/usr_doc/Merlis_risingoopspending_887.pdf.

Mian, Atif R., and Amir Sufi. "Household Leverage and the Recession of 2007 to 2009." Working Paper 15896, National Bureau of Economic Research, Cambridge, MA, 2010. http://www.nber.org/papers/w15896.

Modigliani, Franco. "Utility Analysis and the Consumption Function: An Interpretation of Cross-Section Data." In *Post-Keynesian Economics*, edited by Kenneth K. Kurihara, 388–436. Rutgers, NJ: Rutgers University Press, 1954.

Montalto, Catherine Phillips, and Jaimie Sung. "Multiple Imputation in the 1992 Survey of Consumer Finances." *Financial Counseling and Planning* 7 (1996): 133–46.

Morris, Lydia D. "Redundancy and Patterns of Household Finance." *Sociological Review* 32, no. 3 (1984): 492–523.

Moss, David. *When All Else Fails: Government as the Ultimate Risk Manager*. Cambridge, MA: Harvard University Press, 2002.

Munnell, Alicia H., and Annika Sundén. *401(k) Plans Are Still Coming Up Short*. Center for Retirement Research at Boston College Issue Brief 43b. Chestnut Hill, MA: Center for Retirement Research, 2006. Accessed January 30, 2011. http://crr.bc.edu/images/stories/Briefs/ib_43.pdf.

Munnell, Alicia H., Anthony Webb, and Francesca Golub-Sass. *The National Retirement Risk Index: After the Crash*. Center for Retirement Research at Boston College Issue Brief 9-22. Chestnut Hill, MA: Center for Retirement Research, 2009. Accessed January 30, 2011. http://crr.bc.edu/images/stories/Briefs/ IB_9-22.pdf.

Murray, Sara. "Community College Pays Off for Job Seekers." Real Time Economics (blog), *Wall Street Journal*, May 5, 2009. http://blogs.wsj.com/economics /2009/05/05/community-college-pays-off-for-job-seekers/.

National Federation of Independent Business. *Access to Credit. National Small Business Poll*, Volume 8, Issue 7. Nashville, TN: National Federation of Independent Business, 2008. Accessed February 1, 2011. http://www.411sbfacts.com/ files/Access%20to%20Credit.pdf.

National Opinion Research Center. *General Social Surveys, 1972–2006: Occupational Prestige*. Chicago: University of Chicago, 2007. Accessed January 24, 2011. http://www.norc.org/GSS+Website/Data+Analysis/.

National Sleep Foundation. "2009 Sleep in America Poll: Highlights & Key Findings." Press Release, March 2, 2009. http://www.sleepfoundation.org/sites/ default/files/2009%20POLL%20HIGHLIGHTS.pdf.

Neustadter, Gary. "When Lawyer and Client Meet: Observations of Interviewing and Counseling Behavior in the Consumer Bankruptcy Law Office." *Buffalo Law Review* 35, no. 1 (1986): 177–284.

Newman, Katherine. *Falling from Grace*. New York: Free Press, 1988.

Newport, Frank. "Just Why Do Americans Attend Church?" *Gallup*, April 6, 2007. Accessed January 24, 2011. http://www.gallup.com/poll/27124/Just-Why-Amer icans-Attend-Church.aspx.

New York Times. *Class Matters*. New York: Times Books, 2005.

———. *The Downsizing of America*. New York: Times Books, 1996.

Nguyen, Eric S. "Parents in Financial Crisis: Fighting to Keep the Family Home." *American Bankruptcy Law Journal* 82, no. 2 (2008): 229–51.

Noonan, Mary C. "The Impact of Domestic Work on Men and Women's Wages." *Journal of Marriage and Family* 63, no. 4 (2001): 1134–45.

Norberg, Scott F., and Andrew J. Velkey. "Debtor Discharge and Creditor Repayment in Chapter 13." *Creighton Law Review* 39, no. 3 (2006): 473–557.

O'Hare, William, and Barbara Clark O'Hare. "Upward Mobility." *American Demographics* 15, no. 1 (1993): 26–32.

Oliver, Melvin L., and Thomas M. Shapiro. *Black Wealth/White Wealth: A New Perspective on Racial Inequality*. New York: Routledge, 1995.

Pahl, Jan. "Household Spending, Personal Spending and the Control of Money in Marriage." *Sociology* 24, no. 1 (1990): 119–38.

Pardo, Rafael I., and Michelle R. Lacey. "Undue Hardship in the Bankruptcy Courts: An Empirical Assessment of the Discharge of Educational Debt." *University of Cincinnati Law Review* 74, no. 2 (2005): 405–530.

PayScale. "Salary Survey for Employer: United Parcel Service (UPS), Inc." Accessed February 1, 2010. http://www.payscale.com/research/US/Employer=United _Parcel_Service_%28UPS%29,_Inc./Salary.

PBS. "Changing Face of Unemployment." Accessed January 20, 2011. http://www .pbs.org/now/politics/unemployment.html.

Peirce, Robert S., Michael R. Frone, Marcia Russell, and M. Lynne Cooper. "Financial Stress, Social Support, and Alcohol Involvement: A Longitudinal Test of the Buffering Hypothesis in a General Population Survey." *Health Psychology* 15, no. 1 (1996): 38–47.

Pew Social Trends Staff. *Inside the Middle Class: Bad Times Hit the Good Life*. Washington, DC: Pew Research Center, 2008. Accessed January 2, 2011. http://pewsocialtrends.org/pubs/706/middle-class-poll.

Porter, Katherine. "Bankrupt Profits: The Credit Industry's Business Model for Postbankruptcy Lending." *Iowa Law Review* 93, no. 4 (2008): 1369–1421.

———. "Life after Debt: Understanding the Credit Restraint of Bankruptcy Debtors." *American Bankruptcy Institute Law Review* 18, no. 1 (2010): 1–42.

———. "Today's Consumers Prefer Chapter 7 Bankruptcy 3 to 1." Credit Slips: A Discussion on Credit, Finance, and Bankruptcy (blog), March 22, 2010. http:// www.creditslips.org/creditslips/2010/03/todays-consumers-prefer-chapter-7 -bankruptcy-3-to-1.html#tp.

Porter, Katherine, and Deborah K. Thorne. "The Failure of Bankruptcy's Fresh Start." *Cornell Law Review* 92, no. 1 (2006): 67–128.

Pottow, John A. E. "The Nondischargeability of Student Loans in Personal Bankruptcy Proceedings: The Search for a Theory." *Canadian Business Law Journal* 44, no. 2 (2006): 245–78.

Prater, Connie. "Poll: Credit Card Debt the New Taboo Topic." CreditCards.com, July 8, 2008. Accessed January 21, 2011. http://www.creditcards.com/credit-card-news/talk-about-credit-cards-the-new-taboo-1276.php.

Pribesh, Shana, and Douglas B. Downey. "Why Are Residential and School Moves Associated with Poor School Performance?" *Demography* 36, no. 4 (1999): 521–34.

Project on Student Debt. *White Paper: Addressing Student Loan Repayment Burdens; Strengths and Weaknesses of Current System.* Oakland, CA: Institute for College Access and Success, 2006. Accessed February 1, 2011. http://projectonstudentdebt.org/files/pub/WHITE_PAPER_FINAL_PDF.pdf.

Ramsay, Ian, and Cameron Sim. "Personal Insolvency in Australia: An Increasingly Middle Class Phenomenon." *Federal Law Review* 38, no. 2 (2010): 283–310.

RealtyTrac. "More than 430,000 Foreclosure Filings Reported in Q1." Press Release, April 25, 2007. http://www.realtytrac.com/content/press-releases/more-than-430000-foreclosure-filings-reported-in-q1-2007-2551.

———. "Record 2.9 Million U.S. Properties Receive Foreclosure Filings in 2010 Despite 30-Month Low in December." Press Release, January 12, 2011. http://www.realtytrac.com/content/press-releases/record-29-million-us-properties-receive-foreclosure-filings-in-2010-despite-30-month-low-in-december-6309.

Reinberg, Steven. "With the Economy Down, Sleeplessness Is Up." *HealthDay*, March 2, 2009. Accessed September 12, 2009. http://news.health.com/2009/03/02/with-economy-down-sleeplessness-is-up.

Renaud, Bertrand, and Kyung-Hwan Kim. "The Global Housing Price Boom and Its Unwinding." *Housing Finance International* 22 (December 2007): 3–15.

Rochelle, Bill. "Business Bankruptcies Rise More Than Individuals'." *Bloomberg*, January 6, 2010. Accessed January 6, 2011. http://www.bloomberg.com/apps/news?pid=20601110&sid=aBUz3iZl11wA.

Rockefeller Foundation. *American Worker Survey: Complete Results.* New York: Rockefeller Foundation, 2007. Accessed January 24, 2011. http://www.rockefellerfoundation.org/uploads/files/1f190413-0800-4046-9200-084d05d5ea71-american.pdf.

Rosenbaum, James E. *Beyond College for All: Career Paths for the Forgotten Half.* New York: Russell Sage Foundation, 2001.

Ross, Stephen L., and John Yinger. *The Color of Credit: Mortgage Discrimination, Research Methodology, and Fair-Lending Enforcement.* Cambridge, MA: MIT Press, 2002.

Rubin, Lillian B. *Worlds of Pain: Life in the Working-Class Family.* New York: BasicBooks, 1976.

Scherer, Ron. "Number of Long-Term Unemployed Hits Highest Rate Since 1948." *Christian Science Monitor*, January 8, 2010. Accessed January 6, 2011. http://www.csmonitor.com/USA/2010/0108/Number-of-long-term-unemployed-hits-highest-rate-since-1948.

Schoen, Robert, and Vladimir Canudas-Romo. "Timing Effects on Divorce: 20th Century Experience in the United States." *Journal of Marriage and Family* 68, no. 3 (2006): 749–58.

Schoen, Robert, and Nicola Standish. "The Retrenchment of Marriage: Results from Marital Status Life Tables for the United States, 1995." *Population and Development Review* 27, no. 3 (2001): 553–63.

Schor, Juliet B. *The Overspent American: Why We Want What We Don't Need.* New York: Basic Books, 1998.

Schwager, Jack. *Stock Market Wizards: Interviews with America's Top Stock Traders.* New York: HarperBusiness, 2002.

Schwartz, Nelson D. "Jobless and Staying That Way." *New York Times*, August 8, 2010. Accessed February 4, 2011. http://www.nytimes.com/2010/08/08/week inreview/08schwartz.html.

Scott III, Robert H. *The Use of Credit Card Debt by New Firms.* Kansas City, MO: Kauffman Foundation, 2009. Accessed February 2, 2011. http://www.kauffman .org/uploadedFiles/kfs_credit_card_debt_report.pdf.

Shane, Scott A. *The Illusions of Entrepreneurship: The Costly Myths That Entrepreneurs, Investors, and Policy Makers Live By.* New Haven, CT: Yale University Press, 2008.

Shapiro, Thomas M. *The Hidden Cost of Being African American: How Wealth Perpetuates Inequality.* New York: Oxford University Press, 2004.

Shellenbarger, Sue. "Break It to 'em Gently: Telling Kids about Financial Woes." *Wall Street Journal*, March 24, 2009. Accessed January 20, 2011. http://on line.wsj.com/article/SB123794190752432769.html.

———. "When Tough Times Weigh on the Kids." *Wall Street Journal*, September 24, 2008. Accessed January 20, 2011. http://online.wsj.com/article/SB 122220949327768879.html.

Shenn, Jody. "Housing Crash to Resume on 7 Million Foreclosures, Amherst Says." *Bloomberg*, September 25, 2009. Accessed January 20, 2011. http:// www.bloomberg.com/apps/news?pid=20670001&sid=aw6_gqc0EKKg.

Simon, Ruth. "Grave Errors as Undead Rework Loans." *Wall Street Journal*, July 23, 2010. Accessed January 1, 2011. http://online.wsj.com/article/SB1000142 405274870442130457538354001791920202.html.

Simon, Ruth, and James R. Hagerty, "House-Price Drops Leave More Underwater." *Wall Street Journal*, May 6, 2009. Accessed February 4, 2011. http:// online.wsj.com/article/SB124156804522089735.html.

———. "One in Four Borrowers Is Underwater." *Wall Street Journal*, November 24, 2009. Accessed February 4, 2011. http://online.wsj.com/article/SB 125903489722661849.html.

Slaughter, Mai Lang. "Foreclosures Hit Record 2.8 Homes in 2009." MSN Real Estate (blog), January 14, 2010. http://realestate.msn.com/blogs/listedblog post.aspx?post=1551458.

Stanley, David, and Marjorie Girth. *Bankruptcy: Problem, Process, and Reform.* Washington, DC: Brookings Institution Press, 1971.

Stettner, Andrew, and Sylvia A. Allegretto. *The Rising Stakes of Job Loss: Stubborn Long-Term Joblessness Amid Falling Unemployment Rates.* Washington, DC: Economic Policy Institute and National Employment Law Project, 2005. Accessed January 24, 2011. http://www.policyarchive.org/handle/10207/bit streams/8088.pdf.

Stiglitz, Joseph E. *The Roaring Nineties.* New York: W. W. Norton, 2003.

Stolberg, Sheryl Gay, and Peter Baker. "Obama's Measures for Middle Class." *New York Times*, January 25, 2010. Accessed January 1, 2011. http://www .nytimes.com/2010/01/26/us/politics/26obama.html.

Stone, Michael. *Shelter Poverty.* Philadelphia: Temple University Press, 1993.

Story, Louise. "Home Equity Frenzy Was a Bank Ad Come True." *New York Times*, August 15, 2008. Accessed February 4, 2011. http://www.nytimes.com /2008/08/15/business/15sell.html#.

Stouder, Michael, and Bruce Kirchoff. "Funding the First Year of Business." In *Handbook of Entrepreneurial Dynamics*, edited by William B. Gartner, Kelly G. Shaver, Nancy M. Carter, and Paul D. Reynolds, 352–71. Thousand Oaks, CA: Sage, 2004.

Sullivan, Teresa A. "Debt and the Simulation of Social Class." Paper presented at A Debtor World: Interdisciplinary Academic Symposium on Debt, Champaign, IL, May 2008.

Sullivan, Teresa A., Elizabeth Warren, and Jay Lawrence Westbrook. *As We Forgive Our Debtors: Bankruptcy and Consumer Credit in America.* New York: Oxford University Press, 1989.

———. "Bankruptcy and the Family." *Marriage & Family Review* 21, nos. 3 and 4 (1995): 193–215.

———. *The Fragile Middle Class: Americans in Debt.* New Haven, CT: Yale University Press, 2000.

———. "Less Stigma or More Financial Distress: An Empirical Analysis of the Extraordinary Increase in the Bankruptcy Filings." *Stanford Law Review* 29, no. 2 (2006): 213–56.

———. "The Persistence of Local Legal Culture: Twenty Years of Evidence from the Federal Bankruptcy Courts." *Harvard Journal of Law & Public Policy* 17, no. 3 (1994): 801–65.

Surowiecki, James. "Home Economics." *New Yorker*, March 10, 2008. Accessed February 4, 2011. http://www.newyorker.com/talk/financial/2008/03/10 /080310ta_talk_surowiecki.

The Tarrance Group and Lake Snell Perry Mermin and Associates. *Battleground XXVII.* Washington, DC: George Washington University, 2006. http://www .lakeresearch.com/polls/pdf/bg305/charts.pdf.

Taylor, Mark P., David J. Pevalin, and Jennifer Todd. "The Psychological Costs of Unsustainable Housing Commitments." *Psychological Medicine* 37, no. 7 (2007): 1027–36.

Tedesco, Phillip. "In Forma Pauperis in Bankruptcy." *American Bankruptcy Law Journal* 84, no. 1 (2010): 79–102.

Tejada-Vera, Betzaida, and Paul D. Sutton. "Births, Marriages, Divorces, and Deaths: Provisional Data for March 2008." *National Vital Statistics Reports* 57, no. 6. Hyattsville, MD: National Center for Health Statistics, 2008. Accessed January 1, 2011. http://www.cdc.gov/nchs/data/nvsr/nvsr57/nvsr57_06 .pdf.

Tennessee Student Assistance Corporation. "College Pays." Accessed January 1, 2011. http://www.tn.gov/CollegePays/.

Theil, Stefan. "The Urge to Splurge." *Newsweek*, December 6, 2010. Accessed February 4, 2011. http://www.newsweek.com/2010/11/29/the-urge-to-splurg e-is-creeping-back.html.

Testerman, Mary M. "Paralegal Regulation and the Bankruptcy Reform Act of 1994: Legitimate Legal Assistance Options for the Pro Se Bankruptcy Debtor." *California Bankruptcy Journal* 23, no. 1 (1996): 37–48.

"Text: President Bush's Acceptance Speech to the Republican National Convention." *Washington Post*, September 2, 2004. Accessed January 24, 2011. http://www.washingtonpost.com/wp-dyn/articles/A57466-2004Sep2.html.

Thorne, Deborah. "Extreme Financial Strain: Emergent Chores, Gender Inequality and Emotional Distress." *Journal of Family and Economic Issues* 31, no. 2 (2010): 185–97.

———. "Personal Bankruptcy and the Credit Report: Conflicting Mechanisms of Social Mobility." *Journal of Poverty* 11, no. 4 (2007): 23–43.

Thorne, Deborah, and Leon Anderson. "Managing the Stigma of Personal Bankruptcy." *Sociological Focus* 39, no. 2 (2006): 77–97.

Treiman, Donald J. "A Standard Occupational Prestige Scale for Use with Historical Data." *Journal of Interdisciplinary History* 7, no. 2 (1976): 283–304.

Turner, Margery Austin, and Stephen Ross. "How Racial Discrimination Affects the Search for Housing." In *The Geography of Opportunity*, edited by Xavier De Souza Briggs, 81–100. Washington DC: Brookings Institution Press, 2005.

Twiggs, Joan E., Julia McQuillan, and Myra M. Ferree. "Meaning and Measurement: Reconceptualizing Measures of the Division of Household Labor." *Journal of Marriage and Family* 61, no. 3 (1999): 712–24.

Uchitelle, Louis. *The Disposable American: Layoffs and Their Consequences*. New York: Knopf, 2006.

U.S. Census Bureau. "America's Families and Living Arrangements: 2007." Accessed January 2, 2011. http://www.census.gov/population/www/socdemo/hh -fam/cps2007.html.

———. *Current Population Survey: 2007 Annual Social and Economic (ASEC) Supplement*. Washington, DC: U.S. Census Bureau, 2007. Accessed February 3, 2011. http://www.census.gov/apsd/techdoc/cps/cpsmar07.pdf.

———. "Homeownership Rates by Race and Ethnicity of Householder." Accessed May 21, 2010. http://www.census.gov/hhes/www/housing/hvs/annual09/ ann09t22.xls.

———. "Housing Vacancies and Homeownership (CPS/HVS) Annual Statistics: 2007." Last revised February 20, 2008. http://www.census.gov/hhes/www/ housing/hvs/annual07/ann07t12.html.

———. "Median and Average Sale Prices of Homes Sold in the United States." Accessed January 30, 2011. http://www.census.gov/const/uspriceann.pdf.

———. *Statistical Abstract of the United States 1993*. 113th ed. Washington, DC: Government Printing Office, 1993.

———. *Statistical Abstract of the United States: 2009*. 128th ed. Washington, DC: Government Printing Office, 2009. Accessed May 25, 2009. http://www.census.gov/compendia/statab/2009/tables/09s0224.pdf.

———. *Statistical Abstract of the United States: 2010*. 129th ed. Washington, DC: Government Printing Office, 2010. Accessed July 22, 2010. http://www.census.gov/compendia/statab/2010/2010edition.html.

———. "U.S. Census Bureau Reports on Residential Vacancies and Homeownership." Press Release, February 2, 2010. http://www.census.gov/hhes/www/housing/hvs/qtr409/files/q409press.pdf.

U.S. Courts. "Bankruptcy Forms." Accessed January 1, 2011. http://www.uscourts.gov/FormsAndFees/Forms/BankruptcyForms.aspx.

———. "Bankruptcy Statistics: Filings." Accessed March 1, 2010. http://www.uscourts.gov/Statistics/BankruptcyStatistics.aspx.

———. "Business and Nonbusiness Bankruptcy Cases Commenced, by Chapter of the Bankruptcy Code, during the Twelve Month Period Ended Dec. 31, 2007." Accessed March 1, 2010. http://www.uscourts.gov/uscourts/Statistics/BankruptcyStatistics/BankruptcyFilings/2007/1207_f2.pdf.

U.S. Department of Education, National Center for Education Statistics. *Students Entering and Leaving Postsecondary Occupational Education: 1995–2001*. Washington, DC: U.S. Department of Education, 2007. Accessed February 3, 2011. http://nces.ed.gov/pubs2007/2007041.pdf.

U.S. Department of Health and Human Services. "The 2007 HHS Poverty Guidelines." Accessed January 25, 2011. http://aspe.hhs.gov/POVERTY/07poverty.shtml.

U.S. Department of Housing and Urban Development and United States Department of Commerce. *American Housing Survey for the United States: 1999*. Current Housing Reports H150/99. Washington, DC: U.S. Government Printing Office, 2000. http://www.census.gov/hhes/www/housing/ahs/ahs99/tablecc.htm.

Vigeland, Tess. "What Is the Middle Class?" *Marketplace*, January 11, 2008. Accessed January 24, 2011. http://marketplace.publicradio.org/display/web/2008/01/11/what_is_the_middle_class.

Vise, David A., and Mark Malseed. *The Google Story*. New York: Random House, 2005.

Vogler, Carolyn. "Money in the Household: Some Underlying Issues of Power." *Sociological Review* 46, no. 4 (1998): 687–713.

Vogler, Carolyn, and Jan Pahl. "Money, Power and Inequality within Marriage." *Sociological Review* 42, no. 2 (1994): 263–88.

Warren, Elizabeth. "Financial Collapse and Class Status: Who Goes Bankrupt?" *Osgoode Hall Law Journal* 41, no. 1 (2003): 115–47.

———. "What Is a Women's Issue? Bankruptcy, Commercial Law, and Other Gen-der-Neutral Topics." *Harvard Women's Law Journal* 25 (2002): 19–56.

Warren, Elizabeth, and Amelia Warren Tyagi. *The Two-Income Trap: Why Middle-Class Mothers and Fathers Are Going Broke.* New York: Basic Books, 2003.

Wedoff, Eugene R. *Report of the Advisory Committee on Bankruptcy Rules.* Washington, DC: Committee on Rules and Practice of Procedure of the Judi-cial Conference of the United States, 2010. Accessed February 4, 2011. http://www.uscourts.gov/uscourts/RulesAndPolicies/rules/Reports/BK12-2010.pdf.

Weller, Christian E., and Jessica Lynch. *Household Wealth in Freefall: Americans' Private Safety Net in Tatters.* Washington, DC: Center for American Progress, 2009. Accessed February 3, 2011. http://www.americanprogress.org/issues/2009/04/pdf/wealth_declines.pdf.

Wheary, Jennifer, and Viany Orozco. *Graduated Success: Sustainable Economic Opportunity through One- and Two-Year Credentials.* New York: Demos, 2010. Accessed February 3, 2011. http://www.demos.org/pubs/graduated_success_Final.pdf.

Wheary, Jennifer, Thomas A. Shapiro, and Tamara Draut. *By a Thread: The New Experience of America's Middle Class.* Waltham, MA: Demos and the Institute on Assets and Social Policy at Brandeis University, 2007. Accessed January 24, 2011. http://archive.demos.org/pubs/BaT112807.pdf.

White House. "Remarks by the President and Vice President at Middle Class Task Force Meeting." Press Release, January 25, 2010. http://www.whitehouse.gov/the-press-office/remarks-president-and- vice-president-middle-class-task-force-meeting.

———. "White House Announces Middle Class Task Force." Press Release, Janu-ary 30, 2009. http://www.whitehouse.gov/the-press-office/obama-announces-middle-class-task-force.

White, Michelle J. "Abuse or Protection? Consumer Bankruptcy Reform under 'BAPCPA.'" *University of Illinois Law Review* 2007, no. 1 (2007): 275–304.

———. "Bankruptcy and Consumer Behavior: Theory and Evidence from the U.S." In *The Economics of Consumer Credit*, edited by Giuseppe Bertola, Richard Disney, and Charles Grant, 239–74. Cambridge, MA: MIT Press, 2006.

———. "Why It Pays to File for Bankruptcy: A Critical Look at the Incentives un-der U.S. Personal Bankruptcy Law and a Proposal for Change." *University of Chicago Law Review* 65, no. 3 (1998): 685–732.

Whitford, William C. "The Ideal of Individualized Justice: Consumer Bankruptcy as Consumer Protection and Consumer Protection in Consumer Bankruptcy." *American Bankruptcy Law Journal* 68, no. 4 (1994): 397–417.

Williams, Brian K., Stacey C. Sawyer, and Carl M. Wahlstrom. *Marriages, Families and Intimate Relationships: A Practical Introduction.* 2nd ed. Boston: Allyn and Bacon, 2008.

Williams, Richard, Reynold Nesiba, and Eileen Diaz McConnell. "The Changing Face of Inequality in Home Mortgage Lending." *Social Problems* 52, no. 2 (2005): 181–208.

Willis, Lauren E. "Will the Mortgage Market Correct? How Households and Communities Would Fare If Risk Were Priced Well." *Connecticut Law Review* 41, no. 4 (2009): 1177–1256.

Wolfe, Alan. *One Nation, After All*. New York: Viking, 1999.

Wolff, Edward N. "Recent Trends in Household Wealth in the United States: Rising Debt and the Middle-Class Squeeze—An Update to 2007." Working Paper no. 589, Levy Economics Institute, Bard College, Annandale-on-Hudson, NY, 2010. http://www.levyinstitute.org/pubs/wp_589.pdf.

Wray, L. Randall. "Lessons from the Subprime Meltdown." Working Paper no. 522, Levy Economics Institute, Bard College, Annandale-on-Hudson, NY, 2007. http://www.levyinstitute.org/pubs/wp_522.pdf

Yinger, John. "Cash in Your Face: The Cost of Racial and Ethnic Discrimination in Housing." *Journal of Urban Economics* 42, no. 3 (1997): 339–65.

———. *Closed Doors, Opportunities Lost: The Continuing Costs of Housing Discrimination*. New York: Russell Sage Foundation, 1995.

Yingling, Edward L. "ABA Statement on House Passage of H.R. 5244." Press Release, September 23, 2008. http://www.aba.com/Press+Room/092308House PassageHR5244.htm.

Zagorsky, Jay L., and Lois R. Lupica. "A Study of Consumers' Post-Discharge Finances: Struggles, Stasis or Fresh-Start?" *American Bankruptcy Institute Law Review* 16, no. 1 (2008): 283–320.

Jerry Anthony is associate professor in the School of Urban and Regional Planning at the University of Iowa and the director of the Housing Policy Program at the University of Iowa's Public Policy Center. He researches housing, land use, and international planning. His article "The Effect of Florida's Growth Management Act on Housing Affordability" was named one of the most influential papers published in the planning profession's flagship publication, *Journal of the American Planning Association*. He has received the "Excellence in Planning Education" award for teaching from the Iowa chapter of the American Planning Association.

Brian Bucks is an economist at the Federal Reserve Board where he works on the Board's Survey of Consumer Finances. His research focuses on household finances and financial decisions, including the measurement of household wealth and well-being. Bucks received his Ph.D. in economics from the University of Wisconsin–Madison in 2004.

Dov Cohen is professor of psychology at the University of Illinois, where he also has an appointment in the College of Law. He is coauthor of *Culture of Honor* and coeditor of *The Handbook of Cultural Psychology* and *Culture and Social Behavior*. He was previously on the faculty at the University of Waterloo.

Marianne B. Culhane is dean of Creighton University School of Law, where she has long taught commercial law and bankruptcy. She has served as the Robert Zinman Scholar in Residence at the American Bankruptcy Institute and as the Southeastern Bankruptcy Institute Distinguished Visitor at Georgia State Law School. She is a coauthor of *When Worlds Collide: Bankruptcy and Its Impact on Domestic Relations and Family Law* (2005, 3rd ed.) and *BAPCPA: Evaluation of Using IRS Standards to Calculate a Debtor's Monthly Disposable Income* (2007).

Jacob S. Hacker is the Stanley B. Resor Professor of Political Science at Yale University and a resident fellow at the Institution for Social and Policy Studies. He is the author of several books, including *The Great Risk Shift: The New Economic Insecurity and the Decline of the American Dream* (2008, rev. ed.), and with Paul Pierson, *Winner-Take-All Politics: How Washington Made the Rich Richer—and Turned Its Back on the Middle Class* (2010). He is an expert on economic security, the privatization of risk, and the politics of U.S. health and social policy.

Robert M. Lawless is professor of law and codirector of the Illinois Program on Law, Behavior, and Social Science at the University of Illinois where he specializes in bankruptcy, consumer credit, and business law. He is the author of numerous scholarly articles and the coauthor of *Empirical Methods in Law*. Lawless also administers and contributes to Credit Slips, a blog discussing bankruptcy and credit issues.

Kevin T. Leicht is professor and chair of the Department of Sociology and director of the Iowa Social Science Research Center at the University of Iowa. His research examines the relationship between globalization and economic development. His recent books include *Post-Industrial Peasants: The Illusion of Middle Class Prosperity* (2007, with Scott Fitzgerald), *Handbook of Politics: State and Society in Global Perspective* (2010, with J. Craig Jenkins), and *Social Change: America and the World* (2010, 6th ed., with Charles L. Harper).

Angela Littwin is assistant professor at the University of Texas School of Law. Her research and teaching interests include bankruptcy, consumer law, and commercial law. Her recent work includes research on credit card use among low-income women and the relationship between the consumer credit system and domestic violence.

Katherine Porter is professor of law at the University of California Irvine School of Law. In 2010–2011, she was the Robert Braucher Visiting Professor at Harvard Law School. She is an expert in consumer credit law and has testified several times before Congress. Her published research addresses mortgage servicing, financial education, and consumer bankruptcy.

Deborah Thorne is associate professor of sociology and Wagner Teaching Fellow at Ohio University. For the past decade, her research agenda has focused on economic inequality—specifically, consumer debt and consumer bankruptcy. She has authored articles on social mobility, stigma, gender, medical debt, reasons for elder debtors' bankruptcy, and financial well-being after bankruptcy.

Elizabeth Warren is the Leo Gottlieb Professor of Law at Harvard Law School. She recently served as an assistant to President Barack Obama and the special advisor to the Secretary of the Treasury on the Consumer Financial Protection Bureau. From 2008 to 2010, Warren was the chair of the Congressional Oversight Panel for the Troubled Asset Relief Program. She is the author of more than one hundred scholarly articles and several books, including *The Two-Income Trap* (2004, with Amelia Tyagi Warren) and *The Fragile Middle Class* (2000, with Teresa A. Sullivan and Jay Lawrence Westbrook).

STUDIES IN SOCIAL INEQUALITY